BEAUTY REGIMES

Studies of the Weatherhead East Asian Institute, Columbia University

*The Studies of the Weatherhead East Asian Institute of Columbia University were inaugurated in 1962 to bring to a wider public the results of significant new research on modern and contemporary East Asia.*

# BEAUTY REGIMES

# A History
# of Power
# and Modern
# Empire
# in the
# Philippines,
# 1898–1941

GENEVIEVE ALVA CLUTARIO

Duke University Press   *Durham and London*   2023

Project Editor: Bird Williams
Designed by Courtney Richardson
Typeset in Warnock Pro, Briem Script, and Briem Akademiby
by Westchester Publishing Services

Library of Congress Cataloging-in-Publication Data
Names: Clutario, Genevieve Alva, [date]- author.
Title: Beauty regimes : a history of power and modern empire  in
the Philippines, 1898-1941 / Genevieve Alva Clutario.
Description: Durham : Duke University Press, 2023. | Includes
bibliographical references and index.
Identifiers: LCCN 2022040843 (print)
LCCN 2022040844 (ebook)
ISBN 9781478019640 (paperback)
ISBN 9781478017004 (hardcover)
ISBN 9781478024279 (ebook)
Subjects: LCSH: Beauty, Personal—Social aspects—Philippines. |
Beauty, Personal—Political aspects—Philippines. | Clothing and
dress—Social aspects—Philippines. | Clothing and dress—
Political aspects—Philippines. | Philippines—Colonization—
Social aspects. | BISAC: SOCIAL SCIENCE / Gender Studies |
HISTORY / Asia / Southeast Asia.
Classification: LCC GT499 . C58 2023 (print)
LCC GT 499 (ebook)
DDC 391.609599—dc23/eng/20221205
LC record available at https://lccn.loc.gov/2022040843
LC ebook record available at https://lccn.loc.gov/2022040844

Cover art: *Maganda*. 11" × 8.5". Oil on Canvas, Cotton Pearle
Embroidery on Piña. © Jeanne F. Jalandoni. Courtesy of the artist.

Interior: Details of *Maganda*. With alterations.

Duke University Press gratefully acknowledges the Weatherhead East Asian Institute at Columbia University, which
provided funds toward the publication of this book.

Publication of this book is supported by Duke University Press's
Scholars of Color First Book Fund.

For Glenn

Contents

Archival research and writing often seem like solitary and even lonely processes. In reality, this book would not have happened without the generosity and support of my family, friends, and colleagues. I am indebted to the work of so many librarians and archivists who helped me locate materials, guided me through seemingly never-ending boxes of documents, and shared their expertise and insights that profoundly shaped my research. I am especially grateful to Waldette Cueto, Von Totanes, and Dhea Santos at the Rizal Library at Ateneo University; Mario Feir at the Mario Feir Filipiniana Library; Jon Labella and the Filipinas Heritage Library; and Jina Park at the Fairchild Archive.

I thank Ken Wissoker for believing in this project. His unwavering support and vision gave me the push to complete this book during a pandemic. I am grateful for the editorial guidance and support of Ryan Kendell, Lisl Hampton, Bird Williams, Steph Attia, and the editorial board and staff at Duke University Press. Thank you to Ross Yelsey and the Weatherhead Center for East Asian Studies at Columbia University for your enthusiasm and investment in my work. I am deeply thankful to the anonymous readers for their extraordinarily attentive comments and careful reading that strengthened my writing. I am indebted to the editorial support and incisive feedback of Roxanne Willis and Megan Bayles.

I am fortunate to have had the guidance of mentors at the University of California, Irvine (UCI), who encouraged me to pursue graduate school and an academic career. My thanks to my undergraduate professor, Fatima Rony, whom I hope to emulate in all things. To Anna Gonzalez, who has guided me in all aspects of my life, you are never wrong, and I thank you for being the best and most generous mentor and now dearest of friends.

My research began in earnest at the University of Illinois at Urbana–Champaign (UIUC). There, I was fortunate to have the very best advisor, Augusto Espiritu, who challenged me to push my research, enjoy the intellectual journey, and teach and write with integrity, and who also always took the time to read the messiest of drafts, talk through ideas, and help me make important and difficult decisions. Kristin Hoganson was the epitome of generosity who helped me navigate my first history conference, gave critical and encouraging feedback, and who mentored me as I grappled with motherhood and graduate school. My thanks to JB Capino, who connected me with archives in the Philippines and always had the uncanny ability to provide the exact book or document that I needed. Leslie Reagan, Yutian Wong, Soo Ah Kwon, Kent Ono, Junaid Rana, Lisa Nakamura, Fiona Ngo, Richard Rodriguez, David Roediger, Clarence Lang, Marc Hertzman, Tamara Chaplin, Kevin Mumford, Kathy Oberdeck, and Antoinette Burton provided encouragement and invaluable wisdom. I was lucky to have incredible and brilliant friends. My thanks to Nile Blunt, Ed Onaci, Sonia Mariscal-Dominguez, Sarah Park, Anna Kurhajec, Judy Estrada, Frank Galarte, Aidé Acosta, Constancio Arnaldo, Norma Marrun, T. J. Tallie, Yaejoon Kwon, Vince Pham, and Shantel Martinez. Long Bui, my spiritual guide, has a remarkable ability to know just when I need to be reminded of my strengths and not to be afraid of the future. To my graduate-school *kapatid*, Mark Sanchez, Christine Peralta, and Tessa Winkelmann, I am grateful for the family and community that we created that continue to sustain me. Tessa Winkelmann, I am so lucky to have you as my comrade in arms, from UCI to UIUC, and beyond. I thank Mimi Nguyen and Martin Manalanslan for their warm and generous counsel as I navigated new institutions and new challenges. Mimi has been instrumental in transforming my research into a book, reading my early drafts and messy ramblings, and talking with me of all things beauty.

The research and writing for this book were made possible by the support of several institutions. At Harvard University, my thanks to the Charles Warren Center; the Mahindra Center; the Asia Center Jeffrey Cheah Fund for South-East Asia Studies; the William F. Milton Fund; and the Anne and Jim Rothenburg Fund for Humanities Research. Thank you to the Wellesley Suzie Newhouse Center for the Humanities, and especially to Eve Zimmerman and Lauren Cote, and Olga Shurchkov and the Knapp Fellows Program in the Social Sciences. Thank you to colleagues who have invited me to share my work and provided invaluable feedback. Thanks to Mae Ngai and Charles Armstrong for organizing the Asian Migrations in the Pacific World Symposium at Columbia University, and thanks to the symposium participants Sascha Auerbach, Gordon H. Chang, Kornel Chang, Peter Hamilton, Davide Maldarella, and Andy Urban for their insightful feedback. Thanks also to the following individuals and organizations: Anne Cheng, Tessa Desmond, and Brittany Cooper for their incisive readings and comments at the American Studies at Princeton University workshop; Victor Mendoza and Deirdre de la

Cruz at the Center for Southeast Asian Studies at the University of Michigan; the Southeast Asian Seminar at Yale University; Francis Taglao Aquas and the Asian and Pacific Islander American Studies Program at William and Mary; the Southeast Asia Program's Ronald Janette Gatty Lecture Series at Cornell University; the American Studies Department at Oberlin College; Pacific New England Group Symposium at Brown University; and Min Song, Nitasha Sharma, and the Association for Asian American Studies Junior Faculty Retreat; and, finally, thanks to Naoko Shibusawa; Paul Kramer and Walter Johnson, who read the earliest iterations of the manuscript at the Charles Warren Center, and whose wisdom and extraordinary feedback helped usher this project to fruition.

At Harvard, I had the good fortune of meeting wonderful colleagues, many of whom have become mentors and friends. My thanks to Mary Lewis, Jill Lepore, Afsaneh Najmabadi, Maya Jasanoff, Walter Johnson, Vince Brown, Kirsten Weld, Sunil Amrith, Phil Deloria, Jane Kamensky, David Armitage, Elizabeth Hinton, Nancy Cott, Evelyn Brooks Higginbotham, Allison Frank-Johnson, Erez Manela, Amanda Claybaugh, Robin Bernstein, George Paul Mieu, Ajantha Subramanian, Tey Meadow, Tessa Lowinske Desmond, Mayra Rivera, Todne Thomas, Kimberly O'Hagan, Kelly Rich, Annabel Kim, Angela Allen, Brandon Terry, Jennifer Ivers, Robin Kelsey, and Claudine Gay. Thank you to the Pan-Harvard Filipino Network, especially to Myrish Cadapan Antonio and Geraldine Acuña Sunshine. I met Katherine Marino, Megan Black, and Juliet Nebolon while they each lived in Cambridge; they have become intellectual interlocutors and great friends. To my Cambridge family, Lorgia Garcia-Peña, Durba Mitra, Ju Yon Kim, and Lauren Kaminsky, I cannot express just how grateful I am for your life-giving friendship.

My colleagues at Wellesley College have welcomed me to a community of conviviality and exciting intellectual engagement. My deepest thanks to my wonderful American Studies colleagues Paul Fisher, Petra Rivera-Rideau, and Michael Jeffries. To Yoon Sun Lee and Elena Tajima Creef, thank you for creating a vital and exciting space for Asian American Studies. I am grateful for the comradeship of Natali Valdez, Sabriya Fisher, Susan Ellison, Chipo Dendere, Becca Selden, Irene Mata, Soo Hong, Smitha Radhakrishnan, Mala Radhakrishnan, Kelly Carter Jackson, Kathya Landeros, Michelle Lee, Baafra Abeberese, Nadya Hajj, Quinn Slobodian, Ryan Quintana, Becky Belisle, and Kaleb Goldschmitt.

I am grateful to be a part of the thriving community of Filipinx studies scholars. These scholars have been tremendous sources of inspiration. My thanks to Vernadette Gonzalez, Christine Balance, Denise Cruz, and Cathy

Ceniza Choy for their brilliant scholarship, commitment to feminist approaches to Filipinx studies, and their wise counsel. A special thanks to Allan Isaac, Lucy Mae San Pablo Burns, Robert Diaz, Ferdie Lopez, Josen Diaz, Gina Velasco, Joyce Mariano, Nerissa Balce, Mina Roces, Gary Devilles, Robyn Rodriguez, Cynthia Marisigan, Karen Hannah, Rick Baldoz, Allan Lumba, Neferti Tadiar, Victor Basra, Theodore Gonzalves, Rhacel Salazar Parreñas, Celine Parreñas Shimizu, James Zarsadiaz, Tom Sarmiento, Gina Velasco, Joyce Mariano, Jan Padios, Paul Nadal, Sony Coráñez Bolton, Adrian De Leon, Thea Quiray Tagle, Joi Barrios, Joy Sales, Mike Atienza, Alden Marte-Wood, Karolyn Ejercito, Stephanie Santos, Lorenzo Perillo, and the very much missed Dawn Mabalon.

I am indebted to colleagues and friends who have taken the time to read, converse, and think with me about this project. My thanks to Mary Lui, David Eng, Shelley Lee, Arissa Oh, Rachael Joo, Minh-ha Pham, Emily Raymundo, Christine Mok, Wendy Lee, Doug Ishi, Tanisha Ford, Laura Briggs, Anjali Vats, Chris Cappazola, Manan Ahmed, and Rana Jaleel. Special thanks to Kristin Oberiano, Sara Kang, Ruodi Duan, Jiahui Zhang, Joelle Tapas, Nora Krinitsky, and Isi Miranda, whose contributions and assistance were so instrumental to pushing my research forward. I thank Judy Wu for taking an early interest in my career, starting in graduate school, and for her unwavering support, attentive comments, and kind words of encouragement. Thank you to Lisa Lowe for her tremendous generosity, brilliance, and wise counsel. My daily online writing group, organized by the brilliant Lili Kim, fostered a vital and supportive community that allayed the isolation of the pandemic. My thanks to Lili Kim, Naoko Shibusawa, Heather Lee, Perin Gurel, and Patrick Chung for their critical engagement, laughter, and kindness. Jeanne Jalandoni, I am in awe of your artistry and talent. Thank you for visualizing and transforming my words into beautiful and moving art.

My friends and family have sustained me during the many years it took to complete this project. To Eden Picazo, Joanne Jose, and Jina Park, thank you for your unfailing friendship, for helping me with childcare, for keeping me company during research trips, and for your patience and understanding when I get lost in my work. Maraming maraming salamat to Kuya Junjie, Ate Majal, Ate Minerva, Kuya Michael, Kuya Bong, and Sam for helping me navigate Manila and Northern Samar. Kuya Junjie, thank you for keeping us alive during Typhoon Ondoy. Manay Elsa and Ate Yang, I am forever grateful for your care, and I will keep you both forever in my heart. My thanks to the entire Clutario family. Although my Lola Aster and Lolo Waling have long since passed, I am thankful for their care and their confidence in me; I know that they would be proud. To the Lopez family, especially to my mother- and father-in-law, Susan Lopez and Efren Lopez, without your help, especially with taking care of Ethan, I would not have been able to make it this far.

My mom and dad never wavered in their love and encouragement. Even when I bewildered them with my decisions and when I declared I would be moving quite a distance away to attend graduate school for almost another ten years, they remained steadfast in their support and have never doubted me. I owe my love of reading, stories, and history to my mom, who introduced me at an early age to the beauty of libraries and bookstores. Her own enthusiasm for books and her intellectual curiosity are tremendous sources of inspiration. There are no words that can fully express my gratitude for my parents.

Glenn Lopez and Ethan Clutario-Lopez bring me joy every single day and fill my life with light and love. When Ethan came into our lives, he and Glenn would accompany me to libraries and archives in far-flung locations, from Madison, Wisconsin, to Manila. They did so without a complaint and instead they made what could have been lonely endeavors into fun adventures. I am grateful for Ethan's cheerful encouragement, like spontaneously shouting, "Go for it!" when he sensed I needed motivation. Glenn has read every word I have written since my first research paper at UCI, has gotten me through countless computer disasters with quiet aplomb, has driven me to archives while waiting patiently around the corner at a café, and has made sure I was properly fed when I could have easily lived on coffee and Pocky. It is to him that I dedicate this book.

# INTRODUCTION

## *A Queen Is Crowned*

On February 24, 1938, the popular Manila-based magazine *Graphic* published a multipage feature on eighteen-year-old Guia Balmori: "A Queen Is
Crowned: Guia Balmori, Daughter of a Manila Labor Leader Crowned Guia
I, Miss Philippines and Queen of the Philippine Exposition." The article
provided an intimate look at how the beauty queen was made publicly
presentable.[1] Balmori appeared "smiling and serene" after winning a cut-
throat competition that included soliciting votes and sponsorships.[2] Balmori
defeated the other young women contestants from all over the Philippines,
earning the much-coveted title of Miss Philippines. Balmori's coronation was
the climactic spectacle of the 1938 Philippine Exposition.

The article begins early in the morning on the day of the pageant, documenting the behind-the-scenes process of becoming a beauty queen. Alongside
a full-length photograph of Balmori adorned in her coronation regalia, the
*Graphic* article offers a detailed description of Balmori's *terno*, a formal gown
consisting of a floor-length skirt, with a long train and matching bodice, and
its most recognizable feature, the "butterfly sleeves." Lucy Mae San Pablo
Burns aptly refers to this gown as an "overprivileged icon of ideal womanhood

and of the mother nation," symbolizing the "feminized, demure, and upper-class Filipina."[3] Designer Ramon Valera, along with an unacknowledged team of seamstresses and embroiderers, created Balmori's dramatic garment with hand-sewn gold and green sequins and rhinestones that created a stalactite effect on the skirt, long train, and standing collar.[4] The *Graphic* article also details Balmori's beauty regimen as she is prepared for her public appearance by a crew of hairstylists and makeup technicians who flex their skills: a professional hairstylist meticulously curls and pins Balmori's hair into a stylish coiffure; a "deft" Max Factor beautician artfully pencils in eyebrows, applies lipstick, and flicks on a last dusting of face powder.[5] Balmori's public face requires the work and expertise of many. These beauty workers labor toward the moment when Balmori stands "regal" in all her "splendor" outside her well-to-do Ermita home. There, the *reina* greets her public. The article reported that Balmori waved to the crowds of onlookers who "crane[d] their necks" and clapped their hands in excitement before a number of attendants and military escorts whisked her away to the coronation.

This article is just one of thousands celebrating Filipino beauty contests and winners published in the mainstream Philippine media between 1908 and 1941, during the years of US colonial rule before World War II. In many ways, *Graphic*'s multipage feature on Balmori substantiates what historian Ambeth Ocampo calls the "Filipino obsession with beauty contests," referring to the pervasiveness of beauty pageants across barrios, towns, and regions in the Philippines and throughout the diaspora that have developed into a mainstay of Filipino life.[6] In 1994, Philippine secretary of tourism Vicente J. Carlos declared, "Beauty contests are part of Philippine culture. They say if you want anything to succeed in the Philippines, hold a beauty pageant or a cockfight."[7] Just a decade later, the Philippines swept two out of four titles in the Big Four international beauty pageants (Miss Universe, Miss World, Miss International, and Miss Earth), making the Philippines the only Asian country to have multiple title winners in all four categories. In 2015, Filipina Pia Wurtzbach won the Miss Universe title; this was followed by Catriona Gray's Miss Universe victory in 2018. News pieces and social media show a staggering number of Filipino fans dedicated to these beauty queens and also to the industry itself. Beyond the large international pageant circuit, which features mainly young, single, able-bodied, cisgender women who embody a very narrow definition of beauty ideals, there is also a "larger constellation of Filipino gay, *bakla*, and transgender beauty pageants," and there are pageants for overseas domestic workers in places like Hong Kong and Milan.[8]

It might be easy to dismiss Filipinx cultural obsession with beauty pageants as frivolous.[9] But Robert Diaz invites us to take this interest more seriously by asking, "What does it mean to commit to articulations of biyuti even when such a commitment seems frivolous and risky to do so?"[10] Here Diaz refers to *biyuti*, an astute riff on the word *beauty* that "marks the flourishes, humorous asides, and idiomatic expressions that many queer Filipinos in the diaspora utilize to negotiate the travails of daily life," or what Martin Manalansan refers to as the exigencies of "kinship and family, religion, sexual desire, and economic survival."[11] Diaz's provocation can be extended not only to Ocampo's declaration of Filipinos' obsession with beauty contests but also to a broader collective passion for beauty. In other words, what can we gain by taking beauty seriously?

*Beauty Regimes* does just that. It tracks emotional, physical, and financial investments in Filipina beauty production. By beauty production, I mean the products made by Filipinas, the performances of beauty, and the strategies to control and define beauty. Indeed, it takes power to declare that something is beautiful. Processes of self-beautification can also function as self-empowerment.[12] Beauty can serve as a source of pleasure, fulfilling aesthetic desires; or, as Jennifer Nash illustrates, resistant beautification rituals provide delight and care in the sensorial fulfillment of physical touch and connection.[13] Efforts to define what is beautiful depend on concepts of the able body, race, gender, class, and sexuality. However, knee-jerk associations between beauty and frivolity misrecognize or ignore the levels of influence, control, empowerment, and resistance embedded in concepts of beauty. Beauty is powerful and functions as a structuring force that determines individual and cultural practices. It influenced national and transnational politics and policy formation during the overlapping imperial regimes and rise of Filipino nationalism between 1898 and 1941. Aesthetics, fashion and dress, and the labor of beautification "[cut] across national and imperial boundaries."[14] Beauty as a force impacted individuals as well as imperial and national cultures, production and consumption, politics, and transnational labor.[15]

At the turn of the twentieth century, beauty and fashion were contested measures of modernity in the Philippines. During the turbulent transitions between the Spanish, US, and Japanese imperial regimes (from 1898 to 1941) and the simultaneous Filipino nationalist movements, beauty, fashion, and personal appearance were central to the concomitant projects of imperial expansion and modern nation-building. During these years, the Philippines remained a colony despite winning a revolution against Spain and declaring its independence. The United States seized the Philippines in addition to Spain's other island colonies, claiming that Filipinos were not yet ready for independence. The Commonwealth period of the 1930s, a so-called transitional period to prepare for and anticipate national independence after colonialism, was interrupted by World War II. The Philippines then found itself under the control of a new regime—the Japanese Empire. In this time of overlapping empires and repeated denial of Philippine national independence, "Filipina beauty" developed into a highly charged political, economic, and cultural force at the center of global change. Thus, I tell the untold story of beauty work and empire and show how gender became the lens through which Filipino nationalist aspirations and modern empires were understood.

Filipina beauty structured what it meant to be a modern subject of a modern empire and how Filipinos envisioned their new nation. Beauty also proved to be a powerful political tool for controlling and managing bodies and desires. Beauty, dress, and fashion provided instruments with which to discipline subjects, establish norms, and structure hierarchies of difference. At the same time, laying claims to beauty or finding pleasure in beautification could function as resistant acts against the disciplinary imposition of norms.[16] Deep investments in and aspirations to beauty and its promises of status and power also reworked, expanded, and at times developed into new industries and systems of beauty work and production. The Philippines became both a source of and resource for beauty, though not always for Filipinos themselves.

In defining and considering "beauty," I am less interested in philosophical inquiries such as Immanuel Kant's notion of the sublime; instead, I am more focused on the social and political contexts and constructions that inform self-presentation.[17] I use the concept of beauty to address the practices of personal appearance and self-presentation that encompass beauty, dress, and fashion. These distinct categories worked in tandem with one another in the construction of modern beauty cultures. Beauty tells us a great deal about social formations, commerce, consumption, labor, social interactions and control, and policy. Tracking practices of constructing personal appearance sheds light on the changing relationships between the production, marketing, and consumption of articles of dress and beauty commodities and services.[18]

My study of beauty explores its location at the interstices of culture and political economy.[19] Popular and scholarly discourse more often than not treats beauty, fashion, and dress as frivolous and therefore apolitical. As Mimi Nguyen warns, though, "Much might be lost in dispensing with (what is dismissed as) mere ornament, or subtracting from the surface."[20] My work examines Filipina appearance in order to locate and connect seemingly disparate local and transnational circulations of ideologies, people, capital, policies, material culture, and the labor of constructing femininity. Examining the framework of beauty as encompassing the economies of fashion and beautification considers beauty a force that traverses culture, commerce, and politics rather than a passive thing to behold.[21] Beauty and beautification are action, performance, and interaction.

Examining the Philippines under overlapping empires during the late nineteenth and first half of the twentieth centuries reveals a deep investment in Filipina beauty. During this era, individual women sometimes wielded their personal appearance as weapons or defenses against colonial racism. They also leveraged beauty and fashion to solidify their social and economic class statuses. During the US colonial period, the colonial state and the private sector viewed Philippine feminine dress and adornment as lucrative transnational enterprises. At the same time, beauty's affective power rallied communities and created new forms of belonging and colonial subject formations, as in the case of the Filipina beauty pageants.[22]

Historian Mina Roces's work on Philippine national dress and politics stresses that beauty encompasses character, respectability, tradition, modernity, and status.[23] Indeed, the Tagalog word for beauty, *maganda*, is as much about virtue, family background, heritage, and individual achievement as it is about aesthetic appeal. Aesthetic practices and values provide a sensorial index of what is considered normal, valuable, and desirable—and what is not. Thus, I understand beauty in terms of physical appearance and as a cultural force that, as Manalansan argues, "extends to other realms of social and personal life" as well as to political and economic arenas.[24]

The phrase "beauty regime" might seem like a malapropism for "beauty regimen."[25] But as Emily Raymundo argues, "Beauty regimens are never separate from beauty regimes."[26] I use the word *regime* much in the same way as Inderpal Grewal, whose approach to studying empire, power, and "networks" focuses on the "transnational connectivities" between subjects, technologies, and ethical practices.[27] In other words, *regime* identifies the beauty practices and forms of labor operating on individual, national, and transnational scales.[28] There is no shortage of studies of political regimes, and the majority of these studies focus on authoritarian regimes in contrast to democratic state formations. Others take a liberal approach, asserting that regimes are simply neutral states or even that regimes encourage benevolence and voluntary cooperation from constituents.[29] Susan Strange offers an important critique of regime theories, saying they "exclude hidden agendas and to leave unheard or unheeded complaints."[30] In step with newer scholarship on political regimes, such as studies on "local" regime formations in Southeast Asia, my work homes in on factors often overlooked in the production and maintenance of regimes. I look specifically at the network of knowledge and power involved a complex constellation of players, including the insular state's bureaucracies and bureaucrats, private industries, individuals who held no official titles but who nevertheless advanced political agendas, and the subjects whose everyday lives were predicated on their ability to navigate colonial regime change.

I use regime as a framework to account for what Raymond Williams calls "social formations" and to understand beauty's relationship to power and its role in the accumulation of power. Beauty and fashion encapsulated specific networks and arrangements that maximized political, economic, social, and cultural power that converged in the Philippines during the late nineteenth and early twentieth centuries. Beauty and fashion provided the tools to control how bodies should look and how bodies should operate. In thinking about beauty regimens *and* beauty regimes, I identify the various colonial and private institutions involved in forming what political scientists identify as regimes' power to structure patterns of principles, values, procedures, and norms.[31] The conceptualization of beauty regimes provides a powerful lens through which to understand modern empire's "ensemble of practices, institutions, force, and contradictions."[32] Beauty and fashion operate in both formal and informal capacities to normativize appearance, behavior, and beliefs.[33] Philippine beauty regimes relied on processes of normalization to regulate gender roles, racial hierarchies, and colonial operations in everyday life. For example, with the expansion of the public school system, the matriculation of girls increased and so did the degree of surveillance of their bodies. Schools increasingly policed students' everydaywear, discouraging Filipina-style dress and later pressuring students to wear American-style white cotton uniforms. School officials argued that Filipina dresses were unhygienic and cumbersome and would hinder girls' performance and productivity in the classroom. In addition to larger forces, historical agents—embroiderers, seamstresses, consumers, beauty contestants, and government officials—actively participated in the work of building and maintaining the Philippines as a colony and as a nation *and* changed and challenged the disciplinary norms of empire's beauty regimes.

Much of the beauty regimes' tactics focused on modes of dress and ornamentation. Expanding on Roland Barthes's work on fashion systems, I trace sartorial presentations and meaning-making as well as the Filipina labor that went into producing the materials of fashion and beauty from 1898 to 1941. In his book, *The Fashion System*, Barthes argues that "written clothing," that is, the written discourse on clothing in fashion periodicals, and processes of signification do the work of fashion. Beyond "real clothing," or actual garments themselves, written clothing in various forms of media such as magazines assigns fashion a "supercode," or a system of words and meanings that "take over" the clothing.[34] In my chapters I examine the supercodes of garments and other forms of adornment and modes of constructing personal appearance. At the same time, each chapter examines the *production* and *use* of actual materials of dress and ornamentation, which Barthes dismisses, but which actually emphasize how Filipinas embodied and actively participated in the connected systems of labor, production, and meaning-making at the heart of the concomitant projects of empire and nation-making. My focus on Filipina beauty regimes asks how shifting constructions of race, gender, sexuality, and class informed colonial power structures and modes of control as forms of resistance to modern imperialism. For example, at the turn of the twentieth century, elite Visayan women drew from their arsenals of luxurious garments made by local seamstresses and embroiderers as well as from their dresses procured in fashion centers like Paris to visually perform and preserve their statuses at the pinnacle of local hierarchies of power. They also wielded fashion as a weapon with which to directly counter US presumptions of white American women's superiority during the rocky transition from Spanish to US colonialism.

Through the framework of beauty and fashion systems, *Beauty Regimes* tracks the formal state actors involved in the structuring of US empire and its new colony, the Philippines, and how such processes were inextricably connected to the Philippines as a "nation-to-be" or "in development" as well as to the development of Philippine nationalism from 1898 to 1941.[35] However, the production and governance of values, norms, and practices goes well beyond state actors. Beauty regimes take into account how nonstate actors across geographies and from various economic, ethnic, gender, and racial positions influenced how the regime worked. I look to the colonial state's arrangement with other entities, including militaries, nonstate groups and organizations, and private industries and institutions. Beauty and fashion industries that flourished during the colonial period depended on information networks between the United States' Office of the Secretary of War and US consuls in European fashion-production centers who circulated design samples back to the Philippines. These samples were then further distributed through informal networks of homeworkers and shared with public industrial schools. Workers were then required to copy these styles in their work to meet American market demands. These networks of labor and material culture influenced the negotiation and implementation of tariffs and the regulation of imported and exported materials that went into the making of a garment outprocessing system during the early twentieth century. In accounting for fashion and beauty systems as core parts of imperial operations, I outline the contours of these overlooked arrangements, bringing into sharp relief the connections and convergences—or what Lisa Lowe calls the "intimacy"—of modernity, empires, and capitalism. Tracing the threads of empire, *Beauty Regimes* illustrates how coloniality "operates through precisely spatialized and temporalized processes of both differentiation and connection."[36]

Whether intentionally or unintentionally, Filipinas, from beauty queens to the embroiderers, contributed to imperial and colonial nationalist formations. The majority of these Filipina subjects did not physically traverse national borders. Nevertheless, they navigated and shaped transnational and global flows, networks, and infrastructures.[37] Their lives and labor were part of the complicated forces structured by intertwined histories of Philippine nationalism, legacies of Spanish empire, US imperialism, and the shadow of Japanese empire on the horizon. *Beauty Regimes* accounts for the complex matrixes of institutions, actors, resources, commodities, behaviors, signs, and symbols that worked to regulate rules, procedures, norms, and principles formed under conditions of empire.[38]

FIGURE I.1. Manila, 1919. Mario Feir Filipiniana Library, Metro Manila, Philippines.

I do not present an exhaustive history of Filipina beauty and fashion, Philippine nationalism, or US empire. Rather, I provide alternatives and possibilities for understanding how empires overlap, how nationalism and nations formed against and with the colonial state, and how colonial subjects navigated dramatic shifts in power. This is a history that takes into account both formal and informal responses to structures of authority and that uncovers connections and relationships between seemingly disconnected people and institutions. Pushing at the boundaries that keep these fields and histories separate forces us to reckon with the messiness of overlapping imperial and national formations.[39] The links, networks, and relationships can appear overwhelming. Yet, it is a worthwhile and rewarding endeavor to delve into the messiness of arrangements, links, and networks.

*Graphic's* piece on the 1938 Philippine Exposition and Miss Philippines contest reveals the complex contours of empire's connections and conjunctures. The piece tracks Balmori's impact as a beauty queen through not only her physical appeal but also her familial, political, and social connections. It juxtaposes descriptions of Balmori's personal life and connections with political and economic developments, using pictorials and detailed textual descriptions of her education, her social clubs, and her family's involvement in politics and Filipino labor movements to bring readers into the excitement of the world of pageantry.[40] The article's many questions concerning Balmori's familiarity and involvement with the labor movement directly targets major political and economic concerns. This was particularly relevant as the second election for the presidency of the Commonwealth was set to take place later that year. The piece's title, "A Queen Is Crowned: Guia Balmori, Daughter of a Manila Labor Leader, Crowned Guia I, Miss Philippines and Queen of the Philippine Exposition," makes obvious reference to Balmori's father, Joaquin Balmori, a labor leader, government official, and journalist.[41] Balmori's uncle, Jesús Balmori, was a well-respected and award-winning Spanish-language poet, playwright, and journalist. Her "pedigree" lent credibility to the article's accounts of Guia's "regal" demeanor. To this, she added her own accomplishments. *Graphic* reported to readers that she was enrolled in a secretarial course at the University of Santo Tómas and aspired to work at a Manila business firm upon receiving her degree. Her social circle included a popular group of young women, referred to as "sub-debs," short for "sub-debutantes," a term that referred to upper-class young women approaching the age to be "presented" into Manila's high society. These sub-debs socialized at luncheons, teas, parties, and balls. In other words, Balmori fit the image of the beauty queen and embodied 1930s Filipino notions of *maganda*—beauty and good character. To contemporary readers, the inclusion of questions of labor organizing and politics in an article celebrating the newly crowned Miss Philippines may seem jarring. Considering the long trajectory of the deeply intertwined relationship between pageantry and politics, though, this piece was in no way unusual.

Balmori's victory sheds light on the economic and political currents of the time. As Miss Philippines, Balmori possessed the power to gain the attention— admiration and perhaps criticism—of the nation-to-be. The year 1938 marked the fourth year of the Commonwealth, a "trial period" intended to ready the Philippines and Filipinos for national independence. Philippine nation-building had developed after roughly four hundred years of Spanish coloni-zation, culminating in the Philippine Revolution. It continued to take shape throughout the Spanish-American and Philippine-American Wars at the turn of the twentieth century and throughout the US imperial period. Even before the United States government passed the Tydings-McDuffie Act, which set a date for Philippine independence, declarations of a Philippine nation as an "imagined community" had already manifested.[42] Claims to a Filipino na-tional identity had emerged in the second half of the nineteenth century, and Philippine independence was first claimed by the Political Constitution of 1899, also called the Malolos Constitution. The creation of a Miss Philippines title was thus also an assertion of a national identity. However, the pageant title was an emblem of *Filipina*-ness.

*Beauty Regimes* focuses on the connections and relationships between overlapping empires and nation-building and uses the framework of Filipina beauty to examine the process by which the colony became a nation. At the turn of the twentieth century, the United States presented itself as *the* model for the Philippines to follow. In this narrative, the United States, a former British colony, won independence and fashioned itself into a modern demo-cratic state. The Philippines therefore could achieve modern nationhood only under the tutelage of the United States—a project the United States called "benevolent assimilation."[43] For Americans, the making of a Philippine nation was a derivative process, and the Philippines was seen as perpetually in a state of development. To be sure, there were many visions and divergent enterprises active in the move toward Philippine nationhood. But from the onset of its imperial takeover, the United States invested heavily in shaping the Philippines as a profitable colony and military stronghold in Asia. If there was to be an independent Philippine nation, the United States intended to continue to benefit from it.

The uncertainty around when and if national independence would be realized further complicated the formation of Philippine nationalism. In the second half of the nineteenth century, reformists sought enfranchisement through the acquisition of Spanish identity and citizenship rather than through the formation of a separate independent Philippines. As historian Vicente Rafael contends, Philippine nationalism "began as a movement among groups uncertain about their identity and anxious about their place in society."[44] Radical nationalists like Andrés Bonifacio and the members of Katipunan drove nationalist movements to shift toward a fight for sovereignty and independence, which provoked the formation of a Filipino identity. The Philippine Revolution against Spain was victorious, and the Malolos Constitution declared Philippine independence and sovereignty. However, the 1898 signing of the Treaty of Paris, which marked the United States' victory in the Spanish-American War, resulted in the United States purchasing and claiming a number of Spain's colonies, including Puerto Rico, Guam, Cuba, and the Philippines.[45] Thus, Filipinos remained colonial subjects—but now of the United States—and were neither fully citizens of the Philippines nor fully citizens of the United States.[46] The United States positioned itself as a "big brother" ushering the Philippines into modern nationhood in its own likeness.[47] This process made "the social and territorial space for the formation of a 'Filipino nationality.'"[48] Nation-making was, therefore, a project of empire.

By forging together analyses of culture and political economy, I track the inextricably connected developments of empire-building and colonial national identity formations to multiple forms of gendered labor.[49] *Beauty Regimes* identifies the making of the *Filipina*, building on the work of Filipina suffrage movements, women's clubs, labor movements, and histories of feminism.[50] The term *Filipina* also serves as an important analytic beyond the years of formal colonialism. Colonial and postcolonial developments in gendered labor, violence, and exploitation in the Philippines and throughout the ever-growing diaspora not only depended on the concept of the *Filipina* but also contributed to the formation of a Filipina subject. *Beauty Regimes* traces the threads that bind empire, nationalism, Filipinas, and ideas of Filipina womanhood. Though undeniably engaged with Philippine histories of militarization, the hard labor of colonial infrastructure-building, Filipino migrant laborers, and the work of colonial and Filipino political leaders, in its focus on beauty and fashion systems, *Beauty Regimes* uncovers the overlooked connections between the labor of performance and the concomitant work of colonial historical subjects as producers, consumers, colonial agents, and entrepreneurs.[51] For instance, elite Filipinas' performances, such as public gestures of collaboration and friendship between colonial subjects and their colonizers, were vital to preserving Filipinas' wealth and status while maneuvering around colonial campaigns. Additionally, for US colonial agents, testaments to the success of colonial projects were couched in narratives of Filipinas' beautification and "modernization." Chosen modes of dress and accessories had the potential to exhibit visual, physical, and material claims to wealth, respectability, and modernity and functioned as testaments to the "triumphs" of colonization and of nationalism. Conversely, comportment, along with clothing, hairstyles, and a lack of jewels, could signify being underprivileged, marginalized, or in need of becoming modern. Examining the details of fashion and beauty systems at the intersections of gender, race, class, religion, and ethnicity provides a new and more nuanced story of modern empires and nation-making.

In initial confrontations between Americans and Filipinos at the turn of the century, images of Filipina womanhood became strategic tools with which to counter the US stereotypes of Filipino backwardness and savagery that justified the colonial project. For example, elite Filipino nationalists relied on Filipinas as proof of Philippine civilization, countering characterizations of barbarity in the Philippines by citing Filipinas in entrepreneurial positions as legacies of matriarchal precolonial societies.[52] In other cases, Filipinas were expected to tout their moral superiority over white American women, as conveyed through their ability to preserve "traditional" values and shun American women's wild modern ways. Such "traditional" values, however, were often rooted in elite Spanish colonial culture. In other moments, Filipino leaders and the Philippine media celebrated Filipinas' modern "achievements" in education and the workplace. Filipinas were both objects of nationalist projects and subjects of a colony and a nation-to-be. In addition to suffrage movements and the growing number of Filipina civic organizations, beauty and fashion emerged as a critical arena in which Filipinas navigated their status as colonial subjects.[53] At the same time, these very sites where Filipinas asserted and negotiated their statuses and positions took place in the tenuous state of a nation deferred. The need to demonstrate their capacity for modern subjecthood shaped their demonstrations of belonging to either the metropole or the Philippines. It also spoke to their desire to cement their status in rapidly changing transnational cultures.

Excavating evidence of colonial beauty regimes always reminded me of the tenuous relationship between the archive and scholarship. At the beginning of my research journey, some warned me that my research would most likely bear little fruit because the archive was constructed against the very subjects of my research. The archive both sustains historical scholarship and reproduces hegemonic systems of knowledge. Saidiya Hartman exposes the brutality of archives in her argument that it indexes the violence inflicted upon enslaved Black women and "deposit[s] these traces in the archive," thus committing another form of violence in the reduction of Black women to "fragments of discourse."[54] Hartman's work on "critical fabulation" pushes against the limits of archives to write the stories of Black women's lives without reproducing the harm of dishonoring life and the violence of slavery. Challenging the conventions of archives and archival research, postcolonial feminist scholars also caution us to be suspicious of the archive, pointing to its organization—the ways institutions select and preserve particular documents and not others.[55] Traditional archival systems depend on the existence of documents, their submission, and their methods of categorization and preservation. These methods silence and erase as well as preserve. Moreover, preservation technology is not always accessible, adding to the vulnerability and eventual vanishing of sources. Critical archival scholars such as Lisa Lowe remind us that archives are "organized to preserve government records and information for the public; its imperatives are classification, collection, and documentation, rather than connection or convergence."[56]

I shifted my methodological approach by not presuming what might be contained in particular categories and titles and by questioning my own assumptions about where femininity and feminine worlds would appear in the documentation or evidence. Once I did, sources began to accumulate—bit by bit, fragment by fragment. Archival research requires bringing together seemingly unrelated and disparate collections and documents.[57] These sources were scattered across libraries and personal collections between the United States and the Philippines and were often hidden in mislabeled folders. In the face of what turned out to be archival excess, I experienced a kind of archive exhaustion. The numbers and lengths of descriptions and images of Filipinas were overwhelming. Boxes and folders not overtly labeled "women," "girls," "gender," or "dress" contained images and promotional literature for Filipina fashion, documents and receipts tracking transactions between the United States and the Philippines for materials and labor for beauty commodities, and even suggestions for implementing dress codes as a means by which to discipline young women.

My search for historical sources on beauty and fashion uncovered a broad range of documents written in Tagalog, Spanish, and English, including colonial government reports, personal letters and memoirs, prison intake records, anthropological photograph collections, portraits, women's magazines, and advertisements through which I tracked the diffusion of colonial, imperial, and nationalist systems.[58] Empire- and nation-building operated in the structural realm in spectacular displays like beauty pageants as well as in day-to-day experiences. My sources gave me insight into arenas typically considered "private" and "personal," such as clothing and beauty choices. Indeed, the archives revealed an obsession with Filipina appearance—with beauty as well as with ugliness. Durba Mitra calls for historians to pay close attention to obsession through repetition, as "repetition is purposeful and a way to constitute knowledge."[59] It became clear to me that a range of individuals, agents, groups, and institutions were obsessed with Filipinas and, more specifically, with Filipina appearance.

And yet, even with the hypervisibility of Filipinas in newspapers, photographs, and government documents, many questions about and gaps in their histories remained, exposing the paradoxical limits of historical "visibility."[60] I argue that we cannot understand the relationship between colonial projects and nation-building without examining how colonial subjects, like Filipinas, were not only impacted by such projects but also actively shaped colonial and nationalist ventures within and beyond national borders. But traditional archives, particularly colonial archives, make it difficult to find the "voices" of many of the Filipina subjects in this book. Even with the numerous appearances of Filipinas in anthropological photographs, souvenir postcards, and stereographs as well as in descriptions in diaries and government documents, with a few exceptions, it was difficult to ascertain from these sources the individuals' agendas, emotions, and personal backgrounds—the very details that give insight into their lives as people. Even with my net cast wide, my research required weaving together "fragments" and rereading documents to excavate the experiences and viewpoints of Filipinas across racial, ethnic, and class lines.[61]

The Contours of a Beauty Regime

Through the prism of beauty, *Beauty Regimes* looks at the years between 1898 and 1941—a time of overlapping empires. During these years, colonial powers shifted between Spanish, US, and Japanese control. These years marked rapid change that heightened the desire to structure and enforce social order. To many Filipinos, especially elites, nationalists, and members of the growing middle class, when regimes were changed, the location of power seemed to be in flux. The uncertain state of Filipino national independence increased, in many Filipinos, the desire for structures of order with which to secure and consolidate or gain power along shifting hierarchies of difference.

My focus on regimes as a way to understand social formations moves away from more standard periodization of Philippine and Philippine-American history. It looks not only at big events or episodes but also at the mechanisms of empire- and nation-building in everyday life. The book starts at the beginning of the US colonial regime and moves forward chronologically. Each chapter emphasizes temporal overlaps, highlighting that the making of "the Filipina," "Filipina beauty," and Filipina beauty work occurred under the conditions of overlapping empires. I frame the US-Philippine relationship within the context of transimperialism. That is, I do not separate the historical narratives of the US regime from the Spanish or Japanese empires. Rather, I use a transimperial framework to highlight the imperial residues and tensions that lingered and continued to shape colonial life even after regime changes.[62] Beyond its chronology, each chapter takes on one fashion or beauty domain, tracing the local and transnational arrangements and connections made between Filipinas, colonial agents, state institutions, and private industries to fuel beauty economies. The chapters closely investigate overlooked instruments of discipline and control that were implemented by agents of empire and nationalism as well as by Filipina/o subjects seeking survival and empowerment.

Chapter 1 tracks the consequences of the shift from the Spanish to the US regime as a result of the Spanish-American and Philippine-American Wars at the turn of the twentieth century. It centers encounters and confrontations between Filipina *mestiza* elites and white American women. American women who accompanied their husbands on the Second Philippine Commission were tasked with befriending Filipinas as a means of strengthening Filipino-American relations. The Commission brought women together in a range of social settings, from elegant ballroom dances to casual conversations in sitting rooms. But the intended friendly encounters were often rife with tension that manifested in sartorial descriptions and displays. In the memoirs, diaries, and letters written by white American women in the Philippines, imperial aggression engendered by the collision of hierarchies took place in the context of sartorial competition. Gowns and accessories became the weapons used to undermine the others' sense of privilege. Embedded in gossip and expressions of jealousy and disdain were competing ideologies of whiteness, privilege, and respectability that the change in imperial regimes threw together. Diamonds, pearls, and gowns became the battlegrounds over which shifting definitions of whiteness and superiority were negotiated.

Moving beyond traditional narratives that describe beauty pageants during and after the colonial period as a manifestation of colonial mimicry, chapter 2 narrates a much more complex history. Examining the development of the Manila Carnival Queen contests that ran from 1908 to 1939, this chapter tracks the US colonial government's hand in the secularization of pageantry and the establishment of the Carnival Queen contests to make money, gain public attention, and perform colonial success through the presentation of beauty queens. These contests, which started as a showcase of colonial progress, paradoxically became a potent site for Filipino national identity formation. Filipino pageantry breached the disciplined choreography of the Manila Carnival Queen contests. Queens developed into powerful figures of ideal Filipina femininity that continued to shape gendered and sexualized performances of beauty and desirability well beyond the American colonial period.

Chapter 3 moves from the labor of performance to the labor of production. By the 1910s, the US colonial government initiated infrastructural changes to expand local industries into a much larger import-export business model. This chapter zeroes in on the United States' targeting of the Philippines as a resource for beauty production through the building of a transnational embroidery industry. Filipino-made embroidery paved the way for a new feature in US garment labor: outprocessing, in which American merchants would ship materials from the United States to the Philippines to be sewn and ornamented by Filipina needleworkers. Philippine dealers would then send the finished products back to the United States for American consumption. The establishment of a transnational embroidery industry based on import and export required political, social, and economic maneuverings in both the United States and the Philippines. The alliance between the US colonial and federal governments and the private sector expanded a cheap Filipina labor force whose "exotic" talent for handcrafted ornamentation was marketed aggressively to American consumers. The result was a transnational embroidery industry that linked the Atlantic and Pacific worlds. This chapter examines the relationship between Filipina-crafted embroidery and American style and consumption, illuminating the seemingly unlikely intimacies between colonialism, global capitalism, and a transnational industry of feminized and racialized labor and commodities intended for mainly white American consumers.

A major feature of the developing transnational Philippine embroidery industry was its reliance on public colonial disciplinary institutions—namely public schools and prisons—to help expand and regulate commercial enterprises. Chapter 4 examines the disciplining of beauty workers in the intertwined public school and colonial prison system. These public institutions of reform functioned as a central nervous system for the embroidery industry. Through industrial education and labor, particularly in embroidery and other fine needlework, the new colonial state promised to usher Filipinos into a modern and industrialized life. However, an examination of embroidery, one of the most profitable exports, in industrial schools and prisons reveals a troubling story of racialized and gendered exploitation. While colonial institutions promised Philippine women and girls the education and skills to thrive in an advancing and industrializing society, in actuality, prisons and schools provided a controlled environment in which educating "pupil workers" and women prisoners constituted, in fact, the disciplining of a vulnerable and exploitable workforce for the profit of the colonial state and American investors. By linking embroidery and labor to colonial education and prison systems, this chapter questions the "benefits" of American colonialism and explores the hidden cost of uplift.

Despite the "Americanization" of Philippine embroidery for American markets, embroidery in *Filipiniana* wear, like the terno, not only continued but produced Filipina high fashion. Chapter 5 homes in on the terno, a formal gown worn by mestiza elite women, that came to symbolize class status as well as a specific kind of Filipina high fashion. This chapter traces the constellation of arenas that marked changes in the production of clothing, the development of a Filipina fashion system, and the construction of Filipino national identity rooted in Spanish *mestizaje*, elitism, and cosmopolitanism. I track the transformation that made the terno a high-fashion garment by the 1920s, as well as the glamorous body adornments that changed in conjunction with urbanization, the rise of Filipino fashion designers in local and transnational contexts, and the emergence of concomitant beauty industries.

The epilogue brings the reader into the years leading up to World War II. By examining the business of textiles and fashion, it tracks feelings of anticipation and uncertainty about the possibilities of Philippine independence, the potential consequences of imperial competition between the United States and Japan, and the threat of war. The epilogue looks at fashion as a space in which protectionist policies reflected not only growing economic and political tensions between the United States and the Commonwealth of the Philippines but also anxiety over what a postcolonial Philippines would look like. The chapter also follows the competition between the US and Japanese empires that manifested in the Philippine textile markets. The epilogue ends by showing how dress became a critical tool to shore up feelings of anxiety against the uncertainty of impending war.

The histories presented in each of the chapters uncover the wide range of historical actors who worked to solidify, gain, or contest power and authority through beauty. Their deep investment in Filipina beauty, beautiful bodies and visages, and their potential to create consumable beauty generated political, economic, cultural, and social technologies that were unevenly advantageous—in terms of financial gain, power, and status—for US agents and industries and, to a lesser and yet still significant degree, for some Filipina/os. *Beauty Regimes* examines the everyday and spectacular performances that, linked with consumption, sartorial presentations, and beauty practices, uncover the multiple and previously overlooked circuits that cross and converge through Filipina bodies. In doing so, it reconfigures the geographies of colonialism and nationalism and accounts for the transpacific and transatlantic movements of bodies, ideas, goods, and capital.

# 1

## TENSIONS AT THE SEAMS
### *Petty Politics and Sartorial Battles*

In the spring of 1901, a prominent family in Bacolod hosted a lavish feast for members of the second Philippine Commission and their entourage.[1] In the colonial record, the family and Filipinos in attendance remained unnamed. The event was one of many colonial encounters in the form of balls, banquets, and afternoon teas held across the Philippines at the turn of the century. Throughout the nineteenth century, Filipinos of means had regularly held lavish social events such as *bailes* and banquets. Two years into the racial and physical violence that characterized the Philippine-American War, the Philippine Commission capitalized on the norms of the Philippine social landscape in its efforts to establish a civil government and end anticolonial resistance.[2] The Commission's tour impacted elite nationalist politics, Philippine political party formation, and the implementation of a colonial state.[3] At every stop of their tour, the Commission arranged social activities with local elite families in an attempt to assuage tensions and build friendships between Filipinos and Americans.[4] These events occurred against the backdrop of the United States' continued denial of Philippine independence and sovereignty.

In well-appointed ballrooms and with feasts laid out under the glow of hanging lanterns, guests sized each other up. The social events became battle-grounds of another kind; sometimes the encounters became confrontations. In one such situation, a Visayan woman at the Bacolod party approached Mabel LeRoy, the (white American) wife of the man who served as the secretary to the head of the second Philippine Commission, and pointedly asked why the American ladies in attendance had not brought their "diamond necklaces and tiaras" with them.[5] The question underscored the sartorial differences between Filipino and American women: wealthy Visayan women wore elaborate gowns made from luxurious materials and were bedecked with jewelry of gold and diamonds, while American women wore much simpler dresses and little to no jewelry.[6] The contrast in sartorial styles and the pointed questions about their appearance bothered the American guests. Almost as a reflex, LeRoy made a quick mental inventory of her wardrobe, which consisted of white cotton and linen dresses, the colonial uniform of white American and European women, but which unfortunately included no diamonds. She found herself lacking. The awkward conversation continued, with Filipinas asking questions that might have indicated interest; but their faces expressed disappointment in the American woman's appearance. The bombardment of questions, expressions of dissatisfaction, and backhanded compliments paid to LeRoy's one accessory—a small gold crown—were acts of aggression, eliciting what Sianne Ngai calls "ugly feelings": insecurity, inadequacy, and jealousy.[7] Nerissa Balce designates the ugly feelings of "rage, rancor, and irritability toward the Philippine colony and 'the natives'" generated in the colonial context as "colonial racial affect."[8] These emotions contradicted ideologies of American white supremacy and chipped away at the white American woman's sense of self-importance and confidence, and her presumption of superior status.

LeRoy's admission that there were, in fact, "no diamonds" calls attention to her own class status. She and her husband were middle class and therefore of a different social and economic status than the Filipino elites with whom they rubbed elbows. Helen and William Taft, the heads of US colonial society, were at most upper middle class. William Taft complained that his income as the head of the Commission, and later as governor-general, was insufficient to live in the archipelago.[9] Taft relied on his brother Charley, who had come into money through his wife's inheritance, to compensate for what he considered an insufficient income. Helen Taft's biographers point out that her family, the Herons, had stretched their income to perform the image of wealth in Cincinnati. They characterize Taft as insecure in her fringe status between the middle class and more elite classes.[10] The elite *hacienderos* mentioned in American accounts were some of the most prominent families in the Philippines, and their wealth exceeded that of the Americans. These wealthy, landowning families were connected to global agricultural export industries such as sugar.[11] Filipina elites displayed their wealth through their clothing and jewelry as well as through their houses and home decor.[12] Such displays of material wealth also exhibited their Hispanism and the cosmopolitan nature of their lives.[13] Elites spoke Spanish and were educated in Spanish schools in Manila or sent abroad to universities in Spain and across Europe; their churches and homes were influenced by Spanish architecture, and they danced Spanish dances at bailes.[14] Their locally embroidered and tailored gowns were made from imported Chinese and Indian silks as well as from luxurious local textiles such as *piña*; their hats were purchased in Paris; and women and girls flaunted their dresses as well as their musical skills by playing on imported German pianos. Thus, at this moment of colonial encounter, LeRoy's appearance, which she described as "simple," was in sharp contrast to the appearances of these wealthy women. Perceiving the question about her absent diamonds as a threat, the American woman retaliated. She responded to her Filipino hosts that American women did not bring luxury items with them to the Philippines because "we were afraid they would be stolen."[15] The barb countered any suggestion, whether true or not, that American women lacked style and access to material wealth. She also insinuated that American women were not safe in what they characterized as a "barbaric" and "savage" place—a direct insult to the Filipino elites who sought to demonstrate their civility, refinement, and worldliness as evidence of their capacity to self-govern. Deflecting the threat to her image with an accusation of potential thievery was a discursive strategy LeRoy deployed (a strategy similarly deployed by other women of the Commission) to protect her white American superiority. The Filipinas' unexpected luxury, wealth, and array of styles elicited a range of reactions from the women of the Commission. The realities American women faced in their individual encounters did not mirror their already-formed racialized and gender conceptions of white womanhood and Filipinaness and engendered what Minh-hà Phạm calls "racial resentment," which was exhibited as an absolute denial of racial others' capacity for taste.[16]

The tense exchange between the two women laid bare the many hierarchies under which women on both sides of the colonial divide operated. Veiled insults masquerading as innocent questions often fall into the realm of feminized social interactions labeled as "petty" and therefore considered inconsequential. The curation of appearances, practices of gossip, and the dishing out of insults are treated as petty acts. Pettiness suggests triviality and energy wasted on inconsequential, as opposed to real and important matters. Concern over personal appearance and material culture is often dismissed as a feminized form of frivolity.[17] Feminized acts of aggression are typically not seen as impactful power moves. But what is the politics of pettiness? Materialistic questions and slights about personal appearance and the very process of curating appearances can be assertive and aggressive acts. Indeed, as Carol Tulloch points out, "style" connotes "agency—in the construction of the self through the assemblage of garments and accessories, hairstyles and beauty regimes that may, or may not be 'in fashion' at the time of use."[18]

This chapter considers sartorial conflict in social scenes of colonial encounters. Rather than dismissing tense exchanges between women as mere squabbles, I examine the stakes and agendas behind behaviors and practices to situate and trace confrontations in complex fields of power. Lucy Mae San Pablo Burns argues that colonial encounters were dynamic and volatile given the "uneven relations of power that undergird[ed] these exchanges and events."[19] Building off Tessa Winkelmann's, Vicente Rafael's, and Cecilia Samonte's work on intimacy, domesticity, and colonial encounters in the Philippines, I specifically focus on the ways elite Filipinas and the white American women who accompanied the Philippine Commission took part in and contributed to fashion systems—the complex matrices of capital, materials, and conceptions of taste that circulated locally, regionally, and globally.[20] The sartorial confrontations and instances of petty politics in this chapter tell the story of tensions created by overlapping empires, the building of a Philippine nation, and the reliance of both empire and nation-to-be on beauty regimes.[21] When Filipina elites questioned the simplicity of the Americans' fashion, the American women felt envy, jealousy, and insecurity about their positions as colonizers. These conflicts show how colonial encounters were often also colonial confrontations filled with judgment, worries about identity presentation and concerns over whether they were admired, and mutual recognition of and competition between women.

The social events that took place in the more than twenty towns on the Commission's tour produced a range of intimacies as Filipinos and Americans came face-to-face with one another.[22] Colonial contact was not just about strangers meeting and acting upon mutual curiosity. Rather, these encounters—in ballrooms, *salas*, and bedrooms—produced an incredible amount of tension borne of the unrecognized political work of tricky social maneuvering, pettiness, and performances of power.[23] Securing power and authority was a central concern for both Filipinos and Americans at the turn of the twentieth century. In these engagements, challenges were not issued in prepared public orations or manifestos, and battles were not fought with guns or knives. Rather the "interactive, improvisational dimensions of imperial encounters" where "subjects get constituted in and by relations to each other" materialized through gendered, racialized, and class discourses of self-presentation—namely fashion and dress.[24] For both Filipino and white American women, fashion, dress, and personal presentation were "contact zones": the intimate spaces and interactions in which we can actually see and understand the stakes, desires, and risks of the historical agents of empire.[25] In these intimate sites, women mobilized practices of self-presentation and its evaluation to assert and interpret meanings and messages. The codification of sartorial practices was fundamentally important to the brokering of hostility, politeness, and empathy. Thus, rethinking pettiness as political reframes our understanding of colonial conflict. Taking gender and the interactions between white American and Filipino women seriously exposes the personal stakes of empire and nation-building.

Accounts documenting these occurrences reveal how women navigated and executed their own agendas. As the writings of the women who accompanied the second Philippine Commission show, the curation of impressions through personal style played a crucial role in asserting both Filipina elites' and white American women's statuses and backgrounds. White American women's documentation, in the form of personal letters, diaries, and memoirs, describe "paradigms of aggression" practiced by both Filipina elites and white American women.[26] Analyzing these feminized acts of aggression reveals how the women in these encounters strategically used appearance to demonstrate and measure their own and each other's worth, power, and authority. Viewing the feminized acts of aggression through the framework of beauty regimes provides new insights into the social, cultural, and economic structures that converged in the acts of dressing and self-presentation. Such regimes also constituted claims to the authority to judge, compare, and rank one's own and others' appearances. Tensions over power manifested in the ways clothing and ornamentation were, as Emma Tarlo puts it, "self-consciously used to define, to present, to deceive, to enjoy, to communicate, to reveal and to conceal."[27] Getting dressed is like donning a particular kind of armor and its accompanying declaration of power. To insult someone's appearance is to cut into their armor, point out their weaknesses, and attack their authority, worth, and status. Thus, the women involved in these colonial encounters asserted their authority and legitimacy through deliberately cu-rated modes of personal appearance. The valences of material culture, aes-thetics, rules of conduct, and power all intersected in Filipina and American women's sartorial practices and discourses on feminine appearance. Modes of dress were not simply metaphors for empire, but real and material mecha-nisms of imperial domination and resistance.[28]

Physical appearance provided an arena in which differences and similari-ties between white Americans and Filipinas were articulated, accepted, or contested and were part of the process of creating colonial identities. The politics of appearance force us to consider bodily adornment not as a super-fluous component of culture but as a significant material artifact of colonial reality, with its own corporal, material, and visual language of signification.[29] Furthermore, because "dress as both a social and personal experience is a dis-cursive and practical phenomenon," by analyzing dress, we can understand the convergence of discourse and practice in technologies of colonialism as well as in its material impact on Filipinas.[30] Using dress as a central frame-work of analysis places Filipinas at the center of narratives of US imperialism.

The politics of fashion attend to the relationship between capital and power and to how feminine acts of consumption and display are intentional performances of position and power. The articulation of status for Filipina elites and white American women took place through conspicuous con-sumption and through the assertion of knowledge of how to buy, how to wear, and how to put wealth on tasteful display. The presentation of wealth, then, increasingly fell within the realm of the feminine. The presentation of class status and worldliness became the responsibility of women whose conspicuous consumption was funneled into ornamenting the feminized do-mestic space of their homes as well as their bodies.[31] At the turn of the century, Filipino and American women's consumer practices reflected the rapid indus-trialization and commercialism that impacted not only the markets of Eu-rope and the United States but also the colonies that contributed these global economic developments. Thus, to understand the threads of and tensions around power, it is critical to explore the tensions and competitions between women. Through their modes of self-presentation and their assessments of each other's appearances, Filipino and American women alike embodied and therefore defined modernity and civilization by projecting gendered, racialized, and class norms. These women demonstrated the importance of appearances and first impressions during a period of uncertainty, suspi-cion, competing agendas, and weak relations. They also understood the effectiveness of pettiness and gossip in asserting their own or undercutting the other's status and power.

## Preparing for Colonial and Postcolonial Life

To understand the behaviors and actions of Filipina elites and white American women in their encounters with one another, one must recognize the complex transimperial and colonial nationalist historical developments that directly shaped their interactions. In other words, women's sartorial battles embodied competing colonial and postcolonial aspirations. The obsession over appearances played a critical role in negotiating power and establishing authority during the transition from Spanish to US colonialism and concomitant Philippine nation-building. These tumultuous shifts produced what Lisa Lowe calls a "colonial uncertainty."[32] Sartorial acts of aggression were strategies through which Filipinas and white American women navigated the uncertainty of their colonial futures. Sartorial battles between Filipina elites and white American women also transpired amid the context of multiple wars.

In just the span of one year, from 1898 to 1899, the Philippine Revolution and the Spanish-American War concluded and the Philippine-American War began.[33] The demise of the Spanish empire after the revolution and the Spanish-American War led Filipino nationalists to believe the United States would continue to play the role of ally in the formation of an independent Philippine nation.[34] However, with the onset of the Philippine-American War and the denial of Philippine independence, differences in the competing visions for Philippine nationhood and organizations of power emerged and strengthened. As anticolonial movements unfolded across the Spanish empire, the United States secured its global power through imperialism.[35] As many scholars have underscored, US "expansion" included seizing land from and asserting control over indigenous peoples.[36] Though the "frontier" of the American West had officially closed in the late nineteenth century, this did not signal the end of expansionism but rather a continuation of empire-building beyond the continent as the US aggressively extended its power and claimed islands in both the Atlantic and the Pacific as its colonies and territories.[37] This expansion entangled with other forms of imperial profit and power garnered from the enslavement and continued exploitation of Black people, along with racist settler colonialism and land dispossession.[38] Its imperial expansionism both within the continent and overseas entailed military expansion, active warfare, investments in capitalist development through the expansion of markets, and the ongoing racist and patriarchal exploitative extraction of resources and labor.[39] United States efforts to reconcile colonialism with the purported national ethos of freedom and democracy exposed modern empire as a complex set of contradictions. The US obfuscated its pursuit of empire through the ideology of exceptionalism that promoted the United States as the bestower of freedom, modernity, and democracy. The onset of the Spanish-American War early in the spring of 1898 was thus portrayed to Americans and to the world as a freedom mission: releasing the Philippines, Guam, Cuba, and Puerto Rico from four hundred years of Spanish "tyranny."[40]

The Philippine-American War was experienced throughout the Philippines as a continuation of a state of precarity. Farmers who had already suffered from starvation, poverty, and exploitation under the Spanish regime, and whose lands had been destroyed during the Philippine Revolution against Spain, continued to face economic instability. During the war, some provinces established provisional revolutionary governments similar to those instituted during the revolution against Spain. Others joined or supported guerrilla units to combat the US military. Christine Doran's work demonstrates how women of varying economic classes smuggled munitions, carried confidential messages, and set up a Red Cross to tend to the wounded.[41] Many people evacuated their towns and barrios to avoid being caught up in the fighting. Others were killed when whole villages were slaughtered by the US military, such as in the Balangiga Massacre in Eastern Samar.[42] Indeed, the war took a massive toll; approximately 100,000 were killed in Mindanao, and 20,000 Philippine soldiers and 500,000 civilians were killed in Luzon and the Visayan regions.[43] Nationalists employed a range of strategies from negotiation to collaboration to resistance. Other Filipinos created new businesses to cater to the influx of American soldiers into the Philippines, opening restaurants and entertainment venues in Manila. From 1902 to 1913, the United States also waged war against Muslim communities in the southern Philippines. These were wars of imperial subjugation and anticolonial resistance, in which resistance encompassed a range of often competing agendas of sovereignty and nationalism. As a result, this period was marked by rapid change and colonial uncertainty that set off a range of reactions and struggles between Filipinos and Americans and across class, ethnic, and geographic lines.

For many Filipino elites, US aggression and efforts to institute a new colonial authority demanded, in turn, new strategies to acquire and maintain power and their privileged statuses. Their power, rooted in colonial Philippine hierarchies, was not necessarily antithetical to US notions of civilization. Elites in the Philippines also saw Europe and the West as the centers of the civilized world; and they saw themselves as connected to Europe and thus also as bearers of civilization. However, American white supremacist ideologies, the Philippine-American War, and the US colonization of the Philippines threatened this perspective.[44] While many elite Filipino families' wealth eclipsed American families' and individuals' wealth, the new colonial regime brought with it a stronger military and an insular government designed to exploit Filipinos and curb elites' power. At the same time, elite Filipinas worked toward a *postcolonial* life in which they could increase the power and wealth they had accumulated at the end of the nineteenth century in a Philippine nation that they envisioned would be run by a Christian Filipino ruling class. In these colonial encounters, Filipino women displayed their status and worth to showcase their readiness and capability for Philippine nationhood and citizenship.

White American women understood that their unofficial function in the second Philippine Commission was to secure a colonial and imperial future. In 1900, as the Philippine-American War wore on, US President William McKinley commissioned a group of Americans, led by William Taft, to establish a centralized colonial civil government in the Philippines. The second Philippine Commission wrestled power away from the US military by shifting from martial law to a civil government. McKinley also tasked the mission with identifying potential allies among the Filipino elites who would ultimately join the Commission. In its early years, the second Philippine Commission consisted of a group of colonial officials, Filipino political and business allies, members of the press, and an entourage of fifty-seven people that included the members' wives, sisters, children, assistants, secretaries, dressmakers, servants, and other staff.[45] While presented as a kind of "getting to know your new island possession" tour, much of the work of the Commission focused on building a social and political base for the US colonial regime.[46] The group followed an intense itinerary, traveling through various towns and barrios throughout the Philippines. The majority of the Commission's trips aimed to establish municipal governments and vet local prominent Filipinos to fill in new civil government positions. Much of this itinerary focused on social events, from luncheons to balls to more casual interactions. This work was vital to US colonial statecraft. These social events constituted important arenas for political work where hierarchies of power collided. In contrast to the violent encounters between US soldiers and Filipino insurgents and civilians, Taft attempted to create a different culture of interracial encounters based on "sociality." Interracial sociality—which began prior to the outbreak of the Philippine-American War—fostered civilized interactions to help establish the foundation for a US-controlled civil administration.[47] Building connections between US colonial agents and elite Filipinos normalized the presence of Americans and American colonial rule.

The social work of "friendship" between Filipinos and Americans was not a task of establishing mutual admiration. For Filipinos, organized meetings and social events provided an opportunity for colonial maneuvering. During a time of great uncertainty about their future, proximity allowed them to evaluate American officials, learn more about proposed policies, and assert their own political and economic agendas and goals. For their part, the Americans sought to establish relationships with influential Filipinos and local elites in each town in the hope of implementing a cooperative government and electing supportive municipal and provincial officials.[48] According to Ruby Paredes, although US colonial officials "dismissed municipal politicians as caciques, or corrupt local autocrats, the Americans nonetheless worked with them to extend the electoral system from the municipality (1901 to 1903), and thence to the national legislature (1907)."[49] For members of the Commission, a "successful" American mission had the potential to catapult their careers and create pathways for upward mobility. The white women who accompanied the Commission understood that their success in establishing US power and authority would in turn elevate their own political, social, and economic statuses.[50] Their participation in the Commission also coincided with their political aspirations as well as those of their husbands.[51] Their obsession with appearances stemmed from their desire for control and their deep investment in the promises of power.

The confluence of revolutionary wars, imperial wars, and colonial regime change undoubtedly made Filipinos and Americans alike feel anticipation and anxiety. When the Commission was formed and the plans for the tour were made known, Helen Taft, the wife of William Taft, described the preparations for the sojourn: "The first thing the ladies all asked, of course, was 'What shall we wear?' It was a most important question."[52] Far from insignificant, sartorial concerns loomed large in the minds of Americans traveling to colonial territories. Taft was not the only woman asking herself how to pack for the Philippines. It was a question for all the women of the Commission, including teachers and women accompanying their families to their military and colonial government posts in the Philippines.

On September 27, 1900, in the midst of the Philippine-American War, one white American officer's wife sought advice directly from the fashion experts at *Vogue* magazine. In her letter, she asked a series of questions: "Would you advise for a young matron's wardrobe for traveling to the Philippines and going about while there? . . . What hats shall I require? . . . What are the necessary items for the trip? . . . What would you advise my taking that I am unable to purchase there?" *Vogue*'s reply asserted, "It must be remembered that the climate is almost always warm, or at least summer is the prevailing season's mood," and therefore she must wear dresses "suited to a moderately warm climate as your income will permit." *Vogue*'s advice reassured the reader that such dress practices were common. "Men and women consequently dress in any tropics" in "light, gauzy materials."[53] The sartorial advice was couched in the language of practicality—dressing for the climate. Light materials such as cotton and linen would indeed be more comfortable than thick wool, for example. Helen Taft and the rest of the women of the Commission followed this logic. Taft recalled in her memoir that she selected her wardrobe for "going to the tropics" and "got a supply of white muslins and linens."[54]

Expectations for dress, though, went well beyond practicality; they also established rules for how white people should present themselves. Imperial fantasies informed by dominant US imperialist discourse and notions of the Philippines as a new colonial acquisition influenced white Americans' sartorial practices. The white uniform did not just keep them cool and comfortable in the humidity and heat. Rather, the rules of colonial style were designed to showcase white colonial agents as distinct from colonized nonwhite people. Their claims to aesthetic superiority were as much about the aesthetics of white feminine bodies as about white dresses. The colonial uniform of the nineteenth and twentieth centuries was plain and simple in comparison to garments deemed fashionable in Western metropoles. Yet, while understood as different from fashion in the metropole, white women still perceived themselves as desirable and aesthetically admirable.

The American wardrobe of white linen, cotton, and muslin sartorially expressed ideologies of difference and white superiority in the colonies. Across modern Western empires generally, white dresses and suits evolved into a colonial uniform that cemented in the minds of white colonizers the white woman as the model woman in contrast to the imagined nonwhite native other.[55] A uniform suggests a compulsory component in which the wearers do not necessarily have choices but wear what is expected of them. The rules of the uniform organized difference and reaffirmed colonial racial hierarchies. In her work on intimacy and colonialism, Ann Laura Stoler describes the romanticization of white femininity in the colonial setting as "white linen nostalgia," referencing not only the white linen white women wore in colonial settings, but the power they wielded as white women colonizers. Stoler references Marguerite Duras's 1950 novel, *The Sea Wall*, which vividly describes the sartorial presentation of white people in Vietnam during French colonialism. Duras wrote, "[They] learned to wear the colonial uniform suits of spotless white, the color of immunity and innocence[,] . . . white on white, making distinction among themselves and between themselves and others who were not white."[56] The idea of the spotless white uniform stemmed from what Anne McClintock refers to as the "Victorian obsession with cotton and cleanliness," which manifested in the "middle class Victorian fascination with clean, white bodies and clean, white clothing."[57] The sartorial practice of the white uniform constructed a romanticized vision of white women in colonial nonwhite spaces that bolstered a fantasy of white superiority. In this fantasy production, the ideal woman was appropriately feminine in her innocence and cleanliness. Through the purchase of white garments, these women invested their money in white femininity and privilege.

For white American women, the unofficial colonial uniform also solved the problem of what to wear. The formulaic wardrobe provided rules that urged American women to stick to garments with simple cuts and made of cotton and linen. Style uniforms provided a sense of preparedness and the illusion of confidence in the expected physical, sartorial, and political outcomes. Preparing a colonial capsule wardrobe provided comfort and assurance during times of uncertainty. American and European discussions of women's dress practices in colonial spaces stimulated and reified US racial norms, which placed white Americans in a position of superiority and dominance over colonial subjects. The problem of what to wear was actually the challenge of how to present oneself in the messiness of anticolonial war and imperial transition. Sartorial practices became the mode through which white American women anticipated interactions between white Americans and Filipinos.

These were sartorial practices based on fantasy. "Fantasy," as Neferti Tadiar argues, is a "field of symbolically structured meanings . . . that shapes and regulates our desires, our modes of acting 'in reality.'"[58] Planning one's wardrobe required imagining the Philippines and the Philippine colonial subject. Selecting clothing and accessories for self-adornment also demanded introspection; white women had to envision themselves as white women in a white supremacist racial hierarchy and anticipate their roles as white American colonial agents.[59] This speculation was rooted in fantasies of what Allan Isaac calls the "American Tropics."[60] *Vogue*'s response to the officer's wife's letter tells us much about how Americans imagined their newly seized territories. They describe the Philippines as "so far removed from home, Americans there are unable to keep in more than partial touch with prevailing styles in New York, Paris, or London."[61] The *Vogue* article's language of remoteness and isolation suggested that the Philippines was cut off from what were considered the fashion capitals of the West at the turn of the century. While it is true that the Philippines is geographically more than eight thousand miles from the western coast of the contiguous United States and a transpacific voyage there by steamship took over a month, Americans viewed the distance between the United States and the Philippines not only in terms of geography but also in terms of disparities in intellect, politics, culture, economics, and ability.[62] For them, the Philippines was a tropical hinterland, disconnected from the modern world and therefore unaware of the latest fashions.[63] White American anxieties over dress practices in the Philippines were informed by and fed into what Allan Isaac describes as the broader "legal and political terrains" that "structure the fantasy and imagination to fill the temporal and spatial distance assigned to them."[64]

United States–based writing and visual culture created the fantasy of the Philippines and galvanized American women's anxieties over being severed from the fashion world—and therefore from civilization. Fashion writing on the Philippines was part of a much larger phenomenon: the rapid increase of American print discourse on the Philippines. At the turn of the century, American readers and viewers were bombarded with texts and images depicting the Philippines. With the start of the Spanish-American War, the Philippines increasingly made appearances in news reportage. When it became clear that the United States would take over as colonizers of the Philippines, both pro- and anti-imperialist discussions and descriptions of the Philippines began to circulate. One thread of anti-imperialist writing decried US expansion on the grounds of protecting the nation from "unwanted" nonwhite people. Another vein criticized the hypocrisy of bestowing democracy and freedom through war and colonialism even as pro-imperialists claimed that US expansion was based in liberation and democratization. African American journalists and intellectuals such as W. E. B. Du Bois and Ida B. Wells decried US imperialism, critiqued the practices of torture used against Filipinos during the Philippine-American War, and exposed the racist foundations of US colonialism.[65] But the majority of American depictions of Filipinos and the

Philippines circulated and recirculated what Victor Mendoza calls the "metroimperial fantasy" of the exotic, uncivilized "racial others somewhere out there, off the US metropolitan grid."[66] Texts about the Philippines and US colonial expansion, from the trashy novel to travel writing to social science texts, all shared common tropes about the Philippines that ranged from the savage native and the hypersexual Filipina to the childlike and naive colonial subject.[67]

In her memoir, Helen Taft confesses that she knew nothing of the Philippines and turned to sensational travel novels to fill that void. Taft describes a popular novel set in Manila as a "trashy thing and stupid in the bargain," but nevertheless says it gave "some idea of life" there.[68] Travelogues and travel novels claimed to give American readers insight into far-flung and "exotic" locales and cultures.[69] Travel writing, novels, and journalism mirrored the language of the social sciences. Like the American press, ethnographic works often circulated descriptions of difference that cemented notions of white Western (namely Anglo) superiority over the nonwhite "uncivilized" "savages" of the Philippines.[70] Textual and visual social scientific reports explored this new American "frontier," the mysterious terrain of the island tropics, and the nature of its inhabitants.[71] These texts presented the Philippines as a large-scale diorama of human evolution, from the primitive to the (almost) civilized.

White Americans latched onto descriptions of Filipinos' appearances and clothing to rationalize racial ideologies of difference. Writing and photographs by white Americans showcased a range of portrayals of Filipinas and their clothing. These texts offered contradictory images of Filipina dress. Photographs depicting nude Filipinas from the outlying areas of the islands rendered them hypersexual and savage.[72] Other photographs and image captions portrayed Visayan and Tagalog Filipinas from the Christian lowlands as less civilized than white women but as more modest and demure than the naked "savage" women from the "hinterlands."[73] Each description of Filipinas in these texts projected and reaffirmed a sense of white American racial superiority. These ethnographic photograph collections—which, unbeknownst to American viewers, were often staged and choreographed—made racial classifications easily identifiable and racism more palatable.[74] The "visual cliché in colonial photography," alongside detailed visual descriptions, also bolstered ideas of the Philippines and Filipinos as frozen in time and therefore devoid of fashion and fashion sense, hallmarks of modernity and civilization in the West.[75] As other scholars have argued, the practice of creating knowledge about "Others," particularly in the new colonial possessions, tells us more about the United States' perception of itself and less about Filipinos.[76] Modes and judgment of self-presentation articulated the logics of white superiority used to justify imperial expansion and US colonization of the Philippines.

Discourse on the Philippines and its populations treated fantasies of the "Other" as scientific data. The process of treating fantasy as reality relies heavily on reframing what is imagined as "knowledge." Hegemonic American "knowledge" of the Philippines depended on a layering of authoritative discourses, whose borrowing of codes and lexicons produced a sense of "truth." The belief in the power of the white American authoritative voice assured the women of the Commission's entourage and gave them confidence in their "knowledge," even if their sources were "dubious" and "trashy" novels.[77] Armed with science, white American women planning to journey to the Philippines, no matter their social and economic standing, felt confident in their white superiority. They could combine what they considered to be expert knowledge in science and fashion with fiction and travel journals to structure fantasies and imaginings of the Philippines as real. And they could plan their wardrobes accordingly.

In the beauty regime of empire, the American model of womanhood was also an assertion of control over norms and practices across gender, class, ethnic, and racial lines. The women of the Philippine Commission were invested in white American superiority, traditional gender norms, and upper-middle-class values. The Philippine Commission presented these norms and values as evidence of US superiority and colonial authority in the Philippines. Helen Taft's husband's political and professional advancement hinged upon his "success" in establishing American colonial rule in the Philippines and thwarting Filipino resistance through military aggression and diplomatic negotiations with ruling classes of Filipinos.[78] Likewise, Mabel LeRoy was invested in her husband's role as the secretary of the second Philippine Commission. Edith Moses accompanied her husband, a University of California professor, whom the United States government had tasked with organizing a colonial Philippine system of public education.[79] The success of the Commission presented to these families the possibility of moving up economically and socially from their middle-class ranks.[80] Although white women in the Philippines occupied roles ranging from supportive, unofficial positions like military wives to authorized positions such as teachers, they were each tasked with the responsibility of upholding US colonial dominance. The appearance of white superiority bolstered the project of white American control over the Philippines. These women, too, had their own desires for upward mobility, which fed their feelings of anticipation and their need for reassurance. The woman who wrote to *Vogue* asking for sartorial advice expressed anxiety about meeting other American women of her station. She hoped her manner of dress would materially and visually establish her status among other officers' wives.[81] Similarly, the other women accompanying the Philippine Commission regarded their supportive roles to their husbands, fathers, and brothers as a pathway to increasing their own social power; their work as agents of empire in the Philippines offered the potential for them to reap political, social, and economic gains.

## Impressions and the Power of Appearances

Hot? You never imagined the real meaning of that word, yet the thermometer marks only ninety-nine; the moist atmosphere makes it seem many degrees higher. Thin clothing and excitement are helping us to beat the heat, for there is a sense of exhilaration in the thought that we are at last in Oriental America.     —EDITH MOSES, "FIRST IMPRESSIONS," JUNE 3, 1900

In her published letters, Edith Moses shared her first impressions of the Philippines on June 3, 1900, while docked in Manila Bay.[82] After a forty-six-day journey, she expressed both her relief and excitement about her arrival. Her confident words make it seem as if this first moment in the Philippines was a favorable sign for how the rest of their journey from Manila to the provinces of Luzon, the Visayas, Mindanao, and Sulu would pan out. She conveyed the simultaneous condition of anticipation and discomfort in her vivid descriptions of the environment, the climate, and—just as importantly—her clothing. Moses's travel preparations proved beneficial; the thin material of her dresses helped her adjust to the new and unfamiliar.

Moses and her counterparts felt self-assured in their capacity to establish a civil government and US colonial authority. But this larger mission entailed several specific objectives for the "ladies" of the Commission.[83] They needed to gain support for the Commission's political authority among Filipinos as well as among the American troops and military officials. As unofficial members of the Commission, they were tasked with modeling white American ideals for everyone in the Philippines: Filipinos, Chinese residents, and Europeans as well as other Americans. Moreover, their personification of proper and modern womanhood played an important role in the management of racial hierarchies.

Presentations of idealized femininity did the political labor of offering an image of superiority and strength while at the same time functioning as an invitation for sociality and bridge-building. When Helen Taft and a number of other women were called upon to accompany their husbands in the second Philippine Commission, they took up the labor of collecting information about the Philippines and Filipinos, establishing relationships, and upholding a specific image of American civilization. The tableau of white women accompanying white men also presented to Filipinos a highly curated racial visual of the United States, erasing the realities of the US racial landscape, including its long history of settler colonialism and chattel slavery. The public face of America did not include Black, indigenous, brown, and Asian people, whose labor and lives were shaped by the same global capitalism that America's empire hinged upon.[84] This curation effectively erased racial conflict and any anti-imperialist discourse written by Black intellectuals and activists. In this racial schema, white women embodied ideal modern womanhood. They were agents of empire.[85] Under the auspices of getting to know their new colonial "possessions" while touring the archipelago, the Commission constructed hierarchies of difference by categorizing people, regions, ethnic groups, and religions and by separating Christians from non-Christians. This racial hierarchy measured proximity to and distance from whiteness and civilization. White women's ideological work fed into and bolstered colonial state-building.

The Commission and its members attempted to soften the image of colonial governance by presenting themselves to Filipinos as friendly and hospitable. Through the rhetoric of "friendliness," the Commission took on the mantle of "US exceptionalism," the idea that the United States embodied democracy and freedom, and sought to distinguish itself from European empires, particularly the "despotic" Spanish imperial regime.[86] The rebranding of US colonialism as a gift of democratic tutelage also required disassociating the Insular Government from the horrific ongoing violence of the Philippine-American War. Mabel LeRoy was told that simply interacting with Filipinos would fulfill the Commission's policy of "draw[ing] no color lines."[87] The Commission's take on the color line was based on a narrow and inaccurate view of white supremacy and on racism that simplified systemic oppression into race-based social division.[88] The Philippine Commission and its attendants frequently wrote about the challenges of "race prejudice" and how it might inhibit their goals to establish a civil government and gain support from Filipinos, particularly from members of the elite. As head of the Commission, William Taft encouraged official and unofficial Commission members to openly socialize with Filipinos.

Taft's social tactics were also motivated by his ambition to wrestle power away from the military government. In the summer of 1900, Manila, like much of the Philippines, was under martial law. The Commission attempted to portray itself as the embodiment of democracy and justice, and it associated racism with the US military. LeRoy and her counterparts noted that Manila high society demanded that any events hosted by US officials and army officers would be closed to Filipinos. At the same time, white Americans would not attend any festivities organized by Filipinos. "The army," Edith Moses noted in her diary, "has tabooed the native socially."[89] Moses recounted how a wife of a high-ranking army officer remarked, "I pity you Commission people: thank heavens the army has no social duty towards these natives."[90] Moses contended that these attitudes were "perhaps natural, for a conqueror seldom feels an equality with such a race with whom he has recently been in conflict."[91] For her, the problem was not that racism was wrong but that the color line posed a challenge to the overall project of US imperialism. How could the Commission cultivate relationships with Filipinos and convince them to accept and support a US colonial state?

Moses framed this challenge in the language of feelings, claiming that "Filipinos are sensitive on this point" and that this resulted in Filipinos equating American with Spanish colonial rule. The designation "sensitive" neutralized reactions and critiques of racism under the new colonial regime, reducing them to a nuisance. The Commission's strategies toward overcoming such obstacles simultaneously upheld white supremacy and performed gestures of uplift and support for Filipinos together with promises of peace, friendship, and collaboration. The Commission and its entourage praised themselves for organizing events such as the Commissioner's Banquet, held in Manila in late July 1900, at which there "were all kinds of conditions of men and women: black, brown, yellow, and white."[92] While the social choreography of the Commission relied on a different mode of pacification from that of the military, it nevertheless reaffirmed and cemented white American superiority and power.

Although the Commission's social events were racially integrated, the majority of white attendees refused to dance with Filipinos.[93] It seemed the color line was difficult to erase. One attempted solution was to create social clubs "for the purposes of bringing Americans and natives together socially."[94] These clubs, like other quick fixes to assuage animosity, fell short of their goals. One such club adhered to the American ideology of "benevolent assimilation" and promised to bring together Filipinos and Americans for the purpose of uplifting Filipinos. But the promise of elevation aggravated the elite Filipinos.[95] The language of civilizing and tutelage was an insult to the social status they had attained during the previous regime as well as to their wealth and their investment in their mestizo identities and cosmopolitanism—to use Raquel Reyes's term—their *urbanidad*.[96] The Commission's misrecognition of or refusal to acknowledge established social hierarchies in Manila engendered difficult consequences. Moses feared that the sustained insult would encumber American women's social standings in the Philippines. While they were able to penetrate some Filipino elite social circles, they could not gain access to all powerful and prominent Filipinos. She writes, we wished "we might know more of different social circles here."[97] Nevertheless, the Commission deliberately hosted and sought out invitations from those considered to be in the "elevated" classes in the hope of creating a circle of reciprocity.

The discourse of success and the public performances of the Commission and their entourage obfuscated the difficulties they faced in establishing an American civil government. The Commission's presentation of American women and families sharply contrasted with the more familiar image of Americans in the Philippines: the military. As the Philippine-American War continued far longer than the United States had anticipated—and as the Filipino death toll increased exponentially—the United States was anxious to distract both Filipinos and Americans from the carnage.[98] The 1900 *Report of the Philippine Commission* states that "the presence of ladies seemed to be especially gratifying to the people whom we met, as evidence of our confidence in the sincerity of their friendly reception."[99] Women did the diplomatic work they hoped would counter Filipino perceptions of Americans as linked to the martial masculinity and hostility of American soldiers in active combat. As wives, daughters, and sisters of Commission officials and staff, these women conveyed an intimate portrait of family and nonthreatening femininity. Moreover, placing white women, whom white Americans considered the most vulnerable or precious members of American society, in proximity to Filipinos symbolized a gesture of trust and good faith.[100] Official reports made by the Philippine Commission in addition to private writings recorded examples of welcome and enthusiasm as proof of the Commission's success in forging friendships and garnering support.

Beyond constituting gestures of goodwill, Americans considered the appearance of white women to be a pleasurable gift to Filipinos. While white colonial officials took on paternalistic roles in uplifting their "little brown brothers," white women framed their position by representing notions of American "grace," "generosity," and benefaction. Colonial imaginings and expectations of the Philippines and Filipinos imbued white women with the confidence that their presence in the archipelago would be appreciated. White American women expected admiration as their due. In their writing, the women conveyed a tone of maternalism.[101] Filipinos needed to be taught and conditioned to emulate their American colonizers to gain the capability of self-rule and to thereby be included in American definitions of modernity. In her memoir, Helen Taft reassures her readers that Filipinos were "not slow to grasp" the "significance" of seeing and sometimes meeting the wives and children of colonial officials, noting that "Filipinos were greatly pleased."[102] While touring the western Visayas, James LeRoy, William Taft's official secretary, described the arrival of American women as causing a "disturbance," interrupting the latter part of a public speech. In his travelogue he elaborates, writing that "native women . . . who had never seen an American woman before, were striving to repress their curiosity."[103] For LeRoy, this curiosity signaled more than mere interest; it underscored Filipinas' strong desire to know these white American women. LeRoy thus emphasizes the power of white American women's presence in the Philippines. Putting white women in white dresses, the garb of Victorian white normativity, was like displaying live artwork of the Victorian ideal of femininity and womanhood. The Commission's choreographed public events throughout the duration of its tour presented white women in a series of dramatic reveals. James LeRoy played up this anticipation and the impacts of "firsts." He recounts how a crowd gathered in the streets of Tayabas to witness his wife's ascent up the town's steep belltower.[104] He describes her trek as a brave and adventurous undertaking, underscoring that she was the "first lady to climb the tower at all."[105] The rhetoric of "firsts" suggests that Mabel LeRoy's actions garnered crowds and attention as a form of admiration rather than as novel spectacle. Her climb up the stairs represents the leadership roles Americans saw white women taking: leading Filipinos by example into a "new" and "unknown" world of modernity and Western civilization.

The details provided in these very same accounts, however, also reveal cracks in American fantasies of white femininity. Counter to the avid curiosity described by James LeRoy, Mabel LeRoy's letters home describe feeling disconcerted about the ambivalent attitude of some Filipinos they encountered. In a marketplace in Cotobato, Mindanao, for example, she witnessed a number of women shopkeepers seated next to their goods, "watching the strangers indifferently," showing "neither interest or surprise" at seeing the first white American women in their town.[106] Here, the market women's lack of reaction and interest in Americans' presence in Filipino towns contrasts with the friendliness and festive welcoming described in other accounts. LeRoy expected her presence to elicit a reaction—any reaction—from the Filipinos she encountered. But the countenance of indifference was part of the emotional colonial repertoire in the Philippines.[107] Filipinos' ambivalence stemmed from the realities of overlapping empires and war and unpredictable conditions, including ad hoc governance, violence, dramatic economic destabilization, and hunger. The transition between Spanish and US imperial power, the ongoing Philippine-American War despite the United States' initial rhetoric of assisting and freeing Filipinos from imperial tyranny, produced feelings ranging from dread to uncertainty.[108] Thus, disinterest was also a form of "sullen defiance"—a nonverbal expression of dissatisfaction and distrust of the Americans whose intentions regarding the Philippines appeared contradictory.[109] Indifference was effective. For Mabel LeRoy, the reactions of townspeople—or lack thereof—came as more of a shock than the outright resistance of guerrilla conflicts. Until this moment of encounter, in LeRoy's mind, there had been a clear demarcation between "peaceful" cooperation and violent ("savage") resistance. Ambivalence and the vacillation of reactions blurred this distinction. For women of the Commission, these encounters made small but critical fractures in their presumptions of white women's status in the Philippines, weakening their dual fantasies of the Philippines and of themselves as models of white womanhood and modernity.

As the trip went on, Mabel LeRoy's confidence in her own white superiority wavered. Like many women, she expressed her unease by focusing on the problem of what to wear. In a letter to her family in Michigan, she confesses that the "hardest question of all to meet in all this traveling is one of clothes."[110] She explains that the humidity and saltwater encountered when traveling by boat ruined the starch from the "American style of dress," making the white American women's outfits of pique skirts and shirtwaists look "worn." She laments how the weather "often leaves us looking like drowned rats."[111] Their dresses were supposed to appear pristine in color, well-tailored, with every fold and pleat kept stiffly in place with starch. The reality of the conditions of the Commission's travels in the Philippines eroded this pretty image. As her dress drooped and sagged, LeRoy's confidence in the presentation of white womanhood also began to wilt.

But beyond humidity's toll on starch and pleats, judgment from elite Filipinas intensified LeRoy's insecurities. She felt increasing pressure to rethink her style because "the better class natives cannot understand such simple choices."[112] LeRoy thought that lightweight silk dresses and more "fancy style" would "create a much better impression."[113] Filipinas' critical assessment of white women's clothing had called into question the value of the white colonial uniform. As previously mentioned, the white colonial uniform promised to do the symbolic and material work of reinforcing American ideologies of white supremacy. But in the Philippine context, the medium's message did not translate. The colonial uniform of the white linen or cotton dress had promised to present white American women in a favorable light and leave a dramatic and positive first impression. However, to Filipino onlookers, all-white clothing conveyed neither ideal womanhood nor American racial and class superiority. Feelings of insecurity deeply disrupted white women's faith in their white superiority. As colonial agents, white American women expected that their presence in the Philippines and attendance at events, social functions, and in towns and barrios contributed to the Commission's strategy of engaging in "acts and gestures of the self-consciously symbolic."[114]

## Filipinas, Appearances, and Securing Power

For Filipinas and their communities, American military and civilian occupation of the Philippines elicited anticipation, concern, and, for some, deep unease. The Philippine-American War threatened not only the power structures created during the Spanish period but also the elites' agendas to consolidate power through the vehicles of nationalism and independence. At the time of the second Philippine Commission's formation, Filipino perceptions of Americans were primarily informed by militarization and conflict. The United States' plans were unclear to Filipinos. Historian Resil Mojares writes that the "coming of Americans stirred anxieties among Filipinos even as it raised hopes of a quick end to Spanish rule through the Filipino-American Alliance."[115] Doubts and speculation manifested in the form of gossip and rumors.[116]

If the Philippine Commission designated the continued denial of Philippine independence and the implementation of a new colonial state, and if the Commission's presence produced uncertainty, how can we understand Filipino elites' participation in the Commission's social itinerary? How do we explain Filipino elites hosting Commission members in their homes and celebrating them through parades, banquets, and bailes? How can we explain the contradictory American reports of being fêted and of experiencing ambivalence and hostility? One way to make sense of the colonial encounters between Filipino elites and Americans is to frame them through the power of appearance and what Julian Go refers to as the "elite semiotic system."[117] By the power of appearance, I refer to the methods of conveying power and authority through personal style, the presentation of one's home, and public pageantry.

Throughout the US colonial period, fiestas, celebrations, and smaller, more intimate gatherings of the Spanish colonial period continued to be part of the social milieu in many parts of the Philippines.[118] Fiestas had a long and dynamic history in many regions and towns throughout the Philippines. Vernacularized Catholic pageantry in the form of weddings, baptisms, and annual celebrations honoring patron saints and the Virgin Mary drew people into town centers to watch and participate in religious processions, parades, sermons, theater performances, banquets, and other attractions.[119] This remained constant both during and after the Philippine-American War. American teenager Eva Johnson described life in the Philippines as being full of entertainment and parties: "It seems these people are giving 'bailes' and dances all the time. There is hardly a week passes that I don't go to some party. And often during the 'fiesta' times, three and four balls are given a week."[120]

These events were woven into the Commission's itinerary while in Manila and while on tour throughout the Philippines. The intensity of the social schedule across the archipelago was felt by Filipino hosts as well as by members of the entourage. In Pampanga, for example, prominent local families arranged meals for the Commission and its entourage. After attending speeches by Filipinos and Americans, the women of the Commission were treated to a second luncheon where they were introduced to even more locals. Then in the evening, Ignacio Naval hosted a large banquet for the entire Commission and their entourage. The Commission's work in Tayabas followed a similar schedule. A band playing "The Star-Spangled Banner" greeted the Commission members as they made their way to a midday reception, where they met a dozen of the town's prominent women, part of a committee that had prepared for the Commission's visit. The committee had organized accommodations and had even embroidered pillows with flowers and greetings of welcome for the American women to use and take as souvenirs.[121] Hearing that Americans loved whiskey, the hostesses purchased generous amounts of it and offered it liberally to their guests. The same committee arranged an elaborate evening reception and ball to honor the Commission. The anticipation of such colonial encounters spurred Filipinas from prominent local families to procure one-of-a-kind gowns from local dressmakers and embroiderers for the occasion.[122] For one fiesta, a Filipina wore an *escuadra Americana*–style custom-made gown in the colors of the US national flag: a gown of red satin, trimmed with white lace, and embellished with blue bows.[123] Elite Filipinas prepared for meeting members of the Commission as they would have for any special occasion; they dressed for ostentation—to make powerful first impressions. Many of these women would have helped design their own gowns, and they employed *costueras* (seamstresses) and *bordadoras* (embroiderers) already established in fashion labor systems to construct luxurious skirts with long trains and finely made *pañuelos* or *alampay* (shawls) made of piña ("pineapple silk") and embellished with ornate embroidery.[124]

Americans regarded the flamboyant gowns and exuberant events as positive messages of welcome. They interpreted gestures like the aforementioned gown made up in the motif of the American flag, the mass of decorations, flags, banners, and lanterns, and the invitations to dine with Filipinos as an acceptance of their presence and a celebration of American rule.[125] At times, the records of these events are patronizing in tone, conveying amusement about what they considered "quaint" and endearing gestures. At other times, they depict feelings of admiration and awe for the exuberance, abundance of food, and luxurious dress and décor. Commission members expressed a sense of satisfaction with the celebrations, accepting them as part of their due.[126] Such celebrations were seemingly in line with the white Americans' self-image of racial superiority and benevolence. These signs were important to the Commission—evidence of their mission's success—and bolstered their feelings of authority. As Ruby Parades astutely argues, however, Filipino-American interactions and politics constituted "a complex narrative of colonial politics and how Filipinos and Americans ranged themselves as allies, or as rivals calculating, shifting, and maneuvering for control."[127] These interactions reveal shifting commitments and identities that provide a framework to better understand the contradictions in colonial encounters. Appearances, from the American flag-themed dress to embroidered pillows, shifted between messages of welcome and threat.

Some scholarship on Philippine nationalist history frames Filipino and American relations during the years of imperial transition and the beginnings of US colonization as either collaboration or resistance.[128] Filipino members of the second Philippine Commission would form the Federalista political party, who were also referred to as *Americanistas*, elites and political leaders who saw working with the US colonial government as advantageous politically, economically, and socially.[129] But as Victor Bascara points out, "Collaboration is a complicated and uncomfortable aspect of empire . . . a defining feature that makes an empire an empire, a complex manifestation of the consent of the colonized."[130] The gestures and signs of consent and welcome, while perhaps interpreted as acceptance and even loyalty to a new colonial regime, were "not really loyalty at all." In actuality, Bascara continues, "The result is a colonized subject who may perform compliance, even in settings of extreme intimacy, while holding the potential for menace."[131] Rey Ileto frames this apparent social shapeshifting as "amigo warfare," or the "ability to shift identities in changing contexts," and being "adept at handling tricky situations that demand shifting or multiple identities and commitments."[132] If we pause to consider the "systematic repertoire" of elite political culture, apparent contradictions and shifting commitments collide, and Filipino and American political cultures and ideas come to a head in the fiesta setting.[133] As Go writes, in Manila and throughout the Christian lowland provinces, the power and privilege of patron-client systems "manifested in social functions." Events like town fiestas, baptisms, and weddings sponsored by landowners for their tenants were organized around social hierarchies and public performances of *utang na loob* (debt of gratitude), patronage, and loyalty.[134] Similar styles of negotiations marked the itinerary of the Philippine Commission with "rituals of recognition" that Americans hoped would signal the war's end.[135]

In each of the locations of the Commission's tour, townspeople of all ages and social positions would have participated in the public processions and public festivities. Americans might have interpreted this exuberance as welcome and acceptance of US officials and colonial authority; however, understanding fiestas, feasts, and pageantry genealogy in the Philippine context provides a more nuanced perspective of Filipino attitudes toward Americans in these colonial encounters. As Doreen Fernandez's work on the long history of Spanish Catholicism, colonialism, and vernacularization of theatricality and pageantry in the Philippines shows, *"pompas, solemnidades, pistahan, bonggahan* (pomp, solemnity, feasts, and over-the-top exuberance) entailed many layers of labor, performance, social cues, and interactions. The repertoire of fiestas and feasts included food and the aesthetic and sonic details of spectacle—spectacular displays of lights and banners, dazzling ornamentation of vestments, recitations of poems and hymns, public theater in the form of *komedyas* and *sarsuwelas*, music performed by bands, processions, dances, and feasts. While the theatrical repertoires of fiestas and feasts were largely built on a history of Catholic pageantry to reinforce Spanish colonial power and create "collective attitudes and behavior," the practices of constructing and performing collective attitudes were also vernacularized and localized.[136] Pageantry and celebrations were not just about colonial dominance and the internalization of colonialism. During the Philippine Revolution against Spain, Filipino nationalists utilized the repertoire of fiestas and celebrations to simultaneously host Spanish government bureaucrats and officials and express nationalist agendas and critiques of colonial rule.

In these events, Filipino elites displayed and created cultures of power through the ostentation of pageantry and entertainment. They conveyed information about individuals, families, and their respective degrees of wealth and influence. Fiestas took on and adapted local and indigenous practices of display, and indigenous communities utilized them to "assert themselves culturally under changed political and economic conditions."[137] Thus, the dynamic repertoire of the fiesta—what Doreen Fernandez describes as "splash and glitter, bravura and the *bonggahan*"[138]—flexed the image of elite power. Fernandez addresses the genealogy of fiesta culture using a *kablakaan* term, *bongga*: a class-specific form of celebrations characterized by "exuberant excess that are also often laced with power dynamics."[139] Fernandez's adoption of the term underscores the deliberate mobilization of extravagance without the connotations of gaudiness or pretentiousness that "ostentation" does in English.

Fiestas exerted power in the presentation of abundance through a combination of luxurious sartorial displays, decor, and food. Hostesses deliberately laid out an abundance of food on expensive dishes and wares. The details—from the dazzling lanterns to the dishes on silver platters on the buffet tables—present a live diorama of Philippine power structures. In fiesta cultural practices, the "excess of sumptuous food and flamboyant décor were marks of social status. It was a way for women to show off their skills in food preparation and to display opulence through the amount of food and careful presentation."[140] Thus, to invite strangers or even one's enemies to celebrations was not a concession of power. Rather, the invitation opened up opportunities to project images that countered American perceptions of Filipinos as backward, behind, or not as civilized as white Americans. Just as in the times of the Philippine Revolution against Spain, elites—even those who were deeply entrenched with anticolonial guerrilla movements—mingled with their colonial enemies. While the Philippine Commission understood its presence as an important actor in establishing Filipino-American colonial relations, Filipino elites used these encounters to display their power and resources and, through grand entertainment, to confront their American colonizers.

In addition to the politics of public spectacle, elite Filipinas asserted their status and wealth through the appearances of their homes, thus conveying to both white American onlookers and other Filipinas the already established class and ethnic hierarchies. Women played a large role in the way elite culture conveyed status through appearances.[141] Filipina style was part of a material and visual repertoire of performing the wealth that had been accumulated during the late Spanish colonial period. Filipino and American women depended largely on the communication of status through the curation of style within the domestic space, especially as they often did not speak the same languages.[142] In addition to the local vernacular and Spanish, elite Filipinas were often educated in European languages like German, French, and to a lesser extent, English. With few exceptions, the women of the Philippine Commission could communicate solely in English.[143] The language of commodities and exhibition, though, made strong impressions. American women cataloged in their letters and diaries what they found familiar and valuable. In Iloilo, a local elite family entertained the Commission in what LeRoy described as a "very fine" house filled with "handsome" decorations.[144] Through decor, Filipinos displayed their access to wealth and purchasing power that inserted them into global economic flows. Just as importantly, the types of commodities on display asserted an image of elite Filipina cosmopolitanism.[145] Although Edith Moses dismissed the decor in elite homes as "bric-a-brac," her diary's detailed catalog of items indicates a recognition of coveted, valuable, expensive, and luxury items.[146] She made note of an Érard grand piano imported from Paris (Érard pianos were the best and finest pianos of the nineteenth century, and pianos were a centerpiece in elite homes). Young Filipino women were expected to learn to play the piano and to showcase their skills and training as an exhibition of proper and refined femininity. Moses also recognized "artistic and valuable" Sèvres porcelain pieces.[147] Mabel LeRoy remarked that in the "elaborate sala" of a Western Visayan home, she enjoyed viewing displays of "feminine beauty and wealth."[148]

The displays of luxury and taste were also didactic: they documented the complicated hierarchical structures developed under Spanish colonial rule.[149] Through these feminized exhibitions of wealth and power, Filipinas attempted to concretize and strengthen their status despite the colonial regime change. The curation of appearances was part of what Edgar Wickberg calls "social Filipinization," or the formation of a Filipino national identity controlled by elites through the growth of status by wealth and occupation.[150] In the latter part of the Spanish colonial era, Filipino elites amassed and leveraged capital, land, and assets. In the 1830s, the Philippines had shifted toward an agricultural export economy.[151] Landowners and laborers moved from locations like Iloilo to "settle" Panay Island, displacing indigenous populations including the Ati and Tumandok. This island was considered a frontier by Visayan settlers seeking to expand sugar cultivation and export—even though it was already inhabited by indigenous ethnic groups.[152] By the 1880s, prominent sugar elites, the majority of whom were Chinese mestizos, took over as the moneyed group, which previously was exclusive to the Spanish (*peninsulares* and creoles) political elites.[153] In the Western Visayas, then, the expansion of the sugar industry gave rise to a new prominent class of hacienderos, whose family members became influential during both the Spanish and US regimes. "Sugar capitalism" rearranged racial barriers and constructed new ones.[154] Mestizos began to view themselves as *Filipinos*, a term originally designated for people of Spanish descent born in the Philippines.[155] The elasticity of the landowning class even beyond the Western Visayas produced changing concepts of whiteness that also included Spanish and Chinese (Sangley) mestizos.[156]

To receive recognition and power in the Spanish racial system that disenfranchised indigenous, non-Christian, Chinese, and mixed-race peoples in uneven ways, eliteness hinged upon the creation of a separate privileged category. Elite identity was very much rooted in the formation of mestizo identity.[157] Mestizo culture and identity was not just about phenotypic features such as light skin or a long nose; it was an identity created around access to capital to produce an aristocratic class with many European lifestyle features.[158] Their increased personal wealth meant elites could attend European schools and travel to and live in European cities.[159] Access to capital gave them access to global routes between the Philippines and Europe. Particularly during the nineteenth century, *mestizaje* was largely a strategic claim to ties with Europe that demonstrated civility and modernity. In her study of *ilustrados* (middle-class and elite Filipino men studying and living in Europe), Reyes writes about how transnational networks bridged mestizo Filipinos with Europe. She argues that "the attractions of nineteenth-century Paris, of course, were not unknown to Filipinos passing through Europe."[160] In letters sent home to their families and friends, ilustrados shared their new urban experiences through detailed descriptions of the "shops and department stores everywhere; passersby animate and throng the streets, the restaurants, cafés, *bouillons* [French restaurants that offer fast, affordable, good quality food], beer halls, parks and monuments."[161] Like ilustrados, Filipinas who traveled through Paris also wrote letters and brought home clothing and accessories in the current European styles. Their demand for European wares also led to an increase in purchasable imports at the shopping centers of Manila, like Binondo and Escolta.[162] These items were also made available in Visayan port cities like Iloilo that were originally part of the Manila Galleon. Thus, the European furniture, musical instruments, and home wares found in elite homes were expressions of the accumulation of wealth, purchasing power, and access to global commercial and economic channels.

Filipina elites applied the same strategy they used to showcase their wealth in the domestic space to showcase their wealth in their personal style. Personal style amplified the messaging of Filipina elite culture. Filipinas, like American women, felt deeply invested in the power of their sartorial practices and codes. During colonial encounters, Filipina elites used their appearance to showcase their taste in adornment and access to precious jewels, recognized by Americans as luxury items. According to Maria Kalaw Katigbak, for Visayan women, "jewelry was *the* status symbol. The larger the stones, the better. Only diamonds were worn."[163] These sartorial choices made strong impressions on the members of the Philippine Commission. During social functions—both in Manila and on tour—white American women were struck by the luxury of elite Filipinas' style. At gatherings, Filipina elites were "resplendent in many jewels."[164] Elite women in Manila were "dazzling in immense pearls set with diamonds" and impressed the Philippine Commission.[165] Filipinas, according to LeRoy, were "proud to wear diamonds in the morning."[166] Moses described Visayan mestizas as "cultivated" and was struck by how the women of the "'upper classes' dress[ed] with great elegance and [wore] gorgeous jewels," with "pearls like pigeon eggs and diamonds without number."[167] Both American and Filipina women considered diamonds to be status symbols, and without having a shared spoken language, these Visayan hostesses sent out clear messages about their social standing.[168]

The stylization of their personal appearances, homes, and lifestyles was not simply a vacuous mimicry of European fashion and customs. Rather, these women were producing a specifically Filipina mestiza elite identity. In their consumption and curation practices, they relied on "modification, adaptation, and selection . . . between local customs and Europeanness."[169] Mestiza eliteness was articulated through a kind of cosmopolitanism and the development of signs and codes that marked not only their knowledge of but also their relationship to Europe. At the same time, through mestizaje, these elites repackaged their careful adaptation into a form of ideal Filipina identity.

In addition to home decor and ornamentation with precious jewels, Filipina elites put forward a definition of mestiza cosmopolitanism through their modes of dress, which combined local, European, and Chinese styles and materials.[170] The richness of the fabrics used to make the Filipinas' clothes also stunned white American women, who commented on the quality of the brocade and the "exquisitely painted and embroidered" silks and piña, a local fine textile handwoven from pineapple fibers.[171] The dresses seen in Filipina hostesses' wardrobes ranged from *baro't saya* (blouses and skirts) to Parisian gowns.[172] By the end of the nineteenth century, nationalist movements influenced trends, and for formal occasions, women more commonly donned the *traje de mestiza* (mestiza dress), a nineteenth-century, ever-evolving style that combined the indigenous elements of the baro't saya and European styles.[173] While both the imported European clothing and the traje de mestiza signified class privilege, the latter also contributed to the formation of a Filipina identity built upon what Stephanie Coo describes as an uneven "convergence" between "Spanish or creoles, the mestizas, and native women."[174] By the American colonial period, the gown was often referred to as the Maria Clara gown, thus named after the main character in José Rizal's *Noli me tangere* who, over time, would come to symbolize ideal femininity—a Spanish mestiza with light skin and hair and a slim, long nose; virginal, devout, and demure.[175] As nationalist movements intensified, this same style of dress was also called the Filipino dress, *Filipiniana*, or *traje del país. El bello sexo*—a Spanish-language magazine that targeted a Spanish-speaking elite Filipina audience—described the Filipina formal gown as a "model of wealth and good taste" and it became the standard for formal events of what was referred to as *alta sociedad* or high society.[176] While this type of dress evolved over time, there were consistent distinctive features of the traje de mestiza: a voluminous skirt made of high-quality fabrics, a *baro* (blouse) with wide and loose sleeves, and a pañuelo (shawl) made of piña and typically ornamented with elaborate embroidery.[177] The cosmopolitanism reflected in the materiality of the dress translated into what Raquel Reyes refers to as social and cultural urbanidad, the knowledge of foreign and urbane sophistication.[178]

Although dressing the part of a cosmopolitan and urbane Filipina was practiced in the urban space of Manila, Filipinas also wore the traje de mestiza in towns and barrios scattered across the provinces. This style of dress provides a different understanding of the geography of Filipina cosmopolitanism, one that expands beyond the colonial capital. Manila was indeed a central, dynamic, and cosmopolitan space; but the display of such luxury during the Philippine Commission's provincial tour also demonstrated the crossing vectors of influence, trade, and travel that connected the provinces to a global network, and it forced the Americans to reconsider their assumptions about the Philippines as *provinsyana*, or provincial. Immigration, global trade, and kin networks connected Philippine provinces and cities to China, Hong Kong, and Europe.[179] This mestizo cosmopolitanism extended beyond the elite classes, influencing the middle class, who worked in import/export

FIGURE 1.1. A Filipina in her traje de mestiza. Mario Feir Filipiniana Library, Metro Manila, Philippines.

firms, trade centers, and Manila. Connections to global trade required that these employees be conversant in English.[180] They were in no way provincial; they were not closed off to the larger world.

The dress code of the mestiza gown was a manifestation of a mestiza cosmopolitanism that embodied "the formalization of conduct and comportment" that "expressed new values of the Christianized and Hispanized emergent bourgeoisie: decency, respectability, and civility."[181] Sartorial presentations amplified the message that this class of Filipinas personified respectability and civility. In doing so, they asserted their authority to dictate social norms and rules of conduct. Through Filipina elites' cosmopolitan sartorial performances, gestures, and practices, they also forged a concept of Filipina national identity. In this construction of Filipina national identity, their glamorous sartorial statements were also declarations that they were not just in proximity to civilization but connected to and inheritors of a civilized and more refined European heritage.

In their strategic mobilization of mestiza elite appearance and identity, Filipina elites did not necessarily disagree with the Philippine Commission's categorization of difference that separated Christians from non-Christians and that created hierarchies along a spectrum from "savagery" to "civilization." Filipino and American women alike had limited knowledge of one another. While Filipino elites had connections to the West through travel and living in European cities—or through transnational family and friend networks maintained by letter-writing, gift-giving, and the consumption of imported goods—they would have had limited interactions with Americans, who up to this time had been mainly soldiers and soldiers-turned-merchants. Filipinos, then, defined Western civilization through Europe, not the United States.[182] Elite Filipinas' curation of beauty and style in their personal appearances and in their homes strengthened their grip on legitimacy and control over Philippine societal norms. This social and cultural authority, in turn, fortified their claims to political and economic power, an important safeguard when potentially threatened by a new colonial regime's intention to elevate all Filipinos in the "image" of white America.[183]

Women in these prominent families were not just canvases or symbols of privilege. Filipinas from elite backgrounds with varying degrees of social, political, and economic power played critical roles in stabilizing and strengthening their statuses during the turbulent and uncertain period of colonial regime change and revolution. Despite patriarchal structures, women across various classes were also deeply involved in the entrepreneurial and accounting aspects of their families' businesses.[184] Haciendero economic structures were often built upon close-knit families and had a "long tradition of male intellectuals and female entrepreneurs."[185] Family, business, private, and public life overlapped. Although white American women often failed to name and represent Filipinas in their records, it is still possible to have a better understanding of Filipino elite cultures and to speculate about the kinds of social and economic positions held by the Filipinas the Americans encountered. To do so, I turn to the documented family histories of the haciendero families of the Western Visayas visited by the Philippine Commission. For example, it is quite likely that the Commission met with elites like the Lopez family. While Eugenio Lopez was considered the head of a powerful Western Visayan landowning family, Eulogia Lopez, Eugenio's sister, served as the "banker," overseeing the accounting and distribution of the family's finances. She permitted and gave large sums of money to her two brothers, who needed capital to purchase and operate land.[186] Her last will confirmed that she was the owner of two haciendas.[187] Furthermore, due to their involvement in Philippine economies, Filipinas understood the impact of transitions of power and colonial regimes on their businesses and lives. Although the US colonial state maintained the same gender restrictions with regard to government offices, Filipinas often attended the Philippine Commission's sessions. More than an ornamental form of representation, they participated in the ways available to them. Though women were restricted from speaking, they demonstrated their opinions in reaction to the public speeches and proposed colonial policies by actively listening, nodding, shaking their heads—and probably making side comments under their breaths.[188] Women—particularly those from the elite landowning class—had deep investments in knowing how shifts in colonial power would impact their businesses, livelihoods, and access to power. They would have been determined to preserve, consolidate, and even expand the elite privileges developed during the Spanish colonial period.[189] These economic realities informed assertive performances of Filipina eliteness.

The American women of the Philippine Commission took note of the gender dynamics among the Philippine elite. In Bacolod, Negros Island, the Commission attended a party at the expansive estate of Aniceto Lacson. Mabel LeRoy commented that the "hostess," whom she did not name, was the "true financier of the vast estate."[190] Edith Moses labeled another woman who owned large estates the "dispenser of diamonds."[191] In formal and informal sites of colonial contact, competing notions of status, civility, cosmopolitanism, and claims to superiority collided along gendered and racial lines. The intimacy of social gatherings made confrontations between Filipinas and white Americans and their respective notions of superiority nearly impossible to escape. During their tour, the Commission's retinue had to be housed and fed by locals. They occasionally stayed in monasteries but were more commonly hosted by local prominent families. For example, in Balanga Province, one branch of the Tuason family, a local wealthy family, accommodated the women of the Commission.[192] Filipinas invited the women of the Philippine Commission into the private and intimate spaces of their bedrooms. Their gender, in conjunction with their social standing and roles in colonial service, provided them entrée into these private settings.

It was in these contexts, where intimacy was supposed to produce feelings of trust and the seeds of friendship and collaboration, that tensions arose. Letters home provide a window on such developments. Mabel LeRoy describes resting between social events in the home of a Bacolod family, hoping to drive away a headache. While she relaxed in the bedroom, her Filipina hostess attempted to provide comfort and show hospitality by offering her whiskey, beer, tea, or coffee. The hostess also tried to entertain the ailing LeRoy by making several trips to a large wooden *aparador ropero* (armoire).[193] The hostess proceeded to bring out neatly folded dresses for LeRoy to see. LeRoy was surprised to learn that her hostess had not worn many of them but continued to purchase more, adding a good number of dresses to her daughter's trousseau. This prompted LeRoy to comment in her letter, "so much for the changless [sic] style."[194] LeRoy's offhand comment was made both in admiration and self-derision. She referred to a common attitude held by white Americans and Europeans that while wearing clothes might be universal, fashion—as it was tied to modernity—was an exclusive arena. Nineteenth- and twentieth-century discourses of dress contributed differentiation between colonizer and colonized, white and nonwhite, Western and non-Western. Part of this differentiation derived from distinguishing fashion from costume. For American women, identifying differences between how white and Philippine women dressed distinguished the two racial groups and asserted white superiority.[195] When white Americans referred to "native costumes," they imagined a static mode of dress that reflected their depictions of nonwhite peoples as unchanging, frozen in time, and therefore unfashionable and unmodern.[196] But in the intimate space of the Filipina hostess's bedroom, the revelation of her wardrobe conveyed not only the quantity of her clothing, but also the speed with which she accumulated new clothes and styles.[197] To be fashionable was to be up-to-date, to demonstrate the ability to keep up with changing styles. The Visayan hostess showcased glamour and cosmopolitanism when she exhibited each article of clothing in her wardrobe. Through fashion, Filipinas openly challenged white women's assumptions of their superiority and unmasked white women's fantasies about provincial and less-civilized brown women.[198]

At one baile in Bacolod, LeRoy admiringly described the Visayan women in attendance. She wrote, "All the senoras [sic] were gorgeous in their best bright satins and embroidered camisas, while [many] of the mestizas [sic] ladies wore fashionable European clothes, which differ from ours in that they are very much more costly and elaborate."[199] Moses made similar observations about a Filipino member of the Commission, Benito Legarda y Tuason, and his daughter-in-law, Filomena Roces y Gonzalez.[200] Moses noted that Roces y Gonzalez had just returned from Paris and "wore an exquisite black brocade gown embroidered in jet, and a hat that one had only to see to know where it was made."[201] Access to European fashion embodied cosmopolitanism and worldliness that transcended national boundaries.

Women from both groups recognized the trappings of desirable luxury items. Kristin Hoganson identifies the emergence, at the turn of the nineteenth and twentieth centuries, of an American feminine identity rooted in the crystallization of an imagined community based on a shared desire for consuming Parisian items.[202] In recounting her social encounters with Filipina elites, Mabel LeRoy does not describe Filipina self-presentations as "queer," "novel," or "quaint," but as familiar, beautiful, and coveted.[203] The American women's itemizing of luxury goods in mestiza elites' homes and on their bodies was also a recognition of their own uncomfortable position as part of the same shared imagined community—a community that looked to Europe and to Paris, specifically, as the capital of tastemaking. Despite the mutual recognition of some shared consumption practices, both American and Filipina women did not necessarily want to be a part of the same community. Witnessing luxury alongside recognizably upscale European fashion forced American women to confront extant hierarchies of power and status that resulted from various Philippine regions' ties to trade, global economies, and Spanish colonialism.

In addition to confronting Filipina elite cosmopolitan style and Filipina indifference, white American women also faced Filipina judgment and criticism. After the Visayan woman in Bacolod displayed her impressive wardrobe to her American guest, LeRoy noticed that her hostess appeared "visibl[y] disappointed" in LeRoy. LeRoy caught the expression and wondered if the disappointment was because "I felt ill" or "perhaps because my finery represented only two muslin dresses."[204] Here, the measuring gaze was turned upon the American. LeRoy's interpretation of the look is rooted in ugly feelings of self-doubt. Rather than expressing awe or admiration, this elite Filipina took inventory of the American woman's self-presentation, assessed the value and meaning attached to the sartorial details, and was left unimpressed. In the end, the Filipina hostess found only one of LeRoy's possessions satisfactory. LeRoy confesses in her letter, "The only possession that I had which seemed to please her and which she asked me to display to several young ladies was my gold crown."[205] This encounter lays bare some of the contradictions and incongruities in American claims of inherent and total superiority over Filipinos. The simple colonial uniform of white muslin gowns appeared ineffective in such moments of colonial encounters. The mutual inventory-taking of material possessions exposed the wealth disparities between the two women. Filipinas' disappointment in American women's sartorial presentations were also expressions of doubt in the Americans' capacity or authority to "elevate" Filipinas, which was a central tenet of American empire. In these sartorial confrontations, Filipinas undermined the United States' discourse of progress: that through American tutelage, the US would bring Filipinas and all of the Philippines into the modern world. Rather, Filipinas displayed sophistication, wealth, and style signifying modernity and asserting that they, rather than the American women, were models of glamour and class.[206]

Filipinas' aggressive presentations of wealth and cosmopolitan fashion proved effective. The performance of elite power structures undermined Americans' assumptions of the backwardness of the colonized "Other." At balls and receptions, elite Filipinas adhered to dress codes and practices established during the last decades of the Spanish colonial period; they wore elaborate gowns and fine jewels. In these moments, white American women felt far from sentimental or friendly.[207] In her letters home, LeRoy expresses discomfort, envy, and shame when witnessing elaborate displays of opulence. She writes that the "display of diamonds was wonderful and [made] me wish I had loaded up with a lot of good rhinestones just to be in at these balls."[208] But LeRoy would not have been able to afford diamonds or other precious jewels. Opulent sartorial exhibitions created a sense of envious longing that intensified the tense feelings of not measuring up to elite Filipinas.

LeRoy's accounts expose feelings of envy, longing, competition, and insecurity—feelings that conflicted with the images of American benevolence and maternalism. LeRoy confesses that she had "begun to think that our American style of dress is all together too simple; we would create a much better impression if we left off these pique skirts and shirtwaists and adopt[ed] lightweight silk dresses and more fancy style." She concludes, "the better class natives cannot understand such simple choice."[209] Understanding the power of sartorial codes and the markers of status, she felt embarrassed by the colonial uniform. At one ball in Manila, Americans noted the range of beautiful gowns from "bright satins and embroidered camisas" to "fashionable European clothes." LeRoy points out that this dazzling sartorial display "differs from ours in that they were much more costly and elaborate."[210] LeRoy felt deep frustration with her clothing. The white colonial uniform was not holding up to its promise of performing and signifying infallible white supremacy. She declares, "If those white dresses could have been changed by magic into costly silks and rare jewels then I wish mine could have been."[211] On a separate occasion, LeRoy expresses that when the white American women in their "dusty white piques and shirtwaists" met with women from Iloilo, she longed for something to impress the Filipina women. She wishes that some of her companions "had been artists on the piano or else were very good singers to compensate our appearance."[212] The tension of sartorial confrontations had critical implications.[213] These emotions were not just trivial expressions or feminine shallowness.[214] Rather, in these sartorial showdowns, Philippine-based notions of gender, race, and class differences collided with US social constructions. Between the revolution and the messy transition between colonial regimes, both groups of women needed to navigate multiple hierarchies and solidify their hierarchical positions.

How did white women deal with the fissures in their fantasies about the Philippines and Filipinas? How did they come to terms with or even counter perceived threats to their sense of white supremacy? The textual descriptions of elite Filipinas' sartorial appearances call into question the white women's function in the empire. If white women were supposed to help usher Filipina women and men into modernity and civilization, how would they fulfill this role when Filipinas were just as sophisticated and even wealthier than the white American women? Did they accept their similarities and forge actual connections and true friendships, bolstering the United States' sense of benevolence and exceptionalism? To put it simply, no. American women set hard limits on their "friendliness" and employed a number of strategies to compensate for the evidence of Filipina elites' superiority in terms of wealth and "worldliness." Coming face-to-face with extremely wealthy Filipinas challenged the Americans' ideas of Filipinos as primitive and provincial and also demonstrated the failings of the United States' so-called impenetrable superiority.

In her memoir, Helen Taft provides a teleological narrative of Filipina dress that directly contradicts the accounts of elite Flipinas' fashion, including those written by the other women of the Commission. Taft frames her descriptions of Filipina fashion as becoming increasingly finer and of better quality *as a result of* American colonialism. Taft claims that during the Philippine-American War, Filipinas "didn't display so many jewels and fine garments in those days as now because, in certain quarters, the *insurrectos* were still levying tribute, but the girls and women, many of them quite pretty, were very gay in long, trailing calico skirts and *jusi, sinamay*, or *pina* [*sic*]."[215] Taft's words mirror Mabel LeRoy's lie that she wore no jewels because she feared becoming a victim to theft in the Philippines. At the same time, Taft's memoir runs counter to LeRoy's and Moses's accounts of Filipina elites' fashion and the abundance of wealth exhibited through accessories and ornamentation worn even during the war years. Instead, Taft's recounting of memories creates a narrative that obfuscates the terror inflicted by American soldiers and emphasizes instead that elite Filipinos were being terrorized by *insurrectos* (insurgents) who threatened to take women's jewels. Here Taft's portrayal of Filipino revolutionaries as thieving bandits positions anticolonial nationalists not only as threats to American women but also as threats to Filipina elites. Taft's description of stagnated fashion suggests that a sense of normalcy among Filipina elites could be achieved through allyship with the US colonial government, and that this government would in turn provide law and order. Taft's narrative provides a very specific timeline of moving forward from a time of anticolonial resistance and turmoil to one of peace and the re-establishment of elite, everyday comfort. In doing so, Taft reinforces the image of United States imperialism as successfully modernizing the Philippines.

In addition to Taft's descriptions of Filipinas *not* wearing diamonds and jewels, her memoir records many contradictions to other Americans' descriptions of Filipino style. Whereas Moses and LeRoy both describe the luxuriousness of mestiza gowns and the European gowns found in wealthy mestizas' trousseaus, Taft claims that Manileños "enjoyed emancipation from the tyranny of clothes"; "there were no fashionable gowns to be had, therefore simplicity, or more or less rundownedness [*sic*] of one-time respectability" was embraced—which she attributes to the backwardness of both the Filipinos and Spanish colonial influence. Although Taft seems to praise Filipinos' lack of clothing inhibitions, her underlying tone is one of condescension.[216] The lack of fashionable wear—according to Taft—stems from the scarcity of shops in Manila selling the latest fashions. Taft's account of the lack of fashion supports the overall American portrayal of Filipinos as lacking sophistication and as stagnated in their progress toward civilization. However, she concludes, "It is different now." Taft's memoir published in 1914 conveys her perspective on the impact of fifteen years of US colonization in the Philippines. She posits a story of colonial progress through fashion and writes, "The importer of fashionable millinery and sumptuous garments has invaded the field and the women in Manila to-day are about as finely gowned and hatted as they are anywhere."[217] According to Taft, the arrival of American women exposed Filipinas to current women's styles and brought them into the fashionable modern world. Taft's rhetorical strategy—denying Filipinas' appearances and then suggesting that American women ushered in high fashion—allows her to counter Filipinas' contestations of white American supremacy. Unlike her counterparts, Taft does not express any sense of discomfort with the display of wealth and status in Filipina women's formal dresses and jewelry. Her denial of their ownership of diamonds—something so often mentioned in other Americans' accounts—allows her to avoid the subject altogether. In doing so, Taft's memoir helps reify the culture of US imperial racism, rendering Filipinas as inherently inferior to their white American counterparts, regardless of their social and class statuses.

Although she acknowledges Filipinas' glamorous style, Moses makes sure to qualify it. In her diary, Moses frames elite Filipino culture as absurd. She writes, "There is something astonishing to us in the serious ways these Filipinos regard themselves." She goes on, "Filipinos are extravagant in many ways from our point of view."[218] Her attention to extravagance is not complimentary. Instead, the underlying tone of her descriptions is distaste for "over-doing it" or overreaching one's position. In her view, Filipino natives did not understand their position in the racial hierarchy, and instead performed access to capital. She found such performances disgraceful. Moses argued that the vestiges of European tastes, articles of clothing, and decor stemmed from Filipinas' uncanny ability to "memorize quickly and learn certain things readily." For Moses, Filipinas were "imitative."[219] Mimicry suggests a failure—the lack of access to the origins of taste and style.[220] Moses ridicules the presentations that had impressed others, and that had even made them feel envious and even insecure. For her, the backhanded compliment of being able to memorize quickly puts Filipinas in their place. Though Parisian and other European fashions were popular among American women, Moses ignores this reality and instead focuses on mimicry as an uncouth act. Not only is imitation seen as a kind of failure, but to Moses, Filipina modes of dress are also unnatural. During one social event, she catches sight of the host's children wearing a European dress that "makes one long to see them running about in their pretty brown skins."[221] Moses's backhanded compliment conveys that while Filipinas had access to European dress, they—due to their race—could not achieve fashionability.

Unlike LeRoy, Moses does not convey feelings of envy in reaction to Filipina wealth. Couching Filipina style as a failed attempt at colonial mimicry allows her to channel her reactions into disdain instead. To combat any threat to her own status, she insults Filipina style with contempt. Their sartorial displays of wealth are a testament to Filipinas' gaudiness and lack of taste and knowledge of style. Recounting the fashion at state occasions, Moses remarks that because "brocaded satin skirts . . . are considered the height of elegance," her own "ancient pink brocade is the glory of the party and meets the approval of the natives, who did not suspect its age nor the fact that it is quite out of style at home."[222] Moses makes herself the epitome of style and grace while belittling Filipinas' tastes. She blends the discourse of fashion with the picturesque, putting forth the notion that current styles among the elite Filipinas are passé, merely failed copies of their "betters." Access to capital, according to Moses, does not necessarily imbue good taste. In her formulation, conversely, she has refined taste, even with her family's comparably lower income.[223]

Moses also attempts to reduce the value of luxury goods in the Philippines to explain away the presence of coveted commodities. She declares that the "fact that champagne and diamonds bore very low duties during the period of Spanish rule may account for their abundance in the Philippines."[224] Here, Moses suggests that these imports were easy to obtain, rationalizing Filipinas' displays of wealth by rendering their luxury goods less valuable than if they had been purchased in the West, where tariffs and import taxes made luxury goods more expensive. This strategy of denial depended on a deliberate recanting of the impact of global trade and the Spanish colonial regime's continued influence, which manifested itself in jewelry shops and shops that sold European goods. Racial resentment motived white women to disparage any Filipina practices of demonstrating cosmopolitanism and cultural dexterity through the consumption and display of Chinese, local native, and European materials and styles. This pattern of refusal followed racially coded language that persisted throughout the US colonial period. The American press continued to use ridicule and absurdity to uphold the framework of Filipinos as being perpetually in a state of development.

White American women narrativized fashion to illustrate this racial developmental framework. In her memoir, Taft takes pains to point out the city's inability to meet the standards of what a truly modern urban space should offer. She tells readers that, in the "old days" of the Spanish colonial period, a "really fine Spanish and rich *mestizo* society" existed, but as a result of the Philippine Revolution and the Spanish-American War, "all, or nearly all, of the Spaniards had left the Islands, and the mestizos had not yet decided which way to 'lean,' or just how to meet the American control in the situation."[225] For Taft, fashion and the culture of consumption exemplifies "backwardness" or delay in Filipino modernization. In contrast to other accounts that describe the proliferation of textile stores, boutiques with ready-to-wear fashion imports, tailors, and dressmakers, Taft declares that Manila "lacked" fashion: there "were no fashionable gowns to be had, therefore simplicity, or a more or less rundownedness of one-time respectability, became the fashion" and "there were no hat shops, so women ceased to wear hats."[226] Taft uses commerce and fashion as a way to create a recognizable gauge of modernity both for herself and her readers. Ultimately, these white American women contended, the elements of civility, proper womanhood, and cosmopolitanism were present in the Philippines. But, in keeping with imperialist logic, they agreed that Filipinas still needed white American women to educate them about femininity, fashion, taste, and refinement.[227]

## Persistent Tensions and Collaborations

By 1902, the Philippine Commission's tour had ended, and while resistance continued throughout the archipelago, the United States had officially declared an end to the Philippine-American War. Meanwhile the colonial state firmly cemented Manila as the center of the Philippines. Political sessions moved from the provinces to the colonial capital. "Filipinization," colonial authorities' strategy of incrementally including elite Filipino men in state governance through the Philippine Assembly, drew more people from the provinces to Manila. Consequently, the social makeup of Manila transformed. High-society social life did not simply reflect political and economic developments but was itself political.

By 1905, Manila society was filled with heightened tension between Filipinos and Americans. Many Manileños distrusted and disapproved of the newly formed military police, the Philippine Constabulary.[228] Filipino nationalists also challenged and critiqued Governor-General Luke E. Wright, William H. Taft's successor. American and Filipino newspapers circulated stories about the problems of "race antagonism" and "race prejudice."[229] White American women sought to maintain a sense of authority in the colony and reaffirm their own identity through white supremacy. Aware of the power of "parlor politics," American women went to great lengths to ensure their abilities to contribute to their husbands' political careers and to the maintenance of the United States' authority in the Philippines. At the same time, white women policed racial boundaries in segregated Manila society. While some settings, such as civic organizations, deliberately brought together Filipina elites and white women, in Manila high society, racial tensions between white Americans and elite Filipinas persisted. "Manila Americans" had "little or no social intercourse" with Filipino elites, and many of these racial barriers were policed and upheld by white American women.[230] The women who dictated American "society" in Manila organized the social events, created and enforced guest lists, and set unspoken rules for proximity and interactions. Dr. Elsie Clews Parsons, a sociologist visiting the Philippines, wrote a short article in the New York–based publication *The Independent*. In this piece, titled "American Snobbishness in the Philippines," Parsons comments that in 1905, "Americans perpetuated racial separation." She explains, "Americans led the life of parties, yet most socialized only with others in the white community."[231] Indeed, in many ways the anti-Black racism of Jim Crow and the segregationist logics of the continental United States could be seen in Philippine society under colonial rule.[232]

Much like the racial tensions that arose during the Philippine Commission's tour several years prior, racism and competition over power manifested in the social worlds and interactions between Filipino and American women. Competition between women and petty acts continued to serve as crucial technologies in the maintenance of colonial hierarchical structures. Alice Roosevelt, the daughter of US president Theodore Roosevelt, toured with a commissioned party of US congressional representatives and the US secretary of war. In describing the social realities of racism in the Philippines, one article stated that "each particular woman, whose social importance was larger in her own eyes, tried to capture Miss Roosevelt for some affair."[233] The social competition over Roosevelt's attention amplified the underlying and persistent tensions between white American and elite Filipino women. American newspapers in the Philippines and the United States began to run stories about the antagonism between Americans and Filipinas. Parsons supported the reporting on Alice Roosevelt's visit to the Philippines and described "race prejudice" in the ways that white Americans excluded Filipinos from the events and affairs of Manila high society. In her writing, Parsons divulges, "It was stated to me, and as far as I could I verified the statement, that not a single Filipino lady was invited to meet Miss Roosevelt or the ladies of the party at any of the dinners given in their honor."[234] Parsons goes on to underscore that Filipino women were insulted by petty acts and social snubs. Parsons writes, "The daughter of one of the most prominent native officials, a cultivated and distinguished lad, told me that under no circumstances would she go to the Malacañan (the official home and headquarters of the Governor-General and later the President of the Philippines), as she understood that she was not welcome there. She added that all her friends felt the same way."[235] Another article published in the *San Francisco Argonaut*, "Quarrels of Filipino Ladies—How 'Princess Alice' Bolted Reception," describes "race prejudice" as "in essence the same as in the days of military supremacy" when Manila was under martial law at the turn of the century.[236] People were well aware that the social aggressions between women "all seem small things," but as one news article points out, "it is the small things which count."[237]

Even after the Commission's tour ended and the Insular Government was established, Filipina and American women's relationships remained complex and contradictory. Throughout the US colonial regime, Filipina civic groups collaborated with Manila Americans. Suffragists, for example, worked with American representatives to gain voting rights for Filipina women. This did not necessarily mean that all Filipina women completely internalized colonialism; nor were they "unconscious victim[s] of Modernity," as a prominent journalist and legislator, Teodoro Kalaw, wrote.[238] But it did mean that like the men of their social classes, they sought to consolidate their power and position in a time of rapid change. Filipinization, the expansion of gender-inclusive public education, and the creation of new professions brought dramatic changes to Philippine politics, culture, society, and the economy. Collaborations and negotiations with official and unofficial colonial authorities often cemented Filipinas' status and power.

However, competition over power sustained tensions between white American women and elite Filipina women. Paying attention to drama, gossip, and "petty" interactions shows the slippages and cracks in the image of cooperation and friendship between the two groups. Episcopalian missionary bishop Charles Brent commented that in order to achieve US colonial "success" and to overcome Filipino discontent with the United States, "it also would be well if the character of a man's wife also played [a] part in his qualifications as colonial administrator."[239] Such tensions and resistance manifested in various arenas, especially in beauty, fashion, and dress. And these arenas—as we will see in the following chapters—continued to be inextricably linked to politics, culture, and the local and global economies. The politics of pettiness expressed through style and fashion took place in intimate settings and public venues, demonstrating that women's appearances were used to leverage power and authority and revealed previously unexplored terrains of foreign relations and challenges to American colonizers. Frictions arose precisely because the colonial transition from the Spanish to US regimes threw together power structures built on distinct—yet often similar—ideologies of gender, race, class, ethnicity, and nation. In this context of shifting power, modes of dress became a way to manage tensions and fears. The drama and competition over presentations of "better" femininity also highlight incongruent power, incongruent access, and competing hierarchies. Through the terrain of appearances, Filipina elites and white American women accompanying the second Philippine Commission enacted imperial aggressions through sartorial confrontations.

While this chapter looks at the intimate interactions between women in colonial encounters, the strategies of curating and displaying personal style and appearance extended beyond the private spaces of homes or the ballroom. In chapter 2, we will see how many of the same racial tensions, competitions over power, and weaponization of personal appearance also occurred in the spectacular pageantry of beauty and popularity contests.

# 2

## QUEEN MAKERS

*Beauty, Power, and the Development of
a Beauty Pageant Industrial Complex*

In 1934, the Manila-based newspaper *La vanguardia* published an interview
with the first Manila Carnival "Queen of the Orient," Pura Villanueva Kalaw.[1]
The interview marked one of only a few occasions on which Villanueva Kalaw
spoke of her experience at the first Manila Carnival in February 1908—a
grandiose weeklong celebration and exhibition that was similar to a World's
Fair. Rather than expressing either nostalgia for the first large-scale exhibition held in the Philippines or pride in her title, Villanueva Kalaw expressed
deep dissatisfaction with her experience. In the interview, she compares the
1908 contest to the same event in 1931, in which her daughter, Maria Kalaw
Katigbak, won the Miss Philippines title. She says, "Para mi, el carnaval más
atractivo fué aquél en que fué elegida reina mi hija María, porque era el
carnaval que propiamente podía llamarse de filipinos" (For me, the most attractive carnival was that in which my daughter, Maria, was elected queen,
because it was a carnival that could properly be called Filipino).[2] Villanueva
Kalaw goes on to say that although 1908 witnessed what she called a "carnivalistic spirit," "en aquél novenario de alegría los que más se divirtieron y
también aprovecharon, fueron los extranjeros" (in that period of joy, those

who most enjoyed themselves and also made the most [of the Carnival] were the foreigners).[3]

Villanueva Kalaw identifies the tension between Filipinos and Americans as the source of her displeasure. She describes the first Manila Carnival as inherently flawed, because it catered disproportionately to American foreigners. The juxtaposition between her own title and her daughter's—"Queen of the Orient" as opposed to "Miss Philippines"—also puts forward a teleology of imperial contestations and Philippine nationalism and national identity. In 1908 there were two carnival titles: "Queen of the Orient" and "Queen of the Occident." In many ways, Villanueva Kalaw's 1908 title was a runner-up; although the "Queen of the Orient" was the winner among the Filipino contestants, the title "Manila Carnival Queen" was bestowed upon the American "Queen of the Occident." Over time, the Manila Carnival Queen contest became more Filipino. It was renamed the Miss Philippines beauty contest in 1927. Villanueva Kalaw's brief interview addresses how the platforms of beauty pageantry were shaped by negotiations between the formation of Philippine nationalism and US colonialism. In her interview, Villanueva Kalaw reminisces, "Si bien es verdad que en mi tiempo hubo más espíritu carnavalino y más disfrazados deambulando por las calles, sembrando ruido con sus trompetas: si bien es verdad que la indumentaría que yo me ponía, desde la corona hasta los zapatos, era todo del país, en aquel novenario de alegría los que más se divirtieron y también aprovecharon, fueron los extranjeros" (Although it is true that in my time there was more carnival spirit and more costumed people wandering the streets, making noise with their trumpets: although it is true that the clothing that I wore, from the crown to the shoes, was all of the [Philippines] however, in that celebration of joy those who had the most fun and also took advantage, were the foreigners). Despite the joy of celebration and the pride she had in the fashion that showcased the styles and clothing from the Philippines, her joy was tempered by the colonial conditions that shaped the Manila Carnival. Villanueva Kalaw contends, "Y la razón es porque síendo aquél el primer festival carnavalino, aun desconocido por nosotros, los que lo dirigieron y lo animaron fueron Americanos" (And the reason is because that being the first carnival, still unknown to us, was directed and controlled by Americans).[4] Her feelings resulted not just from her individual experience or interactions with other people at the Carnival; they were a reaction to the larger political forces and tensions that manifested in the very production of the Manila Carnival.

Participants in the Manila Carnival pageant navigated these tensions. They not only negotiated and solidified their social and political statuses through pageantry and titles but also produced specific markers of feminine beauty, along shifting hierarchies of difference, through their spectacular self-presentations. The title of "queen" awarded winners cash prizes along with status and connections that produced many powerful alliances through marriage and bolstered numerous careers.[5] To be a beauty queen meant embodying normative scripts of ideal womanhood and broadcasting successful beauty and femininity.[6] As Dawn Mabalon argues, Filipina beauty queens "embodied the best aspirations and virtues of the new nation."[7] Filipino and American emotional and capital investment in the development of beauty pageants through the Manila Carnival contest—and eventually the Miss Philippines beauty contest—reflected the power of beauty pageantry and beauty queens themselves.[8] Indeed, the Manila Carnival Queen contest, held annually from 1908 to 1939, provided a platform for a broad range of actors to negotiate identity and display fantasies of power.[9] The pleasure and pain that the pageantry evoked therefore must be regarded as political. Filipina beauty pageantry was, and continues to be, shaped by long-standing hierarchies of racial and gendered differences first solidified by modern colonialism and its tensions with anticolonial nationalism.

The Manila Carnival Association, sanctioned by the US colonial state, began making plans for the first Carnival in 1907, when the state was just beginning its next phase of "colonial consolidation."[10] This period marked a huge step toward the implementation of a centralized colonial government. That year, the elections of Filipino representatives to the newly established Philippine Assembly were held. Filipino elites, who had been courted by the Philippine Commission a few years earlier, were fully aware of the new system's potential power.[11] But political infrastructural planning still faced challenges. Public censure of continued "race prejudice," especially from anticolonial nationalists, marred the image of American benevolence.[12] Despite the rhetoric of Philippine-American friendship after the end of the war, "Manila Americans," the American military and civilians who had built businesses and institutions in Manila, continued to maintain racist beliefs and practices such as excluding Filipinos from the highest levels of government and prohibiting Filipinos from entering and joining certain American social spaces and organizations in Manila.[13]

Racism and racial tensions were woven into every aspect of the Manila Carnival. Although the festivities were intended to highlight the success of US colonialism, the Manila Carnival Queen contest projected the existing racial tensions between white Americans and Filipinas onto a very public and spectacular stage. In doing so, the problems and fissures in American efforts to present colonialism as "benevolent assimilation," as an endeavor of friend-ship, were placed in the public spotlight. At the same time, the contest and its subsequent spectacles of feminine beauty demonstrated Filipino reactions to and negotiations with US colonial hierarchies. The public celebration of feminine beauty and ideal womanhood aimed to define the Philippines and its ideals within the context of American colonial subjugation. The spectacle of crowning a beauty queen disciplined normative ideas of proper feminin-ity and messages of modernity and civilization. The title and the idea of the beauty queen asserted varied and often competing images of femininity, con-tributing to the formation of Filipina identity.

Beauty pageants are complex systems. The Manila Carnival contest was entangled with official colonial state organizations, businesses and trade, news agencies, and informal arenas of everyday life. This network coalesced in a regimented machine that effectively functioned as a "queen maker."[14] By 1930, Filipinos promoted the Philippines as a "land of beauty queens."[15] The power of beauty pageants seeped into Filipinos' everyday lives in the archi-pelago and across the diaspora.[16]

This chapter identifies and tracks the interactive components that struc-ture beauty pageantry and queen-making. It examines the development of beauty pageantry as a complex system and explores how the pageant in-dustry and pageant practices were used simultaneously as tools for colo-nial domination, as venues for articulation of Philippine nationalist power, and as arenas for gendered contestation of colonialism.[17] Starting with the Manila Carnival, the modern Philippine beauty pageant has evolved into an industry—or more accurately, an industrial complex—that fused together in-dividual contestants, the colonial state, Filipino elites, private enterprise, and the Filipino public. Queen makers, contestants, their supporters, state offi-cials, and private investors are all invested in the beauty queen for their own gain. While this chapter does not account for all local and global pageants, it conveys a sense of the significance of beauty pageantry in the broader Fili-pino context. Although beauty pageantry was partly used to support the US colonial state, as part of the larger arena of Filipino diasporic performance, beauty pageantry also displayed what performance studies scholars Lucy San Pablo Burns and Doreen Fernandez describe as the brave acts against the "press of the cultures of imperialism" and the consistency of indigenization amid imperialism.[18] Beauty pageants have proliferated and have sustained their popularity among Filipinos for more than a century precisely because they were presented as an arena in which emotional, physical, temporal, and monetary investments would pay off.[19] Beauty pageantry is a lucrative industry, and beauty queen title holders, then as now, find their statuses catapulted in terms of their economic and cultural capital.

In the early twentieth century, the popularity of the Manila Carnival, its ability to attract global attention, and the simultaneous economic growth in Philippine industries as well as the increased presence of new foreign-owned businesses motivated other regions and cities in the Philippines to hold similar exhibitions. After 1912, these smaller fairs hosted queen contests similar to the Manila Carnival Queen contest, making pageantry the main feature of their festivals and adding them to their performative repertoires of theater and religious pageantry. Further, popular news publications sponsored both beauty and popularity contests to increase their sales and advertising revenue. Pageants like the "Miss Pearl of the Orient," the *Philippine Free Press*'s beauty contest, and *Graphic* magazine's popularity contest mirrored the structure of the Manila Carnival Queen contest.[20] The increased availability of photography and portrait studios also allowed news publications to print good quality staged portraits of each candidate. Readers could then rely on photos and descriptions of each candidate to make their selections. Thousands of Filipinos cast their votes for the candidate of their choice and thus demonstrated an acceptance of beauty pageants as a respectable arena for Filipina participants.[21]

To this day, beauty pageants elicit high emotions and intense investment among Filipinos across the Philippines and the diaspora.[22] Pageants place bodies on display for the entertainment, pleasure, and consumption of others. They structure expectations of comportment, dress, and how bodies and faces should look. Yet, despite apt criticisms of mainstream pageants' perpetuation of misogyny and patriarchy through the objectification of women's bodies, beauty pageants remain both ubiquitous and special in the Philippines. In addition to national pageants, barrios, towns, and provinces host a number of local pageants each year. Pageant participants include young cisgender and trans girls in both rural towns and urban spaces. Pageants are also ubiquitous in the Filipino diaspora. As early as the 1930s, Filipino American communities hosted annual beauty contests such as the Queen of Rizal Day in Stockton, California. Dawn Mabalon's work on Filipino Americans in Stockton shows that pageants policed what was expected and acceptable in the formation of Filipino American identity.[23] More recently, overseas Filipino workers (OFWs) in Hong Kong, most of whom are domestic workers, have hosted Sunday beauty pageants.[24] They use their only day off, Sundays, to organize, rehearse musical performances, and make and design costumes to put on elaborate contests. Organizing beauty pageants forges connections, creates community, and provides a source of joy that is needed to survive the highly exploitative nature of domestic work in Hong Kong. As Robert Diaz argues, *biyuti* and beauty pageantry can be powerful forces in moments of survival, fights for dignity, and protests, particularly for marginalized peoples.[25] Pageants are everywhere, and yet they have not become banal. They are always and already spectacular.[26] Pageantry serves as a disciplinary tool that enforces normative scripts for the gain of a select and privileged few. At the same time, beauty pageants have the potential to empower minoritized subjects, even if just through being a "queen for a day."[27]

The emergence of the modern Filipina beauty contest involved multiple uneven forms of power and empowerment. In the Philippines and the diaspora, beauty and politics cannot be easily separated. Filipina beauty pageantry cannot simply be disregarded as frivolous and devoid of political consequence, nor can it be understood exclusively as a residual effect of colonialism or as an internalized colonialism. Scholars of international beauty pageants often trace the advancement of beauty pageants in the Global South to the 1930s and 1940s, arguing that decolonization efforts appropriated American beauty pageants to perform and cultivate national identity.[28] Some critics frame Filipino beauty pageants as imitations of Western contests and as the internalization of Western standards of beauty pageantry, which they regard as a sure sign of blind acceptance of colonial subjugation. However, while the US colonial state organized the first Manila Carnival Queen contest, beauty pageantry in the Philippines cannot be reduced only to internalized colonialism or to mimicry that fails to recognize what Lucy San Pablo Burns calls "the richness of imitation as creative process."[29] San Pablo Burns turns to the concept of *gaya* (mimic), contending that when we take "labors of imitation" seriously, it is possible to see mimicry both as "producing a body of performance riven by historical stress of its own emergence" and as "an act that can be deliberate, an experiential method of learning and a way of knowing the world."[30] In other words, the Manila Carnival was at once a colonial tool, a platform for the performance of emerging nationalisms, and a site at which to appropriate and reconstruct what the title of "queen" could mean for Filipino ethnic, racial, class, sexual, and gender identity formations. Ultimately, beauty contests tell a story of how the Philippines developed an understanding of itself as a nation and how a hegemonic Filipino identity was produced through the formation and disciplining of Filipina beauty.

Beauty contests emerged from a complicated genealogy that brought together aspects of religious pageantry, fiesta culture, and American spectacles of beauty.[31] This chapter traces the emergence and concretization of formal structures and systems that went into making a beauty pageant industry in the Philippines. Recognizing the multiple facets of beauty pageantry and queen-making, we can better understand the role of women, gender, and performances of femininity in processes of national identity formation within the context of colonial domination. This is not a comprehensive history of beauty pageants in the Philippines. Rather, this chapter examines the regime of beauty pageantry and investigates the power dynamics of Filipino beauty contests. In efforts to seize and sustain forms of power and authority in the colonial and nationalist regimes, a wide range of people and institutions invested in the beauty queens' potential to discipline and shape societal norms. Analyzing the beauty pageant system sheds light on the ways in which ideologies of race, gender, ethnicity, geography, and class fundamentally informed the infrastructures of nationalism and empire as they constructed the figure of the beauty queen in the colonial Philippines.

## Pageant Politics

The Manila Carnival had an indelible impact on the development of modern Filipina beauty pageants. In 1907, US colonial officials and entrepreneurs formed the Manila Carnival Association and planned a one- to two-week-long event to project a positive image of the American empire. The event was to be modeled after the exhibitions and world's fairs of the late nineteenth and early twentieth centuries.[32] Western empires wielded world's fairs and other large-scale spectacles to showcase global power. Spain, for instance, organized a World Exposition in Madrid in 1884 and a Philippine Exposition in 1887 as its last gasps of power in the midst of the revolutions and anticolonial nationalisms erupting throughout its empire. In 1904, the Louisiana Purchase Exposition, also known as the St. Louis World's Fair, exhibited the United States' colonial conquest and the expansion of its empire. Live dioramas of "ethnic villages" and constructed schoolrooms where fairgoers could witness the education of new colonial subjects in real time were among the most popular features of the St. Louis World's Fair.[33] For the US colonial state in the Philippines, then, the Manila Carnival would serve two purposes. First, it would draw attention to the natural resources and industry of the Philippines, enticing both local and foreign investors.[34] Filipino Governor-General James Francis Smith made it clear to a large gathering of diverse American, Filipino, and European investors prior to the first Manila Carnival that "though the Carnival would look like it was for pleasure, it was really for business."[35] The president of the Manila Carnival Association,

George T. Langhorne, echoed similar sentiments, claiming that "the Carnival would be good for the country, for its common interests, and would make the world take note of our prosperity and good opportunities for business."[36] The carnival would fulfill imperial capitalist aspirations for American wealth attainment in the Philippines. Second, the Association hoped that the revelry of a carnival would draw attention away from the violence of the Philippine-American War, which had begun in 1899 and had lasted almost a decade.[37] The festivities offered a revised history of colonial violence. A promotional brochure for the 1909 Manila Carnival claimed that the carnival celebrated "a great, beautiful, fertile group of islands, which for centuries had peacefully slumbered apart from the world activities of the day, [that] suddenly, by chance of war found itself in the very middle of the highway of progress."[38] The brochure went on to reduce the Philippine-American War to an insurrection of misplaced anger, claiming, "The insurrectionary army of the Filipinos, brought into existence in the struggle against Spanish supremacy, was, unfortunately, directed by these people against their liberators."[39] The Carnival Association sought to portray the Manila Carnival as a jubilant celebration that would build friendship between Filipinos and Americans, using the same logic that the Philippine Commission had used.[40] But rather than perform friendship in intimate spaces of the home or even in government sessions, the Carnival spectacularized the image of colonial friendship.[41] Manila Carnival pamphlets and endorsements included detailed descriptions of the wonders of the Philippines and its attractions that Western tourists would enjoy, marketing the Philippines as welcoming to Americans. Carnival organizers built opulent structures and staged elaborate festivities to stand as visible proof of US success in modernizing the Philippines.

Early iterations of the Manila Carnival promoted and capitalized on American exceptionalism. The 1909 Carnival's promotional pamphlet celebrated US imperialism, stating, "Into the wonderful process of transformation and development which the United States has undertaken in the Philippines and which is moving forward in such a splendid manner, there has fortunately entered none of the destructive tendency which usually accompanies the efforts of a modern civilization to impress itself and its institutions upon an older one."[42] The Carnival, like other US expositions, showcased the power of the United States as an empire, as a global power to a global audience. At the same time, it was meant to thwart comparisons to other empires and to uphold notions of US exceptionalism by presenting US colonialism as spreading civilization, modern democracy, and progress to an "Oriental race long accustomed to the ways and methods of the easy-going Spaniard."[43] The investment in advertising US altruism and progress in the Philippines stemmed from the Insular Government's desire to bring commercial attention to the Philippines and to promote tourism in the archipelago, entice investors, and advertise Filipino products. In their reports and promotional brochures, Carnival promoters contended that the US bestowed "modern institutions" upon the Philippines, including "the Occidental conception of things, its courage, and its supreme confidence in the power and righteousness of its interpretation of the meaning of civic liberty."[44] Moreover, the large-scale exhibition was seen as an American tool that would modernize "an Oriental race almost without history or traditions and whose only claim to modern civilization is based upon an indifferent contact with the Spaniard during the short period of three hundred years."[45] The Manila Carnival organizers placed a large-scale public spectacle under a global gaze to prove that the United States was, indeed, an international power.[46] By evoking the language of cosmopolitanism and worldliness, the brochure demonstrated how the United States had shaped the Philippines, and particularly the city of Manila, into a modern destination worthy of tourism and foreign investment. The Manila Carnival obfuscated how US colonial projects, conceptualized as modern and progressive, more often than not exploited and subjugated Filipinos. This large-scale production, of course, required capital. Instead of asking the newly formed Philippine Assembly and the colonial state to fully fund the Carnival, Commissioner of Commerce and Police William Cameron Forbes, a leader of the Manila Carnival Association, requested half the total cost from the government and planned to fundraise the additional moneys through subscription campaigns such as the Manila Carnival Queen contest.[47] In doing so, US colonial officials instituted a popularity contest that functioned as a crucial political, economic, and cultural component in support of their colonial endeavors.

The pageant was intended to garner public interest and to raise funds. To gain the privilege of voting in the contest, one had to obtain a coupon by purchasing a copy of one of the Association-approved newspapers.[48] The Manila Carnival Association declared that the Carnival Queen would be a "popularity contest," and that the "lady receiving the highest number of votes, be she American, Filipina, or European, will be proclaimed Queen."[49] With an eye to guaranteeing monetary support for the carnival, organizers understood and tried to capitalize on the segregated sociality of Manila. They deliberately targeted the wealthiest Filipino, American, and Spanish families in Manila, hoping to convince them to enter a family member into the contest.[50] Those with the most money and influence could then campaign and gain support for their selected candidate among their family, friends, and business associates. Thus, Forbes and other Manila Carnival Association members did not organize the pageant simply to celebrate feminine beauty. In these early iterations of the competition, contestants were chosen not for their physical attractiveness but for their economic and social statuses. Carnival organizers hoped that these young Filipinas' families and societal connections would make fundraising easier. Perhaps even more important, the process of selecting Carnival Queen candidates and winners revealed the Americans' dependence on Filipino elites.

## Pageantry and Its Discontents

Although the Manila Carnival Association singled out elite Filipino families to participate in the contest, a number of elements in the Manila Carnival Queen contest disrupted gender norms, which agitated many Filipinos, particularly those of the elite class. That is, Filipino elites upheld Spanish notions that elite women should remain protected in the home and be put on public display only for religious ceremonies. But it was not necessarily the public display of women and girls that troubled them. Indeed, parades and pageantry featuring young Filipina women were certainly not new. In the Christian regions of the archipelago, annual Marian celebrations and acts of devotion to patron saints involved elaborate processions. Girls and young women from prominent families were often selected as the centers of such pageantry, such as in the Flores de Mayo or the Santacruzan.[51] These celebrations couched public presentations of feminine beauty in religious piety— public performances of Marian devotion. Rather, it was the secular nature of the public display that disrupted the elite's gender norms. Critics of the Manila Carnival Queen contest also took issue with the showcasing of Filipina women for profit. Despite promoters' positive rhetoric of friendship and fairness, the Carnival beauty pageant's disruption of gender norms rooted in class and religious ideology provoked contempt and scorn among Filipinos. As evidenced in the news coverage of the pageant, the Filipino public did not immediately accept the Carnival Queen contest. Political cartoons conveyed skepticism and discomfort; one cartoon shows white men—members of the Manila Carnival Association—with lanterns searching for the Carnival queens in Manila's brothels. The cartoon expressed the public's apprehension that a secular pageant would "cheapen" Filipinas. In the early twentieth century, gender ideologies positioned women in public spaces as immoral.

Thus, the Filipino objection was not so much the public display of young women, or that it involved money, but rather that a secular public spectacle would disrupt established ideals of Filipina womanhood and liken the Carnival Queen to a prostitute—the epitome of immorality and vice in early twentieth-century Philippine culture.[52]

The Manila Carnival integrated some Catholic aspects, like holding the festivities in February during the pre-Lenten season, but it eliminated many features of Catholic religious devotion.[53] Instead, the Manila Carnival Association homed in on the revelry of carnivale on the scale of a world's fair.[54] The organizers sought not only to secularize the public display of Filipina femininity, but also to model the festivities held in Manila after exhibitions of "cosmopolitan" cities around the world. As Edward Said argues, imperial spectacles relied on "monumental grandeur" and exotic allure to legitimize the West's visions of the colonized other.[55] The brochure promoting the first Manila Carnival described it as an "oriental adaptation of the far-famed customs of the south of France, of Italy, Spain, and Latin America."[56] Participants and audience members, the brochure boasted, would witness the similarities between these famous festivals and the Manila Carnival's "wonderful display of brilliant costumes, gorgeous processions, magnificent pageantry, gathering of beautiful women, with the attendant revelry, mummery, masked balls, fun, frolic, feasting and sports."[57] Carnival promoters borrowed imagery associated with world-famous, jubilant, and extravagant citywide celebrations, likening Manila to other "advanced" and "worldly" cities. The Manila Carnival Association used these marketing strategies to draw local Filipino participants into purchasing tickets to the festivities. Although the Manila Carnival was mainly an exposition focusing on colonial industry, marketing materials, such as brochures, advertisements in local newspapers, and posters for the Manila Carnival promoted the fiesta-like aspects of the carnival that evoked Filipino connections to Spanish, and therefore European, heritage, inviting Filipino participants to openly display such ties. According to Carnival organizers, like other carnivals in cities ranging from Venice to Rio de Janeiro, the spirit of the Manila Carnival would be guided by "misrule," suggesting the potential for the temporary subversion of power and social hierarchies.[58] Carnivals as interruptions of everyday life manifested in seasonal celebrations (typically before the Lenten season) have a long and rich history; their elements can be traced back to pre-Christian Rome. The carnivals of medieval Europe, for instance, were festivities that included forms of shocking entertainment that pushed at the boundaries of what would be considered socially acceptable. The shocking components of carnivalistic festivities were often called "misrule," an aberration of normal life or social order. And symbols of such misrule—court jesters and masked figures—were emblazoned on the posters and brochures produced by the Manila Carnival Association. The covers of the 1909 and 1910 Manila Carnival brochures featured the "Red Devil," who served as a mascot of the carnival revelry. On the covers, the Red Devil hovers over the Manila Carnival grounds and attendees, showering everyone with glitter and confetti.[59] Brochure covers and posters sought to entice Filipino audience members to participate in the revelry to make American presence, culture, and power palatable to them.

In spite of reservations and criticisms from members of the Filipino community, the contest-organizing carried on. Organizers focused on the Carnival's promise of jubilance, friendship, and the newly bestowed modernity of the Philippines. Following the logic of benevolent assimilation, the Association portrayed the contest as a fair and democratic process open to all women living in the Philippines, regardless of race, ethnicity, or nationality. As such, organizers asserted the contest was a way to observe modern democratic practices. Although ballots were available only for purchase, thus restricting voting to those who had the capital, casting a vote was nevertheless promoted as a way of exercising individual agency, fairness, and democratic spirit. However, the discrepancies and tensions that emerged during the first Carnival Queen competition belied its marketing as a democratic and friendly process. The competition, which touted fairness and friendship, was in fact rife with scandal and unethical behavior. Ballots were counted every week between December 7, 1907, and January 15, 1908. Early on, voting patterns for candidates brought to light racial divisions operating during the American colonial period. During the first few weeks of the competition, three women took notable leads over their competitors: Mrs. Henry M. Jones (a white American woman), Maria de la Cruz Baldasano (a white Spanish woman), and Mrs. Israel Beck (a white American woman).[60] By the second week of the competition, Jones had 4,169 votes, followed by Baldasano with 1,978 votes, and Beck with 1,110 votes. A Filipina candidate, Leonarda Limjap, was in fourth place with 779 votes. The large gap between the top three candidates and their fellow competitors would remain constant during the following weeks of the competition. *Muling pagsilang*, the Tagalog portion of the newspaper *El renacimiento*, the public arm of anticolonial nationalist groups, complained that while the "American and Spanish communities each [had] candidates, the Filipinos [had] several," which explained the wide gap in votes between white Western candidates and Filipina candidates.[61]

The Filipino press regarded the voting patterns for the Carnival Queen as a manifestation of white American racism. Furthermore, Filipinos who criticized the racism of the contest used patriotic and nationalist rhetoric to disparage the election of non-Filipinos. The newly formed Union for the Election of a Filipina Queen sent a letter to *El renacimiento* expressing their awareness of the competition's racist undertones and the perpetuation of a developmental framework placed onto Filipinos that shaped the first few years of the US colonial regime.[62] The letter, which was reprinted in the *Manila Times*, argued, "To elect a foreigner would tacitly admit the absolute lack of Filipina women capable of carrying off such a position with distinction."[63] As the most vocal critics of US colonization and policy, *El renacimiento* would have likely seen an important opportunity in the drama of the Manila Carnival Queen contest. The racist attitudes and disparities within the competition made the contest a convenient vehicle through which to publicly articulate grievances and critique US colonialism. *El renacimiento* continued to act as a media watchdog, closely monitoring the Carnival and reporting on its events for the duration of the festivities.

As the contest progressed, the disparities in votes worsened. In fact, the disparities in the ballot counts were so great that the integrity and fairness of the campaign and voting processes were called into question. Members of the press who were involved in the vote-counting discovered ballot irregularities, including certain American publications that printed four ballots per purchase rather than the single ballot permitted by the rules.[64] The Association also found ballots printed in the *Sentinel*, an unapproved tabloid. Additionally, a significant number of ballots in favor of one or two candidates were found in the Carnival Association's office, which led to allegations that some members of the Association aligned themselves with these candidates.[65] As a result, Carnival officials suspended popular voting and left the selection of the Manila Carnival Queen to members of the executive committee. Beck, who at one point held the lead, withdrew from the competition. Beck's press release stated, "As the contest is admittedly no longer one of popularity or genuine balloting by one's friends, she has today requested the committee to withdraw her name and cancel votes in her favor."[66]

The executive committee not only suspended voting but also changed the number of titles to be awarded in the contest. In addition to the top title of "Manila Carnival Queen," the committee created two auxiliary titles: "Queen of the Orient" and "Queen of the Occident." Carnival organizers regarded the creation of these titles as a way to satisfy the racially divided constituents.[67]

The committee originally declared Leonarda Limjap "Queen of the Orient." However, Limjap withdrew from the contest and relinquished the title. Manila newspapers reported that Limjap had renounced the title because of a previously scheduled trip to Japan. However, historians Alfred McCoy and Alfredo Roces claim that Limjap's father, Mariano Limjap, a powerful Chinese mestizo businessman and politician, decided that the public display of his daughter threatened the family's social standing in colonial Philippine society and pulled her from competition.[68] Eventually Pura Villanueva Kalaw, a young woman from Iloilo, was crowned "Queen of the Orient," while Marjorie Colton became "Queen of the Occident." Carnival organizers hoped that crowning both a Filipina and an American would present an image of harmony rather than animosity. One photograph, which was printed in Manila Carnival promotional literature, in newspapers, and on postcards, showed Villanueva Kalaw and Colton seated side-by-side, emphasizing symmetry. The two women are the same height; their escorts are seated beside them; crowns sit atop each of their coiffed updos; both women stare directly at the camera. The mirrored composition of the photograph attempts to convey equity and fairness.

The rhetoric of fairness and acceptance could not quite disguise the racist underpinnings of the Manila Carnival Queen contest, though. Although Carnival officials changed the contest to assuage tensions and to appear "fair," the creation of two separate titles for a Filipina and an American woman used racialized segregationist logic, negating the message of equality, unity, and friendship between Filipinos and Americans. Public spectacles like the Manila Carnival institutionalized the exhibition of feminine bodies not only as visually consumable objects of beauty but also as symbols of two distinct national and racial identities: white American and Filipina. During the coronation ceremony in the hippodrome, a massive indoor venue specifically constructed for the Manila Carnival, a masked figure, purportedly acting on behalf of the King and Queen of the Orient, announced that the King and Queen of the Occident would be crowned Manila Carnival King and Queen.[69] The coronation ceremony was a performative metaphor for the US colonial logic of benevolent assimilation, revealing how US colonial administrators saw themselves as racially superior and therefore better fit to rule the "kingdom"—or rather, the Philippines. One of the main features of the carnival was a water parade in which the Queen and King of the Orient and their retinue rode richly bedecked barges out into Manila Bay. There, they "most graciously received" the Queen and King of the Occident.[70] Rather than display resistance to multiple colonial regimes, this meeting of the

Queens and Kings portrays Filipinos' welcoming acceptance of the arrival of Americans. The spectacle of the Manila Carnival displayed—on a global scale—the "friendly" concession of power by Filipinos to American colonizers and upheld the myth of American exceptionalism.

The discrepancies between the public treatment of Marjorie Colton, Queen of the Occident, and Pura Villanueva Kalaw, Queen of the Orient, also revealed the racism and racial hierarchies between white Americans and Filipinos. The Filipino press reported the unequal treatment of the two queens. When Villanueva Kalaw and her entourage failed to attend a major ball, a short news piece in *Muling pagsilang* asked whether the "Queen and [her] court [went] on strike."[71] In other words, was this a deliberate form of protest? And if so, against what? According to *El renacimiento*, the public voice of the anticolonial Nacionalista party, Villanueva Kalaw and her consort boycotted the event because "the King and Queen of the Orient, as owners of this land, were not given their due honors."[72] In contrast to the arrangements made for Colton, Carnival organizers arranged no transportation to take the King and Queen of the Orient from the parade marking the first day of the festival to the coronation at the grandstand, leaving them scrambling to find their own transportation. When the couple tried to pass through the entrance gates, the guard demanded that they pay twenty pesetas and refused them entrance, stating, "aunque fueran los Reyes y el mismo Cristo, no podan pasar antes de pagar una peseta" (whether royalty or Christ himself, you cannot pass through these gates without paying a penny).[73] In direct contrast to the carefully coordinated performance of Filipinos ceding power to the Americans during the coronation ceremony, the Filipino press presented these encounters as evidence of racial tension and power struggles. *El renacimiento* claimed that the Carnival revealed the "raza atónicas que luchan por la supremacía en Oriente" (the antagonistic race to claim supremacy in the East).[74] The reality of the racist foundations of imperialism could not be contained by choreographed public displays of revelry.

Regardless of the fact that Villanueva Kalaw came from a powerful Hispanic mestizo landowning family in Iloilo province, which afforded her privilege based on the Spanish colonial racial paradigm, the US racial hierarchy firmly positioned her below her white American counterpart, as was reflected in her poor treatment relative to Colton's. Indeed, the juxtaposition of white American women and Filipinas during the Manila Carnival festivities was intended to highlight white women's "construction of themselves as civilized women."[75] The unequal treatment of the white American and Filipina carnival queens and their retinues continued the "American racial tradition and

FIGURE 2.1. Page from the 1926 Philippine Carnival pamphlet showing the Manila Carnival Queen and her court. RG 350, NARA.

a concern with 'white racial purity' [that] was at the heart of America's domestic and overseas colonial territories."[76] White American racist attitudes shaped the contest. Despite recognizing the diversity of Filipinos, Americans in the Philippines rendered the entire population as racially inferior to and as less civilized than their white American colonizers. The Manila Carnival Queen contest continued to do the work of the Philippine Commission by both performing a veneer of friendship and benevolence and instituting new racial hierarchies based on US white supremacy.

Members of the Filipino colonial elite responded to the privileging of the Queen of the Occident over the Queen of the Orient by using the language of beauty and markers of fashion. Carnival organizers designed the Manila Carnival program and styled Colton's attire and accessories to upstage her Filipina counterpart. Despite such careful orchestration, the Filipina beauty queen and Filipino spectators challenged the representations of American white supremacy in part by praising Villanueva Kalaw's style. One news article describing the pageantry of the parades and the appearance of the Carnival royalty at the grandstand used descriptions of dress to illuminate the apparent disparities between the Queens and Kings of the Occident and Orient. According to *El renacimiento,* the monarchs of the Occident made a sorry impression, appearing "very simple in their attire" and "very ordinary looking," echoing the insults and criticisms elite Visayan women made against white American women in earlier colonial encounters, as described in chapter 1. The article went on, "Not so, however, those of the Orient." Villanueva Kalaw "was luxuriously costumed, beautiful and resplendent in her dignity, affectionate towards all." The piece continued to praise Villanueva Kalaw, describing her as "Altanera sin pedantería, augusta sin pretensiones, producto su distinción de la sangre y de la cuna" (Proud without putting on airs, imposing without pretension, a product of her refined blood and birth).[77] While its descriptions of Americans were curt and unflattering, the article chronicled a long list of Villanueva Kalaw's magnificent traits. Moreover, by using terms such as "blood" and "birth," evoking language used to describe traditional monarchies, the article rendered Villanueva Kalaw and her consort inherently majestic and therefore more authentic.

The discourse about the competition and the carnival queens provided pro-independence voices and nationalist media like *El renacimiento* a vehicle with which to circumvent state-sanctioned restrictions on anticolonial critique and the promotion of Philippine nationalism. The Filipina Manila Carnival Queen allowed Filipino anticolonial nationalists to challenge US racist agendas obliquely. In response to systematic oppression, Filipinos sought ways to defy racist attitudes and ideas projected on them. Elite Filipino nationalists seeking validation for their independence movements saw the Manila Carnival exhibition as a way to project Filipinos' positive qualities to a global audience. They regarded the Manila Carnival Queen as the embodiment of feminine ideals and as a representative of the virtues of Filipino culture as a whole. The process of selecting a Filipina to hold the title of beauty queen and the presentation of a Filipina beauty queen to the public should thus be understood in the context of constructing a Filipino national identity—an identity that would be considered equal to that of their American colonizers.

Sedition laws passed a few years earlier declared advocacy for Philippine independence a form of illegal conspiracy against the United States. Such efforts to squash radical revolutions and anticolonial movements created a culture of fear and punishment and led to the arrests of nationalist playwrights who used the *zarzuelas* (public theaters) to critique US colonialism.[78] Revised sedition acts and the institution of the Flag Law just one year before the first Manila Carnival placed strict prohibitions on displays of Philippine nationalism, including banning the presentation of the Philippine flag. In this first Manila Carnival Queen competition, however, the flag was unnecessary: the Filipina contestant embodied Philippine nationalism. The apparatus of the pageant allowed nationalist expressions to be loud and exuberant while under the surveillance of the insular state. That is, critics could highlight the problems of American control and racism through discourse about the competition. Thus, beauty pageantry became a critical apparatus for the promotion of Philippine nationalism.

## The Institutionalization of the Filipina Beauty Pageant

Organizers had found it difficult to secure financial support for the Manila Carnival from the colonial state, the civil government, and the US military. However, the Manila Carnival Queen contest generated financial sponsorship from the private sector, and ticket sales not only paid for the cost of the festivities but turned a profit. Even with the Carnival's problems and tensions, Governor-General Smith reported in a cablegram to the chief of the Bureau of Insular Affairs of the Department of War that the event was a "magnificent success." Smith concluded that there was almost "unanimous demand for its repetition in 1909."[79] The second Manila Carnival replicated much of the format of the first, but on a much grander scale. Promoters and promotional materials focused on secular forms of revelry and entertainment, likening the Carnival to Mardi Gras in New Orleans. Publicity for the 1909 Carnival continued to convey the US as a generous benefactor bestowing these festivities and their revelry upon the Philippines, boasting that this was the first of its kind in the "Orient." The Carnival Association ignored the scandal of the previous year and once again selected both an American and a Filipino Carnival Queen. Hoping to circumvent the problems with ballots and voting, the winners of the 1909 contest were to be chosen by lottery. At the coronation, a group of ten Filipinas and a separate group of twelve American women, all dressed in fine gowns, walked onto the hippodrome's stage. After two names were drawn, the two respective queens donned their "queenly robes" and were presented to the *carnivalistas*.[80]

In 1909, however, Carnival organizers spent more than their allotted budget and failed to earn enough revenue to cover their costs. Facing a 55,000-peso debt, Governor-General Forbes was forced to take out loans from various banks. As a result, the subsequent annual carnivals practiced "the strictest economy," reusing Carnival structures like the hippodrome. Organizers also eliminated the event that garnered the most attention: the Manila Carnival Queen contest. It is unclear why Carnival organizers chose to not hold the contest when it had been conceived to make money. One possible explanation is that organizers were uninterested in the highly feminized pageant and wanted to focus their attention on showcasing colonial businesses and industries. Yet, despite these economic strictures, the colonial government remained committed to hosting the annual carnival. Over the years, the event accumulated more cultural and social capital in Manila and throughout the Philippines. By 1912, the Manila Carnival Association was on more secure financial footing. The colonial state had established dramatic infrastructural changes, such as the expansion of a public school system throughout the archipelago. The Insular Government wanted to showcase these institutional developments as evidence of US imperial power and their successful control over the colony. Colonial control, they hoped, would signal political and economic stability that would entice American investors to Philippine-based industries like commercial agriculture and mining. These factors all contributed to a much grander 1912 Manila Carnival, which the Association hoped would garner more economic interest in the Philippines.[81]

The 1912 Carnival eclipsed the spectacles of previous years. Building on the infrastructure of the previous carnivals and Philippine Expositions, the 1912 festivities included bigger floats, more elaborate industrial exhibitions, and a fuller program. It also reinstated and expanded the Manila Carnival Queen contest, instituting three separate titles for Filipino, American, and Spanish winners. These distinct titles corresponded with designated themed days in the Carnival's program.

The Manila Carnival continued to inadvertently function as a platform around which a Philippine national identity was constructed. The second day of the 1912 Carnival, Saturday, February 4, celebrated "Filipino Day and Night." According to the English-language American publication the *Philippine Monthly*, "If of the different nationalities who have worked energetically toward the common goal of making the 1912 Carnival a success anyone deserves special attention, it is the Filipinos."[82] The article went on to describe how Filipinos became increasingly excited about the Manila Carnival and "caught the 'Carnival Spirit.'" The article's description of the grandiosity of the Filipino Day and Night echoes historian Doreen Fernandez's accounts of fiestas and feast days, which she describes as a "compound of visual splendor, symbol and allegory, *pasikat* and important personages, richness, music, theater, and exotic dances, and an undeniable spirit of competition or *pasiklaban* between the religious orders."[83] As a secular event, rather than opening with a sermon or blessing from a priest, Filipino Day established a sense of solemnity by first holding an educational conference. Speakers included the president of the University of the Philippines, the superintendent of the School of the Arts, and the director of the Girls' Central School, Libra Aveorino.[84] At midday, carnival goers watched and listened to a festive procession consisting of the familiar markers of patriotism: thirty bands, countless numbers of flags and standards, and decorated carriages. The elaborate spectacle functioned as a performance of Filipino national identity. Filipino Day and Night showcased Filipinos as a unified, civilized, and modern people. The speeches given by prominent officials, though, were overshadowed by the spectacular crowning of the Manila Carnival's Filipina queens. The afternoon featured a grand royal pageant that showcased three separate queens who represented three geopolitical regions of the Philippine archipelago: the Queen of Luzon (Paz de Guzman), the Queen of the Visayas (Amparo Noel), and the Sultana of Mindanao (Rosario Reyes).[85] In the evening, "their majesties" feted the grand prize winner, the Empress (Paz Marquez). Each of the queens had their own escorts and retinues of princesses representing their provinces. Filipino Day and Night put forward a didactic performance of a constructed Philippine geography and nation that collapsed the numerous ethnolinguistic groups, geographies, and religions that informed the heterogeneity of the archipelago, and produced instead a live diorama of an imagined Philippine nation, with Manila at the epicenter.

The grandeur of the 1912 Filipino Day eclipsed both the American and Spanish Day courts with its larger retinues, more majestic titles, and greater magnificence. Carnival goers were told that "while the American and Spanish day will be presided over by queens, the Filipinos will have an empress at the head of their festival, and the Empress will be assisted by three kings and three queens."[86] Participants and organizers of the Filipino Day and Night may have taken up the elements of the carnival and contest introduced by the American-led Carnival Association, but in the exhibition of Filipina femininity and by instituting an "empress," they also creatively played with the performative aspects of the pageant and upstaged the other monarchs. To use the title "empress" was an over-the-top gesture meant to triumph over the queens of the Spanish and American courts. Moreover, the clamor and attention that the Filipina court garnered cemented its central role in the Manila Carnival. Pushing against the careful coordination and choreography of the first few Manila Carnival Queen contests, by 1913, the Manila Carnival Queen contest became an exclusively Filipina competition.[87] In 1915, the contest reverted to voting by ballot and crowned only a Filipina Manila Carnival Queen. Over the years, the contest changed its contestant selection criteria several times, ultimately shifting the event's focus from a popularity contest to a beauty pageant in which the woman who represented the most "ideal" vision of femininity was selected as that year's Manila Carnival Queen.[88]

The Manila Carnival built on multiple forms of ceremony and displays of femininity—parades, coronations, and grand balls—to construct an infrastructure for the beauty pageant industry. Though it was hosted in Manila, the contest organized and maintained a deep and widespread network beyond the colonial capital that connected contestants, prominent families, towns, regions, colonial officials, investors, dressmakers, and workers from the emerging cosmetic and service industries. The Manila Carnival remained the largest platform for beauty pageantry in the Philippines even as beauty pageants proliferated and spread across the archipelago and well beyond Philippine borders. Filipino diasporic communities took up beauty pageants as fundraisers, much like the initial Manila Carnival Queen contests.[89] The repetition and the same pageant format and the continued interest and investment in beauty queens formalized an institution dedicated to the making of beauty queens. After roughly twenty Manila Carnivals, a major Manila-based publication declared, "Whoever invented the idea of the carnival . . . knew his business when the beauty contest was made one of its attractions. It [was] undoubtedly one of the biggest shots."[90]

When the Manila Carnival Association launched its first popularity contest, they did not anticipate their efforts for fundraising would be co-opted and transformed into a complex and powerful beauty pageant apparatus. Pageantry and the making of beauty queens intertwined Filipinaness and Filipina beauty. In this regime, beauty queens performed and embodied characteristics valued as beautiful, feminine, and Filipina. Thus, the emergence of a Filipina beauty pageant industry also produced technologies and tactics of disciplining gender. In the context of Philippine pageants, "beauty" embodies shifting and complex meanings that include and go beyond aesthetics. To unpack the social construction of Filipina femininity, beauty must be understood as having multiple social facets as well as phenotypic or aesthetic features. Historian Mina Roces notes, the "Tagalog word *maganda* does not simply mean beautiful"; it is "also connected with what society considers good or virtuous."[91] To be considered beautiful also means to "exude the virtues of her gender."[92]

Beauty pageants enforced normative ideas of feminine virtue and attractiveness through the institutionalization of contestant criteria. Pageant organizers sought out contestants who fulfilled a set of requirements based on their appearances, social backgrounds, and individual accomplishments. Potential candidates for the *Philippine Free Press* Beauty Contest needed to submit a photograph along with a coupon with the following information: "Name of candidate, home address, now residing at, age, height, weight, accomplishments, address of sender, name of sender."[93] These markers defined the candidate's status in the social hierarchies of colonial Philippine society and were informed by shifting notions of class, gender, race, and ethnicity. In the context of pageantry, to be beautiful meant to be physically attractive. At the same time, desirable physical qualities were linked to markers of privilege. To be privileged was to be refined and civilized. These identifiers signified who did and did not belong in ideal Filipina womanhood.

According to the author of "Meet the 'Misses,'" a magazine article anticipating the 1930 Miss Philippines Pageant, the first question that popped into the minds of Filipinos when the new winner was announced was "What does she look like?" An assessment of her physical appearance would determine whether the winner "deserves the honor of being made queen of beauty in a land of beauty queens."[94] Definite patterns of symbols signifying beauty emerge in photographs and media descriptions of Filipina beauty queens. Perhaps the most intuitive and obvious visual signifiers present in beauty pageantry were

Filipinas' visible physical features. Beauty functioned as an important marker of racial difference and articulated complex, distinct, yet intertwined racial logics in the colonial Philippines. Categories on the application form such as height, weight, and age may appear to be neutral, but coupled with the patterns in beauty queen winners, they show how beauty queen aesthetics structured the normative and desirable body. The selection of beauty contestants reveals a definition of beauty limited to Hispanic mestiza, and in some cases Chinese mestiza phenotypes.[95] Photographs of Filipina beauty contestants and their female entourages show their European-like features, such as light skin, small straight noses, large eyes, and tall, slender frames. Textual descriptions also highlight mestiza features by including visual details like a contestant's "lovely delicate face" or a "queen's fair cheek."[96] The 1909 Empress Paz Marquez's beauty was attributed to the "fineness" and "transparency" of her skin.[97] Estrella Alvarez, winner of Miss Luzon 1930, was described as the "type of beauty that is more Spanish than Filipino. . . . Her complexion is light and her features are Occidental rather than Oriental."[98] Similarly, Rosario Ruiz Zorilla, who won Miss Mindanao that same year, was praised for her "light" complexion and for having features that were "Occidental rather than Oriental."[99] Descriptions of her character, however, praised her for being truly Filipina. Ruiz Zorilla's personality, the article happily claimed, was "devoid of the temperament" associated with the "daughters of Castile."[100] There were rare instances in which winners did not fit the Eurocentric pattern; these women were praised, and yet their wins needed justification and the deviation from the norm was emphasized as an aberration. For example, *Graphic* magazine describes Luz Villanueva, who placed third in the 1930 Miss Philippines contest, as having the "most typically Filipina looks of all the four winning beauties this year." Here, "typically Filipina looks" referred to Villanueva's skin tone, which the article describes as "kayumangging kaligatan, pulsing brown . . . with pink at the cheeks."[101] The article makes it a point to qualify *kayumangging kaligatan*, which roughly translates to "light brown," as "attractive skin" and notes that readers should trust the author's assessment, as "photographs never do justice [to her beauty]."[102]

Demarcating mestiza appearances as distinct from the "typically Filipina" was also a way to exclude other ethnic and racial groups from idealized beauty. Beauty queens' performances on stage and in public discourse provided specific standards for Filipina beauty.[103] Modes of dress and the practice of "costuming" were also ways of marking difference, so that beauty pageants simultaneously reified Spanish racial hierarchies and constructions of *mestizaje* and co-opted the US racial system that divided Christian from non-Christian Filipinos across the archipelago, but especially in the northern and southern regions.[104] The Manila Carnival Queen contests solidified mestiza features as an idealized Filipina phenotype, crystallizing racial and ethnic hierarchical differences that simultaneously accounted for US ideologies of white supremacy and racial difference and for various forms of racial and ethnic mixing. The exhibition of Filipina pageant queens often appropriated US racial taxonomies that classified ethnic and racial groups according to hierarchies of civilization and barbarism. In defining Filipina beauty, pageants also defined and demarcated the nation through hierarchical difference.[105]

Throughout the run of the Manila Carnival Queen contest, beauty queens and their entourages often dressed in clothing from different ethnic groups across the archipelago. Rather than considering different modes of dress as equally part of a heterogenous Filipino heritage, these pageants portrayed the mestiza gown as the symbol of a Filipino identity.[106] Wearing attire from various ethnic communities set up a direct juxtaposition between mestiza bodies and what was described at the time as native, or *indio*, dress.[107] Instead of including indio clothing in the Filipino sartorial landscape—and therefore marking it as part of Filipino identity—this practice was regarded as performative exotic costuming.[108] The costume served as a cultural artifact of an ethnic and cultural other that did not fit the mestizo Christian elite's contemporary imaginary of a modern Filipino national identity.[109] By excluding ethnic groups considered "primitive" from formations of modern Filipina identities, mestizo elites distinguished themselves from minoritized "savage" others, and thereby allowed themselves to make the case that they embodied *modern* Filipina identity and were thus worthy of representing the nation.[110]

Fashion proved to be an important component in beauty pageants not just for its potential to provide aesthetic pleasure but also because contestants' clothing exhibited their ability to afford custom-made, elaborate gowns. Beauty contestants conveyed visually that mestiza Filipinas possessed the ideal qualities of modern women. They usually wore the *traje de mestiza* and, by the 1920s, its modernized version with a matching bodice and skirt, fittingly called the *terno* (matching), as a symbol of true and ideal Filipina womanhood. They also displayed their wealth by wearing diamonds and pearls. These visual markers were meant to be aspirational for onlookers. This style of dress, too, came to represent the Filipino nation. This dress, worn by Filipino elites, adopted silhouettes and cuts from Spanish apparel but used a combination of foreign and local fabrics. The terno was a distinct hybridized style that signified a newly formed Filipino national identity in the late nineteenth and early twentieth centuries.[111] Although it was promoted as an inclusive Filipino national dress, the terno was worn by members of the elite and upper-middle classes. The luxuriousness of the terno signified class privilege, and thus privileged an exclusive mestiza Filipina identity that underscored their Spanish heritage. As Alicia Arrizón argues, the mestiza body itself "is linked with privilege, affirming the identity constructed by adopting the Hispanic legacy."[112] This class privilege was evident in the fabrics worn by mestiza Filipina beauty queens. Fine materials like piña and *jusi*, although native, were expensive fabrics designated for formal occasions. Filipina beauty queens' access to these fabrics was evidence of their mestizo elite class status. Although Filipina pageants showcased women from prominent families, elite women did not have a monopoly on physical attractiveness. Rather, social and class status were significant attributes of respectability and therefore of beauty, too. These women embodied power through symbols of wealth. Enlisting girls and young women from wealthy families or families with wealthy connections was also a practical consideration. Competitions were mostly organized as fundraisers and these connections helped guarantee profits. Moreover, it was "costly to be a queen."[113] The Association's early practice of selecting contestants from well-known families became systematized within the rules of beauty contests. Not only did these contestants have the capital to fund costly wardrobes, but they were also armed with the privilege and esteem that their family names carried. By reaffirming their privileged statuses, Filipina beauty queens signaled their civilized nature and modernity, further distancing themselves from the natives and underclasses.

The attention paid to the costly jewels and crafted accessories adorning Filipina beauty queens' bodies reaffirmed the privilege signified by their dresses. For example, photographs of Pura Villanueva Kalaw from the first Manila Carnival show that—much like Marjorie Colton, her American counterpart—she wore an extravagant gown and a massive amount of precious jewelry. Villanueva Kalaw wore a traje de mestiza, elaborately hand embroidered all along the white *baro* (bodice) and *saya* (skirt), with a long train adorned with embroidery and beading. Adding to the extravagance of her gown, she wore eight layered strings of pearls and diamonds around her neck, a matching crown that draped three rows of pearls across her forehead, and gold bangles and rings. Popular media coverage and photographs of Manila Carnival queens emphasized their fashion choices and accessories. An inscription on the back of a photograph of Manolita Barretto, the 1916 Manila Carnival Queen, reveals that she wore $100,000 worth of diamonds during the pageant.[114] Similarly, the 1921 Manila Carnival Queen, Carmen

Pietro, wore jewels so valuable that she allegedly needed personal guards to protect her.[115] Pietro's crown elicited particular attention: Carnival Director Jorge Vargas designed it especially for her with a solitaire diamond in the central star that was nothing "short of sensational."[116]

Through sartorial presentations of wealth, beauty contests fused together images of normative feminine bodies and prestige to define the ideal Filipina. Promotional materials' narratives and backstories about pageant participants connected the aesthetics of wealth and physical attractiveness to proper feminine character. Publicity for beauty pageants helped pivot away from earlier criticisms of the display of Filipinas by focusing on contestants' accomplishments and achievements, as reflected in the example of the *Free Press*'s candidate nomination form. Admiration for Filipina accomplishments, though, needed to carefully maneuver around heated debates concerning "traditional" and "modern" Filipina gender roles. For example, developments in women's education and employment during the US colonial regime sparked debate concerning proper womanhood and the opportunities—as well as "dangers"—of modernity.[117] The dangers of modernity, as embodied by Filipinas, became a central theme in fraught discourses concerning the dramatic shifts in society and culture during the US colonial period. During the first decade of American colonial rule, colonial officials portrayed Spanish rule as "backward," ridiculing the regime's exclusion of Filipina girls and women from educational institutions. In contrast, the US Insular Government established a public school system all the way up to the university level that was open to both male and female students. United States colonial agents actively promoted this as a symbol of American benevolence; they viewed education as the most effective way to modernize Filipinos and train them for proper citizenship. The changes in the education system instigated a sharp increase in Filipina student enrollment at all levels of education.[118] Consequently, college-educated women from the upper and middle classes increasingly worked white-collar jobs.

Portrayals of 1912 Filipina Day Empress Paz Marquez emphasized her intellectual abilities: even at the young age of sixteen, she surpassed Americans and American-trained *pensionados* (sponsored Filipino students educated at US colleges and universities) in the difficult educational civil service exams.[119] Marquez was described as "intelligent, quick-witted, accomplished, [and] broad-minded," and as a "thoroughly accomplished young lady and very popular among all who [knew] her."[120] Marquez embodied Filipino progress; she had been educated solely in the Philippines and achieved the highest test scores. American colonial officials, including Governor-General

Forbes, acknowledged Marquez's intellectual achievements at a dinner party at Malacañang Palace, placing her in the seat of honor to his right. The inclusion of these details and the tone of the descriptions in Marquez's media coverage projected the image of a true Filipina success story and ignored the fact that the educational institutions were implemented by the US colonial state. Because Marquez exuded physical beauty, came from an elite family, and achieved individual success, she embodied the "perfect type of modern Filipino woman."[121]

As pageants continued, the queens' backstories consistently included lengthy lists of achievements. These lists detailed what schools the contestants attended, the courses they took, the civic groups and organizations they joined or led, and their talents. For example, the *Graphic* magazine article "Carnival Beauties Talk," which aimed to give readers "intimate insight" into the lives of the 1931 Carnival Queen contestants, wrote of one contestant:

> She is at present a Junior in the General Course, College of Liberal Arts, UP. Miss Kalaw's social activities, if enumerated in full, would cover numberless pages. It is, however, not unknown that at present she is the Treasurer of the UP Writers Club, the . . . Vice President of the UP Women's Club, the Secretary of the UP Student Council, the Secretary of the UP Junior Council, the Muse of the Law Bachelor's Club, the Fourth Noble of the Rizal Center Sorority, the Coed Section Editor of the Philippine Collegian, and the "Maria Clara" in the UP Rizal Day. Aside from being a writer, Miss Kalaw sings like a nightingale. And to hear her play the piano is a boon all must well crave.[122]

The beauty queen's worth hinged upon her class and social status, and this long catalog of academic, civic, and social accomplishments rendered Maria Kalaw worthy of her Miss Philippines candidacy. Kalaw possessed talents and skills that were considered elite feminine pursuits during the Spanish period, such as singing and playing the piano. But the signs of maganda and good character had shifted to reflect the social and economic changes during the US colonial period, and to be considered a representative of Filipina beauty, the contestant needed to prove her capability as an individual to achieve success. Attending college became a social accomplishment correlated with one's family status and income—while more colleges and universities allowed young women to matriculate, only those with money could afford the cost of tuition.[123] Kalaw was also heavily involved in extracurricular activities, demonstrating her social networks and participation in circles of influence—an important route to increased cultural capital.

These successes and manifestations of "modernity," however, still needed to be qualified as "Filipina." While proponents of modernization through education praised the increase in the number of girls and women in schools and new forms of employment, others were anxious that American influence would corrupt "traditional" Filipinas. In the 1920s and 1930s, debates around what constituted "traditional" used temporal language to describe tradition in relation to modernization and urbanization.[124] The idea of the traditional Filipina femininity crystallized as antithetical to new forms of entertainment and social life—dancing, going to the movies, socializing, and possibly having intimate relationships with men outside of the normative bounds of marriage.[125] Similarly, apprehension over divorce laws was expressed as a fear of losing traditions and the erasure of an imagined "true" and virtuous Filipina.[126] At the same time, debates on what Filipinas' citizenship would look like increased as the push for women's suffrage steadily intensified throughout the first three decades of the twentieth century.

One example of the tension between a modern Filipina citizen and a "true" and virtuous "traditional" Filipina can be seen in the evolution of the Maria Clara icon. Maria Clara was the main character in Philippine national hero Jose Rizal's late nineteenth-century novel, *Noli me tangere*. The novel portrayed Maria Clara as the Filipina version of the Virgin Mary, embodying her maternal sacrifice and upholding the "sacred duties" of daughters and mothers to their families.[127] Historian Mina Roces writes that by the early twentieth century, Maria Clara had evolved into *the* Filipina ideal.[128] During the American colonial period, a range of historical actors, including Filipina civic groups, politicians, and writers, often pitted the figure of Maria Clara against that of the "modern coed."[129] As Denise Cruz argues, in the 1920s and 1930s, the "coed" became a source of tension in public debate about whether or not highly educated urban women upheld or destroyed the image of the "traditional" Filipina, who was understood as refined, hardworking, and modest.[130]

Beauty pageants needed to carefully navigate the fraught terrain of the "woman question."[131] The Manila Carnival Queen did so by combining and adapting these two oppositional types of Filipinas—the modern and the traditional. During the US colonial period, beauty pageants modified the already familiar Maria Clara icon to appear more modern. The beauty queen combined the modern Filipina's achievements and accomplishments with the traditional Filipina's modesty and refinement. In doing so, new articulations of femininity, education, and work were reconciled with the deeply rooted values of *hiya* (shame) and modesty. Pageants were able to render achievements and accomplishments as signs of respectability by linking them to women from elite and prestigious families. The intentional solicitation of privileged contestants helped legitimate the beauty pageant as publicly presenting "good" Filipina feminine qualities.[132] In turn, accomplishments such as leadership roles in clubs and organizations, college degrees, and academic awards came to signify good character, or *ugali*. Over time, the beauty queen came to represent "the perfect type of modern Filipino woman": educated, civically engaged, and yet still possessing "traditional" Filipina characteristics.[133] Promoting particular types of Filipinas also showed that certain qualities and values were considered not only beautiful but also intrinsically Filipino.

The cultivation of a young woman who had the potential to win the beauty queen title became a tool to police and perpetuate the norms of this ideal Filipina womanhood. In 1934 interview with a *La vanguardia* reporter, 1908 Manila Carnival Queen Pura Villanueva Kalaw noted the differences between her reign and that of the *reinas* of the 1930 Carnival.[134] In the early 1900s, she said, "women did not have to be educated to the same extent as today. . . . [W]omen went to school for a while, got married eventually, and thereafter retired more or less into inconspicuousness."[135] At the time, expectations dictated that "any woman who had more education than the average member of her sex was bound to become outstanding, whereas, had she lived in the present [times, she] would not be regarded as anything extraordinary."[136] By her own standards, Villanueva Kalaw was "outstanding." After attending Santa Catalina College, she began a career as a journalist and helped found the Asociacion Feminista Ilongga, the first feminist organization in the Philippines.[137] In fact, she attributed her election as 1908 Queen of the Orient partially to her "reputation" as a journalist: when she launched her candidacy, she had the backing of the press and counted Commissioner Pedro Guevara among her "boosters."[138]

By the mid-1910s, public discourse about beauty pageants in the Philippines became increasingly respectable in Filipino society. As Mina Roces notes, the "acceptable definition of women in the public sphere was that of the beauty queen."[139] While the first Manila Carnival Queen contests reflected an unreconciled tension between Americans and Filipinos, there were also tensions around debates concerning proper femininity, modernity, and tradition that resulted in wealthy families' hesitation around the pageant. Protests from families and other guardians of young women's morality were commonly reported in the press. For example, 1938 Carnival Queen Guia Balmori's father, together with her Catholic school teachers, objected to her entry in the National Beauty Contest. However, Balmori ignored these protests, entered, and won the title. The press praised Balmori for her accomplishments and popularity in addition to her modesty and humility, describing her as "regal and unsophisticated," carefully cultivating a narrative that allowed her to deflect her family's criticisms.[140] As a beauty queen, Balmori could be a public figure and still retain admired feminine qualities of modesty.

The original intent of the Manila Carnival contests gave no consideration to the "advancement" of women. It was instituted for the economic, political, and cultural gain of the US colonial state. Other institutions, such as the press, also invested in the establishment and maintenance of these contests for their own benefit and profit. Yet Filipinas who competed in and won first the popularity and later the beauty contests through their class status, race, physical appearance, and access to education and training for white-collar jobs—all symbols of respectability—also benefited from earning these titles. Winners gained public attention beyond the pageant stage. Beginning with the first Manila Carnival Queen competition, winners garnered intensive coverage in the press. For the larger public, beauty queens became objects to be looked at and scrutinized both on and off the pageant stage. Their private lives, values, and personal thoughts revealed in interviews became commodities to be consumed by fans and readers at large.[141] Detailed information, often labeled "intimate," gave the public insight into the private lives of these women. An article published in *Graphic* claimed that "public interest in a carnival queen does not die out with the end of her reign. She continues to be the object of popular admiration long after she has relinquished her throne."[142] When beauty queens married, the news of their nuptials made headlines. Articles such as "Miss Philippines 1926 Is December Bride" and "Carnival Queens of By-Gone Days" answered the public's questions about which Filipina beauty queens married and whether they had children.[143] Former beauty queens continued to receive accolades and public adoration if they made successful marriages. As such, media coverage reflected practices that dated back to the Spanish period in which marriage created alliances between elite families—but now, the beauty queen's title helped earn her prestige.[144] Pageants presented Filipina women as objects of admiration and as commodities to be procured for marriages that functioned like business transactions, linking two families for political and economic gain.[145]

The consistent pattern of beauty queens making marital alliances with wealthy or politically powerful men suggests that fulfilling gendered and classed expectations of marriage was another motivator behind entering the contests. Although the spectacle of beauty contests troubled normative gender values that expected Filipinas of the elite class to remain protected and even hidden within the home, patriarchal norms continued to put limits on beauty queens' opportunities and social mobility. A beauty queen's cultural capital more concretely materialized in the "success" she achieved after her reign—which was determined by her ability to not only get married but make a good marriage match. A beauty queen's celebrated beauty, family connections, wealth, and accomplishments rendered her the most desirable of women. As a wife, she could be physically appealing and bring wealth and cultural capital to the marriage. Beauty queen titles were trophies for the contestants themselves and also for the men who could secure marriages with these women. For example, Pura Villanueva bestowed her personal wealth and family influence upon her new husband, Teodoro Kalaw. Although Kalaw was respected in Manila circles as a journalist and later as an editor for *El renacimiento*, he had little personal wealth or political clout prior to his marriage. News articles also gave insight into the private lives and details of marriage contracts. For instance, an article about Virginia Llamas, Manila Carnival Queen 1922, told readers, "Despite the lapse of years she is still a real queen, and is the source of inspiration for her husband, Carlos P. Romulo, editor of the *Tribune*, who was her king consort."[146] Trinidad Fernandez, Manila Carnival Queen 1924, married a wealthy elite mestizo, Benito Legarda Jr.—son of Benito Legarda y Tuason, a member of President Aguinaldo's cabinet and the former resident commissioner of the Philippines. The union cemented both his and her "very prominent status in Manila society."[147] Narratives of beauty queens' marriages portrayed pageantry as a conduit for solidifying powerful alliances and bolstering social status.

At the same time, beauty queen titles did not hinder winners' "advancement" in terms of education or career goals. This is evident in the case of Maria Kalaw, the daughter of Pura Villanueva Kalaw and Manila Carnival Queen 1931. In addition to her prominent lineage, Kalaw's education and status as Miss Philippines opened unique opportunities for her. She was selected as the representative for the Philippines at the first Pan-Pacific Women's Association Conference in 1930.[148] Dressed in a Maria Clara gown, Kalaw led the Philippine delegation in the flag pageant for the conference's Balboa Day celebration.[149] She went on to receive prestigious scholarships, such as the Barbour Scholarship for Oriental Women. Her profile for the scholarship highlighted Kalaw's role as a beauty queen.[150] Perhaps the clearest example of how a Miss Philippines title was the "ultimate status marker" for Filipina women is in Kalaw's use of her title in her political campaigning.[151] Many years after her reign, Kalaw used the slogan, "She Has Beauty, She Has

Brains" for her 1961 senatorial race, leveraging her beauty queen past to bolster her political identity.[152] As a marker of privilege, pedigree, and celebrity, the beauty queen title easily translated as a form of power.[153] Beauty work was firmly embedded in capitalistic processes of advancement and economic gain for both individuals and the businesses linked to the beauty pageant industry that profited from the beauty pageant industrial complex. Indeed, the majority of the Manila Carnival queens came from privileged backgrounds that allowed them to attend colleges and universities. After earning their degrees, many of them embarked on careers newly opened to women. Pacita de los Reyes, Miss Philippines 1929, placed in the top ten of the 1934 bar exam and subsequently practiced and taught law. Paz Marquez became a teacher at the University of the Philippines and perhaps is most well-known for her influential English-language feminist short story, "Dead Stars."[154] Beauty queens straddled multiple forms of gendered expectations placed on women—they fulfilled the presumption that women found respectability through marriage, and at the same time they demonstrated their capacity as high achievers in school and in their careers.

As the pageants continued, organizers negotiated with whether to integrate or reject foreign expectations of feminine beauty. The question of foreign influence centered on concerns over beauty pageants' ability to maintain images of ideal Filipina femininity. In 1930, the Manila Carnival Queen contest added a bathing suit category to the competition. Proponents of this change looked to other major beauty pageants held outside of the Philippines, including the International Pageant of Pulchritude, also known as the Miss Universe pageant, held in Galveston, Texas.[155] They argued that these competitions were celebrations of the "form divine," and that the bathing suit contest was a way of "modernizing their concept of what is beautiful in a girl."[156] Detractors, however, asked if the pageant was to "select a beauty queen or a bathing girl?"[157] Women's groups and influential women from prominent families decried the new bathing suit component, citing it as a violation of maganda. One contestant reportedly wept before donning the bathing suit; another, Violeta Lopez, dropped out of the contest altogether.[158] The bathing suit contest elicited strong emotions and visceral reactions from contestants and the public that manifested in the policing of bodies and notions of appropriate femininity.

Although beauty pageants were regularly used as a means to discipline normative forms of femininity, the powerful notion of the beauty queen as the ultimate performance of femininity would be adopted and adapted in ways that pushed against a Filipina ideal. The image of the beauty queen encompassed recognizable details and markers. Thus, the performance and repertoire of a beauty queen was built on discernible traits: the crown, a regal bearing demonstrated through a rigid posture, femininely styled hair, and a formal gown. All these elements could be found in a photograph of Angeling, for example, who posed with a crown and regal cape. A caption underneath a posed black-and-white portrait-style photograph of the young queen in 1928 reads, "There are Queens and 'Queens.'"[159] Angeling, dressed in white gown, white silk stockings, and an embellished sash, stands regally holding a decorated staff and an elaborate crown atop her head. The photo caption continues, "Have you ever heard of a 'He-Queen' before? Above is 'Her' Majesty Angeling I and consort of the Agusan High School Senior Day celebration. Doesn't he make a lovely 'queen'?" The use of quotation marks in the caption is intended to ridicule the subject's gender performance. But what this caption also indicates is how "queen" signaled a desirable femininity, and how Angeling appropriated and performed the role of beauty queen, producing femininity. In their work on transwomen and nationalism in Venezuela, Marcia Ochoa argues that pageantry and performance were critical venues to "accomplish femininities." By the "accomplishment of femininity" Ochoa addresses the ways that cisgender and transgender women produce femininities with "similar symbolic resources, in dialogue with shared discourses, and employing similar kinds of techniques and technologies."[160] Much in the same way, Angeling accessed the skills of aesthetic curation and took on the symbols and signs attached to Filipina beauty queens: a crown, long hair, and a glamorous gown. Through identification with the queen and artful sartorial and beauty techniques, Angeling stretched the power and lure of the beauty queen well beyond the pageant stage. At the same time, Angeling's production of femininity also created a new kind of beauty queen, one that challenged Manila Carnival Queen and Miss Philippines contests' conventions of crowning cisgendered and wealthy women. Although Angeling's story may appear to be a fleeting moment in the archive, her performance as a queen underscored the cultural labor required in creating a beauty queen.[161] In the complicated beauty pageant regime, Angeling showed that one could produce multiple (queer and normative) and resistant formations of feminine beauty and modes of becoming a queen. This labor would become essential in expanding and institutionalizing beauty pageants as a regime that continuously defined and redefined Filipina femininity, beauty, and performance.

Beauty pageants were not just tangential features of large-scale exhibitions; they evolved into major events in their own right. As they did, the title of beauty queen became the "ultimate status marker" for Filipinas.[162] The title had the power to reaffirm elite status or catapult those from the growing middle and upper-middle classes into "society." Participating in beauty contests and winning were public and spectacular affirmations of Filipinas' respectability and social position—it reflected their class standing, their family connections, their education, and political influence. Their beauty was also articulated through idealized notions of race and gender with praise that wove together adulations over beauty queens' mestiza features with details of their backgrounds and social standing. Moreover, the creation of an adoring public cemented the Filipino beauty queens' cultural meaning and status. Local print media catapulted Filipina beauty contest winners into celebrity status with a public fascination and recognition of their achievements both on and off the pageant stage. The celebrity that beauty queens garnered, in turn, compelled the institutionalization of beauty pageants in the Philippines.

Critiquing the first Manila Carnival Queen contest provided a way for the Filipino nationalist press to air its grievances with the colonial state. But what the members of the press perhaps did not anticipate was that media attention would fuel a public obsession with Manila Carnival Queen contestants and the idea of Filipina beauty. From the first Manila Carnival Queen contest onward, pageant finalists appeared on the front pages of major news publications. These articles had consistent narratives focused on the Carnival Queen's ability to gain public adoration. The *New York Herald*'s article about the first Manila Carnival Queen contest, "Miss Colton and Miss Villanueva Two 'Sure Enough' Queens of the Carnival. Latter Wins Natives," describes how Villanueva Kalaw "was most popular with the masses, that they forgot it was all play and gave her beautiful homage upon her every appearance."[163] Villanueva Kalaw's charisma cultivated not just public attention but also devotion.

The growth of print media and, in particular, the development of pictorial magazines and newspapers facilitated the fascination with beauty queens both on and off the stage.[164] Although society pages consistently published photographs of popular Filipino and American women and the events that they hosted or attended, these women did not garner the same level of attention that was paid to Manila Carnival queens and Miss Philippines contest winners.[165] The Manila Carnival queens were subjects of feature stories that exhibited their portraits in addition to detailed descriptions of their personal backgrounds, what types of gowns they wore, and how they carried themselves during the carnival festivities.[166] Starting with the first Manila Carnival, news sources reported in considerable detail on each contestant's appearance, background, and personal life. This practice would remain consistent, with beauty queens and beauty pageants often making headlines; sometimes entire features would be dedicated to contestants' biographies and social appearances.[167] The fascination with beauty queens and their lives outside the competition crystallized their celebrity status. After the 1938 Miss Philippines competition, *Graphic* published a multipage article titled "Beauties: 1938 Models," detailing the backgrounds and lives of the pageant winners.[168] It focused on the themes of their wealth, prestige, and glamour. For example, the article reported that the winner of the title Miss Luzon (first runner-up to Miss Philippines), Rosario Ferro, "went to school at the St. Scholastica's College. She traveled around the world with Pacita de los Reyes a couple of years ago." As was previously mentioned, Pacita de los Reyes, winner of Miss Philippines 1929, hailed from a wealthy and powerful Manila family and became a prominent lawyer. Here, gossip of who Ferro socialized with added to her glamour and public persona. The article went on to divulge that "Miss Ferro, according to our informant, belongs to one of the wealthiest families in Mauban, Tayabas."[169] Presenting the story as insider information elicited a sense of titillation; the article was catering to the audience's desire to know more of the beauty queen's background.

A 1927 souvenir photo from the Miss Philippines pageant reads, "Beauty is intangible, beyond description. It is simply impossible to portray it, for Beauty is a Divine attribute, the incarnation of all that is good, of all that is pleasing to the heart and the sense; to whom you and I, dear Admirer, bow our heads in sincere homage."[170] This "homage" appeared in a number of public forms within the spectacle of the beauty pageant and in the press. Popular newspapers and magazines published opinion pieces, poems, songs, and tributes celebrating the beauty of contestants and crowned winners.[171] The embellished language of these homages reveals the heightened level of enthusiasm generated among beauty queens' admirers. One admirer from Paco, Manila, felt compelled to write "A Tribute to Beauty" to a beauty queen representing an entirely different island province, Miss Cebu, whom they felt was "worthy of any throne or of any kingdom for that matter."[172]

By the 1910s, developing photography and print technologies made portraits and photographs much more accessible in the Philippines. Portraits of beauty queens could be purchased as collectibles or circulated as postcards.[173]

In this way, beauty could be consumed, and faces and names could become familiar, expanding the beauty queen's public. The mother of Miss Philippines 1930, Consuelo "Monina" Acuña, recalls that pictures of her daughter came in "hundreds daily with most carefully worded notes begging for the 'queen's signature,'" and "clippings from foreign papers bearing Monina's picture poured into my hands."[174] Enriqueta David, society correspondent for *Graphic*, describes accurately what Carnival queens had become by the 1930s:

> As carnival queen, she has become a celebrity. Carnival queens are perhaps the first of female celebrities in the Philippines. She has a public, a large amount of people who admire her, who can look at her (because of the pictures) and who are her fans. This has been made possible not only by the event of the Manila Carnival, but through the mass production of images via photographs. Shouts of "*Mabuhay!... Isana tingin ... Isang ngiti.*" ["Long live [Monina]! ... Look here! ... Smile!"] [A]lmost savage and frightful in tone thundering in the calm afternoon air. Confetti, serpentine, flowers showered upon the lovely delicate face of Monina. . . . She bore them all with smiles of sweet contentment.[175]

Public discourse about Filipina beauty queens' celebrity was not only attributed to developments in technology or the choreography of parades, however. The press described the affective power that convinced Filipinos to submit ballots, beg for photographs, and attend public spectacles as beauty's power to charm, allure, and elicit desire.[176]

The culture of celebrity dovetailed with nationalist politics of the colonial period. Filipina beauty queens' fame also served as an apt vehicle for the expression of Philippine nationalism.[177] Beauty pageants were the first major platform outside of warfare around which to rally masses of people under the banner of "Filipino." The emergence of beauty pageants also coincided with a new phase of Filipino nationalism under the US colonial regime. Indeed, the figure of the beauty queen came to play a key role in embodying and actualizing nationalist sentiments and identities. The "lure" of beauty queens became a rallying force. The beauty pageant and the beauty queen functioned outside of formal nation-building. And yet, contestants, winners, and the spectacle of the pageants themselves each had the power to incite powerful emotions and investment from the public.

The Filipina Carnival Queen contest and its winners embodied the ideal characteristics of an emerging and "imagined" Filipino national community.[178] The idea that a public Filipina figure, whose fame was sourced from beauty, could represent a Filipino nation took root during the first Manila Carnival. One Iloilo-based newspaper praised Pura Villanueva Kalaw, declaring, "If she can occupy the throne of a Carnival, she can also that of a nation."[179] The article directly tied the title of Manila Carnival Queen to a Filipino nation that had yet to be realized. Although Villanueva Kalaw described the first Manila Carnival as an event organized by and for Americans, Filipinos used the Manila Carnival Queen contest to create counterhegemonic discourses of modern womanhood and to express and perform a unified and modern national identity, challenging criticisms that the Philippines was unfit to be an independent modern nation. While under colonial rule, Filipinos rallied together and expressed patriotism through the Manila Carnival Queen contest. Indeed, they were motivated to invest in nationalist productions as the US colonial government and Filipino political leaders presented the US colonial regime as a training period for modernizing Filipinos.

During the first collection of ballots for the first Manila Carnival Queen contest, *El renacimiento* reported, "Miss Leonarda Limjap seems to have the most votes. Rally to her beauty, dignity, and patriotism."[180] However, when just a week later Limjap fell to fourth place, *Muling pagsilang* urged, "Let us all cast our ballots for Limjap."[181] Similarly, letters to the editor encouraged fellow "countrymen" to vote as part of their "patriotic duty."[182] Campaigns also used nationalistic language to describe Filipina candidates, highlighting their *tapatnaloob* (loyalty) and "patriotism" to garner support from Filipinos.[183] In supporting a Filipina candidate, Filipinos also presented an image of a unified Filipino national community, challenging US colonial criticism that the Philippines and Filipinos had yet to reach their full potential because of the religious, ethnic, and linguistic divisions that prevented them from being a modernized cohesive people.

Voting patterns for other competitions also demonstrated visions of a unified Filipino national identity. The beauty contest sponsored by the *Philippine Free Press* included contestants from different regions of the archipelago. The Philippine media claimed that voting patterns for the *Free Press* beauty contestants demonstrated how regionalism was insignificant when it came to admiring true beauty.[184] According to the *Free Press*, "The vast majority of readers vote without the least regard to the province which this or that beauty represents." Instead, the writer states, "Beauty transcends everything and draws its devotees from everywhere."[185] Another article asserts, "Beauty as it appears to each of us recognizes no geographical boundary."[186] This borderlessness extended to the diaspora, as well. Filipinos abroad felt so invested in these competitions that they took the time and effort to cast their votes while overseas.[187] As such, adoration of feminine beauty provided a unifying force that erased the ethnic and geographical boundaries that had been considered divisive. The consolidation of a Filipino public and their celebration of Filipina beauty, then, provided proof of "progress" toward a modern Filipino national identity, challenging US arguments that Filipinos were not ready for self-rule.

The development of the Manila Carnival Queen contest itself reflected the intertwined processes of maintaining beauty pageantry and constructing a version of nationalism through the creation of a "Filipina" identity. Although Manila is just one location in a region made up of thousands of islands, the intent of the Manila Carnival was to present the archipelago as a cohesive whole. While acknowledging different regions, provinces, and ethnicities, the Manila Carnival Queen contest positioned itself as unifying Filipinos despite these differences. It provided visual and performative articulations of a Filipino national identity, even before such a nation existed. In 1926, an invitation to participate in the International Pageant of Pulchritude (Miss Universe) in Galveston, Texas, facilitated the creation of a Miss Philippines title. Although the Philippines did not participate in the Miss Universe contest that year, Manila Carnival organizers instituted two major titles that year: a Manila Carnival Queen and a Miss Philippines.[188] The following year, the Miss Philippines pageant replaced the Manila Carnival Queen contest completely. From 1927 until the onset of World War II, which halted the competition, the top pageant title was Miss Philippines. The national pageant formed prior to the 1934 Tydings-McDuffie Act—also known as the Philippines Independence Act—which officially declared that the Philippines would be an independent nation after a ten-year transition period. The "Miss Philippines" title predated that of the president of the Commonwealth of the Philippines. But performances of nationalism through beauty pageantry were inspired not so much by patriotic duty as by the power of celebrity embodied in the beauty queen.

The Manila Carnival Queen incited, circulated, and encouraged patriotism vis-à-vis the celebration of Filipina beauty. But the Miss Philippines title made an overt declaration of "country" and "nation." This was especially significant as tensions between American officials and Filipino leaders around the question of Philippine independence increased during the 1920s. The pageant industry directly engaged with the complexity of colonial nationalism. The 1926 Manila Carnival promotional poster for "Philippine Beauties," for example, printed all thirty-seven contestants' portraits, scattered across a map of the Philippines. The map was superimposed on the US and Philippine

FIGURE 2.2. The Philippine Beauty Contest, 1927. Mario Feir Filipiniana Library, Metro Manila, Philippines.

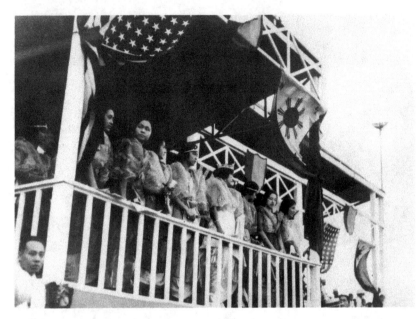

FIGURE 2.3. Spectators at the Manila Carnival Parade, 1924. Filipinas Heritage Library, Metro Manila, Philippines.

flags, positioned side-by-side, with a portrait of Miss Philippines, Anita Noble, placed within the Philippine flag's sun. The two flags reminded onlookers that spectacles of patriotism and Filipino nationalism still required a semblance of allegiance to the United States. By the 1927 Miss Philippines contest, however, the visual symbols had changed: promotional materials began to showcase only Miss Philippines and the Philippine flag. While Miss Philippines had no official political role, she was the figurehead of the Philippine nation.

## Beauty Work

In 1980, Doris Nuyda published *The Beauty Book*, a commemoration of all the Manila Carnival Queen and Miss Philippines contest winners. In it, Nuyda writes that during the American colonial period, "No natural resource . . . so enthused the Filipino's romantic nature as much as the beautiful young women who presided as queens at the annual Carnival."[189] Describing Filipina women—and specifically Filipina beauty—as a natural resource constructs a particular kind of beauty myth. It erases the deep investments of the state, media, and private investors in the development of a beauty queen industrial machine. It also discounts the work that goes into making and being a beauty queen. The production of a Filipino beauty pageant institution in the first few decades of the twentieth century required a specific kind of beauty work: the labor of the beauty queen's performance, the beauty services needed to produce a public figure, and the publicity and promotional work to hype the beauty queens.[190]

Manila Carnival queens and contestants had intensive event schedules. The first few Manila Carnivals set the standard for extravagance, with land and water parades, coronation ceremonies, and galas.[191] The Carnival Queen contestants were not there just to enjoy themselves and be entertained—they *were* the entertainment. The beauty queens' mothers chaperoned and managed their schedules. The chaperones acknowledged the social and cultural capital that came with the titles of Manila Carnival Queen and Miss Philippines. Consuelo "Monina" Acuña's mother, Lutgarda Aldeguer Zaldarriaga, explained that when her daughter "was acclaimed the most beautiful . . . [e]veryone paid her the most profound respect" and her "presence was sought everywhere."[192] Miss Philippines 1926 Anita Noble's mother, Concepcion Zamora de Roa, also described the amount of energy and emotion demanded by her daughter's hectic schedule: "Hardly [taking] meals at home . . . [we] were always out—always at some banquet, party or dance. Often we arrived home shortly after the stroke of two. Yet at seven—just five hours after we had gone to bed—the sala was crowded with eager photographers and reporters."[193] Although she found it a "pleasant year," she and her daughter "got tired of it all before the year was half over." But attending a full schedule of social events was part of Miss Philippines's duty to her title. "We wanted rest but could not have it. Not because we weren't entitled to it, but because . . . we were duty bound to attend the banquets and receptions."[194] A major contributing factor to this social fatigue was the expectation that the beauty queen always be "on." A. E. Litiatco, a reporter for *Graphic*, contended that a "national beauty, especially one designated Miss Philippines, is placed in a difficult position. . . . [She] has to live up to the expectations which her title aroused in the public."[195] For Acuña, these expectations manifested around her appearance: she felt that "she should always be well dressed every day," or "perhaps [she] did not fix up [her] hair well enough."[196] She felt acutely the pressure of constant surveillance and judgment; in an interview published in *Graphic*, she recounted overhearing whispers about her when she attended church. Acuña felt "fear" and was "rather troubled with this publicity stuff."[197]

Their attention to personal style and appearances transformed beauty queens into arbiters of style. The circulation of their images through postcards and later through society and fashion pages in the ever-expanding print media cemented beauty queens' place in the realm of style and fashion. Newspapers and pictorial magazines featured portraits and short descriptions of beauty queens and contestants, showcasing their outfits, their makeup, and their coiffures. The solidification of the beauty queen as an institution had wide-reaching social impact. The efforts behind the production of beauty pageants, along with the work of the contestants and winners, together created new meanings of the word "queen." "Beauty queen" signaled style, fashion, physical beauty, refinement, elitism, and humility.

The pressure to meet public expectations meant that beauty queens constantly needed to attend to their personal style, comportment, and wardrobe, which included enlisting the services of dressmakers and couturiers to create elaborate gowns. During the 1938 Miss Philippines Contest, Guia Balmori's gown garnered almost as much attention as Balmori herself. The press gave detailed descriptions of the design but also named and praised the designer, Ramon Valera.[198] Thus, the beauty queen and the designer entered a symbiotic relationship in which the designer's creations added to the beauty queen's cultural capital and allure, while at the same time, beauty pageants and subsequent events provided a platform for couture ternos. The ternos consisted of various components that were often made of fragile material, making them difficult to put on. Not only did these elaborate gowns demand the labor of designers, along with a team of seamstresses and embroiderers, they also required the wearer to receive assistance in putting on the gown and preserving the gown's shape. Chaperones often came to the beauty queen's sartorial assistance. Consuelo Martinez, who was once a beauty queen competitor and who also served as a chaperone, described in an article featuring chaperones how contestants would cry while being dressed, "because we hardly knew which part of the camisa to pin, which to fold, and all that."[199] Archival photographs of each Manila Carnival Queen and Miss Philippines winner show, too, the careful and meticulous work put into their hair and makeup. Beauty competitors' elaborate updos and tight curls required hairdressers' skills with hot irons. It is no coincidence that the reporting on the 1938 Miss Philippines competition included details about the cosmetic brands and makeup artists who prepared Balmori for her coronation.[200] Imported Japanese and US cosmetic brands like Shiseido, Max Factor, and Coty became increasingly available in the Philippines. Moreover, beauty service became a burgeoning industry in urban centers.[201] Public promotion of Guia Balmori's appearance in the media contributed to the stimulation of capital and affective investment in beauty and fashion in the Philippines. The work done by beauty queens as well as the work done on them highlight that feminine beauty was produced through an amalgamation of performance and comportment, skills developed for a service industry, and the production and consumption of fashionable garments.

Beauty pageantry developed into an industry through the work of the colonial state, the Philippine press, contest participants, and their supporters. Together, they created a machine that produced Filipina beauty queens. The beauty pageant industrial complex forged a deep relationship between pageants and politics, highlighting the long-lasting legacy of Filipina beauty pageants. Contests showcasing an ideal of femininity in the Philippines defined and defended national identity along shifting lines of gender, class, ethnicity, race, and citizenship in the colonial context. Philippine nation-building and American imperial expansion were in constant contact, conflict, and negotiation with one another. The Manila Carnival Queen's prominence in public discourse demonstrates how defining the nation through Filipina femininity was inherently a gendered process that required many forms of labor and work.

The following chapters build on the notion of beauty work in the context of the spectacular beauty pageant industry. As we will see, US colonial officials, manufacturers, and consumers regarded the Philippines as a source of beauty labor. The labor of Filipina embroiderers became increasingly desirable, as they were able to provide fashionable garments for the beautification of American consumers. The formation of a transnational Philippine embroidery industry depended on the racialization and feminization of Filipina beauty work. The industry commodified both the Filipina worker, a figure whom advertisements portrayed as a source of exotic artisanal labor, and the embroidered goods themselves, which followed coveted European fashions. In the hope of creating a lucrative outprocessed hand embroidery industry, US empire capitalized and exploited highly skilled Filipina workers of beauty.

# 3

PHILIPPINE LINGERIE

*Transnational Filipina Beauty Labor*
*under US Empire*

In an open room with large windows and views of trees outside, at least twenty Filipino women sit with thin needles in their hands, embroidering intricate flowers and swirls onto delicate white cloth. An intertitle flashes: "Ten thousands of deft dusky feminine fingers fix the pleasing pattern on miles of fine white fabric."[1] These "feminine fingers" belong to Filipinas and girls whose training in needlework became a hallmark for lingerie, embroidered women's blouses, christening gowns, and white linens made in the Philippines. Close-up shots focus on their fingers busily working, visually amplifying the words "deft," "dusky," and "feminine." The film portrays a distinct image of embroidery work and workers as feminine, nonwhite, and exotic.[2]

The 1920 film *Luzon Lingerie* begins with an intertitle that declares, "This film is not intended to interest the men."[3] From the start, filmmaker Burton Holmes frames *Luzon Lingerie* as a revelation for white American women consumers. Edited as an exposé, *Luzon Lingerie* hopes to answer these consumers' unvoiced questions: how, where, and by whom their underwear was made. It is a silent film that edits together images of Filipinas deftly sewing embroidered patterns onto miles of cotton with descriptive intertitles.

Like Holmes's other films, this particular work on Philippine embroidery and the embroiderers exposes American audiences to far-off and exotic lands. Holmes highlights the transnational intimacy between the Filipina women who create delicate underwear and the presumed white American women consumers who place these garments onto their bodies. In doing so, he reiterates familiar tropes found in wildly popular Victorian travel writing that portray the Philippines and other "island possessions" through images of the tropical pastoral of swaying palm trees and balmy air and, perhaps more importantly, the exotic natives who inhabit these far-off spaces.[4] *Luzon Lingerie* ends with a long shot of women and girls seated outdoors, beneath palm and coconut trees. Each woman sews patterns and designs onto white cloth while a white woman walks between the workers, inspecting their work. Here, in the "murmuring palm groves," "five thousand Tagalog needle workers" labor for an American girl. According to the film, Filipina embroiders and lacemakers produce 1,500 pieces of lingerie per day, "[capturing] the world markets for their Philippine products." The last image of the film is another intertitle that reads: "So here beneath the palm trees is where they make your Luzon underwear."[5]

Although *Luzon Lingerie* was made in the early twentieth century, it echoes much of the present-day discourse concerning multinational corporations and exploited garment workers. In the last few decades, portrayals of garment workers, including immigrant women of color in the United States and workers in China, Bangladesh, and Southeast Asia, seem obsessed with hands and fingers.[6] The workers are praised for their "nimble fingers" and their "visual acuity."[7] This proliferation of discourse about nonwhite women from the Global South that focuses on their presumed biological proclivity for tedious manufacturing tasks reflects the late twentieth-century development of exploitative transnational structures of outprocessing.[8] While outsourcing labor and outprocessing commodities are typically considered phenomena of late capitalism, the outprocessing of delicately embroidered items marketed to American buyers developed during the US colonial period.

In replacing the military government, the Insular Government of the Philippines sought to institute a regime that would foster mutually beneficial relationships between private industries and the colonial state. The turn to the craft industry of embroidery fit the US empire's agenda of maximizing its profits and expanding its markets.[9] During the 1910s and 1920s, embroidery—long established as a practice in the Philippines—evolved into a lucrative transnational industry that largely benefited the colonial state and US businesses.[10] The establishment of a global embroidery industry required political, social, and economic maneuvering in both the United States and the Philippines to establish an alliance between the government and private sector. In the Philippines, colonial trade policies opened up opportunities associated with a new consumer market for American imports. At the same time, the new US colonial regime at the end of the nineteenth century was geared toward a free market relationship, and it cemented existing connections and created new links between the local Philippine economy and American markets.

Starting in the 1910s, "Philippine lingerie" and other embroidered linens grew increasingly popular among American consumers. Philippine embroidery, as it was labeled by American manufacturers, was predicated upon the racialization and commodification of the Filipina embroiderer as a beauty worker who produced coveted and fashionable embroidered garments for American women.[11] This chapter focuses on US empire's investment in building a transnational beauty regime through the formation of the transnational Philippine embroidery industry. This chapter traces the seemingly unlikely intimacies between the colonial state, global capitalism, and the development of a fine needlework industry based on feminized and racialized labor producing commodities destined for mainly white American consumption.[12] Filipina beauty labor lies at the heart of US empire, or at what Neferti Tadiar describes as the convergence of "transnationalization of production" for "capitalist accumulation" and the United States' accumulation of colonial territories, people, and resources.[13] The US colonial state, along with entrepreneurs, saw a recognizable and established industry that—if scaled up—could potentially rival the European embroidery industry. As workers who produce beautiful commodities, Filipinas' appeal as a cheap, feminized labor source was grounded in their colonial status and nonwhite racialization, which together forged a disposable and vulnerable worker identity that persisted long after the formal end of US colonial rule.

The history of the beauty regime of US empire intertwines labor, material culture, gender, and race. As Minh-Hà Phạm states, "The history of fashion capitalism has always been a history of racial capitalism."[14] But it is also a history of empire. Outprocessing—shuttling materials from the United States to the Philippines, adopting designs from Europe, embroidering and finishing pieces in the Philippines, and then selling them to US consumers—transformed the geography of production and distribution and was made possible by new global links and trade circuits produced by imperial expansion. US manufacturers considered outprocessing attractive because it maintained and funneled capital to established textile manufacturing jobs in the

United States while the labor-intensive fabrication process was completed by some of the lowest wage workers in the Philippines and throughout the US empire.[15] The outprocessing of embellished cotton clothing and accessories wove Filipina embroidery labor practices that had been developed under the Spanish empire together with the imperial expansion of US markets and manufacturing.

## The Development of Philippine Embroidery under Imperial Regimes

With the transition from a Spanish to a US colonial regime, the United States sought to capitalize on the Philippines' extractable natural resources as well as on the colony's established trade, commodities, and laborers.[16] A report by the Philippine Commission made it clear that the new colonial regime would concentrate on "the enterprises" that would "develop . . . vast natural wealth."[17] The United States viewed itself as a savvier and stronger economic force than Spain, and it believed Filipinos were unaware of their own industrial potential. The report argued that "capital is waiting" in the Philippines, dormant and available for the United States to profit from.[18] The United States homed in on Philippine embroidery as the source of this waiting capital.

During the mid-nineteenth century, during Spanish colonial rule, Spanish, French, and Belgian nuns from various religious orders introduced various European fine needlework techniques to the Philippines. By the time of the imperial regime change, European-influenced needlework was already socialized as a feminine task performed mainly by Filipina women and girls in the Christian lowland regions. As historian Stephanie Coo points out, the idea of women sewing during the Spanish colonial period "formed part of the idealized image of a compliant and talented colonial woman."[19] In the eighteenth century, Spanish colonial officials established schools for young women and girls at which Spanish Catholic nuns taught "feminine" skills and tasks. A major part of the curriculum focused on needlework, including European techniques for sewing, embroidery, and lacemaking.[20] The nuns taught a variety of laces, including Venetian, English point, *ojetes* (eyelet), *surcido* (similar to Buratto), and *sombrado* (shadow embroidery), in which stitching is applied to fabric turned inside out. These techniques and textiles were applied to women's nightgowns, undergarments, and handkerchiefs, as well as to the *camisas* and *pañuelos* of *trajes de mestiza*.[21] Embroidery was integral to the designs of trajes de mestiza and *ternos*.[22] *Bordadoras* (embroiderers) also produced religious vestments for local Catholic priests that were worn during mass, religious holidays, fiestas, and parades.[23] Girls as young as six became proficient bordadoras, ornamenting imported silks and cottons from China and Bengal as well as locally produced fine and expensive textiles such as *piña* and *jusi*.[24] Not only did Filipina bordadoras' work resemble European styles like Alençon or Brussels lace and Swiss eyelets, they also incorporated Chinese, Indian, and Persian floral patterns.[25] Embroidery combined local and foreign techniques and patterns, reflecting the global circuits that crisscrossed in the Philippines.

The nuns taught embroidery at colleges, institutions dedicated to young Spanish and Filipina mestizas from the *principalia* class, and at charity institutions, including *beaterios* (convent schools), *asilos* (asylums), and *hospicios* (hospices).[26] Handicraft production provided a way for "charity students," such as orphans, to earn their keep and eventually earn a living after leaving the institution.[27] Needlework was also regarded as integral to instilling the characteristics of ideal femininity, such as hygiene, modesty, and propriety, in charity students and elite girls alike.[28] Elite Filipinas did not do needlework to earn wages but to increase their cultural and social capital. After learning sewing and fine needlework in convent schools, young Filipina elites continued their craft in their households—as a form of leisure. For wealthy families, elaborate patterns applied to costly and coveted fabrics exhibited artistry and good taste. Furthermore, women and girls demonstrated their ability to perform "feminine" duties through embroidery, thus showing themselves to be appropriate and desirable wives for elite marriages. They adorned their own bodies with their designs, gifted their work to friends and relatives, and in some cases showcased their artistry at large-scale spectacles such as world's fairs abroad.[29] Not only did embroidered materials convey refinement and artistry, but so, too, did images of elite women or girls embroidering. Nineteenth-century ink illustrations and portraiture commemorated romanticized images of a Filipina in a domestic setting, seated with a needle in hand.

The majority of bordadoras, though, were working-class women, not elites. Some worked in their homes, completing needlework alongside other forms of domestic labor.[30] Others labored in the households of wealthy landowning families or in local shops. The wealthiest families employed bordadoras and *costureras* (seamstresses) to custom-make dresses. In elite household economies, matriarchs would often design gowns and accessories and retain a costurera as part of their household staff. The embroiderers and dressmakers carried out the bulk of the painstaking work. As an industry, embroidery functioned on a hierarchical division of labor. *Sinamayeras* (Filipina textile vendors) and Chinese and Chinese mestizo merchants employed bordadoras to embellish textiles and plain ready-made commodities.[31] Merchants in Manila neighborhoods like Binondo and Escolta procured textiles, such as piña, from Iloilo.[32] In Manila, embroiderers in the merchants' homes or in convents then embellished the textiles. In parts of Manila, such as Tondo, Chinese mestizo entrepreneurs used a debt patronage system (*utang na loob*) to coerce women workers into producing embroidery and lace.[33] Entrepreneurs would lend money to women on the condition that they work in the lender's house. Ornamented work dramatically increased textiles' value, thus also increasing the demand for embroiderers.[34] Elites in the Philippines purchased these expensive and luxurious embroidered goods. In these informal economies, bordadoras produced a limited amount of merchandise for elite and wealthy consumers.[35] At the same time, Chinese and Chinese mestizo merchants sold some of these items to foreign markets, whose circulation reached far beyond Asia and the Pacific.[36] Filipina-made embroidery, while an informal economy, was far from provincial. Its global ties were woven into the very fabric of the textiles. The Filipina embroidery industry encompassed a network of intra-Asian trade in woven textiles from China and Bengal and the transregional circulation of piña and jusi. Designs often blended indigenous, European, Chinese, Indian, and Persian aesthetics.

Despite the high price of embroidered textiles, embroiderers and weavers remained in low-income positions. They received little of the profits from the sale of the expensively ornamented fabric and dresses they produced. While embroidery was a highly skilled form of labor, the bordadoras' artistry and workmanship were attributed solely to their employers. Whether employed in an elite household or a workshop, bordadoras' work was under constant scrutiny and supervision. They had little input in the designs. Instead, employers demanded that embroiderers execute their orders and mindlessly manufacture other peoples' designs.[37] Hierarchies marked by race, class, and ethnicity cemented embroiderers' status as lower class. Embroiderers often entered into patron-client relationships in which wealthy families acted as their benefactors. In many cases, embroiderers were compelled to work to repay borrowed money, and thus entered a cycle of debt peonage.[38] Embroiderers received little compensation for their meticulous work and spent long hours in poor working conditions. Much like the sweatshops of the contemporary US and European garment industries, women and girls worked hunched over a frame for hours at a time in tight, cramped spaces in homes and home workshops.[39] In the mid-nineteenth century, an American naval officer traveling in Manila saw forty embroiderers in a small workspace "busily

FIGURE 3.1. "Bordadoras Filipinas," *Exelsior*, August 20, 1930. Mario Feir Filipiniana Library, Metro Manila, Philippines.

plying their needles, and so closely rated as apparently to incommode each other."[40] Embroidery work was thus a "sweated trade."[41]

The transnational embroidery industry maintained some of the features of this informal industry, such as informal economies, the feminization of labor, and the low socioeconomic status of needleworkers. It radically transformed other aspects, however, introducing new racial and gendered scripts about "Philippine embroidery" and the Filipina embroiderer. The shift from the Spanish to the US colonial regime irrecoverably changed the image and the labor of the bordadora from a symbol of ideal femininity, refinement, and domesticity to that of a productive, dexterous, and disposable brown laborer. These new scripts were central to creating a new market—enticing new consumers and forging new geographies of labor, capital, and goods. A Philippine embroidery industry controlled by the United States emerged from economically driven colonial agendas. Establishing new markets and seeking opportunities for profit played central roles in US imperial expansion. From its inception, the Insular Government focused its attention on regulating industry, trade, and capital in the Philippines. With an eye on extracting wealth for US profit, the government pushed policies that structured an uneven economic relationship between the Philippines and the United States, including tariffs and duties that greatly benefited US industries and, in turn, the colonial and US state. At the same time, the Insular Government quickly moved to take possession of land and resources for corporations and other private entities. US economic interests in the Philippines sought to identify potentially profitable industries and extractable resources.[42] Turning to the Philippines for garment labor was a part of the larger historical phenomenon of extracting Filipino labor for American enterprises. A growing body of literature on Filipino labor emphasizes the roles of empire, colonialism, and neocolonialism in shaping transnational labor histories. Dorothy Fujita Rony, Rick Baldoz, and Linda España Maram trace how US colonialism in the Philippines created transpacific labor networks and shaped the lives of Filipino migrant laborers in other US territories like Hawai'i and Alaska as well as in the contiguous United States.[43] Catherine Ceniza Choy's work on Filipina nurses underscores empire's role in creating pipelines between education and transnational labor demands.[44] Her work contributes to the increasing attention paid to gendered Filipina labor, which is primarily focused on "care work" in the forms of nursing and domestic labor.[45] Filipina embroiderers are another example of a labor force shaped by US empire. These Filipina workers were deeply embedded in global circuits of capitalism, and yet they did not physically cross borders.

In their search for profit, US colonial agents and entrepreneurs turned to Philippine embroidery. In many ways, though, "Philippine embroidery" was a misnomer that veiled the uneven transnational features and structures of the Philippine embroidery industry. The United States' interest in embroidery was not so much about an extractable commodity and more about the skill set of a primarily Filipina workforce that could be folded into the extant US garment industry. The appeal of a potential Filipina workforce was a product of the labor problems in the US garment industry. In the United States, Progressive Era reformers of the early twentieth century targeted the exploitative conditions faced by new immigrant laborers in the garment industry, criticizing factories and workshops for their low wages, excessive hours, and unsanitary conditions.[46] Muckrakers exposed the dark and dirty rooms where workers produced clothing, and brought to the public's attention the kinds of conditions reformers wanted to improve. Reformers sought to regulate the garment industry and eradicate tenement labor and sweatshops, which dominated the New York garment industry. This era also marked the collaboration of union organizations rallying against labor exploitation in the garment industry, as in the cooperation of the International Ladies' Garment Workers' Union and the National Women's Trade Union during the New York Shirtwaist Strike of 1909.[47] This massive reform movement reflected growing anxiety over the intertwining developments of industrialization, immigration from eastern and southern Europe, and the increasing presence of women in the workforce. These issues in the continental United States incentivized looking to the new colonies for labor. *Luzon Lingerie* portrayed the Philippines as the picturesque colonial tropics and offered a dramatic contrast to the horrific conditions of garment work in the United States.

United States manufacturers and retailers sought to compete with European manufacturers over American demand for coveted hand-sewn and embellished garments and linens. Philippine embroidery, as it was referred to by US manufacturers, distributors, and consumers, was a source of handcrafted and hand-adorned garments accessible to a larger swath of American consumers. Private US interest in Philippine embroidery was largely influenced by the desire to lower the cost of producing hand-embellished commodities. Lowering the production costs would secure a lower price point that would entice more American consumers to purchase these luxury goods. Philippine embroidery would thus enable US manufacturers to compete with European producers who had traditionally dominated the market with their products. Up to that point, embroidery, commonly referred to as "Hamburg embroideries," came mostly from European locations like St. Gallen and embroidery centers in France.[48] The colonial state and manufacturers, by adopting and expanding the established embroidery cottage industry, adapted Filipina embroidery work for mass production and American consumption. The system of embroidery in the Philippines had already created a hierarchy that devalued skilled labor while valuing its product.

From the mid-1910s until the late 1920s, American demand for Filipina-made embroidery catapulted. Across the United States, the number of American retailers that sold "Philippine lingerie" increased. Some department stores, such as Marshall Field and Company, went so far as to set up offices in Manila.[49] These American retailers marketed Philippine lingerie and other embroidered goods to middle-class consumers. Advertisements for Philippine lingerie handcrafted by Filipina women appeared regularly in fashion publications such as *Vogue*. *Women's Wear Daily* reported for more than a decade on the development of Philippine embroidery. American consumers knew of and coveted Philippine embroidery in the same way they desired European fashion imports, but Philippine embroidery offered consumers handcrafted, beautifully ornamented shirtwaists, undergarments, and accessories at a fraction of the price of imported products from Europe.[50]

The Insular Government deployed a number of strategies to lure investors' interest in Filipina workers. Starting in 1908, the US colonial state staged large-scale expositions such as the Manila Carnival that showcased resources and industries to draw American investors.[51] These public spectacles displayed potentially profitable Philippine industries. Unlike the copra, sugar, and hemp industries, however, the Philippine embroidery industry did not just center on a particular Philippine-sourced product but featured a labor force that could produce goods based on European styles. The Manila Carnival exhibited tatted lace and embroidered textiles that bore little resemblance to the usual work of the bordadoras who catered to local elites. Such displays promised that Filipina-made needlework could compete with the embroidery and lace produced in Europe.[52] These spectacles also showcased the Filipina labor force itself. Much like world's fairs and expositions in the United States and across Europe, the industrial component of the annual Manila Carnival (later called the Philippine Exposition) exhibited Filipina workers, making their bodies, personhood, and labor part of the spectacle. Live dioramas presented stereotypes of Filipina embroiderers. Fairgoers could witness Filipina women and girls practicing their craft while sitting next to elaborate displays of finished products. The exhibits portrayed Filipina embroiderers as industrious, dexterous, and feminine. As productive workers, embroiderers presented an image that differed from that of the romanticized *doña* of the

Spanish period. The elite Spanish or Spanish mestiza women who were commemorated in paintings and literature, seated at home and creating beautiful embroidery, symbolized the coveted characteristics of *elite* femininity: domestic, feminine, and artistic refinement.[53] The image of the productive Filipina embroidery worker also countered previous American accounts from the early years of the US colonial regime, when Filipina weavers and needleworkers were described as oddly grotesque in comparison to the beautiful products they produced.[54] Nerissa Balce addresses American expressions of racist disgust for Filipinos at the turn of the century, and examines one specific excerpt from the 1904 book-length memoir of Emily Bronson Conger, a white, middle-class American woman visiting her son, a soldier assigned to the Philippines.[55] In her memoir, Conger recounts meeting Filipina weavers and writes, "So many of the women are deformed and unclean, both the makers and the sellers that it seemed utterly incongruous that they should handle the most delicate materials."[56] Balce describes Conger's words as part of the larger lexicon of the "bile of race" in the language of white women's travel writings. This racial language depicting Filipino "savagery," Balce argues, "surfaces in the narratives about Filipino inferiority as either a physical or moral condition."[57] In their quest to lure investors, however, US manufacturers and retailers needed to rewrite this racial script of disgust and present Filipina workers and their wares as beautiful, alluring, and desirable to white American consumers.

By the 1910s, American portrayals of Filipina embroiderers as producers of beauty blended together racial and gendered notions of nature, talent, and the exotic. Education administrators, along with other governmental agents, promoted a "biological" argument, asserting that Filipinas had a predilection and aptitude for embroidery—an "unusual skill" that demonstrated a "native" and "natural aptitude."[58] Being "naturally gifted" gave Filipinas "patience and the delicacy of execution."[59] Walter Marquardt, the director of education from 1916 to 1919, described Filipinas as having "eyes on their fingers."[60] In films like *Luzon Lingerie* and in advertisements published in American fashion magazines like *Vogue* and *Women's Wear Daily*, the imagery of small and nimble fingers, made recognizable by their brown skin, also cemented the idea of the Filipina body's proclivity for fine needlework.[61] Another related but slightly different approach to Filipinas' skill couched their talent in ancient tradition and culture rather than as a biological feature of all Filipinas. American descriptions of Philippine embroidery's history vaguely described its origins as "centuries ago," passed down through convent and matrilineal training.[62] This narrative provides an uncanny mix of exotic others, knowledge production, and kinship systems that already circulated in other American and Western colonial narratives.[63] The idea of a long tradition of embroidery established that the skill existed well before American occupation. The perseverance of tradition over centuries underscored that embroidery was firmly embedded in Filipino culture, and thus constituted skilled labor that could easily be extracted. Moreover, it suggested that there was an almost inexhaustible source of labor for American use.[64] Both threads of the narrative on Filipinas' skill naturalized the association between embroidery work and Filipinaness. Endorsements to grow a Filipina embroidery labor force made use of both the biological/racial and the cultural narratives, likening natural skills to natural resources such as minerals that could be extracted for profit.[65]

In addition to using a Filipina workforce to lure investors, the United States legislature worked to pass policies that benefited US corporate and private economic interests in the newly acquired colonies.[66] Economic historian Onofre Corpuz describes the US-Philippines colonial economy as a "special relationship"—a relationship geared toward the expansion of US trade in the Philippines.[67] A new US tariff law enacted in August 1909 allowed duty-free imports and exports of products between the United States and the Philippines—with the exception of rice. Just two years after the law's enactment, imports and exports between the Philippines and the US more than doubled.[68] At the same time, these tariff laws placed greater strictures on European products, including cotton, cotton materials, and finished cotton products like ready-made garments. Such actions were in line with US protectionist policies.[69] From 1901 to 1913, the Insular Government had a laser focus on facilitating private enterprise that disproportionately favored the United States. Moreover, the transpacific flow of goods was shaped by the Insular Government's strategy of simultaneously creating a Philippine market for US exports and extracting cheap resources and labor for US industries.[70] Luxurious lingerie came within reach of a wider consumer base because of the lack of duties on the import and export of materials and finished goods and the cheaper labor costs made possible by colonial structures. Fashion insiders expressed enthusiasm for the expansion of the lingerie market, which was previously restricted mainly to the wealthy.[71] Promotions for Philippine embroidery promised a hand-sewn "graceful design" at a "reasonable price."[72] Advertisements failed to note that it was low wages and cheap Filipina labor that made these reasonable prices possible.

Investment in Philippine industries was merely one part of larger American ventures in Asia.[73] But to simply generalize the early twentieth century

as a period of free trade glosses over closures, restrictions, and unfree working conditions engendered by the colonial context.[74] What was particularly
unique to the Philippine context was the way colonialism and territorial
"possession" allowed the colonial state and American businessmen to bypass
protectionist policies like tariffs and duties. The Philippines was a territory
of the larger US empire, and therefore it came under US jurisdiction. As a
US colony, its subjects were expected to demonstrate loyalty to the United
States, and yet these very same subjects did not receive the full benefits of
citizenship.[75] The framework of island possession placed ventures in embroidery within the larger US imperial project. As a US possession, Filipina labor
and embroidered products were not considered wholly "foreign." American
garment manufacturers and retailers took advantage of the Philippines' new
colonial status and colonialism's blurred line between foreign and domestic
products. Retailers and manufacturers alike marketed this "in-between" status to entice American consumers. The San Francisco Emporium advertised
its stock of Philippine embroidery, declaring: "Here's a sale we're proud to
announce—an industry of our own possessions—the Philippines."[76]

The blurring of boundaries and colonial tariff policies also incentivized
manufacturers to export textiles like cotton from the US to the Philippines,
extract the labor of Filipina embroiderers, and then ship the embroidered
goods back to the United States for sale.[77] Only a small fraction of embroidered products for American use were made with Philippine textiles.[78] The
transnational embroidery industry was enfolded into a long-established
racist and exploitative system and upheld a geography of empire where technologies of control were shared. The US textile industry was built on long-
standing imperial processes that displaced indigenous peoples from their
lands.[79] Furthermore, the cotton harvested mainly by Black Americans in
the US South and processed in mills scattered across the South and all the
way north to Lowell, Massachusetts, depended on the brutal legacy of chattel
slavery that remained under Jim Crow.[80]

The US's colonial possession of the Philippines meant it had power over
not only land and natural resources but also people, their skills, and their
labor. However, the United States framed possession not simply as a form
of imperial seizure but as a manifestation of the US's "exceptional" form of
empire based on benevolence and uplift. Capitalist interests were couched
in terms of US benevolence through modernization. This line of thinking
projected colonial possession as a necessary form of intervention to "engage"
the Philippines and Filipinos in "productive commercial activity."[81] As one
American entrepreneur put it, the Philippines needed the United States'

colonial tutelage because of the "lack of a developed commercial sense among the people."[82] Advocates for the expansion of Philippine embroidery criticized Philippine needlework that ornamented luxurious and expensive piña as a constrained and limited proto-industry that catered to an exclusive group of wealthy elites. This restricted embroidery industry, according to the US, stemmed from "undeveloped conditions of local resources, [Filipino] temperamental characteristics, and [the] lack of interest in sustained industrial effort."[83] The narrative of limitation also portrayed embroidery as a contained form of production that was so localized that it remained stagnant in terms of style and taste, thus concealing embroidery's genealogies and networks connecting multiple locations within and beyond the Philippines.

These conditions did, in fact, attract entrepreneurs, manufacturers, and retailers who worked with and alongside the US government to expand Philippine embroidery. United States–based embroidery and lace businesses linked to the garment industry began sending representatives to the Philippines in 1909.[84] One such business, the Embroidery Trading Company, characterized their venture in the transnational Philippine embroidery industry as "aiding women of the United States" by "supply[ing] [the] American market with handmade goods."[85] The Embroidery Trading Company transported bolts of cotton cloth and cut and sewn garments produced in the United States to the Philippines. There, some of these products were distributed to factories, but most were sent to subcontracted Filipina homeworkers to be embroidered. Over time, more and more of the production process took place in the Philippines. Factories were concentrated in the Manila area, and handicraft production, including embroidery, took place largely in Manila and surrounding neighborhoods and towns.[86] Manufacturing companies sent agents to manage pieceworkers in Manila districts like Paco, Tondo, Ermita, Malate, Santa Ana Materials, and Singalong, as well as in provinces outside the capital.[87] Unfinished and finished goods were filtered through distribution centers in Manila, which served as a central hub that connected the dispersed embroidery production sites to newly configured global networks. By 1918, the Philippine embroidery workforce included at least 60,000 women located mainly in the Manila area.[88] Embroidered products were then shipped to processing warehouses in Manila, loosely called "factories," though no actual manufacturing took place there. This phase was for quality assurance. Finished goods were then cleaned, pressed, packed, and shipped back to the United States for distribution.[89]

The tariff legislation that ensured cotton goods could move freely between the United States and the Philippines made "Philippine-made merchandise a desirable product to handle."[90] Efforts to expand Philippine embroidery for American consumption, however, went well beyond legislation. Proponents of the embroidery industry expansion aimed to create a workforce through simultaneously teaching and training "natives to work in a systematic way" and developing a market in the United States.[91] Mass production—and, subsequently, consumption—could take place without having to resort to machine manufacturing. Scaling up embroidery to become a transpacific multisited industry depended on colonial ideologies about Filipina labor and skill and colonial policies and bureaucracy that connected private and state interests. It was this alliance of the colonial state and private businesses that institutionalized the disparities in economic gain between the United States and the Philippines and that placed Filipina workers—in this case embroiderers—in positions of structural vulnerability.[92] The United States continued to double down on their image as a generous modernizing force that would steer Filipinos into an industrialized civilization. The US colonial government promised that the United States would liberate Filipinos from Spanish tyranny and radically change and better the lives of Filipinos. However, rather than eroding class and labor divisions, US strategies largely appropriated and adapted previously established labor systems that kept Filipina embroiderers among the lowest-paid workers in Manila and the surrounding provinces.[93] An alliance between the state and private industries created an outprocessing system that had little interest in modernizing or industrializing Philippine embroidery.

## "Filipinisque": Fashioning a Filipina Beauty Workforce for a Transnational Embroidery Industry

The creation of new transnational and beauty industries expanded the Filipina embroidery workforce.[94] These developments placed Filipina embroiderers and their labor at the center of colonial modernizing projects that were intended to boost projects of imperial market expansion and make the Philippines into a lucrative colony for the United States. The US vision for commercial activity was one in which Filipina laborers produced garments for the pleasure and beautification of American middle-class consumers. As beauty workers, embroiderers provided what Millian Kang identifies as "transnational body labor"—service work performed on a local level but "shaped by cross-border economic, cultural, and historical processes."[95] The making of a transnational Philippine embroidery industry depended on the expansion of a small Filipina labor force and on the transformation of the labor force's image for American consumers. United States narratives of Filipina embroidery workforce expansion complemented American ideologies of benevolent assimilation and exceptionalism and posited that the Philippine embroidery industry could become commercialized, global, and profitable only through American intervention. The growth of the Philippine embroidery industry of the 1910s through the 1930s hinged upon the narrative of revolutionizing and modernizing an existing yet "undeveloped" workforce for global "commercial success."

The proliferation of narratives in US publications celebrating the United States for optimizing dormant Filipina talent normalized the expansion of the Filipina workforce and the pivoting of their production toward the transnational embroidery industry. The Powis-Brown Company was one of more than a dozen US firms that formed in the early 1910s in the hope of capitalizing on the transnational embroidery industry, and it received the most media attention.[96] News reporting and the company's own marketing campaign created a gendered narrative that presented the Powis-Brown Company as a truly feminine business—one that fully embodied the business of making beautiful embroidered commodities. American media presented Louise Powis-Brown as the "originator of the great Philippine lingerie industry."[97] An American woman born in Wayne, Illinois, Brown had accompanied her husband, Elwood Brown, to Manila in 1910. One article that ran in a US women's magazine, the *Delineator*, describes how Louise Brown used her allowance to hire Filipina embroiderers. Brown "marveled at the skill" of Filipina embroiderers who went door-to-door selling their wares, but she was "troubled by the coarseness of the design and the coarseness of the material."[98] Brown felt horrified at the thought of the hours of intricate needlework spent "upon ugly and obvious design."[99] It was then, according to the *Delineator* article, that Brown came up with the idea of applying Filipina embroidery to French lingerie, a commodity she had always "longed for" but that was too costly and always out of her reach. Brown sent samples to her mother in Illinois, who worked as a distributor to American department stores. Together, they started the Powis-Brown Company. By 1922, they employed approximately 8,000 Filipina embroiderers who constructed between 1,000 and 1,500 pieces a day.

The success of the Powis-Brown Company was framed in gendered terms—a celebration of American white womanhood and the erasure of Filipina talent and artistry. The *Delineator* article states, "Ten thousand miles separated the middleman from the source of supply, but because they were mother and daughter, and inextricably bound up together, the distance never mattered."[100] Here, global circuits were made intimate and manageable because of the strength of the American mother-daughter bond. Moreover, the narrative of the Powis-Brown Company celebrated not only Brown's mind for business but also her refined taste as an American woman. Brown's "instinct for beauty" gave her the ability to transform something "ugly" into something "beautiful" and desirable: products that in turn "revolutionized the lives of thousands of Filipino women."[101] Although the Powis-Brown Company branding seemed to put a spotlight on Filipina labor, it in fact discredited Filipina embroiderers' skill and taste and portrayed them as faceless masses of extractable labor. This marketing strategy deliberately removed Filipinas as sources of artistic expertise, while still depicting them as almost mechanical producers of beautiful and desirable products. The story does not account for other ways that Filipinas participated in the development of the Philippine embroidery industry. For example, in 1913 the US Bureau of Foreign and Domestic Commerce circulated a trade report on the growth of Philippine embroidery. The report briefly spotlights Trinidad Tobias, a "Filipino expert . . . sent to the United States to make a special study of American style requirements," whose work would contribute to the establishment of new export offices in Manila.[102] Although the trade report made it clear that Tobias was a valuable asset as an embroidery expert, her knowledge and skill did not fit into the popular marketing story that celebrated US creativity and enterprise.

In addition to marketing strategies like that of the Powis-Brown Company, the expansion of a transnational Philippine embroidery industry also relied on the connections and resources of various US government sectors. Using government channels, the colonial state could essentially pirate European designs, send them off to be produced in the Philippines, and then sell them in the United States.[103] General consuls did not just work in "diplomacy," and officers in the Department of War did not just manage the armed forces—they also served as resources and brokers for lingerie and other finely made garments. Director of Education William Marquardt, for example, used his governmental ties to request product samples made by leading European lace and embroidery companies. American consuls in St. Gallen, Switzerland, and Calais, France—considered the centers for fine needlework design and production—retrieved certain laces and other fine work samples and sent these materials back to the Philippines through the Secretary of War's office.[104]

Significant profits were elusive in the early years of these ventures. However, World War I resulted in a dearth of embroidered imported goods from

Europe and thus presented an important opportunity for US manufacturers and retailers. From 1914 to 1918, the amount of lace and embroidery produced in St. Gallen and Calais sharply declined.[105] George Robinson, a representative from the American Dry Goods Co. based in Chicago, asserted, "With France at war and less exquisite lingerie being shipped to America great inroads have been made upon both the domestic and French lingerie by the invasion of the Philippine market." He went on, "This war . . . has given to the Philippine women an opportunity to work for Americans."[106] As a result, an increasing number of US manufacturers invested in Philippine embroidery, seeking to fill in the gap in affordable ready-made goods.[107] One trade news report remarked that "since the importations from the Philippines have been coming into [the United States], handmade underwear has been brought within reach of many others of small means, creating a large, new buying public."[108]

In the early years of World War I, American manufacturers and retailers collaborated with Filipino entrepreneurs, many of whom were graduates of the School of Household Industries, a colonial state-run institution that trained Filipina embroidery instructors and supervisors.[109] United States embroidery firms funneled in money, plain cotton fabric, patterns, and designs and established factories in Manila that functioned as quality control and distribution centers.[110] Reports from the Bureau of Customs document the rapid growth of the handmade embroidery industry, in particular lingerie.[111] The Bureau of Customs underscored that the "great popularity of this merchandise" was "partially due to the inability to get any importations from France during the War."[112] The amount of embroidery exports increased from $34,000 in 1914 to over $2,250,000 in 1918.[113] These numbers might suggest a more industrialized production model. However, US companies maintained the structure created by colonial officials, working with "go-betweens"— Filipino entrepreneurs such as women who graduated from the School of Household Industries—or working directly with the Department of Public Instruction (see chapter 4) to place orders and communicate with embroiderers in the provinces.[114]

At the same time, retailers and manufacturers needed to capitalize on the embroidery shortages from Europe and stimulate consumer desire for Philippine embroidery in US markets. Manufacturers and retailers carefully branded Philippine embroidery as products that met American consumers' desire for European-inspired designs, good-quality materials and craftsmanship, and affordability. The San Francisco Emporium guaranteed consumers that Philippine embroidery was equal to European-made products, claiming, "We get no better from Paris."[115] Products ornamented in the Philippines "combin[ed] the essentials"—that is, the fabrics and styles were familiar to potential consumers, while also remaining distinct from competitors' products. In *Women's Wear Daily* trade reports, US entrepreneurs and retailers described the importation of textiles and designs as "adapting the Philippine embroidery to the needs of the American people."[116] Philippine embroidery needed to be sewn onto the "correct materials," though.[117] Rather than the textiles produced in the Philippines more commonly utilized by Filipino embroiderers, such as piña or jusi, American consumers wanted cotton textiles, spun, woven, and cut in the United States. Consumers also coveted patterns and cuts modeled after European styles.

Fashion newspapers like *Women's Wear Daily* wrote that manufacturers sent European samples, or designs drawn in the United States based on European trends, to the Philippines.[118] These European trends served as reassurances of style, marking Philippine lingerie as "tasteful" and "beautiful."[119] *Women's Wear Daily* descriptions of each item included detailed technical information, documenting "regulation" straps on chemises, and familiar and coveted features like "buttonholing," "embroidered bowknots," and "ribbon run through hand-embroidered eyelets."[120] These details emphasized features recognizable to American consumers and portrayed Philippine embroidery as comparable to European commodities. Philippine embroidery retailers needed to convince consumers that "foreign craftsmen" could produce what the "American public want[ed] and need[ed]."[121] Advertising campaigns made the United States the conduit between the Philippines and what were considered the global style capitals of Europe.[122] They portrayed Filipina artistry as a talent for mimicry, recasting the recognizability in Philippine embroidery as American proximity to European fashion.[123] The discourse of style erased the complicated relationship that Filipina dress and ornamentation had with Europe, however. While Filipina embroiderers' skills were desirable, Filipina styles were not. This global system of fine needlework fashion created a new beauty regime that undercut Filipinas as artists. The system was highly regimented: the talent and labor of Filipina embroiderers was extracted, and their creativity was strictly limited. Embroiderers had no say in the patterns and designs. The system left no room for Filipina embroiderers to contribute their own creative visions. As we will see in the next chapter, this kind of regime would be taken up and reinforced in industrial schools and prisons, where embroidery was produced for profit.

Despite the stranglehold the global embroidery system placed on Filipinas, and despite the imposition of European fashions, manufacturers branded the lingerie and other white goods produced as "Philippine." *Vogue* and the *New York Times* regularly featured advertisements for "Philippine" embroidery products.[124] These ads told consumers that Philippine embroidery was distinct from competing products on the market: embroidery was "Philippine embroidery," lingerie was "Philippine lingerie" or "Philippine envelope chemises," gowns were "Philippine gowns," and so on.[125] In contrast to the marketing strategies for outprocessed goods from the late twentieth century to the present, these advertisements *showcased* the colonial component of the production process while obscuring the manufacturing that took place within the metropole. Promotional strategies specified "Philippine" as an identifier that conferred a number of meanings and enticements for the American consumer. Advertisements for Philippine lingerie, for example, consistently exhibited black-and-white illustrations of white models with short, bobbed hair wearing chemisettes and gowns. An advertisement published in a 1916 issue of *Vogue* instructed consumers on how to analyze the advertisements themselves and evaluate the images promoting pieces of lingerie. Attempting to convince buyers that "Philippine hand-embroidery for underwear has much to recommend," the model on the page showed "the excellent design and workmanship combined with a fine quality of muslin which make this work acceptable to the woman of exacting taste."[126] As a didactic text, the advertisement told women that to have discerning and fashionable taste meant coveting Philippine lingerie.

Advertisements were also careful to correlate "Philippine lingerie" to the luxury of handcrafted garments. Advertisements printed in major newspapers and magazines across the United States underscored that one of the major features of Philippine lingerie was that each piece was "hand-made" rather than machine-made or mass produced.[127] The small, detailed work on underwear gave the illusion of "one of a kind" fashion, in contrast to other ready-to-wear and mass-produced pieces.[128] Embroidery from the Philippines, one retailer assured, would satisfy "a taste among many of the women for daintiness of that lingerie and its pretty hand embroidery."[129]

This intense focus on handmade embroidery also highlighted the beauty labor of Filipina embroiderers. The identification of the laborer became part of the branding of the product. Promotional literature in *Women's Wear Daily* proclaimed that the "work is different, has a beauty of its own, and is all hand-made."[130] The emphasis on "hand-made" centers Filipina embroiderers. American companies adopted the narrative created by the colonial education system, emphasizing the European roots of Philippine embroidery and painting a romantic picture of European nuns passing on the knowledge of artistry and fine needlework to Filipina women and girls. The companies assured consumers of the embroiderers' skill level by regurgitating racial tropes of Filipinas' preternatural talent for needlework. Like other colonial agents, American retailers and manufacturers characterized the workforce as feminine, with "delicate" hands and "deft fingers."[131] The attention to the corporeal aspect to embroidery's production commodified Filipina labor as something coveted and consumable.

The corporeality of hand embroidery on lingerie also suggested a kind of interracial intimacy between Filipina bordadoras and the targeted consumer demographic of white women. White women donned undergarments that had passed through the bare hands of Filipino embroiderers. The lingerie traveled presumably from the domestic settings of labor in the Philippines to the private spaces of American homes. Advertisements confronted the slippery terrain between repulsion and desire, overtly giving the message to consumers that undergarments handled by "brown," "dusky," and non-white fingers were not only acceptable but enticing, thus repurposing racist scripts around beauty and intimacy. In earlier colonial encounters, accounts of American soldiers associated the brown skin and "duskiness" of women in the Philippines with ugliness and feelings of disgust.[132] Particularly during the years of active warfare, American soldiers described "dark," "scowling faces," disdain, and wariness as Filipinos' ugly and unacceptable affect.[133] This discourse of repulsion and grotesqueness also constructed a color barrier that insisted on the protection of white people from the perceived hostility of ugliness. While interracial intimacy in the colonial context typically engendered repulsion and fear, in the case of Philippine lingerie, advertisements displaying white models clad in Philippine lingerie signaled to potential white American consumers that white women could and should wear garments made in the Philippines by Filipina women.

Making Philippine embroidery and Filipina embroiderers a desirable commodity for American consumers meant deploying a mixture of racial and gendered tropes that stemmed from Spanish colonialism in the Philippines, orientalist discourse circulating within the United States, ideas about the "native," and notions of feminized labor.[134] Combining these different ideologies, US manufacturers and retailers carefully constructed an image of the picturesque native woman who transmitted the exotic and beautiful qualities of the tropical islands into the product. Advertisements for Philippine lingerie mirrored Burton Holmes's film, *Luzon Lingerie*, and produced a collective public fantasy of the finished product, the picturesque qualities of an exotic locale, and embroiderers' feminine and dainty bodies that mirrored the way the United States actively created an extractable, cheap, racialized, and gendered feminine workforce.[135] An ad for the Powis-Brown Company, for example, included a photograph of three young Filipina women, dressed in *baro't saya*, embroidering a cloth stretched on a frame. The caption reads, "Natives Making Philippine Hand Embroidery."[136] This image of Filipina bordadoras fueled American fantasies of Philippine embroidery as produced in a picturesque setting by "native" women whose skills flowed in their blood and poured out into the elaborate embroidery work. The marketing of Philippine lingerie thus created dual fantasies of an exotic product and an equally exotic Filipina workforce. The repetition and circulation of such representations built a brand. The allure of Philippine lingerie was not just the beauty of the products but the possibility of consuming something exotic produced in the romantically imagined tropics by exotic Filipinas.[137] By purchasing Philippine lingerie and other embroidered goods, consumers attempted to purchase an intimate connection with far-off spaces and people and thereby attain a kind of cosmopolitanism rooted in exoticism.[138]

Retailers also invested heavily in the romanticization of "native" work to commodify Filipina embroiderers and the workforce as a whole. They regarded the romanticized image of Filipinas plying their needles in their "native" environments as a viable marketing strategy. The behemoth department store Marshall Field and Company borrowed display strategies from exhibitions at the St. Louis World's Fair to bring the exotic into the domestic space. The company created a live diorama. In 1921, a "realistic exhibit" designed to "show natives at work on dainty embroideries" was first erected in Marshall Field's flagship store on State Street in Chicago.[139] A "genuine nipa hut" was erected in the middle of the department store to provide shoppers visual access to embroiderers' "natural home surroundings."[140] The exhibit traveled to other department stores to further popularize Philippine embroidery throughout the domestic United States.[141] At the San Francisco Emporium, bordadoras were described as wearing "quaint" "costumes" and working in a "bamboo grass hut erected for their comfort."[142] The department store also brought in a man named Padra, described by *Women's Wear Daily* as the "native designer" who managed the exhibit and who explained the process of production in "perfectly plain English to the women who gathered 'round the workers."[143] According to the *Women's Wear Daily* article, Padra appeared "like a 15-year-old boy ... dressed in white trousers and plain cloth smock which was embroidered and interesting in design."[144] This exhibit performed the essential branding of Philippine embroidery—a combination of the familiar and the exotic. The live performance sought to make onlookers think they were getting an inside look at the Philippine embroidery industry. Just as in the advertising campaigns, this marketing scheme showcased the recognizable features of a lingerie industry: women workers plying their needles on delicate cloth and a man overseeing the artistry and design.

Despite this familiarity, the exhibit also played up that which made Philippine embroidery exotic, strange, and unfamiliar—and distinct from European competitors.[145] The article's attention to Padra's unusual appearance and his rendering as a young boy, regardless of his real age or his position (we do not know if he did needlework or if he was a manager, for example), maintained the vision of Philippine embroidery as a feminized industry.[146] The exhibition of the embroiderers and Padra in what was imagined as their natural habitat invited onlookers to gaze, covet, and serve almost as patrons by purchasing the products fashioned before them. Moreover, under the auspices of giving consumers a peek into the production of the Philippine embroidery, these major retailers offered a fantasy of production that elided the complex transnational industry, which was mostly owned and controlled by US private enterprise. Instead, the live diorama attempted to deliver a brand of Philippine embroidery that—like the St. Louis World's Fair, the films of Burton Holmes, and popular travel literature—used the spectacle of the exoticized Filipino native not so much for the comfort of the Filipinos on display but to satisfy Americans' curiosity and to bring to life their fantasies about the Philippines. The performance of labor was meant to entice American consumers to own the exotic through the purchase of Philippine lingerie. These performances contributed to the commodification of not just the embroidered goods but also the embroiderers themselves.[147]

By the 1920s, Filipino civil servants also encouraged the investment of American capital in embroidery through the commodification and promotion of the Filipina beauty workforce. Filipino civil servants were just as invested in building the beauty regime of Philippine embroidery, as they hoped the potential profits might extend to Filipino elites, entrepreneurs, and government agents. In 1920, *Women's Wear Daily* interviewed Arsenio Luz, manager of the Philippine Commercial Agency, at the Grand Central Palace, a large trade exhibition hall in New York City.[148] In the hope of securing business relationships with American companies, Luz boasted that Filipina embroiderers could both execute patterns by American designers *and* create original and beautiful designs. Luz reassured potential investors that designs "could be submitted by American designers, and executed by native Filipinos. It is, after all, the execution of the design which counts. You can get nowhere else such delicate color and workmanship as our women can put into embroidery of the finer sorts."[149] Luz also capitalized on American familiarity with Philippine embroidery and depicted Filipinas as artisans. Building on American fascination with handmade products and fantasies of the exotic Philippines and Filipinas, Luz described Filipina embroiderers as "not only extremely artistic, but creative as well."[150] He boasted "this has been repeatedly shown . . . in original designs submitted voluntarily by employees of various embroidery firms now in business in the islands."[151] By emphasizing Filipina artistry, Luz put forth a slightly different image of the embroiderer than other marketing campaigns. Luz underscored the fashionability of Filipina embroiderers' style, stating, "These designs . . . were both original and unquestionably unique."[152] And in response to American critics who might have equated uniqueness as ugly, Luz contended that Filipina designs "were not freakish, but distinctly 'Filipinisque,' and decidedly new."[153]

Despite Luz's adulation of Filipina artistry, for him, the greatest appeal of the Filipina workforce was their cheapness. Luz echoed arguments made by white American colonial agents. He declared that businesses would get "cheaper production, with an assured supply of labor already accustomed to the particular industry in mind."[154] Luz presented Filipina labor as a kind of inexhaustible, extractable resource. Luz extolled the size of the workforce, reporting that "about 70,000 persons are employed at present, with 20 concerns supervising the manufacturing and export end of the business." Luz guaranteed that the colonial state infrastructure would make it easy for investors to tap into the Filipina workforce. Luz boasted, "Our government is ready at all times, either through its agencies such as this one [the Philippine Commercial Agency] or directly, to cooperate with American business interests in any way interested commercially in the Philippines."[155] Luz went on to explain that this "cooperation would consist of furnishing the investor with every facility for getting located; of furnishing a labor supply and seeing to it that our liberal laws in regard to factory establishment be made to apply to him as advantageously as possible."[156] He went on to explain that not only did the Philippines produce an endless supply of cheap labor, but there was also "absolutely no possibility of strikes, since the production could take place in the homes."[157] Luz pointed out that this industry, unlike other urban-based manufacturing trades with unions, coupled the structure of informal home work with the feminization of needlework, and that this inhibited Filipina embroiderers from collectively organizing.[158] Luz rendered the vulnerability and lack of power of workers and the ways in which informal economies prevented labor organization as an exploitable feature.[159] In doing so, he directly preyed upon the growing fear among elite Filipinos and US colonialists of the rising anti-imperialist labor and peasant protests of the 1920s to garner sup-

FIGURE 3.2. Advertisement for the American Undergarment Corporation, 1920.
Filipinas Heritage Library, Metro Manila, Philippines.

port for the Philippine embroidery industry.[160] Luz promoted the Philippine embroidery industry as a good investment precisely because its maintenance of Filipino worker vulnerability sustained colonial order. Filipina embroiderers' vulnerability would ultimately make them susceptible to scapegoating when the global economies shifted and the Philippine embroidery industry began to decline.

## The Decline of the Transnational Philippine Embroidery Industry

The expansion of Philippine embroidery hit its limit. After reaching its peak in 1921, when the industry's value was reported at 19,696,207 pesos, the following year, numbers plummeted to 6,514,597 pesos.[161] Retailers had purchased a large number of orders from the Philippines but were unable to sell much of the merchandise, which resulted in a reduction in orders in 1922.[162] For the next ten years, the industry struggled, with peaks and ebbs in the quantity of merchandise ordered from the Philippines. A number of factors contributed to the slowdown in Philippine embroidery. In the 1920s, the exchange rate negatively impacted the US dollar and consequently the Philippine peso. At the end of World War I, European manufacturers sought to increase their exports and regain their dominance in American markets.[163] Despite the overall profitability of Philippine embroidery in American markets, the brand "Philippine" could not attain the same cachet as "French" or "Parisian." "Paris," "Parisian," and "French" still carried an allure and epitomized the height of fashion for American consumers. The rising costs of materials, the costs of shipping those materials and finished goods between the continental US and the Philippines, as well as the cost of Filipina labor also put a strain on the industry. One manufacturer bemoaned how the pilfering of merchandise in transit and the lack of insurance to cover disasters like fires also impacted profits for manufacturers.[164] By the 1930s, US garment industries began to shift toward mass-produced clothing and began favoring synthetic fabrics. United States protectionism rose in reaction to the Great Depression. Philippine embroidery was reclassified as a luxury commodity and thus lost its duty-free status.[165] Last, as we will see in chapter 5, the shifting relationship between the colony and the metropole as a result of new policies toward Philippine independence radically restricted the free-trade relationship between the United States and the Philippines.

Some manufacturers attempted to defray rising costs and maintain profits by using lower-quality textiles.[166] The standard textile used for Philippine embroidery was cloth with an 88 by 80 thread count, or in rare cases an

86 by 1,000 thread count.[167] Throughout the 1920s, consumers noticed the substitution of coarser and narrower cloth even as retailers promised quality, style, and hand embroidery at low price points.[168] The marked changes in the quality of cloth and the decrease in sales urged some in the industry to demand that policy-makers in the Philippines and the United States regulate the textiles used in manufacturing.[169] Ultimately, efforts to legislate the standardization of Philippine embroidery failed despite aggressive efforts by some lobbyists and colonial officials who argued that state regulation would not only help import and export firms but also become a source of revenue for the government.[170]

Despite the numerous and complex factors that contributed to difficulties in the Philippine embroidery industry—from major wars to shifts in the stock market and global competition—much of the blame fell on the Filipina embroiderers themselves. Although the Filipina workforce had been celebrated and praised for their dexterity and their preternatural skill for delicate work, these women remained vulnerable in their disposability.[171] While some trade reports acknowledged the systematic reasons for the trade's difficulties, many still identified Filipina workers as the root of the problem. Helen Duggan, a buyer for Marshall Field and Company, met with the Embroidery Section of the American Chamber of Commerce on June 22, 1922, to discuss suggestions for and criticisms of the embroidery trade. Duggan told Section members that if the industry were to survive past its initial boom and relative success, manufacturers needed to address buyers' and consumers' concerns over the waning quality of workmanship.[172] The Section took this as an opportunity to discuss its own strategies for maintaining and bettering the quality of embroidery from the Philippines. The Section briefly accounted for factors like the "high cost of material" and glossed over others, like the end of World War I and the reemergence of French lingerie makers, Belgian and Swiss laces, and other European-made white goods.[173] The real problem, the Section argued instead, lay in Filipina workers themselves. It contended that Filipinas' "indifference and carelessness," along with "poor habits," had led to the production of subpar goods that in turn tarnished the reputation of Philippine embroidery.[174] Such descriptions directly contradicted the high praise for Filipina workers that had circulated just a decade before. Whereas previously the laudatory commentary on Filipinas' apparent natural proclivity for fine needlework had functioned as an enticement for US capital and investment, here Filipinas' natural tendency was portrayed as an inability to produce good work and Filipina embroiderers were cast as failed modern subjects incapable of taking advantage of American training. The message implied that workers were already overcompensated for their labor and nonetheless produced substandard products. The problem, then, was not structural but a problem of character, of the intrinsic flaws of Filipino laziness and lack of motivation, a long-standing trope used to describe Filipinos as a whole. But another way of understanding "poor habits" is to frame the decline within a context of labor frustration. The "decline in quality" and "poor habits" in actuality signal unsustainable work conditions. As in other sectors of the garment industry, the rising cost of materials coupled with the pressure to keep commodity prices low to maintain the interest of mass consumers demanded cutting cost elsewhere. Just as in garment industries in New York and textile manufacturing in Europe, manufacturers "sweated" workers, demanding an increase in output without adjusting time or wages. Even without written records that document the Filipina workers' experiences from their point of view, the unsustainability of the demands placed on them manifested in the products themselves.

Blaming Filipina workers eschewed the responsibility of policy-makers, entrepreneurs, and investors who deliberately built an unsustainable industry predicated on cheap labor. Moreover, it glossed over the possibility that the materials and already sewn garments imported to the Philippines from the United States might have been poorly constructed. Further, these critiques ignored the worldwide slowing down of economies. Ultimately, the narrative spotlighting Filipina labor hid the exploitative structure of the industry and the lack of investment in a sustainable infrastructure that would have not only "uplifted" Filipina workers but also provided them upward mobility for a livable life.[175] These reports also failed to mention that the decline in quality was not unique to the Philippine industry. Rather, it was symptomatic of the fast-paced production of ready-to-wear goods. In an effort to keep up with fashion market demands for new style trends, manufacturers made compromises and lowered the quality and durability in order to compete with other producers. Fast-paced fashion produced in the continental United States and elsewhere faced difficulties in maintaining quality when the production demanded "sweating" the labor from workers.[176] Across the board, garment industries were cutting costs and cutting production time to maximize profits. Just as in New York and other textile-making centers where women—particularly immigrant women—took the blame for larger economic and social problems, Filipina embroiderers were convenient scapegoats.

The manufacturers' criticisms of Filipina workmanship and artistry also, however, reveal Filipina acts of refusal against the constraints of the embroidery system. One retailer claimed that the "Filipino girl is strange," she has an "archaic spirit" and "she clings to tradition."[177] The retailer found that Filipina workers tended to "rebel against" the changes demanded by manufacturers. For example, when manufacturers imported linen, they also supplied thimbles, which were commonly used in the United States and Europe for hand sewing with thicker fabrics. However, Filipina embroiderers "refused" to use them and it "was not until a later period that the innovation was brought about."[178] Embroiderers also "refused to embroider on net, and it took a long time to induce them to combine lace or drawn work with embroidery in one garment."[179] Americans' descriptions of Filipinas' refusal to utilize American-introduced tools and their resistance to their supervisors' directions attempted to indicate primitivism. But a closer reading suggests that refusal to comply with certain work practices signaled defiance. Frustrated US agents who lashed out against the perceived stubbornness of Filipina embroiderers reacted to the everyday acts of refusal such as lack of compliance.[180] Bordadoras were not necessarily eager to please or to participate in colonial and capitalist projects. While they may not have completely refused to work, they nevertheless demonstrated their displeasure through these gestures of refusal. To be sure, Filipina embroiderers had little power in terms of their class status, their gender, and their position in a very hierarchical transnational embroidery industry. But as James Scott points out in his work on peasant revolts in Southeast Asia, even if forms of struggle stop short of outright collective defiance, individuals nevertheless use the everyday "ordinary weapons" they have at their disposal. Through these small acts, embroiderers demonstrated their displeasure and showed their trust and confidence in their own skill and craft. Acts of defiance may not have radically altered the transnational Philippine embroidery system, but they did put sand in the gears and had the potential to slow production.

## Impact of the Philippine Embroidery Industry

To manufacturers, investors, and retailers, the Philippine embroidery industry's years of growth and profit may have felt short-lived. But the formation of the industry had deep and serious consequences for Filipina embroiderers and for Filipina labor more broadly. Philippine embroidery left a blueprint for colonial co-optation of established practices and skilled labor for the expansion of transnational industries. It also relied on contradictory racial scripts that made Filipina labor and skills desirable and yet disposable. In the industry's early years, Filipina needlework practices were reimagined through a lens of romanticized exoticism that positioned Filipina embroiderers as a source of beauty for white American consumers to extract. United States manufacturers and the Insular Government worked together to refashion racial scripts to expand markets and spark a desire for handmade goods created by exotic Filipina needleworkers.

The industry consisted of a complicated network that crisscrossed through the Philippines, the Pacific, North America, the Atlantic, and Europe.[181] United States colonial agents borrowed and manipulated gendered and racialized labor structures from both the US and Spanish Philippine colonial contexts to embed Philippine embroidery, and later lacemaking, in a transnational white-goods industry that lasted for more than a decade. The United States' deep economic interest in Philippine embroidery produced uneven consequences. Efforts to scale up a cottage industry kept the wages of highly skilled workers low. Moreover, the transnational structure of Philippine embroidery cemented the Philippines' dependence on US manufacturers, distributers, imports, and markets.

The cooperation between private industry and the US state linked Filipina embroiderers and embroidery to new geographies of empire. Free-trade policies allowed materials to be shipped from the northeastern and southern United States to Manila; ornamented and finished white goods made their way back to US retailers across the continent, fusing together industries built on different modes of exploitation and violence. Consulates and officials from the War Bureau, whose work is most often imagined as providing security intelligence, were woven into private industries for the economic advantage of the US government, businesses, and investors. The Philippine embroidery industry also had a lasting impact on the ways that cheap, nonwhite, and feminine "delicate" labor was imagined and extracted, not just from the Philippines but from other geographies and diasporas linked to the Global South.[182] The story of feminized cheap labor in the Philippines is typically told as a story of free trade.[183] However, the establishment of a multisited Philippine embroidery industry directed toward American consumption is a lesson in the relationship between private and public institutions and the building of modern empires. The expansion of US empire enfolded the Philippines and other colonies into the borders of the United States while not wholly including and enfranchising colonial subjects. Empire opened US access to Philippine resources, including extractable skills, artistry, and labor. Empire and its investment in beauty regimes adapted and co-opted Filipina needlework for the accumulation of US capital and power. In doing so, the making of a transnational Philippine embroidery industry helped set the groundwork for what Robyn Rodriguez describes as the twenty-first-century

Philippine labor "broker state," where "the Philippines offers a reserve army of labor to be deployed for capital across the planet."[184] To the colonial state and US manufacturers, Filipina embroiderers were imagined as skilled, dexterous, feminine, delicate, racially Other, and conveniently cheap.

Filipinas had extractable skills that could be translated for industrial work in transnational industries that ultimately profited foreign investors. However, narratives constructed by the industry also contended that Filipinas and their skills needed to be controlled and regulated to reign in "temperamental characteristics" and "lack of interest in sustained industrial effort."[185] This narrative remained as a characterization of the Philippines. When it was clear that the Philippine embroidery industry was in trouble, the American Chamber of Commerce blamed Filipina embroiderers and pivoted toward disciplinary techniques to revive the industry. The Embroidery Section published a circular warning workers that substandard workmanship would lead to US buyers returning shipments of embroideries. Returned products meant Filipina bordadoras would not be paid. Such punitive measures reified portrayals of Filipinos as lacking craftsmanship and positioned their subpar work as the central reason for the industry's failure. Americans placed the responsibility and blame on a workforce that had, for the most part, been separated from the planning and building of industry infrastructures as well as its profits.

The Embroidery Section circular was also distributed through the colonial public school system. Using colonial structures, the Embroidery Section attempted to reach the embroiderers linked to embroidery centers and public schools. Communicating with workers through education networks may seem like an odd strategy. But as we will see in the next chapter, the Department of Public Instruction was deeply involved in the making and disciplining of the Filipina embroidery workforce. Public industrial schools and colonial prisons both fell under the direction of the Department of Public Instruction. Both institutions created new forms of disciplinary and beauty regimes to train and expand the workforce that drew upon the ongoing gendered radicalization of the Filipina embroiderer. This chapter locates the transformation of the embroidery industry in the regime shift from Spanish to US colonial rule. By the end of the next chapter, thread and needles, lace and lingerie, and schools and prisons will provide new perspectives on US colonialism's role in the transnational contours of the garment industry.

# 4

BEAUTY REGIMENS

*Structure, Discipline, and Needlework
in Colonial Industrial Schools and Prisons*

In 1917, the insular state instituted a number of prison reform actions with
the new Administrative Code of the Philippines. These changes to the Spanish Penal Code of 1887 included Section 1728, the "Assignment of Women to
Work," which stated, "Convicted female prisoners may be assigned to work
suitable to their age, sex, and physical condition."[1] Revisions to the Spanish
Penal Code reflected the already ongoing changes in the insular penitentiary
system, namely the establishment of industrial departments, among them Division H, an all-female division at Bilibid Prison. In Division H, incarcerated
women were put to work embroidering, crocheting, lacemaking, and dressmaking, creating fine needlework to be sold for a profit. Domestic science
teachers and administrators from colonial industrial public schools trained
and supervised the women laborers. Scenes of fine needlework being performed in the colonial prison were even captured by Burton Holmes. His
film *Luzon Lingerie* declares, "Even in Bilibid Prison the maidens and matrons of Manila execute exquisite needlework."[2] The film then shows Filipina
embroiderers dressed in prison uniforms made of drab fabric, with starched

butterfly sleeves and unadorned white collars. The incarcerated women sit in neat rows, plying their needles and thread into cloth.

Director of Prisons Ramon Victorio boasted of the success of industrial work, declaring, "An outsider who pays a visit to Bilibid is impressed by the possibilities of the industrial activities with which the inmates are engaged under rigid discipline."[3] Later, in a paper submitted to the American Prison Association titled "Purposes and Character of Prison Discipline," Victorio would stress the importance of labor as a form of discipline. In the paper, Victorio asserts, "Discipline is the mainstay, the backbone of prison administration."[4] In many ways, discipline was also a central feature of the Philippine embroidery industry. The early 1900s through the 1920s witnessed the formation of a new beauty regime: the systematic controlling and training of Filipinas as workers and producers of beauty commodities in public industrial schools and, not coincidentally, in Bilibid Prison.[5] In 1907, the Insular Government placed the Bureau of Education and the Bureau of Prisons under the same office, that of the Department of Public Instruction. Public education and prisons might appear to be two disparate institutions, but a closer look at the public industrial schools' and the prisons' roles in producing Philippine embroidery provides a clear picture of the intimate relationship between schools and prisons. Under US colonial rule, the beauty regimes of the public schools and prisons targeted Filipinas of the peasant and working classes, weaponizing the US colonial promise of uplift through industrialized handicraft. The beauty regimes of public schools and prisons exercised beauty *regimens*, that is, routinized behavioral and physical disciplining of individuals. Although colloquially beauty regimens are often associated with prescribed treatments and lifestyles for self-beautification, the beauty regimens imposed on Filipina students and prisoners were not designed to beautify Filipina workers.[6] Rather their purpose was to improve Filipinas' capacity for efficiency and proficiency in the production of commodities, from embroidered lingerie, to lace-adorned blouses, to crocheted products intended for purchase and use by American consumers in their own regimens of beautification and ornamentation.

The Insular Government asserted that disciplinary institutions in the form of public education and prisons were essential services of the modern state. Making the connection between Philippine industrial schools and prisons helps us better understand the methods of constructing US empire's authority. Dylan Rodriguez asserts the "overarching political project of portraying the prison as an (abstracted) object of state 'authority': the discursive construction of the prison as a respectable and commanding institution that securely inhabits the realm of an everyday common sense, and enjoys a popular consent around the apparatus of its rule."[7] According to colonial officials, the strict training of Filipina students and prisoners in embroidery would provide the much-needed regulation of colonial subjects and lead them to "normal," productive, modern lives. Disciplinary beauty regimes measured the value of Filipinas in colonial modernization projects, promising them that they, too, would reap the benefits. They made little good on these promises. Ultimately, the normalization of disciplinary institutions supported the colonial state's goal of establishing a long-term regime. The bureaucratization of industrial schools and prisons further cemented their places in colonial society through self-sustaining, revenue-generating schemes. Unlike other handicraft labor, embroidery brought in profits for the Insular Government.

Through industrial work and training, schools and prisons disciplined Filipinas and enforced social order. Beauty work was inextricably tied to colonial reform culture, which in and of itself was designed to control colonial subjects and cement US authority. Through reform, the United States promised modernity, freedom, uplift, and upward mobility. But a deeper examination of the state's role in shaping the embroidery industry from the early 1900s through the 1920s exposes the weaponization of beauty regimens to maintain power hierarchies and the stratification of labor and production. The transformation of the Philippine embroidery industry through the public disciplinary institutions of schools and prisons aimed to expand the workforce and create a replaceable worker. However, unlike other forms of cheap and replaceable labor, embroiderers learned their skills through a strict training regimen.[8] Through the beauty-regime framework, this chapter traces overlooked threads and connections tracking the formation and uses of regimented disciplinary technologies and the consequences of colonial-controlled mobilization in state-run disciplinary institutions.

## Department of Public Instruction: A System for Scaling Up Beauty Work

The deliberate efforts of the US federal government and the colonial state, along with private entrepreneurs, slowly built the infrastructures and workforce for a transnational Philippine-US embroidery industry. The structure of the Insular Government paved the way for the growth and increased importance of embroidery manufacturing in public schools and prisons. The 1907 Reorganization Act created new bureaus, consolidated offices, and moved governmental divisions. In this overhaul of the Insular Government's bureaucracy, the Department of Public Instruction came to oversee the

Bureau of Education, the Bureau of Supply, the Bureau of Printing, and the newly formed Bureau of Prisons. The creation of the Bureau of Prisons gave the Secretary of the Department of Public Instruction jurisdiction over Bilibid Prison—including its shops, quarries, and penal settlement—as well as all provincial jails throughout the archipelago. Prior to this, Bilibid had been under the jurisdiction of the Department of Commerce and Police.

Thus, after 1907, the Department of Public Instruction oversaw the institutions that trained and produced colonial citizens. When the Bureau of Education pivoted toward industrial schools, the bureaucratic system was primed for manufacturing to become a central part of its disciplinary regimes.[9] As disciplinary institutions, schools and prisons sought to form and reform Filipinos into ideal subjects who would contribute to the modernization of the nation-to-be. In the framework of colonialism, US tutelage bestowed upon Filipinos the benefit of becoming thoroughly modern subjects through increased wage-earning potential and participation in global capitalism. The methods by which "pupil workers" and convict laborers were controlled and managed were gendered, classed, and racialized in ways that both reflected and departed from US reform operations in the US metropole.[10] Schools and prisons provided controlled environments in which pupil workers and convict laborers were educated and disciplined to create a vulnerable and exploitable workforce for the profit of the colonial state, American manufacturers, and a select number of Filipinos. An exploration of embroidery training and production among Filipina students and convict laborers exposes the methods of control geared toward optimizing profit, often at the expense of unpaid, underpaid, and often coerced forms of Filipina labor.

Despite the outward-facing presentation of benevolence, colonial public institutions like schools and prisons capitalized on the vulnerability of Filipinas from the working and peasant classes. Under the guise of the betterment of Filipino women and girls, the transimperial Philippine beauty regime produced power hierarchies and fused together public institutions and the private sector. The Department of Public Instruction heavily invested in embroidery as well as in other manufacturing and commercial agriculture industries, promising that "individual enterprise" would bring "prosperity and contentment to the Philippines." The colonial state deliberately involved the Office of the Secretary of Public Instruction with the intention of using institutions of social control, like the state-controlled education and carceral systems, to make greater profits. The US Secretary of War declared, "With increased activity of industrial enterprise and business [would] come the greater revenues for the performance of the proper duties of civil government," concluding that such duties would include "improvements and paved and sewered streets and passable highways and adequate schools and effective police."[11] Public schooling and policing were portrayed as essential public services, needed to maintain social control for the sake of stability and prosperity. Industry would fund the "duties of civil government," and social control would facilitate profits for the state. While congressional reports reveal the amount of federal funds spent on maintenance, offices, bureaus, and departments of the colonial state, the Insular Government still needed to generate supplementary capital to function. For example, after the reorganization of the Insular Government, the Bureau of Education slashed the budget for public schools considerably. Pupil workers thus supplemented an underfunded industrial school system. Some schools lacked the capital to pay for the upfront costs of materials, which resulted in individual students being charged fees to attend school and participate in industrial courses. To pay for supplies such as imported goods and ingredients, schools instructed Filipina students to create arts and crafts for export and to sell prepared foods in their communities—thus using their domestic science skills to pay for their own domestic science education costs. Students made trinkets as well as expensive exportable commodities such as baskets, lace, and textiles that appealed to American consumers.[12] The profits went into a "pupil fund," a cash reserve used to pay for industrial education supplies.[13]

The blending of state-run institutions and industrial trade emerged from the United States' efforts to impose its form of tutelary colonialism, promoting its imperial expansion and accumulation of power while "civilizing" its colonial subjects in the image of the United States.[14] Denise Cruz argues that the US intentionally focused on these categories of "advancement" precisely because such a focus demonstrated the United States' benevolence toward Filipinos.[15] Proponents of industrial training in colonial public schools took up the language and logic of vocational training as appropriate for those they deemed racially inferior.[16] At the same time, they utilized the rhetoric of uplift from US mainland progressive reform movements and industrial schools. Superintendent of Education David Barrows extolled the benefits of colonial education, claiming: "Natural benefits can neither be taken advantage of nor enjoyed by a people illiterate and ignorant. Development of markets and of trade only accompany higher standards of life, and higher standards of life proceed nowhere so quickly as from an advance of education. The successful issue of the public government inaugurated in this country rests more than anything else on the work done in the schools. If the work done by the

Bureau of Education succeeds, the American government implanted in these islands will succeed."[17]

School officials promoted industrial schools in Manila and across the provinces as providing "real" and "practical" skills that could be used to generate industry and employment opportunities. The US empire's drive to identify and expand local manufacturing industries became a key component of colonial education. According to education scholar Roland Sintos Coloma, "The focus on marketable and commercial goods became part of the driving force in the school curricular transformation."[18] The same year that the Reorganization Act took effect, the Bureau of Education published its "1907 Statement of Organization and Aims," which celebrated the implementation of various forms of manual-industrial training at all levels of public schooling. In 1909, the leadership in the Bureau of Education transferred from David Barrows, a proponent of the "three R's," to Frank White, who favored industrial education. White sought to continue to educate Filipinos through literary instruction but also added to their curriculum what he considered as the benefits of industrial instruction.[19]

Industrial schools in the Philippines emphasized the transformation of the masses into industrial workers.[20] Colonial educators boasted that their pedagogical strategies provided students the future benefit of potential earning power. One of the central aims of colonial education was to mold and fashion colonial subjects. Industrial schools targeted students from working- and peasant-class backgrounds and taught them a particular imperial economic vision for the future of the Philippines. Rather than focusing on self-governance and civics lessons, which might have furthered the nation-building project, the industrial curriculum focused on making ideal modern citizens who could fully participate in a capitalist society as producers, wage-earners, and consumers.[21] From 1909 to 1930, the Bureau of Education prioritized manual training classes in primary schools and vocational training in secondary schools.[22] The colonial state's investment in industrial education was demonstrated in the number of students who participated in the program. In 1910, roughly 350,000 students took industrial work classes throughout the archipelago. By 1924, at the height of the program, the number of students reached 900,000.[23]

The Bureau of Education reorganized a large portion of the public school system to model an efficient business operation. In 1909, the Bureau of Education's industrial department, which was housed in Manila, organized, promoted, and supervised industrial training in Philippine schools.[24] The US colonial state, along with private manufacturers, relied on industrial schools and prisons to provide the infrastructure to train and discipline a new workforce that was shaped by race and gender ideologies.[25] Schools organized training programs around notions of feminine (domestic science) and masculine (carpentry and manufacturing) types of labor.[26] "Feminine" work not only focused on the skills needed to effectively run households but also taught needlework as vocational training. Industrial schools taught basic sewing as well as "fancy" needlework—such as embroidery, lacemaking, and crocheting—thus blurring the lines between household labor and manufacturing.

The ramping up of industrial education coincided with the increase in demand for Philippine embroidery.[27] The colonial state's investment in industrial education stemmed from the firm belief that formal training through public schools would foster an export economy.[28] In 1911, just two years into the transition to industrial schooling, the Bureau of Education issued a bulletin titled *Lace Making and Embroidery*, which addressed the economic reasoning behind their vested interest in embroidery and lacemaking; the bulletin was distributed to American teachers in the Philippines. It states that textile production existed in the Philippines prior to US occupation. Philippine weaving as an industry, however, had no hope for growth beyond a local market, as it was unable to compete with English and American cotton mills. Thus, to "add to [the] welfare and prosperity [of] the islands, such training should be given in the schools as will result in the general production of a class of articles for which there is a demand abroad, where better prices can generally be obtained than in local markets."[29] According to this bulletin, the clear answer lay in extant household industries—specifically fine needlework. In other words, fine needlework would be the easiest skill to institute and also the most lucrative handicraft. The publication stated that education officials "desired to amplify the course of study for the public schools in such a manner as to include instruction in remunerative industries for girls," and "the arts of lace making and embroidery appear to offer the best possible medium for giving such instruction."[30] The US colonial education system upheld Spanish-era norms of femininity in the demarcation of appropriate fields of study for Filipinas, including embroidery and other forms of needlework. Moreover, industrial schools endeavored to follow practices similar to those of Spanish colonial convent schools. There, Filipina students honed their embroidery (and lacemaking) skills and sold their wares for profits.

While the rhetoric of the modernization of Filipino students espoused that industrial schools would free Filipinos from the legacies of oppressive Spanish conditions, industrial schools capitalized on established practices and

FIGURE 4.1. Scene from the School of Household Industries, *Philippine Craftsman* 5, no. 3 (September 1916): 189.

industries.[31] A letter from the Department of the Interior to the Department of War stated, "Lacemaking and embroidery are the lines now being taught, and as they command a very large market it is thought that the training given and the natural ability of the students" would earn a significant profit.[32] Institutionalizing training in embroidery production to suit American markets led officials to feel "reasonably certain that by adherence to the high standards taught in the school, the product of the classes organized by these students will not only meet with a ready sale but will establish a new standard of excellence for Philippine lace and embroidery."[33] These departments sought to meet the increasing demand for high-quality work by creating an organized and hierarchal workforce primarily composed of women and girls.

The colonial state structured industrial schools and other public institutions with the intent to produce and manage a Filipino workforce. Officials hoped that existing fine needlework production could be systematically replicated, generalized, and scaled up through bureaucratization and standardization. However, education officials and embroidery manufacturing companies did not want to completely mechanize and industrialize fine needlework. As discussed in chapter 3, Philippine embroideries' allure stemmed from American consumers' desire for handcrafted goods. Officials thus sought to co-opt the informal economies of cottage industries and connect them to the ever-growing bureaucracy of the colonial state. The Bureau of Education established the Sales Agency to oversee the marketing of products made in public trade schools.[34] New ties between the Bureau of Education and larger bureaucratic entities, such as the Office of the Secretary of War and General Consuls, provided a structure of control over Filipinos. Local barrio schools were thus embedded in this larger state network. Superintendents, school officials, and teachers all worked as agents of the state, charged with the managerial responsibilities of maintaining the order and productivity of embroidery and other forms of manufacturing in industrial schools.

## The Bureau of Education's Beauty Regime: Structuring a Workforce

In 1916, General Industrial Supervisor Herbert D. Fisher mapped out what he called the "evolution of industrial supervision."[35] The year 1904, he contends, had witnessed the first stage of industrial education, a phase marked by a "public clamor for education" and not enough teachers.[36] This teacher shortage led to Filipino teachers being hired to work under the supervision of American teachers, which ushered in the second stage of industrial education. Fisher echoed colonial discourses around Filipinas' natural proclivity for delicate needlework, noting that these teachers followed their "natural inclination" and began to "introduce many forms of handicraft," including "fancy needlework."[37] While Fisher glossed over the role of Filipina teachers in introducing needlework into public school curricula, their influence, expertise, and labor were crucial to the expansion of industrial education and its earning potential. Some American teachers viewed the introduction of the handicraft curriculum with "curiosity," while other supervising teachers supported it. Despite the skepticism of American teachers, industrial education developed. Fisher asserted that the emergence of centralized supervision and the need for specialized and qualified teachers marked the third stage of industrial education.[38] The fourth stage, he maintained, "began at the moment when the General Office was in a position to attempt to standardize work of all classes; to require that sections and individual schools specialize in work which was more appropriate for them; to disseminate information along all lines which insure concentrated effort and definite instruction, and to give every consideration to those in the field."[39] The structures of these beauty regimes, in other words, were built upon layers of hierarchies that entangled state officials, manufacturers and owners, middle-women and *tiyenderas* (merchants/shopkeepers), instructors, and needle-workers. The Bureau of Education created a new beauty regime with this network of administrators, industrial supervisors, and teachers who traveled to schools across the provinces, providing instruction, advice, and assistance.

The colonial education system functioned as a kind of central nervous system for commodity production and commerce. In terms of the embroidery industry, the education system functioned as a network to produce workers, systematize labor and production, and distribute information throughout the Philippines. Through Filipina needlework, the Bureau of Education wove together the business of fashion and education.

In 1912, in an attempt to use industrial schools as a platform to scale up fine needlework production, the Philippine Legislature passed Act 2110, which granted the Department of Education the power and the funding (it allocated 100,000 pesos to the Department) to create and maintain the School of Household Industries in Manila, which was to train a class of women middle managers.[40] The School of Household Industries essentially churned out a new labor force of women managers who, in turn, trained and employed embroiderers and lacemakers. The training center admitted only Filipina women who were over age twenty-one and from prominent families. Its purpose was to train them so that they could more easily secure supervisor positions—a status that required power. While public schools throughout the provinces targeted the masses, transforming them into workers, the School of Household Industries concentrated on the "cacique type."[41] The Bureau of Education approached municipal civic leaders and asked them to recommend Filipinas of "good character" to attend the school.[42] Ideal candidates were women of "such character and standing as to insure their being able to assemble and hold under their influence groups of industrious workers."[43] Frank Carpenter, one of the early proponents of Act 2110, originally envisioned the industrial school as focusing on the "instruction and control of adult workers."[44] For Carpenter, the ideal students were neither women from the most elite and prominent families nor women from the peasant classes. Rather, to create a managerial class of women workers, he believed that the program should recruit women who were from families of some means, who might own small businesses and stores and have some influence in their towns as well-respected families. These women, he imagined, would have some education already and would already have reading and mathematical skills. As members of the cacique class, they would hold influence in their respective towns and thus could compel women and girls of the town to take up embroidery work.

The government paid students' tuition and boarding at the School of Household Industries. After completing their training, these young women were required to return to their respective provinces to establish and manage work centers for the standardized production of lace and embroidery.[45]

Many students did not receive provisions to build these work centers, most likely because of the Bureau of Education's limited budget and the amount of overhead needed to establish the school. Instead, these students were required to procure sufficient materials by their own efforts. In other barrios, schools provided only partial assistance and pressed students to rely on their individual efforts and skills to set up a flourishing trade. Designs procured from Europe were sent to the Philippines and distributed at the School of Household Industries as well as to all public schools, where students learned techniques in embroidery and lacemaking in styles and designs that would suit American tastes. Students at the School of Household Industries also learned the administrative and managerial skills necessary to run an embroidery business, including simple accounting systems to keep track of materials used, time spent, costs of production, and the profits obtained for each embroidered article. The School of Household Industries required that students devote any "free time" over holidays and on Saturdays to producing and selling merchandise. Most of the students' profits were used to establish and maintain work centers in the provinces.

At these work centers, former students would hire twelve of the best local needleworkers. Former industrial school teachers-turned-managers selected needleworkers who might have worked for local *sinamayeras* (Filipina textile vendors) or worked independently in informal capacities. Needlework was a common occupation for Filipino women. With such a team, managers could field and fulfill contracts from American manufacturers. To meet the demand for embroidered goods and handmade lace, bordadoras were trained in lacemaking and embroidery based on samples distributed to the industrial schools. In this way, the twelve women quickly became proficient in American designs and could be given commercial work. Subsequently, another twelve women were hired and trained in much the same way, exponentially increasing the number of bordadoras who could produce merchandise to be sold to American buyers. The Bureau of Education contended, "Such departments, without attempting to compete with private enterprises, will in all probability prove beneficial in aiding the people to engage in profitable industrial enterprises and in finding markets for the outpost of the schools and the community."[46] Essentially, the School of Household Industries aimed to transform sinamayeras into a class of middlewomen operating between the localized cottage industries scattered throughout the provinces and the American import-export companies.[47]

The Bureau of Education published the story of Mercedes Lopez's embroidery business as an example and a success story. They hoped that the details of Lopez's story would inspire other Filipino women and believed it would "undoubtedly prove helpful to students of the School of Household Industries."[48] Lopez, a former school teacher from Bulucan Province, did not attend the School of Household Industries, but her experiences served as an "illustration of what can be accomplished along the lines for which the school was organized."[49] Lopez's account, which was told in first person, began with her brother requesting embroidered dresses to give to his friends in the United States. Lopez, a highly skilled seamstress and embroiderer, began to receive more requests. Around the same time, an American buyer arrived in Manila looking for an embroiderer to sew designs on shirtwaists. The buyer was given Lopez's name, and after inspecting her work, established a contract for embroidered shirtwaists. To fill the order, Lopez "began to teach others and allowed them to go to work, and as my mother, during the Spanish times, had been a dealer in embroidery work, I soon had many of her older workers working for me."[50] Lopez's business grew from twelve to roughly eight hundred workers employed year-round—despite an annual lull in orders from January to March. Her workforce grew to the point where she could no longer oversee them all personally. Subsequently, she hired subcontractors to supervise and act as go-betweens.

Lopez's profits were tied to the number of laborers she engaged and to the number of sellable goods produced by her workers. Lopez's financial gains, however, did not trickle down to her workers. Lopez confessed she "would rather have contracts for fine embroidery work than for coarse embroidery work, as there is much more profit in the fine work."[51] She explained that the materials for both classes of work were roughly the same, and yet the price for fine work far exceeded that for coarse work because although fine work required more time, she did not pay workers much more for fine work than for coarse work. Thus, the cost of labor remained the same even as the price of the finished products increased, leaving Lopez to reap the profits. Lopez assured readers, however, that her workers did not protest this practice nor complain of labor exploitation. She contended that "all of them would rather do fine work" as "they are proud of it when it is finished."[52]

As skilled experts, embroiderers took pride in their work. Beautiful and complex patterns did, in fact, require artistry and skill. Bordadoras necessarily had talent and cultivated technical skills to produce such intricate needlework—they were only paid if their products were deemed beautiful and sellable. Regardless of the joy taken in the work and the amount of talent imbued into their products, however, they were not recognized as valuable by the larger embroidery system. Contractors and subcontractors did not regard bordadoras as artists or even as artisans, but almost as machine-like producers. Indeed, Lopez uses affective and emotional value to justify the monetary devaluing of the skilled work of her embroiderers. She frames labor as an opportunity for workers to take pride in their skill but not to be fairly compensated for it. Like the manufacturers and colonial agents supporting the embroidery industry, Lopez and other women who functioned as middle managers benefited from the scaling up of subcontracted labor at the expense of Filipinas' cheap labor.

Despite the allure of Lopez's success story and the Bureau's confidence in their initial plans, the School of Household Industries faced several challenges. It is clear that the Bureau did not fully comprehend Filipina occupations and their class structures and statuses. While officials originally sought out Filipinas from families of influence, they quickly found that girls from the most prominent and elite families were not ideal candidates. The problems with the Bureau's ill-conceived plans based on the idea of uplifting Filipina women manifested in the school's first cohort. As women from wealthy backgrounds, the first round of Filipina students found their new accommodations lacking in comparison to their more comfortable and luxurious homes. For example, they were accustomed to employing servants, a luxury unavailable to them at the school. Students were expected to become familiar with what officials called "communal life," as it was "impossible and undesirable to employ a sufficient force of servants to attend to all the minor work necessary in an institution of this kind."[53] One official asserted that it did not seem "unreasonable to expect each girl to care for her own bed and for a designated period each month to assist in such work as caring for the dishes in the dining room."[54] But in fact, this expectation was unreasonable and failed to recognize local class expectations and norms. School officials tried to mitigate the problems by first changing the students' accommodations. The school moved from the center of Manila, at 266 Calbido, Intramuros, to 2973 Herran in Santa Ana. The superintendent described the new space as having a large dormitory and halls, and maintained that the beautiful grounds and the "ever cool and refreshing breeze of the Pasig which flows at the rear of the premises all contribute their share to the containment of the girls who attended the school."[55] But such superficial changes were not enough to launch and sustain a workforce of middlewomen.

School officials made more drastic changes. In April 1916, it instituted a new system for selecting students, shifting away from recruiting upper-class Filipinas. The school eliminated proficiency in English as a requirement, thus expanding the pool of eligible applicants. While the Bureau of Education enforced English as the primary language taught in public schools, socioeconomic barriers prevented some students from learning English. For example, in rural communities, student attendance was variable as students were expected to tend to work responsibilities that depended upon the farming and harvesting seasons. Also, as they increased in age, Filipina girls were less likely to matriculate in schools.[56] Additionally, rather than choosing one or two girls from different towns spread out through the archipelago, as was the initial selection practice, the school chose a larger cohort of students from each province—so as to provide a larger workforce for provincial work centers. Then, from each cohort, one or two students were selected to take a business training course and assume leadership roles.

The change in policies might appear to be benevolent gestures of inclusion that provided opportunities and upward mobility to a greater number of women. However, the new selection system was motivated not by a desire to eliminate poverty, but rather as a means to solve the problem of "unfit" workers. As suggested by the reports of colonial officials, elite women were difficult to control. One report revealed that it was "deemed advisable . . . to select workers from the more humble homes where each member of the family is depended upon to do his part. It is believed that such a plan assures *pensionadas* that will be more appreciative of the education given to them by the Government, and will put [to] more practical use the knowledge gained in school."[57] Education officials thus capitalized on economic vulnerability, institutionalizing a system of debt and gratitude (*utang na loob*) as the main motivator for students to become workers and to produce sellable embroidered goods and lace.[58]

Despite its rough start, the School of Household Industries continued to operate throughout the US colonial period, meeting the spike in demand for Philippine embroideries in the mid-1910s. The systematization of industrial education led to the growth of the embroidery industry, the proliferation of provincial work centers, and a rise in the number of Filipina needleworkers. The embroidery industry was one of the few "successes" of Philippine trade schools. Between June 1916 and January 1917, the Bureau of Education oversaw 2,266 workers in 130 work centers across 18 provinces.[59] One school official declared that the "industrial division of the Bureau as now organized may be compared to a factory which, instead of being centralized in one plant, is scattered over a territory of 127,000 square miles."[60] In 1916, the Insular Government passed Act 2629, which shut down the Sales Agency and set up a new General Sales Department under the Bureau of Education.[61] This new department gave more power to the Director of Education and allowed him to facilitate cooperation between the Bureau of Education and provincial industrial departments.[62] The General Sales Department also set out to sell the merchandise made in schools and work centers as well as the products made in 4,000 schools by over 600,000 students. The Bureau of Education thus relied on three channels to sell the merchandise made in industrial schools: via sales rooms and school exhibitions in smaller provincial locations and large-scale events like the Manila Carnival or the Pan-Pacific Exposition held in locales like San Francisco, California; through cooperation with local merchants; and by filling orders sent directly to the division by the General Office.[63] Although the Insular Government created policies such as Act 2629 to protect private industry from competition, Filipina students and teachers in fact competed with the "commercial centers" of the Philippine embroidery industry.[64] For example, when an American distributor brought a large order for Italian cutwork to Manila, private contractors and "commercial people" would not accept the order, as they were not trained to do that kind of embroidery.[65] The Bureau of Education, however, took the order and fulfilled it promptly. Education officials felt confident in their students' ability to meet the distributor's request because industrial schools had already introduced Italian cutwork motifs into their needlework curriculum. The viability of industrial schools as a source of fashionable embroidery depended on the schools' ability to keep up with changing styles and industry demands and to train pupil workers in these techniques.

According to one school official, it was a network of Filipina traveling teacher pensionadas who disseminated new patterns, techniques, and fashions throughout the archipelago.[66] Traveling teachers and Filipina pensionadas were integral to the growth of the industry and the training of student needleworkers. Trained at the Philippine Normal School in Manila, an institution established to train teachers, these teachers were government employees and agents who taught industrial courses in provincial schools. United States education officials regarded its teacher pensionadas as the front line of trained technicians tasked with increasing the productivity of pupil workers and the quality of their work in colonial public industrial schools. Teacher pensionadas tested out new designs and techniques that met the industry standards of an American market.[67] Armed with their training and a number of Bureau of Education–approved embroidery and lace patterns and instructions, they instructed students and monitored their performance.

Maria Lamug received instruction in the domestic sciences, including specialized needlework classes like Italian cutwork, at the Philippine Normal School. After completing her coursework, Lamug was sent out as a teacher pensionada to Ilocos Norte, the rural province just north of Manila.[68] In 1914, Lamug, along with a handful of other Filipino students who had completed a number of courses at the Normal School, were selected as scholarship students to take part in the "Artisan Section," a new arm of the Bureau of Education established to fully commit to industrial education. The Bureau of Education organized this new Section to respond to criticisms from "The Field," the corpus of superintendents and supervisors who tried to meet the fashion expectations of buyers. Merchants and buyers from the transnational Philippine embroidery industry communicated any dissatisfaction with handicraft commodity designs produced in Philippine industrial schools to the General Office of the Bureau of Education. The network of teacher pensionadas spread throughout the archipelago linked the provinces to the central General Office, thus maintaining communication between the rural provinces and the urban capital.

Although the Bureau of Education credited its successes to the opportunities they bestowed on Filipina pupil workers and teacher pensionadas, the hierarchical colonial education system also produced discontent. While the reorganization of industrial education under the Department of Public Instruction boasted that it bestowed new opportunities upon Filipinas, these opportunities had hard limits. Gracia Urquiza, a teacher pensionada and needlework supervisor in Ormoc, Leyte, expressed her frustration with the ranking order of industrial supervision. In an essay published in *Philippine Craftsman*, Urquiza unabashedly details the incompetence and inadequacy of the division industrial supervisor. She articulates how colonial institutions reified gendered hierarchies, which were clearly manifested in industrial schools. Urquiza writes, "Supervision of the needlework by the division industrial supervisor, who is usually a man, is sometimes more or less superficial, for while he may understand something about sewing, about embroidery, or about lace, he is seldom, if ever, able to do more than detect and point out errors and irregularities."[69] Urquiza continues to describe the male supervisor: "He frequently cannot explain how errors can be corrected."[70] She explicitly states that while the division supervisor occupied a position of power, his status derived from the privilege of his gender rather than from his knowledge of needlework. To Urquiza, this is made apparent in the subpar work produced under his supervision. To underscore the disparity between quality of work and the actual recognition of skill, Urquiza juxtaposes this mediocre work with the expertise of a specialist needlework supervisor, whom she identifies as a woman. The "special supervisor" draws from knowledge and expertise to be "constructive in nature."[71] Urquiza illustrates, "When she goes into a school her familiarity with the work under her direction place[s] her in a position to enable her to do much more than point out poor work and errors. She actually takes hold of the work that is being done and corrects errors by demonstrating to the teacher how to proceed and how to get results."[72] Urquiza points out that "it is necessary that some competent person be placed in charge of the work."[73] Urquiza's tone of frustration calls into question the unmerited power given to the division supervisor.

Urquiza's essay highlights the disparity between the skill sets of these two supervisors to critique the Bureau of Education's stratified division of labor. The institution reinforced hierarchies based not on expertise but on gender and race. Urquiza's use of feminine pronouns to describe the ideal specialist indicates that those with actual knowledge of needlework were usually women. The records assembled by the Bureau of Insular Affairs in 1916 also confirm that all 208 embroidery and fine needlework teachers at the Philippine Normal School were women.[74] Despite their mediocre skills, male supervisors wielded power and authority but could not guide or teach students needlework skills. Although Urquiza herself possessed the knowledge and talent to correct errors through demonstration, she was unable to advance in the industry.

The Bureau of Education presented industrial education as a system that provided opportunity, social mobility, and uplift to students and teachers. However, industrial schools and the embroidery industry relied heavily on traveling pensionadas, like Urquiza, to circulate fashionable needlework styles and teach techniques across the education system. Teacher pensionadas played a vital role in sustaining embroidery production in industrial schools. They also connected provincial and rural schools to the central offices in Manila, relaying standardized techniques and expectations mandated by the Bureau of Education. Urquiza underscored how travel presented even more challenges to teacher pensionadas, using her own experience of traveling from Manila to Leyte to illustrate the difficulties. Urquiza notes that as a traveling teacher pensionada, her post in Leyte required her to "use every type of transportation of common use in the Philippines, and in some cases, it [became] necessary to walk for long distances over long trails."[75] Urquiza points out that travel was an important and crucial part of the embroidery educational system and it also left one exhausted and thus interfered with one's work. Urquiza was well aware of her level of expertise and the value of her labor. Yet, in her writing, she also highlights the devaluation of her work and the inequity of the beauty regime.

The Bureau of Education combined the Philippine embroidery industry with public education to fashion efficient, productive, and skilled beauty workers. Industrial work had two main objectives: "to train pupils to become proficient with their hands, and to prepare them so that they may be better able to cooperate in the economic and industrial development of their country."[76] "Cooperation" is a vague term, but the many training manuals describe what student cooperation entailed. Pupil workers had to produce and sell merchandise and do so consistently and quickly to meet market demands. Fine needleworkers faced tremendous pressure to create beautiful and fashionable embroideries that suited the tastes of their mainly American customers. Education circulars and magazines instructed teachers to emphasize efficiency and to demand that students produce "the greatest amount of salable lace in the least time and at an expenditure of the least energy."[77] The message was consistent across the industrial education system: through "good teaching . . . [of] proper methods of work, through the development of interest and enthusiasm, and the formations of habit and industry," students would transform into the ideal needleworkers—moldable, fast, efficient, and skilled.[78] Industrial education was therefore structured to execute quality control through the disciplining of students. It aimed for the standardization of production to consistently make commercially sellable merchandise. To achieve this level of mechanized production, teachers managed students' work environments, behavior, habits, and bodily comportment. Teachers and supervisors utilized new modes of surveillance to assess the quality of the products and the speed at which students worked. Such beauty regimens strove to optimize pupil workers to consistently create beautiful products for the beautification of their consumers.

Through circulars, magazines, telegrams, letters, and traveling teachers and supervisors, the Bureau of Education created a network of communication, surveillance, and regimented discipline devised to support the expansion and maintenance of a Filipina workforce. The General Office disseminated approved blueprints and perforated patterns to the scattered networks of industrial schools, ensuring uniformity in size, design, and shape, thus further standardizing merchandise. But beyond that, industrial departments made meticulous recommendations for classroom environments for the optimization of needlework. Classroom designs were intended to increase the capacity of Filipina students to more consistently churn out high-grade embroidered lingerie, shirtwaists, and other adorned articles to raise the capital to purchase the equipment to make more embroidered merchandise. Ideal classrooms had uniform, up-to-date equipment, with rigid racks on which to rest work, embroidery frames for large articles, at least one large table for stamping designs, and a set of drawers in which to store supplies and finished work.[79] Classrooms also needed a sewing machine so that ornamented pieces could be sewn together to create completed garments. School officials advised that supplies and individual equipment should be uniform.

Although the Bureau of Education made recommendations, they could not provide all the schools with supplies. Instead, they prescribed these lists as goals to which each school should aspire. Schools' access to resources often depended on the wealth of the barrios and towns in which they were located. This uneven structure created a cyclical system in which schools felt the pressure to create more goods to sell in order to fund their schools and consequently be able to produce a greater quantity of sellable merchandise. The cycle of pressure further cemented the role of industrial schools in communities. The Bureau of Education presented schools as a necessity to generate more capital. The process of production and selling became more and more naturalized.

Educational systems also deployed biopolitical strategies to fashion students into productive pupil workers. This meant that attention was paid to manipulating students' bodies into becoming machinelike producers of beautifully ornamented articles. One industrial school supervisor advised, "It is desirable that pupils be taught to automatize certain movements early in the year."[80] To do so, this supervisor suggested students move in a uniform manner. He suggested they march to get their work materials and when they stored their finished projects at the end of the day, and that they sit in an orderly manner. Even the furniture in the classrooms was designed to support students' bodies so they might hold the most effective and efficient positions for the performance of their needlework. Education administrators advised teachers that chairs, stools, and racks in embroidery classes should be at "such height that pupils will find it inconvenient to get their eyes too close to their needlework while maintaining a comfortable position."[81] Circulars provided illustrations and instructions for positioning Filipina students' bodies to optimize their work. In one photograph, two Filipina students sit side-by-side as they each embellish a pillow. The student on the left holds the pillow up closer to her face while she bends her neck and head toward it. The student on the right positions the pillow on the desk, sitting straight with her hands and arms close to the desktop. The caption beneath the photograph labels the student on the left "improper," while the student on the right is holding the pillow in the "proper" position. The circular explains that the image illustrates how proper posture and the correct positioning of the pillow allows the forearm to swing and for an "easy and natural wrist movement," whereas in the improper position, "workers make the mistake" of moving their arms from the shoulders.[82] In these ways, students were disciplined to hold and move their bodies in specific ways. Teachers and school officials paid close attention to pupil workers' body comportment and the angles of the limbs; the positioning of the neck, shoulders, and head served as ways to control the students' output and performance. Despite the picturesque imagery of Filipinas elegantly seated at loops and frames with tiny needles quickly piercing fabric, embroidery work demanded physical stamina. While beauty regimens are typically seen as ways to improve bodies, the tedious work of elaborate embroidering required long hours and took a physical toll on women's bodies. Sitting and embroidering for long periods of time could cause back problems, joint pain, and eyestrain.[83]

Methods of surveillance and the regimentation of time reinforced biopolitical control. American and Filipina teachers read widely distributed circulars, bulletins, and magazines that contained detailed instructions and diagrams for lace and embroidery patterns. Teachers also attended summer retreats and read manuals that taught them just how to manage and monitor students to make them ideal learners and workers.[84] To reinforce expectations of efficiency and productivity, students were placed under surveillance. Teachers watched students' techniques with needles, how they handled delicate fabrics, and how they washed and ironed finished textiles. Teachers monitored students' work, checking for their ability to duplicate techniques and patterns, comparing students' work to the diagrams and instructions circulated in the bulletins and magazines.

In the School of Household Industries, students followed a strict schedule—so strict that even their recreation time was carefully managed. Students attended morning lace and embroidery classes for two hours, followed by a short recess, and another two hours of classwork, which included learning how to properly wash and iron finished articles intended for sale. After lunch, students would have a one-hour siesta followed by another few hours of classes. Teachers and chaperones encouraged students to spend recreational time in supervised areas within the school, where they could play music or work on their independent embroidery projects. Students could leave school grounds only with a school-approved chaperone to ensure the "proper" behavior and decorum expected of young women from middle-class and wealthy families.[85]

FIGURE 4.2. Photograph from "In Bobbin Lace Classes," *Philippine Craftsman* 4, no. 7 (January 1916): 486.

Students who graduated from the School of Household Industries or the Normal School replicated these same techniques as teachers in industrial schools for children. Teachers and superintendents visited classrooms and closely inspected industrial classwork. Students underwent formal examinations to assess the quality of their work, dividing products into distinct "classes."[86] Burton Holmes's *Luzon Lingerie* provides visual examples of how teachers monitored student work. Scenes of the interior of a classroom show a white woman and white man in the background closely inspecting yards of embroidered white fabric. In another scene, a white woman looms over a student's shoulder examining her embroidery, monitoring it for quality assurance. At the end of the workday, embroiderers line up to be patted down and inspected for any stolen materials or goods. While it is unclear whether the scene takes place at a school or at an operations center, the film underscores the range of surveillance employed by American teachers and administrators.

Surveillance required a tremendous amount of time and labor. Maria Lamug's job as a teacher pensionada included not only instructing students but also closely supervising and scrutinizing their performance. In her reports, Lamug referred to her students as "artisans." She meticulously logged how much time each student spent on the completion of each product. She also documented the quality of the work, providing detailed notes and comments. Lamug's logs show that young teens enrolled in advanced needlework courses spent hours studying new patterns and techniques. Lamug reported to the Artisan Section, the Bureau of Education committee focused on artisanal production, that her group of students dedicated hundreds of hours bent over their canvases.

The surveillance of student performance also produced new forms of bureaucratic documentation. Lamug reported her observations by filling out for each student four separate documents called "artisan forms," which she used to instruct student workers and evaluate and keep record of their work. Artisan Form No. 1 provided specific designs and materials and was shared with the "artisans" as a guide for their needlework. Artisan Form No. 2 provided supplemental instructions in case any individual "worker" encountered difficulties. Artisan Form No. 3 was a weekly report that documented the progress of all pupil workers in the embroidery class. Last, each artisan filled out Artisan Form No. 4, enumerating difficulties they encountered, methods they used to overcome challenges, and any general comments about their work and progress. The paperwork was meticulous and produced important data for both the Bureau of Education and the embroidery industry about the training of fine needleworkers and the establishment of European-inspired designs for American buyers. The production process was repeated so that over time, Lamug noted, the pupil "artisans" were able to lower their production times. The logged data allowed Lamug, and other teachers like herself, to target problems that slowed down production and decreased the quality of the work. Additionally, strict monitoring helped the Bureau of Education determine what kinds of patterns and methods would be most efficient and produce the most salable products.

If a student failed to meet industry standards as directed by the central office of the Bureau of Education, it was deemed no fault of the education system but rather a consequence of the student's inability to adapt to new standards. Indeed, it was engrained in the minds of American teachers through widely distributed bulletins that the success of a "skilled worker in any line of industrial work [would] be determined in a large measure by certain technical elements to which she [would] inevitably attempt to adjust herself."[87] One circular stated that as the students must "be prepared to meet the conditions under which they will probably work and the commercial requirements to which the product of their workers must conform, full instructions are given regarding essential features of the fabrication and sale for high class needlework."[88] Most reports framed the success of industrial schools in terms of the quality of the merchandise and sales they produced. Very rarely did they speak of individual students or student responses to the industrial education. However, just as Gracia Urquiza found fault in industrial education's hierarchy of authority, she also found fault in the disciplinary techniques, noting that "inspection fills the heart of the inefficient with fear," while "recognition puts new heart into the efficient."[89] Urquiza points out that surveillance and control techniques were not emotionally neutral. While Urquiza does not state clearly what kind of reprimands students faced if they failed to meet their teacher's standards, her use of the word "fear" suggests that censure and even maltreatment might have occurred in the classroom. Urquiza makes a case for appreciation and positive reinforcement to encourage students to maintain high standards. Although she calls for support for students, ultimately, the larger system of industrial schools regarded its work as social control for profit.

Policing students' dress practices also played an important role in transforming Filipina students into pupil workers. During the early years of US colonial schooling, girls and young women living in the Christian lowland areas of the Philippines mainly wore variations of the *baro't saya* (blouse and skirt), including *trajes de mestiza* or, more commonly, the *balintawak*. Photographs of children in schools and during public presentations such as the 1904 St. Louis World's Fair and the annual Manila Carnival document Filipina students wearing *camisas* with starched tulip sleeves, draped with *pañuelos*, and long skirts. However, by the time school officials fully implemented embroidery and lacemaking as formal curricula, schools began to phase out this mode of dress that represented Filipina identity. Borrowing from already established colonial strategies of pacification, public schools began to institutionalize dress codes.[90] American colonial hegemonic practices regarded regulating colonized people's clothing as a form of Americanization. In the late nineteenth century, Indian boarding schools established in the continental United States, such as the Carlisle Indian Industrial School, demanded that Native American students wear uniforms and cut their hair short. Disciplining indigenous students' appearance played a part in the systemic erasure of Native American cultures. The Bureau of Indian Affairs' imposition of dress codes, in tandem with the prohibitions against speaking native languages and practicing religious and cultural customs, was a form of cultural genocide practiced alongside other forms of settler colonial violence.[91] Some of the same education officials from the Bureau of Indian Affairs and teachers who had worked at Carlisle took up positions in the Philippines, bringing with them similar ideologies and colonial strategies that they applied to pupil workers.[92] Colonial public schools in the Philippines implemented regulations requiring students to wear white cotton dresses with shorter hems and sleeves, which American teachers and officials regarded as looking more American.[93] Over time, white, cotton, one-piece frocks replaced the baro't saya. Using white cotton imported from the United States, Filipina students were expected to sew these garments in their classes—producing the very garments used to discipline their bodies.[94]

Dress served as an important disciplinary tool in constructing a workforce. Uniforms and dress codes in American industrial schools had less to do with regulating feminine modesty and more to do with efficiency. The Americans believed that these uniforms physically made Filipinas better students and workers. According to American bureaucrats, the differences in skirt lengths and fabrics between Filipina gowns and American-style uniforms granted Filipina students more freedom of movement. They portrayed Filipina gowns as cumbersome, with their diaphanous sleeves and long trains, and therefore impractical because Filipinas would be too distracted by their own dresses to focus on the American curriculum. The Filipina-style dresses, in other words, might hinder students' ability to produce embroidered merchandise. One bulletin published by the Bureau of Education, *Good Manners and Right Conduct for Use in Primary Grades*, argued that a shorter skirt "leaves both hands free for work. It looks neat. It looks business-like. It does not hinder play. It does not annoy others. It shows that the wearer is a sensible girl."[95] This description conveyed the message that to be modern, Filipino girls and women needed to possess a sense of practicality and sensibility. Furthermore, promoting US clothing styles as a method for liberating Filipinas from the constraints of cumbersome dresses associated with Spanish cultural influences supported the American colonial civilizing mission, which promised to liberate women from the patriarchal tyranny enforced by the Spanish colonial regime. The primary motivation behind modernizing Filipinas, though, was to make them more efficient. Dress regulation was intended to help Filipina women and girls concentrate on studying and working and, therefore, producing better results in their schooling and in their productivity in the workplace.[96]

Racialized notions of hygiene and cleanliness also motivated the push to abandon the baro't saya. The *saya* (skirt) portion of the ensemble typically included a train, the length of which signified social and class standing—the longer the train, the wealthier and more elite the wearer. However, American educators disliked trains, as they dragged on the floor whether their wearers were sitting or walking. Unlike the long Filipiniana gowns, the hem of American-style dresses "clear[ed] the floor" and educators considered this a "good thing, because it is cleanly. It carries no germs."[97] In other words, the baro't saya's length made it a sanitary hazard. While discussions about dress styles did not specifically talk about Filipina students' bodies per se, the criticism of these gowns made inference to a perceived lack of hygiene on the part of their wearers. As mentioned previously, the issue of sanitization and labor loomed large over colonial officials' heads.[98] The nonwhite native Filipina body, in the American imagination, was unhygienic in and of itself.[99] The enforcement of dress codes adhered to the larger narrative of transforming Filipinos from uncivilized natives to US wards. Sartorial changes helped carry out a US colonial policy that was rooted in long-established ideologies of eroding the "native."[100]

Education officials like William Marquardt paid close attention to the politics of dress in industrial schools. In his reports, Marquardt described the changes in American educational institutions and their impact in the Philippines through observing students' changing modes of dress. Marquardt writes, "In 1901, with the exception of schools in large cities, little girls were allowed to wear long skirts with trains, just like their mothers. Provincial schools made no effort to restrict the graceful native costume of Filipina women, which had been retained for social purposes. But little by little the advantage of the one-piece dress of walking length for school purposes became appreciated."[101] Domestic science students constructed dresses from imported cotton woven in the mainland United States. They fashioned uniforms based on American patterns and distributed the dresses to the other students. For Marquardt, the evolution of Filipina students' dress exhibited the successful Americanization of students in schools.[102] What his anecdote also demonstrates is the reticence on the part of Filipinas, and perhaps also of their families, to abandon the baro't saya. The fact that it took years to transform dress expectations suggests that there was a struggle. United States cultural dominance was not an instant or a totalizing force. While hesitancy might not equate to resistance, acts of dressing required careful consideration and decision-making that demonstrated skepticism and critical evaluation on the part of Filipinas. This paints a much different picture than Filipinas as mindless "victims" of Americanization, who were unwittingly duped.[103]

Dress codes also designated class boundaries. For example, when first establishing the School of Household Industries, Frank Carpenter, executive secretary to the governor-general, expressed his serious dismay at the selection of students who exceeded the class boundaries he had envisioned. A number of superintendents and town officials selected young women from the most elite families rather than from the cacique class, who would be "content with simple food and accommodations."[104] Whereas the "native costume [was] much more expensive and require[d] many accessories," the white uniforms were affordable and easy to clean and maintain.[105] Fifteen years after the Bureau of Education released the bulletin on proper appearance and behavior in public schools, Paz Mendoza-Guazon, a prominent Filipina feminist, writer, educator, and doctor, penned similar sentiments concerning Filipina women's appearance in schools and places of work. Because of her accomplishments, which also included being the first woman to graduate from the University of the Philippines College of Medicine and founding the National League of Filipino Women, Mendoza-Guazon's writings were considered authoritative.[106] Mendoza-Guazon, herself a product of the American colonial education system, regarded the modifications to Filipina dress implemented by US bureaucrats as positive changes. In *My Ideal Filipino Girl*, Mendoza-Guazon advises Filipinas to consider the "Place, Time, Occasion, Age and the Size of your Income."[107] She went on tell her readers that "you go to school or to the office to work and study, not to display the wealth of your wardrobe. . . . Wear, then, a simple dress for the school or office. The present white uniform for our school girls is the best, because it is simple, economic and easy to launder."[108] Mendoza-Guazon's attitude toward dress regulations reflects how some Filipinas appropriated American ideas to serve their own desires. Concerns over how Filipina students should dress applied not only to privileged members of the elite or to middle-class students, but also to a broader group of Filipinas, particularly those who attended trade or industrial schools across the archipelago.

Looking closely at interconnections among industrial schools, US colonial efforts to normalize school among Filipinos, and disciplining workwear provides insight into how US officials and educators envisioned and fashioned pupil workers. Altering sartorial practices meant radically changing the social and cultural underpinnings of dress. Enforcing dress codes and physically eliminating Filipina dresses through the production of uniforms went only so far in altering emotional and social expectations tied to dress. Educators attempted to slowly transform dress practices by having students supply new uniforms for distribution. They also established Dress Reform Clubs with American teachers, Filipina teachers, and Filipina students as members. Dress Reform Clubs in the metropole were tied to women's dress reform movements of the late nineteenth and early twentieth centuries and were intended to consolidate and circulate ideas about what women should wear. White American dress reformers believed sartorial practices should reflect the "progress" and "liberation" of women. For example, some dress reformers advocated for an end to corset-wearing. Others argued that women should wear pants and pantaloons, which would free them to take part in activities deemed unfeminine, like riding a bicycle and other athletic activities. In Philippine public schools, Dress Reform Clubs activated a similar rhetoric around dressing for the progress and uplift of Filipina girls and women. Clubs gave cultural credence to these shifting ideologies of dress and created a sense of social imperative and social belonging that encouraged Filipinas to take up new modes of dress at school.

## Embroidery and Convict Labor

In August 1914, the *Philippine Craftsman* published a statement by O. Garfield Jones from the General Office titled "Bilibid Industrial School." Describing the implementation of an industrial school in the Philippines' prison center, Jones compares and contrasts the purpose of industrial training in prisons and in public schools. He writes, "Public schools are, of course *formatory*, and reformatory, but aside from that their aim is about the same as that of the prison . . . to prepare the pupils for good citizenship and gain for them an honorable position in the community."[109] Jones celebrated the systematic implementation of "rigid social discipline."[110] Just as in colonial public schools, industrial labor and enforced beauty-work training functioned as a means of imposing control under the guise of betterment. Jones believed that discipline through labor would make students "real producers" and transform prisoners who had "already proven themselves antisocial and therefore need[ed] rigid social discipline to make them normal."[111] Through surveillance and regulation, Bilibid Prison enforced a beauty regimen on incarcerated Filipinas that was intended to transform them into efficient producers of beautiful handcrafted embroidered goods. Advocates for convict labor argued that work—particularly productive work—played a vital role in rehabilitating incarcerated people. Prison reform, in conjunction with policing and adjusting civil codes, produced highly gendered, racialized, and classed conceptions of vice, immorality, and rehabilitation associated with incarcerated Filipinas.[112] While women made up a small fraction of the total prison population throughout the Philippines, their presence, work, and performance in Bilibid drew much attention in US colonial and penal reform campaigns.

Unlike in industrial schools, the needlework division—known as Division H—was the smallest of the industrial work sections in Bilibid Prison. In its inaugural year, Division H housed the prison's sixty incarcerated Filipinas.[113] Bilibid organized and divided the prisoners into different labor groups such as laundry, carpentry, basket weaving, and needlework. Despite the minor profits it earned, it nevertheless received enormous amounts of attention in prison reform discourse. While manufacturing in colonial prisons helped financially support operations, the bottom line for industrial divisions was not solely monetary, but lay instead in political and social capital gains. Incarcerated women's labor played a large role in branding US penal reform as a successful model of modernity. Further, Division H was held as an example of the efficacy of US imperialism in the Philippines. In her work on the US carceral system and the criminalization of Black women during the Jim Crow era, Sarah Haley demonstrates how "gendered temporal frameworks informed a colonial culture order" that "popularize[d] the idea of linear national progress" and how these US gendered and white supremacist racial ideologies were critical to justifying exploitative labor "in the service of industrialization."[114]

Likewise in the Philippines, the colonial state was invested in portraying prison discipline and labor as key tools in colonial modernization's success.[115] In the Philippines, the campaign aimed to distinguish the United States from Spain as a "benevolent" imperial power. Criminalization and disciplinary regimes also helped define Filipina gendered norms that fit into US colonial visions for modern citizenship. For American audiences, colonial penal reform and disparagement of Spanish colonial rule obfuscated the decades-long national progressive prison reformists' censure of the savagery and brutality of convict labor in US prisons, which was itself deeply linked to the long history of slavery, antiblackness, and white supremacy.[116] This narrative strategy of portraying prisons as an extension of US benevolence positioned the United States as *the* model of modernity and democracy.

Bilibid Prison was a behemoth facility that served as the center of the prison system during both the Spanish and US colonial regimes. The Spanish colonial government constructed Bilibid during the latter half of the nineteenth century; it was meant to symbolize power, a kind of last gasp, during the Spanish empire's demise. The prison was constructed as a panopticon, designed by Jeremy Bentham. A guard tower stood in the center of the octagon-shaped prison with a full view of the surrounding barracks, fields, and buildings. Bilibid's central tower gave prison guards an omniscient view of prisoners and prison grounds, while the prisoners could not see guards in the tower. Bilibid took up Bentham's strategies of using surveillance as a method of discipline, believing that knowledge that guards could be watching would motivate prisoners to self-regulate their behavior to avoid punishment.[117] The United States continued surveillance practices begun by the Spanish, adding prison guards first with rifles and later with machine guns stationed along the prison walls. After the colonial regime change, the Bureau of Prisons oversaw Bilibid in addition to thirty-nine provincial prisons, a juvenile reformatory, and the Iwahig penal colony. A separate women's correctional facility was not established until 1931. When the US regime took over in 1899, Bilibid became the largest prison under US control. The massive prison covered seventeen acres and was made up of more than forty buildings, with a potential to house up to five thousand prisoners. Bilibid served as a long-term penitentiary with a population usually around 2,600 to 2,800 prisoners. It was also a sorting center, where incarcerated people stayed temporarily before being transferred to smaller provincial prisons or to Iwahig.

While Bilibid was built as an apparatus of discipline, it brought together and was sustained by systems of colonial control.[118] Bilibid adopted disciplinary techniques developed by the US military, including total body searches of prisoners performed by prison wardens.[119] Additionally, Filipinas were wrapped up in dominant American ideologies of the early twentieth century that associated crime with filth and disease. Such ideologies precipitated the systematic subjection of prisoners to disinfecting baths.[120] The dehumanizing entry process at Bilibid Prison concretized criminals' place at the "lowest" rungs of society, which then justified the use of US intervention through penology.[121] Afterward, prisoners were sorted and cataloged through colonial technologies of surveillance under the Bertillon international system of identification: their fingerprints and photographs were taken and placed on prison intake cards.[122] The cards also documented their criminal offense, age, height, gender, hometown, and occupation.[123] After inspection and sorting, Filipina prisoners were sent to barrack-like dormitories that mimicked military camps. In addition to single-gendered sleeping areas, women also occupied designated work and "recreational spaces" that were intended to separate them from men in Bilibid. Every aspect of their incarceration aimed through a "semimilitary training to teach them to obey orders."[124] However, upon their arrival, prisoners were "given to understand that the prison officials [had] their welfare at heart."[125] Officials asserted that it was in the prisoners' best "interest to observe the rules and regulations of the prison and occupy their time to the very best of advantage."[126]

Prison directors contended that Bilibid "differ[ed] from ordinary penal institutions," and was instead "reformatory in character."[127] A 1910 *Los Angeles Herald* piece describes how Bilibid under Spanish rule had been "the worst prison on earth—veritable survival of the horrors of the Middle Ages," harkening back to the Spanish Inquisition.[128] The piece then recounts how US prison authorities removed chains and whipping posts and hired "humane guards."[129] This 1910 piece echoed the language used by US legislators and the news media during the Spanish-American War (1898) to portray Spain as a tyrannical colonizer of the Philippines, Guam, Puerto Rico, and Cuba as a way to shore up national support for US warfare against Spain. Even after the end of the Spanish-American War, the US colonial government continued to rely on the image of a despotic Spain to underscore US exceptionalism and portray US actions as benevolent even as it maintained colonial institutions first established by the Spanish empire, like Bilibid Prison.[130] Although its residents remained incarcerated, the United States narrated the takeover of Bilibid Prison and the change in imperial power as freeing prisoners from the chains of Spanish penology.[131] United States colonial prison authorities condemned the "punitive character" of Spanish penal laws.[132] Toward the end of Spanish colonialism, punitive technologies like convict labor were put in place to maintain colonial order and curb anticolonial resistance.[133] United States officials publicly criticized the Spanish employment of "hard and burdensome labor" that did not "afford [the prisoner an] opportunity of regaining his lost freedom by reforming himself, but to aggravate his suffering, thus killing manhood and self-respect."[134] In practice, however, US colonial officials like W. Cameron Forbes aggressively implemented hard labor in Bilibid for development and modernization projects.[135] In their view, liberation and freedom came in the form of productive industrialized labor. For the Americans, Bilibid functioned as a source of cheap labor in an array of industries, from infrastructure projects, like road building, to handicrafts.[136] In 1905, Bilibid officials shifted manufacturing in the prison from what they called Spanish trinket work and "old styles" of furniture work toward the establishment of the same types of manufacturing taught in public schools.[137] Two years later, as part of the 1907 Reorganization Act, officials partitioned Bilibid into two separate sections: the prison division and the industrial division.

Under the Reorganization Act, US colonial officials also combined the industrial education and production implemented in colonial public schools with convict labor practices modeled on those employed in US penitentiaries, particularly those in the North that fulfilled private manufacturing contracts to fund and maintain daily prison operations.[138] In 1909, out of the 2,783 convicts in confinement at Bilibid, just over eleven hundred worked in various shops dedicated to manufacturing such as carpentry and producing rattan furniture. Prisons thus became de facto factories operated and funded by the state. The Office of the Secretary of Instruction established similar industrial production systems in both colonial public industrial schools and Bilibid Prison. Both physically housed training centers and produced merchandise. Both schools and prisons took imported materials and refashioned them into export commodities, tourist souvenirs, and supplies for other colonial agencies throughout the archipelago. The rules and regulations of the prison heavily attended to industrial work and manufacturing, which promised to ingrain "habits of sober industry."[139]

The 1907 Reorganization Act transferred the Bureau of Prisons from the jurisdiction of the Department of Commerce and Police to the Office of the Secretary of Public Instruction. This bureaucratic restructuring solidified industrial education as a "feature of the penal institution."[140] It also made it easier to shuttle personnel between institutions. For example, Bilibid hired Fannie McGee, who had overseen the instruction of household industries in Manila public schools. McGee introduced needlework instruction for incarcerated women.[141] She brought with her industrial education experience; she taught incarcerated women needlework techniques that would appeal to American consumers and created a workforce of efficient producers. Bilibid also hired Alice Fuller, who, along with Susie Butts, had written the textbooks for domestic science training at the Philippine Normal School.[142] The placement of industrial school instructors in Bilibid Prison eventually resulted in the establishment of Division H—an industrial division composed solely of incarcerated women—in 1912.[143]

In many ways, Bilibid's industrial division operated similarly to US penitentiaries, instituting a strict and highly regimented daily schedule. Alongside the guards and wardens, instructors provided another layer of prison discipline. Bilibid's beauty regimen required women prisoners to attend one hour of English lessons and spend at least six hours a day engaged in lace or embroidery work. Bilibid provided the materials and equipment necessary for the production of finished goods. McGee, Fuller, and other teachers selected by the superintendent of Manila public schools were charged with the task of training incarcerated Filipinas in embroidery and lacemaking. Instructors were employed at Bilibid for anywhere from two weeks to six months.[144] At the prison, women workers cut, sewed, embroidered, and ironed finished pieces. The women of Division H crafted lace, embroidered handkerchiefs, bed linens, infant wear, and women's wear.[145] Unlike other prison garment divisions, in which men created uniforms for other sectors of the colonial government and military, Division H's products were for personal and even intimate use. Private buyers and manufacturers could purchase finished products, make special orders at the sales department showroom, or purchase items from an annually published catalog. Division H implemented an internal hierarchy based on differences in the quality of work produced. Those deemed the best workers executed more intricate or "high-class" embroidery, while short-term prisoners, women with poor eyesight or other physical disabilities, and those who lacked overall skill produced pillow lace.[146] Over time, needlework expanded to also include crocheting and weaving.

As in industrial schools, Division H implemented disciplinary regimens that supported normative ideas of feminine industries—producing feminine products and crafts. In Division H, embroidery training and production evolved into a disciplinary tool and a vehicle with which to transform women prisoners into normative and acceptable women citizens of a Philippine nation-to-be. Unlike "hard labor," which was still used in Bilibid to punish "unruly" prisoners, Bilibid officials never considered embroidery and needlework punishment. Instead, the discipline of strictly scheduled daily routines and strictly monitored productive work was considered a vehicle for rehabilitation. Through Division H, the United States could showcase the possibilities of penal reform. Bilibid was meant to stand as an exemplar of the United States' ability to transform and civilize even the "lowliest" of Filipinos.[147] Prison discourse positioned incarcerated women as the epitome of racial and gendered abnormality. Government reports and writing in the burgeoning field of criminology presented incarcerated Filipinas as the antithesis of ideal femininity and as foils to both Filipino and American gender norms. In these writings, women who rejected societal norms succumbed to vice and other forms of immorality and eventually turned into "hardened" criminals. Early twentieth-century penology, they argued, could reverse their criminalization, and in doing so, make them more womanlike. In many ways, rehabilitation techniques shared the same disciplinary forms practiced in industrial schools. Despite these shared disciplinary technologies, officials underscored that public schools were *formatory* whereas prisons were *reformatory*.[148] Colonial officials regarded public schools as a means of directly shaping young minds and bodies; youths, because of their age, were viewed as easily moldable. These same officials promoted incarceration as an opportunity to reform, or transform, prisoners from their so-called lives of vice and crime into what they regarded as moral and respectable colonial subjects.

## Criminalization and the Making of Filipina Subjects of Reform

Reform projects required subjects to improve and transform themselves. The implementation of penal reform went hand-in-hand with the discursive construction of Filipina vice and crime. In the early twentieth century, discourses on Filipina crime blamed the combination of poverty and aberrations of ideal femininity for Filipina vice.[149] However, these conversations paid little attention to the structures that perpetuated poverty among the peasant and working classes. In the rural lowlands, during the nineteenth century, peasants were often caught in spirals of debt as Spanish friars and mestizo elites consolidated land ownership and moved the Philippines toward an export economy. Land reform policies implemented by the US colonial state perpetuated these systems of debt, carrying cycles of poverty well into the American colonial period.[150] These conditions marginalized Filipinas of the peasant and lower classes while strengthening the power of Filipino elites and the US colonial state.

Prison officials worked hard to render entire classes of women as deviants whose predilection for vice disrupted societal norms and ideals of femininity. Criminal activity was the antithesis of *maganda* (beauty, moral behavior, and respectability) and thus blemished the landscape of idealized Philippine society.[151] Feminine vice was *pangit*—not just physically unattractive but also unattractive in character—perverse, nasty, and immoral. In addition to Bilibid officials and other Insular Government agents who supported the colonial prison system, American sociologists like John Lewis Gillin positioned crime in the Philippines as a symptom of poverty as well as a gendered and racial predilection for vice.[152] They treated crime as a manifestation of Filipina savagery. This recidivist logic disregarded the specific conditions that might have led to women's "crimes." However, rare traces in archival documents suggest and possibly offer a glimpse of the points of view of incarcerated women themselves, thus offering a more nuanced understanding of Filipina criminality. Such documents suggest that many women housed in Bilibid and in provincial prisons had been found guilty of adultery.[153] However, women expressed that their "crimes" or "dereliction," as one 1917 report of the Philippine Health Services in prisons disclosed, was the result of the "ill treatment of their husbands."[154]

In addition to adultery, the majority of offenses of which women were convicted were theft, gambling, and prostitution, which according to Insular Government documents on law and crime in the Philippines were considered "crimes against public morality."[155] A recurring figure in the discourse on Filipina crime is that of the prostitute, who embodied the antithesis of idealized womanhood, the Madonna or Maria Clara.[156] Colonial officials depicted sex workers as "vicious" women, and sex work regulations aimed to keep women sex workers at the fringes of mainstream society. Discourses of Filipina viciousness rendered these women as predators who tempted and coerced others to practice any number of vices and forms of immorality. Colonial ideologies around the ugliness of feminized vice in the form of prostitution, adultery, gambling, and theft shaped colonial officials' and prison administrators' generalizations of women in Bilibid. They described these women as having a "low degree of intelligence" and as embodying the "lowest type" of women in Philippine society.[157]

Gambling also signaled inherent immorality and low character. It was what Dean Worcester referred to as Filipinos' "besetting sin."[158] For US colonial officials, gambling encapsulated what was perceived as Filipinos' inherent childishness, irresponsibility, and predilection for vice.[159] For example, *jueteng*, a type of game, was primarily associated with the lower and peasant classes; in jueteng, women worked as collectors and also outnumbered male bettors.[160] These women were seen both as corrupters, who duped those without money to go further into debt to feed their gambling addiction, and as gambling addicts themselves. Rather than addressing debt as a symptom of poverty, the consolidation of land ownership, and tenant farming, the colonial state adjusted penal codes and intensified aggressive policing of prostitution and gambling that criminalized women, especially among those of the lower classes. Discourses on criminology identified social problems as rooted in heredity and environmental causes.[161] The racialized and gendered characterization of Filipina deviance also supported US colonial arguments for the necessity of prison discipline. Advocacy for US colonial control and penal reform painted a before-and-after picture that underscored the process of transformation for incarcerated people. Hyperbolic language such as the "lowest type" dramatized the seemingly miraculous efficacy of US systems of discipline and helped cement prisons and carceral systems in Philippine society.

## Division H and the Case for Prison Discipline

Colonial ideologies that positioned Filipinas as immoral and savage bolstered the colonial state's claim of Bilibid's and the larger carceral system's essential role in modernizing the Philippines. As previously mentioned, prison advocates regularly published reports and manuscripts describing the vices and immorality of Filipinas, which contributed to the systematic criminalization and dehumanization of Filipina women; and these discourses were then used to make a case for the necessity of incarceration and prison discipline. They portrayed Bilibid as providing the necessary and effective rehabilitation that could transform once derelict women into "upstanding" citizens of both the colonial state and the Philippine nation-to-be. Officials contended that through the regimentation of life and labor while incarcerated, Filipinos could be fully transformed and re-enfranchised into mainstream society upon their release. The question of crime and its relationship to Filipino citizenship formation treated societal problems as impediments to the actualization of modern nationhood and independence. The beauty regime of Bilibid Prison, implemented in the form of Division H and embroidery work, provided a public-facing platform from which prison officials and supporters could advocate for the necessity of prisons in modernizing the Philippines. While women prisoners made up a small fraction of the total population of Bilibid Prison, Division H nevertheless regularly appeared in prison officials' and prison supporters' writings extolling the efficacy of penal rehabilitation.[162] Beyond the fiscal contribution of convict labor, industrial labor—and, in particular, the beauty work conducted in Division H—played a significant role in constructing a case for prisons.

As with prisons in the continental United States during the Progressive Era, the colonial state propped up Bilibid as a model institution of correction and rehabilitation.[163] Combining the rhetoric of uplift used in public schools with the discourse of penal reform, Bilibid's beauty regimens were intended to transform incarcerated Filipinas into proper women who could not only practice feminine industries—namely fine needlework—but also become productive workers. Prison discipline promised to rehabilitate deviant women—to shift them from a "life of crime to a life of usefulness."[164] Usefulness served as a catchall that encompassed the reproductive work of caretaking, hygiene, cooking, and cleaning, as well as productive labor.

Further, according to the assistant director of the Bureau of Prisons, these women could become "useful companions of men."[165] Convict labor, in this estimation, would produce "softened" women who could perform womanly skills and duties. Prison labor as a form of discipline relied on a series of promises for the future—transforming criminals into upright citizens for an independent nation. In the meantime, these women could practice acceptable feminine work that resulted in beautiful goods that earned money for the prison.

The public face of Bilibid bolstered convict labor as an exemplar of the efficacy of US colonial technologies.[166] It opened a showroom on prison grounds, publicly exhibiting commodities made by convict labor, where visitors might even get a glimpse of prisoners themselves. Additionally, visitors could enter the sections of Bilibid where industrial training and production took place. The Sales Division published annual catalogs from 1912 to 1927 that boasted the quality of their lace and embroidered items, claiming, "Women prisoners [have] already made [a] reputation as some of the best class work on the Islands."[167] Prison officials put forth an image of Filipina criminals who had been transformed from hardened women into an ideal of Filipina femininity, as exhibited by their ability to construct beautiful and dainty works of embroidery. In this context, incarcerated women in Division H embodied the efficacy of US colonial prisons and the success of colonial rehabilitation for American and Filipino onlookers.

The public face of Bilibid proved to be a powerful force. Beyond the Philippines, Bilibid was seen across the United States as a model modern prison. So confident were prison officials in Bilibid's penal technologies that they welcomed visitors and observers—mainly white tourists—into the prison.[168] Travel literature encouraged visitors to witness the progress of uplift in Bilibid, promoting it as a must-see site in Manila.[169] Visitors could enter Bilibid and witness disciplinary routines, thus adding yet another layer of surveillance and extending the public display of the Sales Division's showroom and catalogs.[170] The colonial government funded promotional literature that circulated photographs similar to those in the catalogs of busy women embroidering intricate ornamentation on yards of fabric. Products from Division H and other industrial departments were also put on display annually at the Philippine Exposition, the industrial unit of the Manila Carnival.

For the most part, American consumers, including entire colonial divisions and departments, sought out goods made in Bilibid to take advantage of their low cost. Distributors and retailers in the continental United States made efforts to purchase items in bulk, hoping to take advantage of the gray

FIGURE 4.3. Scene from the Manila Carnival Parade, 1924. Filipinas Heritage Library, Metro Manila, Philippines.

areas of protectionist laws. While such laws prohibited the importation of goods made by convict labor in a foreign country, the Philippines, they argued, was part of the United States and therefore not wholly foreign.[171] Despite American retailers' efforts, the Bureau of Insular Affairs advised against selling and shipping Bilibid products to the metropole. At the same time, travel literature and advertisements conveyed a kind of excitement over the purchase of lace and embroidered goods made by incarcerated women. They expressed a kind of thrill and titillation derived from the ability to consume ornamental goods made by Filipino women in prison.[172] One white woman remarked that the products did not stand out or differ from those that could be purchased from other vendors and shops. Perhaps their allure was in the satisfaction of buying what they regarded as proof of American benevolence, beautifully handcrafted products as the manifestation of the efficacy of American discipline and prison reform. Moreover, consumers' acceptance of and enthusiasm for the disciplining of prisoners through commercial needlework reaffirmed the state's efforts to justify colonial prison systems. Such support was just as valuable as the money used to purchase goods from Bilibid.

Although prison advocates and imperial agents worked hard to build a solid case for US colonialism and prison discipline, there were troubling issues with Bilibid's rehabilitation campaign. Justification for the colonial carceral system relied on the racist portrayals of incarcerated Filipinas as completely abject, in need of redemption and rehabilitation, to point to the efficacy and success of the empire as embodied in this type of penal discipline. In addition to portraying Filipinas as savages, official reports claimed that they had neither the training nor the skills for industrial work. One report stated, "The female convicts were with rare exception women of a low degree of intelligence and untrained in the use of a needle, nor had they had other mental or manual training helpful for the purpose."[173] These reports falsely claimed that women had no productive skills prior to their incarceration and therefore industrial training was greatly needed.[174] The narrative of rehabilitation ignored that many of the women in Bilibid had been employed prior to their incarceration. The intake cards on which prisoners' crimes were recorded provide evidence that, on the contrary, these women held a range of occupations, including working in the industries they were supposedly learning in prison. Francisca Acoba, for example, had been a dressmaker. Vicenta Santos, Emilia Isuy-Sayco, Alfonsa Carahun, Maria Sevilla, and Anselma Piñeda had been seamstresses.[175]

Women prisoners may have had a "voluntary" spirit, as one prison official described it, and it is entirely possible that they enjoyed their work and gained satisfaction from the exercise of their skills and craft. By its very definition, however, convict labor is a form of compulsory labor.[176] Thus, these modes of survival and self-empowerment still must be looked at within the context of carceral systems and the seizure of rights. That is, prisoners had no rights and few choices. If women prisoners were able-bodied, they were forced to work in Division H. Their daily routines were outlined for them, and their bodies were subjected to prison and colonial state authorities.[177] If they gave birth in prison, their children were removed from their care.[178] Though prison literature makes vague references to women enjoying monetary and emotional compensation for their labor, women prisoners faced restrictions regarding pay. Embroidery and sewing did not have an apprenticeship system with a workmanship classification, unlike some of the industries conducted by men.

It remains unclear whether women prisoners could earn wages or what kind of access they had to their pay during their incarceration; though, as with other handicrafts, the majority of the profits from the sale of the embroidered white goods went back to Bilibid Prison and specifically funded salaries under the industrial division.[179] Prison documents refer only to the potential for male prisoners to bank wages and remit money to their families. The logic supporting remittances rested upon the idea that men were breadwinners for their families, which in fact contradicted earlier colonial literature that identified women as largely assuming responsibility for the earning and accounting of household income. Even in cases where girls and women were not "breadwinners," they nevertheless contributed to family earnings.[180] Prison policy reflected US-centric assumptions concerning gender roles and therefore did not regard women as having the same kinds of financial responsibilities and needs as men.[181] Although Bilibid portrayed convict labor as rehabilitative, it was Filipina elites and American reformers who lobbied for the Bureau of Labor to assist women released from Bilibid in finding employment.[182]

## Realities for Women in Bilibid Prison

At the turn of the century, Bilibid officials portrayed the prison as a site of wholesome learning and rehabilitation, where the environment was simple yet clean and comfortable. They described prisoners as efficient and military-like in their ability to follow orders. Photographs and films that show the interior of Bilibid portray the prison as orderly and clean. Such depictions supported the overall image of the prison as a manifestation of the United States' success in creating the model institution of penal reform. Reality, however, was a far cry from the almost bucolic image that prison officials touted. Indeed, one American medical official declared that Bilibid was a "dreary sort of place."[183] John Lewis Gillin echoed the same sentiments, writing that the "discipline is quite severe" in Division H.[184] Filipina prisoners' daily realities contradicted Bilibid's public image.

A 1916 Philippine Health Services report noted that several women prisoners gave birth. Officials decided, "for the sake of [the] mothers and children, that short-term pregnant women be sent elsewhere than Bilibid Prison for punishment, as it hardly seems just that a prison sentence be inflicted upon a child before it is born, and that it be burdened with this stigma throughout life."[185] Missing from the narrative was any concern for the conditions of the pregnancies, including whether or not they resulted from rape, abuse, or sexual coercion within or outside the prison. While the Director of Health showed concern for the care of both mother and infant, and in particular for women who went into labor pre-term, the language of illegitimacy, that is, childbirth outside of the bounds of marriage, questioned women's rights to make decisions concerning their health care or the lives of their children.[186] The reports reflected no consideration for mothers' wishes or needs and instead declared that Bilibid and other facilities were not fit for child-rearing and immediately separated mothers from their infants.[187] Prisons are *not* fit places for living and child-rearing. But it is also important to note that the prison system prioritized incarceration and the fulfillment of prison sentences as a form of uplift and a means of improving society, rather than offering any kind of recourse to women prisoners and their children.

The report also hinted at questionable health and safety conditions in Bilibid. Contrary to the idyllic environment of rehabilitation put forth by prison administrators, critics took issue with the potential dangers and threats women prisoners faced. John Lewis Gillin contended, "Women prisoners here, as in the United States, are poorly handled," thus hinting at the potential abuse women faced from male prisoners and advocating for stricter segregation between women and men inmates.[188] Colonial government reports on Bilibid and other smaller prisons conveyed that problems in keeping genders segregated gave rise to the abuse of women. While the language is vague, the reports allude to the possibility of physical, psychological, and sexual abuse occurring, such as assault and rape, in addition to other crimes being committed within the prisons. While not specifically addressed, the question of gendered abuse faced by women prisoners also raised the possibility of other forms of mistreatment and cruelty, not just between prisoners, but also at the hands of those in power.

Poor conditions in Bilibid also led to an outbreak of tuberculosis that spread through the women's ward in 1912, five years prior to the implementation of state-endorsed efforts to cope with tuberculosis and other highly contagious infections and diseases not only in Bilibid but also throughout Manila and across the Philippines. Eighty-six of the 193 prisoners diagnosed with tuberculosis died in Bilibid's hospital; eighty of the eighty-six mortalities were women. Medical records provide few details and little context for the spread of the bacterial lung disease beyond the number of cases and deaths, and the gender and marital status of each person afflicted. The reality of tuberculosis, though, paints a portrait of deaths that directly conflicted with Bilibid's public promise of better lives for its inmates. The number of recorded patients and mortalities during this short period of time provides a glimpse of the conditions in the women's ward.

According to some sources, including Burton Holmes's film, women's working and sleeping barracks were bright, open, and airy. *Luzon Lingerie* emphasizes neatness, depicting evenly distributed rows of women seated at individual embroidery frames. In the film, incarcerated Filipinas diligently work in an outdoor open space that is not quite beautiful, but at least clean and comfortable. But if this were truly the environment Bilibid prisoners lived in, Bilibid would not have had a tuberculosis outbreak. In reality, living quarters were overcrowded and cramped.[189] A 1925 article published in *Mid-Pacific Magazine* remarked that upon entering the embroidery department, "[a group of Americans] found scores of Filipino women seated on the floor."[190] To have impacted that many women and caused that many deaths in such a short period of time, it is likely that Filipino women inmates lived in overcrowded, dark, damp, and poorly ventilated quarters.[191] Poor nutrition would have also weakened their immune systems and exacerbated the troubling spread of tuberculosis.[192] Despite the existence of the prison hospital, admitted patients would not have received effective medical care. At the time, there was no cure or prophylactic available to treat tuberculosis.[193] Medical staff administered mercury, which we now know was a form of poisoning and could have also contributed to their eventual deaths. The disproportionate number of women afflicted with tuberculosis in Bilibid is perhaps a reflection of the broader treatment of incarcerated women.

The possibility of medical neglect reflects the colonial government's lack of care and investment in Filipino prisoners' lives and well-being.[194] Tuberculosis continued to plague the prison for years following the 1912 outbreak. The spread of tuberculosis only became a crisis, however, when the infection spread beyond the women's ward and impacted the larger prison population.[195] Despite the high rate of mortality in 1912, the reports convey no sense of alarm or concern. It was only when tuberculosis spread throughout the male prison population a few years later that the director of Bilibid appealed for assistance from health officials.[196] United States medical campaigns in the Philippines blamed sickness and disease on racial failure and pinned the cause of illness on backward native character, habits, and primitive dwellings.[197] For several years, the colonial state instituted sanitation and hygiene regulations to combat infectious diseases and launched public campaigns to reprogram Filipinos' habits that were deemed insanity.[198] But tuberculosis outbreaks occurred even as the colonial state surveilled and regulated Manila residents for their supposed lack of hygiene.

For Filipinas, regimented reform and racial uplift in fact contributed to the spread of disease, debilitation, and death. Outside the prison, health officials blamed Filipino habits, culture, and style of dwellings as the main culprits for the spread of infectious diseases. However, in the prison, colonial state and prison officials regulated the environment and determined medical treatment and diet. Prison officials had the capacity to deal with and change the living conditions that contributed to the spread of disease. Instead, they created the very same living conditions US colonial officials had attributed to Filipino savagery to justify US intervention. Ultimately, the image of cramped and disease-filled spaces embodied the antithesis of American modernity and progress. United States colonial discourse portrayed illnesses and disease as the result of backwardness and poor habits. Medical reports attributed sickness to racialized character flaws. Therefore, the outbreak of disease in Bilibid Prison, which was completely controlled by the Americans, undermined multiple and concomitant images of US superiority. Above all, it brought to light the fissures in US penal reform. Bilibid was not the pristine emblem of reform prison advocates praised.

## Legacies and Unfulfilled Promises

In many ways, the colonial state and embroidery industry entrepreneurs regarded the Philippine embroidery as industry a profitable success. The field of embroidery, in fact, was the only "successful" handicraft to be implemented in the industrial school system. Unlike other trades, embroidery turned a substantial profit. Colonial officials saw the promise and opportunity to disseminate disciplinary methods labeled as "uplift" for the purposes of making a profit. The institutionalized link between the education and penal systems created when the Department of Prisons was placed under the Department of Public Instruction made the sharing of disciplinary methods and the cultivation of a workforce easy. The strongly forged links between private industry, the colonial state, and public institutions produced methods and infrastructures that could be borrowed and adapted in other settings beyond the Philippines. So confident were they in their "success" that US colonial officials in the Philippines urged agents in Puerto Rico to adopt similar systems of industrial schooling and labor.[199]

These institutions put into place disciplinary practices that fashioned workforces out of vulnerable populations such as incarcerated women and young girls, mostly from the poorer classes, who attended the newly established industrial schools. United States colonial officials and Filipino supporters of these public institutions framed disciplining students and prisoners as methods of reform and benchmarks of progress that would ultimately benefit those who learned these new norms. Incarcerated laborers had little say in what work they were assigned. While a good number of Filipina children did not attend colonial public schools, once enrolled, their days were highly regulated and organized toward productivity and profit. Moreover, pupil workers and convict laborers received little or no wages for their work. Pupil workers and incarcerated laborers were disciplined for productivity and profit but did not benefit from upward mobility or even stability.

The framework of providing training in public schools and prisons helped obfuscate the exploitative features of industrial education. Officials argued that through education, Filipinos had access to training that would allow them to become productive workers imbued with the skills to reach the goal of capital gains. As "pupil workers," child labor was positioned as learning exercises, a much more acceptable framework than busywork.[200] Working in Division H was positioned as teaching habits of industry that would rehabilitate women. Documents praising the success of colonial programs used the vague language of benefit and the promise of wealth. Records never actually quantified such benefits. For both pupil workers and incarcerated women laborers, working in the present offered the promise of a better future.

The introduction of embroidery and lacemaking as part of systematized vocational training promised uplift but not upward mobility. In other words, education in skilled labor would give embroiderers the potential to earn wages and therefore better their lives and their families' lives. However, earning wages did not necessarily facilitate a boost in social status. In fact, managing and maintaining class divisions was a central concern for colonial officials, educators, and Filipino elites. While students were expected to reach the level of "skilled professional," the industry itself enforced class constraints on needleworkers by keeping their wages low.[201] In rare cases, government records marked a general increase of wealth.[202] To be proper colonial subjects, embroidery workers needed to remain in their subject positions in the hierarchy of global capitalism. Embroiderers in schools and beyond remained manufacturing workers, becoming neither capitalists nor entrepreneurs themselves. It is unclear whether students were compensated once their work began to turn a profit. Instead, the kinds of benefits students received were spoken of in general terms. In learning "modern" domestic science, Filipina students became "assets" at home and could be seen wearing "modern" dresses of their own making.[203]

Some colonial officials saw industrial training as a technology of population control. According to them, earning an extra income would prevent Filipinos from abandoning agricultural work and leaving the provinces to seek employment in Manila. Apprehension about rural to urban migration reflected that US discourses about the danger of increasing "degeneration" in urban life had a transnational reach.[204] Such discourses argued that unskilled workers without motivation would only add to urban poverty and exacerbate problems with crime and moral degradation, potentially leading to the proliferation of vice.[205] Officials cautioned that provincial Filipinos would succumb to the "greater social activities and pleasures of the large towns."[206] Thus, educational training could provide women and girls the tools to better the lives of their families. But perhaps even more important, alternative forms of labor would keep Filipinos of the peasant class in their respective provinces and prevent the immorality so closely associated with racialized others from moving into urban spaces. The colonial structure of the industrial schools made it clear that embroiderers were never meant to own their means of production.

Even with the demise of the Philippine embroidery industry, the end of industrial school programs, and the closure of Division H in Bilibid Prison and the opening of the Correctional Institution for Women in Mandaluyong in 1931, many aspects of the transnational Philippine embroidery industry and the disciplinary methods of creating a gendered and racialized workforce remained.[207] Throughout the twentieth and twenty-first centuries, entrepreneurs continued to view the Philippines as a source of cheap labor, particularly Filipina workers. Outprocessed manufacturing would continue even after Philippine independence in 1946 in the form of factories linked to multinational corporations, particularly in the realm of fast fashion.[208] Filipinas became the "heroes" of the Philippine economy, and their education and work ethic were regarded as coveted qualities for overseas work.[209] The alliances between states, nations, and big businesses continued to operate within the frameworks first introduced by imperial expansion.

# 5

## "THE DREAM OF BEAUTY"

### *The Terno and the Filipina High-Fashion System*

In 1915, Rosenda de Alba began making embroidered lingerie for a small number of private customers.[1] Unlike many of the embroiderers in the Philippines, Alba quickly earned a reputation for her artistry and design. Her popularity gained her a growing clientele among the growing population in Manila. Between 1915 and 1927, Alba turned her focus away from embroidered lingerie to custom-made formal gowns. In 1927, she moved her business out of her home, opening a new shop, Lyric Fashion, on the fashionable Rizal Avenue—the heart of Manila's shopping and entertainment district. Intricate hand embroidery and beadwork sewn onto a new version of the *traje de mestiza* that emerged in the 1920s—the *terno*—was all the rage for formal and special occasions and would later become the national dress of the Philippines. Terno, meaning "matching," referred to a new style of *Filipiniana* dress in which the bodice and skirt matched in material and color.[2] Women in Manila, as well as those from the provinces, coveted Alba's luxurious and beautifully constructed ternos. At the time, Alba was one of a small cohort of Filipino fashion designers who created couture gowns for Filipinas. Over the next decade, Alba expanded her shop's services and products. By the 1930s,

Lyric Fashion had become a central hub for Filipina fashion and beauty, providing not only exclusive, made-to-order gowns but also beauty services, like haircuts, perms, and manicures. Alba was able not only to transform a handicraft that had been systemically limited to a cottage industry, but also to establish and expand a new kind of business: a boutique dedicated to Filipina fashions and beauty services. The demand for her dresses and the increased reliance on her expertise as a trendsetter reflected the material and cultural changes that occurred in conjunction with dramatic political and economic shifts in the colonial relationship between the United States and the Philippines.

The simultaneous rise of the Filipino couturier and the appearance of the terno were deeply imbricated in the rapid economic, cultural, and political changes of the 1920s and 1930s. As businesses like Alba's expanded, the majority of *bordadoras* and seamstresses continued to receive low wages—despite the promises of economic uplift made by industrial schools. But other arenas of public schooling provided social mobility, shuttling students from primary to secondary schools and eventually on to university. The expansion of higher education focused on training for white-collar occupations. A large number of graduates moved into civil service as a result of the Insular Government's pivot toward *Filipinization* of the colonial state, a process undertaken, starting in 1912, in preparation for independence.[3] Others found employment in the growing number of commercial firms in Manila. Meanwhile, as Filipino elites continued to consolidate their power, they were increasingly drawn to the colonial capital of Manila. Filipino participation in government widened, the numbers of universities increased, and commercialization and urbanization increased. Dramatic economic shifts and difficulties were intertwined with questions about the colonial relationship between the Philippines and the United States.[4] Manila had become the center of Philippine commerce and power during the Spanish colonial period and remained so during the US colonial regime as well as after Philippine independence. Over time, economic and political changes transformed the social landscape of the colonial capital. Work, entertainment, and sociality were often intertwined, and each setting demanded specific sartorial forms and styles. Filipina women relied on Alba and other designers to dress and groom them to appear at these different functions.[5]

This chapter traces the development of a fashion system. It draws on the work of Roland Barthes. In the colonial beauty regime, the production and consumption of the terno as high fashion resulted from the accumulation of wealth brought into Manila, and it was a tool used to structure and police class-based hierarchies in a rapidly changing Philippines. Alba, her ternos, and Lyric Fashion were part of a Manila-based fashion system that on the surface seemed centered only on elite clientele. The question of what Filipina elites wore, however, reveals a system of Filipina high fashion that was distinct from the systems of dress in previous years. As a beauty regime, Filipina high fashion was a tool for cultural and material negotiation of elite Filipinas' status in colonial Philippine society.[6] The colonial sociality of Manila two decades before the outbreak of World War II involved a complex matrix of people, institutions, practices, and materials. Barthes's work on meaning-making and semiotics focuses primarily on the discourses of fashion in print media.[7] The growth of print media was indeed a central force in the building of fashion in general and high fashion in particular. Expanding Barthes's concept of the fashion system, I explore the world of high fashion and the Filipina beauty regime, connecting print media and fashion writing to the labor of terno production, the rise of the Filipino fashion designer, and the role of fashion and aesthetics in assembling a colonial social world. In addition to discourses about fashion and garment production, fashion and dress practices, as Emma Tarlo argues, were an amalgamation of "people making decisions, choosing to some extent their own self-image, playing with identities and recognizing the role of clothes in image construction and interpretation. In other words, clothes are not merely defining but they are also self-consciously *used* to define, to present, to deceive, to enjoy, to communicate, to reveal and conceal."[8] This chapter examines discourses on Filipina clothing, acts of wearing Filipina high-fashion gowns, and the production of such garments as self-conscious efforts to construct Filipina modernity.

Fashion became a critical tool with which Filipinas exercised their control during a time of rapid change, dramatic shifts, and uncertain futures. Navigating the social landscape influenced decisions about what to wear, how to cut and curl one's hair, and what methods of cosmetic applications to employ. As shown in the previous chapters, beauty and fashion regimes have always been tied to larger issues. In the 1920s and 1930s, new fashion industries and practices demonstrated the gendered ways that Filipina women reckoned with decades of American power in the Philippines, the sudden shift from the long-unfulfilled promises of national independence to a ten-year Commonwealth period, the fraught process of defining a national identity through constructions of Filipina identity, the increased presence of Filipino elites in Manila and their consolidation of power, and the changing roles of women and contentious notions of Filipina womanhood. The terno and the development of Filipina high fashion illustrate US political, economic, and military power and the impact of two decades of US colonialism in the Philippines, and how fashion production and dress practices were cultural, economic, and corporeal responses to continued and unresolved questions of Philippine independence in the 1920s and 1930s.

## Urbanization and the Terno Industry

The production and distribution of the terno as fashionable wear for Filipinas played a critical part in the development of a Philippine fashion system. Sewing, mending, weaving, and other skills related to clothing construction have often been categorized as domestic, feminine tasks. I focus on these forms of clothing production under the system of formal dressmaking in the colonial Philippines.[9] Colonial regime changes, global connections, and technological developments all changed the production processes involved in the creation of Filipina formal gowns. Dressmaking grew from a small, localized economy of skilled seamstresses to a commercialized, Manila-based industry. Dressmakers were transformed into celebrated designers by the 1920s. These developments played a role in making sartorial claims to Filipina modernity and power through fashion authorship.

The commercialization of the terno and the making of a high-fashion system were deeply tied to colonial urbanization and industrialization. The boom of the export industry also precipitated the expansion of businesses in Manila, which had been established as the links between Philippine-sourced products and the global market during the Spanish period and subsequently maintained into the American colonial regime. There was continuity between the two colonial regimes, but there was also dramatic change. As seen in chapter 2, Manila developed a new identity and spirit with the change in regimes, bringing in droves of people and drawing attention through its hosting of the Manila Carnival and Philippine Exposition. Under the US colonial regime, Manila continued to serve as a major hub for global trade, where goods from abroad would first land and be redistributed, and from which Philippine-sourced commodities would be shipped overseas, mainly to the United States. Manila was also the center of political power. During both the Spanish and American regimes, Manila was the nucleus of both the Spanish colonial state and the Catholic Church. Malacañang Palace housed the governor-general's office and later the office of the president of the Commonwealth. After independence, it held the office of the president of the Republic of the Philippines. The Philippine Assembly also congregated in Manila. As such, more people were coming into Manila for work, play, education, shopping, or simply to see and to be seen. Raquel Reyes's work on Manila shows that the social activities and conspicuous consumption that fully emerged in the 1920s were markers of "urbane sophistication" and conventions of urbanity that were classed and gendered.[10] In this rapidly changing world, demonstrating urbane sophistication relied heavily on dressing the part.

During the US colonial period, Filipina elites' investments in their appearances developed in response to changing social formations of high society that produced an elite Manila culture, one that was distinct from that of the *ilustrados* of the nineteenth century. The consolidation of a Philippine export economy meant that the majority of Philippine-based wealth continued to come from hacienda agriculture.[11] While capital largely remained tied to provincial resource extraction and tenant farming, Filipino elites increasingly moved to Manila to lead urban lives for at least part of the year. They also sent their children to attend the growing number of colleges and universities. Manila high society in the 1920s and 1930s saw a greater number of elite families (including men, women, children, and extended relatives) who maintained their sense of elitism based on their wealth, mestizo identity, and urbane attitudes. This growing population of elites interacted based on a specific calendar, which revolved around congressional sessions; the Filipinization of the government had increased Filipino participation in a new representational system and thus granted these "national oligarchs" the political power that had eluded them during the Spanish regime.[12] Benedict Anderson provides a glimpse of Manila social culture during this time. He writes that elites "might [have] dislike[d] one another, but they went to the same receptions, attended the same churches, lived in the same residential areas, shopped in the same fashionable streets, had affairs with each other's wives, and arranged marriages between each other's children."[13] But what Anderson glosses over is that, more often than not, *women* were at the center of these social events. The popular media paid specific attention to the activities and appearances of elite Filipinas, listing who attended which events and giving detailed descriptions of what they wore. The performance of feminine dress was an effective means by which to put status, wealth, and power on public display.

The influx of Filipinos into the urban capital gave Filipina elites the impetus to construct a high-society culture in Manila. In their work on Filipina magazines, Salvador Bernal, Georgina R. Encanto, and Francis L. Escaler link the economic and social changes in Manila to fashion demands: "The outgoing Filipinos now had social clubs, theaters, races, and bazaars to frequent.

The fashion-conscious woman, thus, needed a wider wardrobe for these diverse occasions: *vestidos* or western style clothing for informal gatherings like afternoon teas and civic group meetings, and the traje for formal affairs like the balls in Malacañang."[14] While Western dress was considered appropriate for the new types of social affairs that emerged in first few decades of the twentieth century, the terno remained the dress of choice for formal functions. In her memoir, Purita Kalaw-Ledesma describes the Kahirup Balls, the exclusive annual events hosted by Visayan elites at the Manila Hotel, as the setting where "Visayans could be lavish on the social front."[15] She recalls the sartorial expectations of high society: "Ladies had to have sumptuous ternos made for every ball," and "family jewels were splashed on to out sparkle those of other members."[16] Kalaw-Ledesma's recollections sound remarkably similar to the balls and fetes described in chapter 1. Indeed, many of the people who received invitations to the exclusive annual balls held in Manila in the 1920s and 1930s were from the same prominent families of Manila and the provinces who had been targeted by the Philippine Commission at the turn of the century. Despite the continuities of elite life, beginning in the 1920s, the consolidation of elite culture in Manila also firmly established the city as the center of high society and elite power. Changing fashion and dress practices reflected the dynamic modification and shifts of colonial urban life. Whereas at the turn of the century, women had been expected to don luxurious trajes de mestiza, in the 1920s and 1930s, they wore ternos to assert their social status. Women attending the exclusive formal events of the Manila social season tried to meet the expectation of having a new terno made for each event. Fashion emphasized the rhythm of elite Manila life.

The ternos worn at exclusive formal occasions were adaptations of the traje de mestizo. The fashion system that evolved around the terno policed the boundaries of who could wear Filipina high fashion. The very name traje de mestiza, which means the dress of the mestiza, indicates that the gown was meant to be worn by mestiza elites.[17] Starting in the seventeenth century—and continuing to the present day—the traje and its many manifestations, ranging from the Maria Clara gown to the terno, have epitomized exclusivity. Ternos signified a woman's privileged status, rooted in claims to a Spanish legacy. Considering Filipiniana gowns in the context of colonial regime change and impending national independence, one can see how signs and signifiers both stayed the same and changed over time. Leading up to the 1930s, the terno came to define privileged womanhood in the Philippines. For Filipinas, the luxurious textiles and meticulous hand embroidery of the terno signified wealth, privilege, and access to local and foreign commodities.

Ternos differed from the traje de mestizo of the late nineteenth and early twentieth centuries. The separate and distinct pieces of the shawl, bell-sleeved blouses, and skirt evolved into a matching bodice and skirt and above-the-elbow butterfly sleeves. Although most commonly recognized by its butterfly sleeves, the terno has taken on multiple silhouettes, materials, and styles. Bernal, Encanto, and Escaler argue that the terno "did not have a single, definite form."[18] Rather, the term was "used for whatever was the prevailing fashion, which *mestizas* followed."[19] The terno had an ever-evolving form, producing new trends for the events of the newly formed social season. The demands of urban social life animated a significant change in the production of the terno itself. As shown in chapter 1, to meet these demands, Filipinas purchased clothing and accessories from European fashion capitals and appropriated changing styles into their own dress creations. Starting in the 1920s, however, the fashion system took a dramatic turn. The fashion system in the Philippines—influenced by industrialization and urbanization—embraced the sewing machine and transformed into an industry that resembled the one in Paris.[20]

Terno production combined local and imported textiles, embroidery work, and dress construction by skilled seamstresses. The construction of the terno required training, skill, and artistry. However, *costureras* and bordadoras were not considered style-makers. Although the demand for ternos and other commodities created a steady need for needlework and textile making, the actual producers continued to be denied both artistic credit and proportional compensation. They continued to be viewed as skilled but were undervalued as manual laborers who merely executed the artistic vision of the elite patron. Art and style were classed concepts, considered manifestations of being "cultured." A 1936 *Woman's World* editorial arguing for vocational training in the Philippines claimed, "Our weavers, both in the Visayas and in the Ilocos, are mostly of the unlettered class with no idea of how to create new designs and fashions to meet the public taste."[21] This Manila-based magazine article continued, "Our weavers lack a direct mind. Being ignorant and untutored, they are content with their meager earnings. Fashion has very little place in the plans of their tasks."[22] Although weavers, embroiderers, and sewers were trained and skilled, their labor continued to be considered mindless and without creativity. Needlework training in industrial schools and Bilibid Prison had promised economic uplift and social mobility. And while bordadoras and costureras might have found new work in these nascent fashion houses, these occupations continued to pay low wages. Embroiderers, weavers, and seamstresses continued to be viewed with disparaging disdain by the *matapobré* (one who looks down on the poor).[23]

The production and consumption of luxury Filipiniana gowns distinguished between costureras, who were considered hired labor, and mestiza patrons, who were considered the source of fashion and style.[24] Prior to the establishment of high-end boutiques in Manila, these formal dresses were constructed in highly localized settings; dressmaking was part of the feminized domestic labor of individual households.[25] In an interview, journalist and socialite Pura Villanueva Kalaw—the first Manila Carnival Queen—reminisced over the dresses of her youth, saying, "When I was a young girl, all my dresses were selected and made under my mother's direct supervision. The most beautiful dress I remember that she chose for me was apple green in color, hand-embroidered all over, and made of Filipino woven material."[26] Well-off families could also solicit the services of local dressmakers and embroiderers. It was common practice for a costurera to visit her clients' homes to design, measure, and fit the gowns.[27] Or, depending on their wealth, a family could employ one or more seamstresses as part of their household staff—typically "a fastidious elderly woman of the house" who translated the household mistress's desires into elaborate dresses.[28] In all these situations, the elite Filipina patrons took credit for the beauty and style of the gowns.

Although the majority of dressmaking production continued to take place on a household scale, changing class dynamics and the growth of conspicuous consumption sparked the opening of high-end terno shops in Manila.[29] If a dressmaker garnered enough popularity and high enough demand for their gowns, they could earn enough capital and project enough economic security to open their own studio and shop.[30] While there were a few men, such as Ramon Valera, whose ternos were in high demand, the industry and work remained largely dominated by women. During this time, a select few terno producers, most of whom came from middle- and upper-class families—including Rosenda de Alba—went from being dressmakers to being couturiers. Terno designers became style authorities and dramatically changed the fashion system of the Philippines, thus cementing their foothold in Philippine beauty regimes. They and their oft-overlooked employees churned out the newest and most desirable one-of-a-kind gowns for an urbanized, elite class of Filipinos. At the same time, couturiers presented themselves as arbiters of cosmopolitan high-fashion knowledge. In turn, designers' brands and creations became critical tools in defining elite culture.

In the 1920s and 1930s, Filipina fashion discourse freely switched between the terms *modiste, modista, couturiere, couturier,* and designer. These differed from the terms used to describe other forms of dressmakers, like seamstress. The fashion system continued to make class distinctions, differentiating designers from seamstresses, patternmakers, and embroiderers, and insisting that only the designer embodied the craft and artistry of making high-fashion gowns. By the 1930s, the popular press—along with elite clientele—had elevated only a select number of individuals from dressmakers to couturiers. Notable designer Juanita Mina-Roa described this period as when "there appeared for the first-time fashion experts and couturiers."[31] In addition to Mina-Roa, the designers most popular with the Filipina elite were Pacita Longos, Ramon Valera, and Pura Escurdia.[32] Longos—the most celebrated designer of the 1920s—owned a shop in Quiapo, the commercial district of Manila, where her clients could purchase made-to-order gowns. Other popular designers soon followed suit, establishing their own dress stores in shopping districts around Manila. Pura Escurdia ran a similar establishment called the P. Escurdia Shop. In the 1930s, Rosario de Guzman ran a store called the Filipina Dress Shop in Sampaloc, which was frequented by beauty queens whose sartorial presentations garnered much public attention and praise. The source of beauty and style shifted from elite matriarchs of households and haciendas to couturiers who owned their own shops.

Departing from the convention of the patron supervising the dressmaking process, in these shops, designers took part in the construction of gowns while supervising teams of seamstresses and embroiderers.[33] Terno construction took considerable work. Designers' shops and studios employed a team of mainly women who expertly cut, pleated, sewed, and embroidered fabric. An article featured in the *Woman's Home Journal* gave readers insight into the inner workings of Pacita Longos's studio:

Mientras habla y borda y da órdenes a sus auxiliares y operarias—estamos en el entresuelo de su propia casa, que le sirve de taller—con una facilidad encantadora y versatilidad extraordinaria, como de una mujer acostumbrada a hacer varias cosas a la vez y dirigir la costura de muchos trajes a un [al mismo] tiempo.[34]

(While talking and embroidering and giving orders to her assistants and female employees—we are on the ground floor of her house, which serves as a workshop—with extraordinary ease and versatility, like a woman accustomed to doing various things at once and directing the sewing of many dresses at the same time.)

Terno designers built their reputations and businesses on having the technical skills to construct elaborate gowns while at the same time distinguishing themselves from the embroiderers and seamstresses they employed. Longos— who earned the titles "Queen of the Needle" and "dictadora de la elegancia feminine" in the prewar era—regarded modistas, or designers, as a distinct class with discerning taste, artistry, and fashion knowledge above all others.[35] Juanita Mina-Roa compared her ternos and trajes de mestiza to other art forms. Mina-Roa considered her work to be like other works of art, filled with deeper meaning and beauty that could only be created by someone with talent and exceptional skill. She asserted that "in every dress creation there is a hidden message, a meaning, a living personality, just as in a poem there is a soul, and in music, a heart."[36] The person behind the craft was as important as the designs and gowns themselves. However, the *sinamayera* who designed the embroidery patterns and oversaw the construction of gowns differed from the designer in that they did not cultivate the same kind of status and branding as the designer. Designers placed themselves in positions of power and as sources of style, creativity, and beauty.

Filipino designers cultivated identities as fashion creatives with the power to set trends for the Filipina elite. The designation of fashion designer, usually assumed by white Westerners, manifested a "racialized presumption of authorial positionality and power."[37] To be a source of style and fashion authorship, Minh-Hà Phạm argues, was to make a claim to a kind of power and authority.[38] Thus, the declaration of the emergence of the Filipino fashion designer or couturier was a power move that used the same signs and symbols as the European fashion system.[39] In 1931, the *Tribune Society* newspaper and fashion journalist Corazon E. Grau chronicled the exclusive Kahirup Ball, lamenting, "The day of the clever-fingered Filipino woman who could proudly boast that the gown she had worn at a smart soiree was her own creation, designed by her own very self, is as good as gone. . . . The dictatorial hand of leading Manila modistes . . . has emerged triumphantly."[40] Grau's brief observations mark the significant shifts in the politics of Filipina dress that occurred in the decade before her column was published. First, she concisely summarizes how the production of Filipina formal gowns had changed from an intimate form of labor carried out in the home to a commercial system of production and consumption. In earlier cases, the woman wearing the gown would normally have claimed creative ownership of the design. By the 1920s, however, a new standard for formal dress production emerged, in which the more coveted gowns were those designed and created by official dress designers. The changes in the mode of production that led to the establishment of Filipina high fashion also gave rise to Filipina couture. Grau refers to designers as "dictatorial" modistes based in Manila. Her word choice emphasizes terno designers' power as fashion and style authorities. These couturiers became authorities whose choices in fabric and designs dictated what was considered stylish in Filipina fashion. Designers marketed their craft as high fashion.

In interviews, terno designers highlighted their talent for generating new styles at a rapid pace. Pura Escurdia claimed, "Modistes like me cannot afford to stand still. . . . Women like newer ideas."[41] Filipino designers drew from many sources, both local and global. For example, Escurdia dug "into the past for some ideas, bringing out certain past trends that will appeal to the present."[42] At other times, she took from European styles, which were "always changing, always new."[43] Fashion columns included images and descriptions of new traje de mestiza and terno designs and explained the innovations needed to make these gowns, making sure to note that the pictured gowns were products of designers' innovations. *Graphic* magazine labeled the gown worn by Manila Carnival Queen Guia Balmori as a "Valera creation" and praised him for conceiving of a "stalactite effect," a look achieved by having the "whole *camisa* and *pañuelo* covered with gold and green sequins that continued down the skirt."[44] Couturiers like Escurdia and Valera demonstrated that unlike Western portrayals of Filipina formal dresses as unchanging and static—and therefore excluded from the category of high fashion—Filipina formal gowns underwent rapid stylistic changes and offered a myriad of designs.

By the 1930s, the development of a Filipina high-fashion industry marked the departure from the practices of formal gown making of the nineteenth and early twentieth centuries, where the artistry and style of the traje de mestiza was attributed mainly to the patron who commissioned the work. Much like Parisian haute couture houses, Filipino studios and shops served as central hubs of Filipina high fashion. With the emergence of shops specializing in one-of-a-kind and made-to-order gowns, "It became fashionable for the well-dressed women to go to the *costurera*'s shop, rather than employ a seamstress to sew up a ball gown at the client's house."[45] Valera, whose prominence as a Filipino fashion designer lasted from the 1930s to the 1960s, had the "luxury of picking and choosing who he would dress"; to "be attended on at his atelier by Valera himself with tape measure in hand was not so much by 'appointment' as 'by invitation.'"[46] As a designer, and therefore an unquestioned style authority, "girls who go to him do not have to do any thinking at all, because they are sure Ramon can do more to glamourize them than all the heads in their family put together."[47] Filipino designers made claims to high fashion by portraying themselves as artists whose talents were made available only to a select, wealthy, and elite few—the power to exclude and include cemented their status.

Claiming this status also meant usurping the authority of those who had previously held it: the Filipino elite. Although Filipina socialites were still considered fashionable, designers claimed an even higher style authority. Longos was open in her claims to style authority and superiority over others. Exclusive balls, such as the Club Filipino's New Year's Eve Ball, held "best dressed" competitions. At these competitions, selected club members and their wives chose the best-dressed women in attendance. Longos, though, questioned club members' abilities to judge style and fashion.

No creo en la competencia de muchos que son nombrados jueces para juzgar cuál es el traje más elegante o más original, en un baile dado. Con frecuencia se dejan guiar más por el brillo y por los colores llamativos que por el verdadero mérito.[48]

(I do not believe in the competence of many who are appointed judges to judge, which is the most elegant or most original gown, at a given ball. Often, they are guided more by brightness and bold colors rather than the real merit.)

Here, Longos challenges the style authority that mestiza elites had claimed in the nineteenth century, and instead positions designers—namely, herself—as having superior taste in fashion.

Designers were charged with the task of teaching their clients, and subsequently a larger Filipina audience, how to be fashionable. Pura Escurdia also gave style advice to larger audiences. Writing in a column titled "Woman's Fashion," published in April 1920, Escurdia gave "Fashion Hints" to her readers. High fashion, according to this logic, necessitated not only artistic and technical ability but also sophisticated knowledge of style and taste. Designers' sartorial creations defined the most current trends. When Juanita Mina-Roa used cellophane ornaments to decorate the terno she made for Aurora Reyes Recto—a former beauty queen and socialite most remembered in Philippine history as the wife of prominent Filipino politician Claro M. Recto—a fashion column told its readers to "try cellophane, if you like glitter but not too much of it."[49] In addition to making fashion news through their gowns, couturiers also provided fashion advice in Filipina news publications. Escurdia gave her readers insights into the latest trends, telling readers, "There is a new fad, and that is to have the embroidery of the camisa [blouse] match the tapiz [fabric draped at the waist]."[50] To illustrate her suggestions, the article included sketches of Escurdia's designs and embroidery along with detailed descriptions of her designs. Escurdia told her readers, when looking at the second image, "note the conventional design on skirt and camisa. The design is hand-embroidered in long stitch in a combination of reds, greens, and browns. The tapiz is embroidered with colored steel beads."[51]

By the 1930s, designers had solidified their collective identity as the makers of high fashion. Popular media likened Filipino designers to famous and celebrated French haute couture designers. A government-sponsored handbook on local industries dubbed Ramon Valera "the Lucien Lelong of Manila."[52] Similarly, popular media called Pacita Longos the "Madame Paquin of Manila."[53] These comparisons marked a careful negotiation between performing ties to Paris, the acknowledged fashion capital, while maintaining a sense of a Filipinaness.[54] Contrary to the critiques of women's fashion in the colonial Philippines as merely aping Western haute couture, Filipino designers selectively adapted the latest trends and made them useful for Filipina consumers. For example, Escurdia considered the diversity in the phenotypic appearances among Filipinas when she offered advice on the prevailing colors for women's dress. In one article, she explains the fashionable colors for elegant dresses, stating, "fair-skinned ones affected a very trying color— sort of brownish gray with reddish tones called top. . . . This is a very rich color, but as I said, very unbecoming to dark complexions. The pendulum no doubt, will swing back to lighter colors, in justice to the darker-skinned. Whatever the shade chosen, however, it should be an unusual color: not so easily described."[55] Here, Escurdia's advice on fabric colors is based on her understanding of the diversity of skin pigmentation among her Filipina audience as well as on her knowledge of global fashion trends. In a 1938 interview, Escurdia claimed that her gowns "hinged on her giving local girls a taste of the [European] Continent, while clinging to what by nature suits them best, the Filipina dress."[56] Escurdia complicates the notion that Western style was simply transplanted into the colonial space. Instead, her column demonstrates a complex translation of trends to be usable to Filipinas.

With the public platforms of fashion magazines made available to them by fashion writers, designers positioned themselves as the best source of knowledge of both Filipino and European fashion. Designers regarded themselves as the link between the Philippines and the global fashion community. Although Filipinas had access to foreign fashion trends before the 1920s, that era marked the beginning of Filipino designers as legitimate—if not preferred—

sources of international style. While working and visiting with clients, Longos recounted the latest Parisian trends. Longos's clients came to regard her studio as a key place to keep up with current styles. Although Longos asserted that her creations did not mimic the styles emerging from Parisian fashion houses, she explained, "Me gusta estar siempre al tanto de las tendencias modernas en los trajes. Además, me aprovecho muchas veces de los 'motivos' en boga para los adornos, las combinaciones de colores, etc."[57] (I like to be always just abreast of modern trends in dresses/gowns. Also, sometimes I take advantage of the "motifs" for fashionable ornaments, color combinations, etc.).

The demand for ternos persisted alongside a desire for European fashion. As fashion authorities, then, designers like Longos regarded keeping up with European styles as part of their professions as couturiers. Longos received fashion magazines from Paris to keep informed of the latest trends.[58] In taking advantage of the transnational circuits that allowed her to receive foreign media, Longos claimed connection with the global fashion industry. For Longos and other Filipino designers, "global" meant European—and to a much lesser degree, American—fashion systems. Her duties as a couturier went beyond the labor of dressmakers; her knowledge of Western fashion trends crystallized her as a trendsetter.

Filipinas of the 1920s and 1930s used similar strategies, demonstrating that, despite a few decades of American colonial rule, they continued to consider Europe—rather than the United States—the center of high culture. Writing about her travels in the United States and Europe, former pensionada (sponsored US university student), first Filipina PhD, historian, professor, and feminist Encarnación Alzona surmised, "Though the United States represented modernization, Europe represented the dignity of culture."[59] In Filipina high fashion, the same held true. While Filipinas acknowledged that the United States regarded itself as the cornerstone of modernization, in terms of fashion, they continued to see Europe as the source of high culture, as shown in their investment in Parisian haute couture trends. As one fashion article put it, "We learn from the latest fashion books to arrive from Paris—which is the place where fashions originate, although Hollywood has been claiming that distinction for . . . years."[60] Although American popular culture was ubiquitous in the Philippine media, Paris reigned as the primary source of high fashion and culture.[61] Filipiniana styles in fashion pages frequently referenced Parisian trends and designers. When doling out advice to readers, style columns mixed descriptions of ternos with the latest trends by haute couture designers like Jeanne Lanvin, Jean Patou, and Madeliene Vionnet.[62]

The tone of intimate familiarity with the big names of the Paris fashion world reinforced Filipinas' sense of cosmopolitanism. With their knowledge of European fashions, Filipinas affirmed their taste in clothing. Moreover, the act of switching back and forth between Western and Filipina gowns suggested that Filipina fashions were on par with Parisian haute couture styles.

Consequently, if Filipinas did not wear ternos to society events, they wore Parisian or Parisian-inspired gowns. One article, "The Vogue in Fashionable Manila," revealed that "evening ensembles for Manila wear vary from light-shaded Parisian gowns to Philippine creations in heavy crepes and velvets."[63] The article placed the terno in the same category of high fashion as Parisan haute couture. Just like the mestiza elites of the turn of the century, terno designers and consumers projected an affinity with European fashion, especially to that of Paris fashion houses. They continued to invest in mestizaness as an indicator of a Hispanic and, more broadly, a European heritage. This sense of Europeanness echoed the legacies of the ilustrados and elites studying and living across Europe, and most especially Paris, who saw themselves as the embodiment of a cosmopolitan and therefore modern identity that white Americans had denied them because of their racial ideologies. In maintaining an investment in a mestiza elite identity, Filipinas provided a more complex perspective on American colonial culture in the Philippines. With respect to culture, US colonization was not a complete process of imitation, where all Filipino women and men simply aped American culture. Filipina designers and their customers consciously connected ternos made in Manila with Paris-based fashion systems. In the 1928 article, "Well-Dressed Manilan Could Feel at Home in Paris or New York," society editor for *Graphic* Lolita Sollee contended that the Philippines "is not backwards in fashions of the day. Frequently, one meets stylishly-dressed women and young girls at the social affairs . . . in up to date frocks, and we would be proud to know that their gowns are not always imported creations but are designed right here in Manila by our own clever designers."[64]

The terno's changing styles demonstrated that Filipina fashion was current with Paris-based fashion trends while still maintaining a distinctive Filipina style. Rosenda de Alba of the popular Manila-based atelier Lyric Fashion approved of adapting foreign styles with the caveat, "We cannot afford to spoil it . . . with too radical ideas."[65] The process of appropriation incorporated careful selection and rejection of various Western influences. The terno, as well as fashion discourse about the terno, provided material evidence that challenged the notion of Filipina fashion blindly imitating foreign styles.[66] Through their work as creators and style aficionados, terno designers carefully

FIGURE 5.1. Advertisement from *Woman's World* (September 1935).

negotiated what Thuy Linh Nguyen Tu calls the "delicate balance" between "persistent tensions" that Asian designers continuously face—namely, the tensions of trying to connect Filipina fashion to the international arena, most especially that of Parisian fashion, while still perpetuating a Filipina identity.[67]

Filipina cosmopolitan modernity was expressed in the fashion system's ability to hybridize fashions with the terno. In 1947, Mina-Roa wrote a brief history of the terno in which she explains, "Our own racial characteristics are also obviously in our native costume. The camisa of an airy, cool, graceful, and gossamer beauty is a key to the character of the woman whose softness, grace, modesty, and daintiness are innate. But of all Filipino racial characteristics, the most striking, in Rizal's own estimate, is mental adaptability—the capacity to absorb alien ideas and ideals without losing what is inherent."[68] Thus Mina-Roa uses the language of a "natural" and essentialized essence of Filipina character to contend that terno designs have the capacity to take on outside styles and influences while still retaining Filipino identity. The regular feature "Creations by Belen," in *Woman's World,* showcased illustrations of fashionable styles of dress and demonstrated this technique of selective adoption. The January 1936 issue of *Woman's World* featured fashion plates titled "Grecian Lines Influence Filipino Dress," which highlighted two ternos that "feature[d] the latest lines" with a "full skirt slightly longer at the back to simulate a train; a band at the waist . . . ; a tight-fitting slip below the knees—these usher the new mode in the Filipino dress."[69] While the gowns borrowed lines from the Grecian column dresses popular in Western evening wear, Belen Gana's designs could still clearly be identified as ternos. The hybridization of the terno with the careful selection of European influences allowed for the Filipina fashion system to provide the succession of change that being fashionable deemed necessary. Even after decades of US colonial rule, elite Filipina culture worked hard to maintain that it had a close link to Europe. Perpetuating a mestiza Hispanic legacy as a link to Paris fashion systems challenged the notion that Filipinas depended on American tutelage to civilize the Philippines.

## The Social Stakes of the Terno

As the numbers of Filipinas in Manila for school, work, and the social season grew, the Filipina formal dress industry shifted from a locally based trade to one centered on Manila. In 1928, an anonymous columnist known as A. B. Legislator wrote about the inextricable relationship between women's fashion and new formations of Manila high society, offering a blistering critique of women's "frivolity" and their judgment of one another. Legislator's articles provide a glimpse into the inner workings of gender, fashion, and high society in the Philippines. Legislator describes how elite Filipinas divided themselves into cliques that carefully observed, judged, and discussed "how one member of this or that group dances, sings, wears her skirt, rouges her face, appears in her picture in her papers."[70] Taking part in Manila social scenes demanded participation in a system of assessing feminine appearance and comportment. Filipinas "take up matters such as the embroiderers of their dresses, who makes their shoes . . . where they buy their skirts, what brand of corsets they wear, if they do, how much were the silk stockings they wore in the last Malacañang tea-party, from what jeweler they have bought their vanity cases and bracelets, etc."[71] This indictment of perceived feminine vacuity as a symptom of the urbanization of Manila joined the chorus of patriarchal discourse linking consumption and the materiality of fashion and beauty to shallowness.[72] But Legislator's catalog of complaints also brings to light the structure of the Manila-based beauty regime—what it meant to be and look elite and how to appear powerful. Expectations around femininity and elite identity circulated in the exchange of style information among women in the forms of gossip, designer gowns and jewelry, and the press writing about women's personal appearances.

Filipina elites' deep investment in designer ternos and the styling of their outfits dovetailed with the efforts of Filipino elites to consolidate power. Elites needed to maneuver around US colonialism's continued questioning of Filipinos' fitness to lead an independent nation. Just as in their initial encounters with American colonial agents at the turn of the century, Filipinos in the 1920s and 1930s objected to the ongoing racial and classed misrepresentations of their privileged status.[73] They resented the racial segregation and culture of exclusivity practiced by Manila Americans.[74] This racial exclusion occurred in the realm of politics and within social spaces. For the first few decades of American colonial rule, many society clubs and luxury hotels, such as the Manila Hotel, banned Filipinos from entering.[75] Only Filipino employees who served the white patrons were excepted. This attitude of exclusivity rendered wealthy mestiza Filipinas as undesirable—or at the least, beneath white American women—in colonial high society. At the same time, securing elite power also required negotiations with the new and dynamic formations of a growing middle class and continued exploitation of the peasant and working classes.

Fashioning high society utilized gendered tactics to solidify class differences among Filipinos and to delineate space and power for elite Filipinos.

Through the cultivation of sartorial expectations, elite Filipinas constructed exclusivity around the places and events in which only they could circulate.[76] Taking part in a system of high fashion helped elite Filipinas redefine Philippine—and more specifically, Manila—high society. High fashion became a strategic tool for challenging what elite Filipinas felt was a misrepresentation of their privileged status and for making claims to an exclusive and cosmopolitan modern womanhood. While historically the traje de mestiza had stood for Filipina wealth and luxury, during the 1920s and 1930s, the terno embodied privilege, exclusivity, and a specific kind of Filipina modernity, countering Americans' misrecognition of Filipina elites' privilege. At the same time, the gown distinguished elites from women of the working class and, most especially, from members of the growing middle class.

According to Philippine fashion historians, only the "more moneyed *mestizas*" could be up to date on all the style mandates.[77] Consequently, the fashion and society pages of increasingly popular Philippine news publications featured only women from prominent families. These articles included news of society events, including weddings, galas, and dinners attended by the Filipina elite. Photographs from these events or portraits taken at the growing number of photo studios, such as Sun Studio in Manila, portrayed Filipinas in their finery, including the latest styles of ternos. Such photos were presented to readers with captions such as "Miss Monina Acuña, a celebrated beauty in the Philippines," "Miss Marina T. Lopez, winner of the *Liwayway* Popularity Contest," and "Mrs. Susana P. Madrigal, the manager of the Philippine Cotton Mills and wife of the Filipino Magnate, Mr. Vicente Madrigal."[78] These descriptions included information about each woman's background. Fashion writing and society pages helped construct signifiers such as beauty queen titles, the names of companies, and family names to associate the visuality of high fashion with prestige.

Print media provided an unofficial catalog of Filipina women in elite circles and mapped out the new social landscape of Manila. Captions in the society pages to photos from high-society events—like the Gala des Diademes at the Rho Alpha in January 1936—included both the names of attendees and descriptions of what they wore. One photograph, for example, featured the adviser of a fraternity, "Mrs. Salvador Araneta," whose "Filipino dress was of white jusi with borders of gold lame studded with tiny green and red flowers."[79] The discourse concerning women's fashion presented the women as leaders of society and as trendsetters in style and high fashion. Indeed, their fashionable garb visibly marked their high status in Philippine society. The media attention paid to the details of the ternos emphasized the luxuriousness of each gown. A 1936 photo editorial in *Graphic* reported on high-society events and detailed women's style, writing, "The ladies were dressed in velvet of different colors with diadems of diamonds, pearls, gold, flowers, sequins, and silver leaves."[80] Although the photographs were in black and white, the detailed descriptions conveyed the splendor of the ternos. The array of fabrics, such as velvet and jusi, were materials that only the very wealthy could afford. The embellishments also revealed the value of the gowns—these dresses were decorated with diamonds and pearls. Furthermore, the labor required to create such detailed embellishments also added to the ternos' worth. These elaborate gowns communicated the fact that the woman under the fabric came from a wealthy background.

Dressing in fashionable ternos and earning praise for her sartorial performances in the popular media also helped solidify a woman's place in high society. Most often, the women recognized and labeled as the best dressed in Manila were also women from the most prominent families. The "Fashion Revue," an invitation-only fashion show held at the Manila Carnival on February 24, 1936, demonstrated this relationship between fashion and status. There, young Filipinas from prominent families participated in a parade in which "charm, grace, modernity, and elegance were exemplified in attractive creations by the country's leading modistes."[81] *Graphic's* fashion and society pages chronicled the event, especially honoring the coordinators: "Mrs. Carmen Melencio, chairman of the Fashion Revue, deserves special credit for the success of the affair. Herself one of the best dressed women in Manila, she was a most appropriate chairman for the evening. She was ably assisted by Mrs. Augustin Liboro, another good dresser among Manila's matrons."[82] Although this fact was not mentioned in this article, both women came from powerful families: Carmen Aguinaldo Melencio was the daughter of Emilio Aguinaldo, the first president of the Philippines; Soccoro Lopez Liboro came from the wealthy and politically powerful Lopez family, often referred to as the "Lopez dynasty" by Philippine historians.[83] By dressing in the current styles created by the popular Filipino modistes, these women performed their status in society.

At the time, modeling was not yet a profession in the Philippines. Instead, society debutantes and matrons modeled the latest modes in high fashion. Although these women—shown in images published in society and fashion pages—wore imported gowns and Western-inspired styles, they also wore ternos. *Graphic's* article on the 1936 Fashion Revue described ternos in the same way they did Western gowns: three debutantes "wore what were adjudged the most stylish evening dresses made of native material."[84] Ligaya

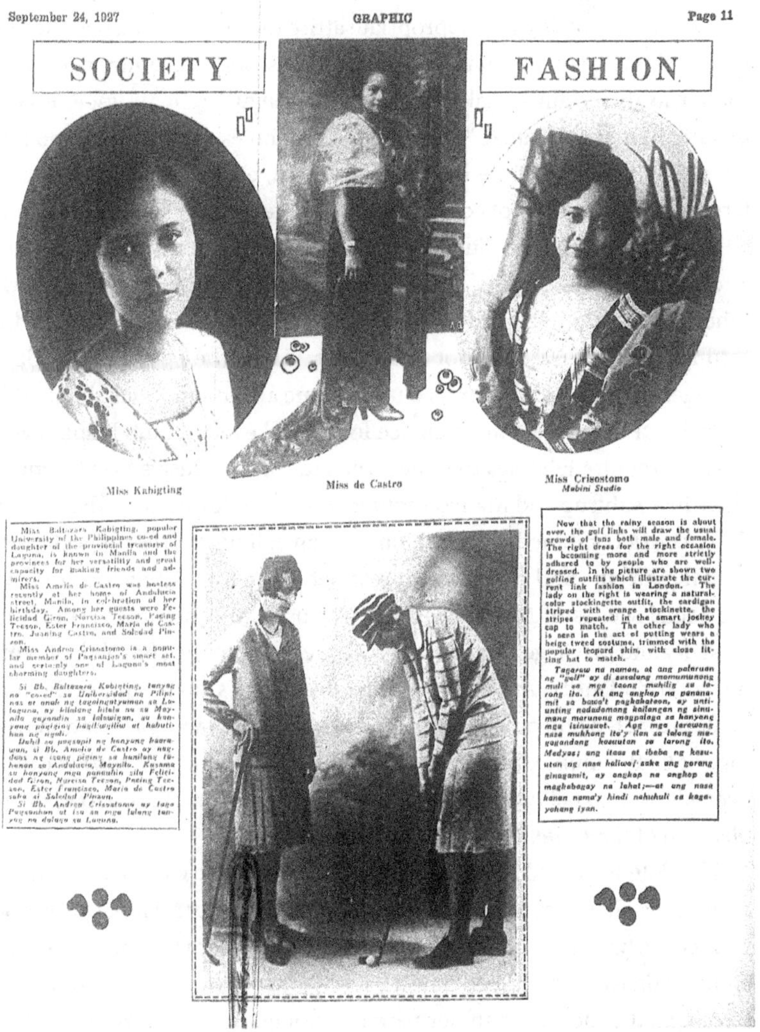

FIGURE 5.2. Page from *Graphic*, September 24, 1927, 11.

Victorio-Reyes wrote that "Schiaparelli and Lelong themselves could not have created more scintillating dresses than those worn" by the elite young Filipinas in the Fashion Revue.[85] Another *Graphic* pictorial, "Fashion of Manila," featured popular and influential women like Pura Villanueva Kalaw modeling Filipiniana formal dresses.[86] By selecting ternos as their dresses of choice, these women helped to make Filipina high fashion. Their ability to switch between ternos and Western gowns made a sartorial statement: Filipina gowns were on par with European designs.

The process of defining appropriate attire for socialites shaped the Filipina high-fashion system. Filipino fashion experts often recommended wearing the terno in certain social situations. The August 5, 1931, issue of *Graphic* included an article titled "Enchanting Ensembles for Late Afternoons and Evenings," featuring three Manila debutantes, each wearing a distinctly different terno. A gown of "dark-hued crepe georgette charmingly incrusted with lace to match" was "just the thing for evening occasions," while the late afternoon dresses "typifie[d] the favorite among the younger set."[87] Unlike other settings that demanded women be "practical" and "productive," formal settings emphasized splendor and beauty. Thus, the terno, which US colonial agents had critiqued for its cumbersome and voluminous silhouette, was considered the correct dress choice for formal events. Club Filipino went so far as to require Filipinas to wear ternos to their exclusive events, and other clubs like Kahirup and Mancommunidad soon followed suit. These enforced dress codes combined with fashion writing solidified dress expectations for the Filipina elite and reflect how dress became a tool with which to navigate the social scenes of Manila. Fashion was used to construct a culture of exclusivity and privilege. Appearances were central to the consolidation of elite power and identity. At the same time, dress codes that required Filipiniana dress protected and preserved the terno as a fashionable garment. In her history of Club Filipino, Felice Santa María contends, "If the *mestiza* dress had been allowed to fall into antiquity, the future would not have experienced the pleasure of the *terno.*"[88]

Elite Filipinas used dress to construct a hegemonic national identity based on cosmopolitanism and modernity. Part of their sartorial performance depended on wearing the coveted designs of well-known couturiers. For example, Mina-Roa described how a Pacita Longos gown "usually did more for a young lady, socially, than her parents' money or social position."[89] Indeed, the regime of the Filipina fashion system was composed of complex relationships between Filipina elites, the media, and couturiers and couturieres. The media published articles about Filipino couturiers and couturieres and featured new designs in fashion spreads. Thus, they presented sartorial displays to a larger audience and helped to cement the position of elite Filipinas—and Filipina/o designers—in popular culture. Society pages and fashion spreads published in Philippine newspapers and magazines named designers as a way of signaling the value of the ternos worn by the women of Manila's high society. Articles that named those in attendance at important social events paid just as much attention to which designer the women wore as they did to the dresses themselves. For example, the society and fashion writer for

*Woman's World*, Ligaya Victorio-Reyes, typically featured ternos worn by "leading ladies" of Philippine society, such as young debutantes, Carnival Queens, and powerful matrons. Victorio-Reyes also used textual description to provide more information than a simple black-and-white photo could convey. Victorio-Reyes insisted that aspiring fashionistas needed to understand details like texture and color, in addition to who designed the dress.[90] Photo captions all followed a similar formula: the end of each description always included the name of the designer.[91] For example, Bubut Valdez, described as a "debutante," is shown in a studio shot, accompanied by the text, "Gown by Valera." Conchita Tirona's photograph displays her wearing a gown by Juanita Mina-Roa. To place the names Juanita Mina-Roa or Ramon Valera next to the detailed descriptions of luxurious fabrics—"the expanse of the gold satin" or the "[p]ink symphony of pleats for a July debut"—placed value on the couturier's signature, which was woven into the very design of the gowns.[92] The name of the gown's creator—just like the rich fabrics used to the make the terno—gave the dress its luxury and glamour. Moreover, society and fashion pages made it seem like the name of the dress's creator was just as important as the name of the wearer herself.

### Fashion as a Tool for Managing the Threat of the Middle Class

The impetus to control normative femininity went hand in hand with demarcating exclusivity. The stakes for defining high fashion and high society rose with the growth of the middle class, especially in Manila. The proliferation of print media spread the latest styles in women's wear, making fashion knowledge available to women (and men) outside the elite class as literacy rates rose and the middle class grew. The newspapers and magazines that published on elite fashion and high-society life had a large readership that included the growing middle class.[93] While members of the middle class did not attend exclusive balls or fashion shows, the media gave them insights into the world of high society and taught them how to decode the signs of wealth presented as style in high fashion. The construction of high fashion—including the designers, the ternos, and the wealthy women who wore couture—presented elite Filipinas as aspirational models of idealized femininity.

New technologies (like sewing machines), the proliferation of fashion schools, and the influx of Filipina manual laborers into Manila made ready-to-wear ternos more available to more women—particularly those in the growing middle class.[94]At the same time that designers established their studios and shops in Manila, so too did dressmakers who sold ready-to-wear garments, mass-produced with sewing machines.[95] According to historian Alfredo Roces, "Doñas in a hurry—or those who could afford P5 to P 25—shopped for the *ternos* in Tabora, Manila's garment district."[96] In the garment district, consumers could find "rows of white boxes containing ready-to-assemble *camisas* [blouses] and *alampay* [shawls]."[97] These developments prompted elite Filipinas to make clear distinctions between high fashion and ready-to-wear garments available to people of lower socioeconomic classes. With the growing availability of ready-to-wear gowns, Filipina elites grew increasingly anxious about how the formal gowns they wore, which signified their wealth, glamour, and cosmopolitanism, could be distinguished from those cheaper, mass-produced dresses. The answer to this dilemma came in the form of the Filipino designer—the "dictatorial modiste" that Grau lamented.

Anxieties over ready-to-wear garments were deeply tied to class formations during the US colonial period. The defining of elite society took place alongside and against significant changes in other class formations—namely the growth of a middle class sparked by a surge in educational opportunities and the appearance of new occupations in white-collar sectors.[98] During the Spanish colonial period, the state and the Catholic Church established schools mainly in the vicinity of Manila. One of the marked changes that accompanied the transition to a US colonial regime was the expansion of the education system within and beyond Manila. In addition to the industrial schools, primarily located outside Manila, the Insular Government instituted primary and secondary schools as well as universities like the University of the Philippines, modeled after US land-grant public universities. More private colleges were also founded, joining the long-established University of Santo Tomas.

The social world of Manila changed as middle-class urbanity gave people access to new ways of life. New storefronts selling goods and services catered to a growing population. More people moved to Manila to attend schools. Filipina students entered a new social environment. Advertisements for automobiles flooded print media. Cars were seen as a means to navigate the changing configurations of urban spaces. Consumer centers grew beyond Escolta. Department stores expanded. The nascent middle class of the turn of the century grew exponentially, and they could afford to send their children to schools to receive the training and prestige to enter newly formed career paths. The Insular Government's strategy of Filipinization, initiated in the early 1900s and carried into the early 1920s, opened up bureaucratic employment opportunities in the Philippine government through the creation of a Filipino civil service. The number of Filipinos employed in permanent positions in the civil service rose from roughly 3,000 in 1903 to 22,000 in 1931.[99] Additionally, the growth of an import-export economy centered in Manila increased the demand for college-educated Filipino workers in positions such as clerkships. New careers in education became attractive as teaching salaries were on the same level as government clerkships. Employment opportunities in pharmacy, medicine, and health care were also deemed attractive and lucrative careers that would lead toward upward mobility. While the matriculation rates for girls and women were significantly lower than those for boys and men, their numbers nevertheless shot up dramatically in the 1920s. The establishment of private universities for women, like the Philippine Women's University established in 1919, added to the number of Filipina college students. University education provided women the training for new careers in fields such as nursing and education. Catherine Ceniza Choy's work on the history of Filipina nurses offers important reflections on the dramatic changes to gendered and classed labor during the US colonial period. She argues that the US colonial agenda in establishing schooling and careers for women was "both liberating and exploitative."[100] Professional training "involved an imposition of control" and the regulation of feminine professions, while also expanding employment opportunities that gave women greater earning potential and increased other forms of mobility such as travel.[101]

The investment in differentiating between social classes was tied to much broader discourses on the appearances and behaviors of middle-class women in the colonial capital. The blurring of boundaries between classes was articulated through dress practices. In the 1920s, the image of the flapper circulated in the Philippines as emblematic of an urban and "modern girl." The editors of the *Modern Girl around the World* identify global iterations of this new gendered identity. The modern girl embodied a new youth culture—a "contested status of young women no longer children."[102] The modern girl was "unmarried but not a child" and therefore was regarded as having a "subversive relationship to social norms relating to heterosexuality, marriage, and motherhood."[103] In the Philippines, this subversive feminine youth was identified by her cropped hair, sometimes styled in a marcel wave or an edgy bob. These new hairstyles represented a new feminine modernity as they required the use of electric curling irons offered at one of the growing number of salons at Manila. Electricity had just been introduced in the colonial capital, a manifestation of Manila's modernization.[104]

At the same time, "flappers" garnered a reputation for wearing dresses that revealed too much of the shoulders and legs. Take, for example, an article published in *Graphic* in 1927 instructing readers on how to identify

Filipina flappers. "Kung nakabestida ka nang maikling pumapagaspas sa iyong mga hita, kahit hindi man maging eskotada o 'sleeveless' ay kasuutang iyang katulad ng karaniwang ginagamit ng ating mga dalaga ngayon—ang tawag sa iyo'y 'flapper'" (If your dress is short and brushes your thighs, even though the dresses commonly worn by our young girls now are not low cut or sleeveless—you would be called a "flapper").[105] These instructions were not simply about aesthetic elucidation. Rather, such descriptions of the flapper's dress came with moral judgment and warnings. Revealing body parts, mainly the shoulders, legs, and ankles, suggested a subversive sexuality and sensuality. The flapper style was a sartorial sexual invitation. The appearance of the flapper signaled a loss of ideal Filipina femininity. The *Graphic* article's title, "'Kiri' nga kaya ang kahulugan ng salitang 'flapper'?" ("Flirt" Is It the Meaning of the Word "Flapper"?), demonstrated that in the Philippine context, "flapper" was synonymous with the Tagalog word *kiri* (flirt).[106] In everyday vernacular, *kiri* means flirtatious in a playful, coquettish sense. However, the article positions flirtatiousness as a dangerous pastime that undermined "traditional" values of Filipina femininity—as the opposite of valued youthful "innocence." It lamented, "Very young girls and the shining pure and innocent souls, now lack consciousness, one that is cowardly and offensive in whatever name you call it it's not a nice connotation in reference to the young adolescent meaning."[107] Modernity, as embodied by the flapper, was associated with immorality, sexuality, and vice.

Even as the era of the flapper faded moving into the 1930s, anxieties over the "modern girl" persisted. Denise Cruz points out that public discourse concerning proper femininity and tensions around modernization and urbanization focused on the figure of the "coed." While the modern girl in the Philippines "eagerly consumed global capital and American popular culture," Cruz argues that she differed from other global and regional iterations of the modern girl in that "her access to university education" was the source of her modernity.[108] For many, the university and its promises of upward mobility were regarded as positive manifestations of modernity. The inclusion of young women marked Philippine progress. At the same time, universities also produced new forms of sociality, including courtship and heterosexual romance. A prominent clinical psychologist and secretary of the Cabinet of the Philippines from 1971 to 1977, Estefanía Aldaba-Lim, reflected on her time as a college student at the University of the Philippines during the 1930s. Aldaba-Lim recalled, "You get your 'crushes' only at campus affairs," and the "most popular girls got invited to be the muses of fraternities, or to serve on the ladies' committees of fiestas at boys' colleges."[109] But for some, the proliferation of the coed threatened to disappear the "traditional" Filipina. For these detractors, "the university," as Cruz argues, was "the site of the [modern girl's] dangerous replication."[110]

Attending university in the big city introduced Filipinas to a world of temptation: the cinema, jazz clubs, and dance halls, just to name a few. One of the coed's most vocal critics was Perfecto Laguio, who wrote a series of articles in the *Manila Tribune* followed by his 1932 book, *Our Modern Woman: A National Problem*. In his sensationalized writing, Laguio extolled the virtues of ideal womanhood, represented by fictional literary figures such as "the demure type of Celia of Balagtas and of Maria Clara of Rizal."[111] Denise Cruz's work on constructions of Filipina modernity and femininity demonstrates how Laguio deliberately used these celebrated literary characters to differentiate the moral from the immoral modern girl and woman, whom Laguio associated with the modern woman and coeds.[112] In his lengthy descriptions, Laguio also used coed aesthetics to underscore the differences between the modern girl and the demure "traditional" Filipina. Although flapper dresses were no longer in style by the 1930s, shorter dress hems remained in vogue. College students wore what were considered "Western"-style dresses in more casual settings. Like his predecessors, Laguio regarded these styles as sartorial evidence of the United States' bad influence and corruption of Filipino society. Laguio used detailed descriptions of the coed's appearance to denigrate her character. He wrote, "To use the vulgar term; in short morning and sport dresses barely covering the knees and leaving almost nothing of woman's mystery for the imagination to explore; in low-necked dresses of transparent silk, so tight-fitting as to reveal every curve of the body; with flesh-colored stockings: all calculated to excite the animal instinct in man."[113] The way coeds dressed dangerously revealed their bodies to the male gaze and threatened to eviscerate self-imposed masculine discipline. These dress choices, according to Laguio, were coldly calculated and intentional—hoping to ruin men's civility and reducing them to base animal instincts. Laguio joined the chorus of patriarchal ideologues who viewed women as the root of sexual temptation.[114]

Laguio's writing was part of a larger discourse that regarded the control of women as key to combating Americanization. The flapper and the coed joined another fraught image of Filipina femininity, the suffragist, whom critics argued also threatened to destroy the traditions and values of family and home. Each of these types of Filipina women aroused anxieties about the negative impacts of US modernization on Filipino values. The response to voices like Laguio's varied. Some, like Encarnación Alzona, a well-respected historian, professor, and at one point chair of the history department at the University of the Philippines, defended young women attending college and emphasized in her teaching, writing, and speeches the importance of their contributions to the making of an independent nation.[115] Others defended the importance of women receiving a college education while simultaneously demanding that these young women embody "traditional" Filipina values of propriety and moral behavior.[116] Another reaction to criticism of the modern girl doubled down on the power of the terno. Elite Filipinas depended on the terno to foil the flapper and the coed. For example, elite women fighting for voting rights in the 1930s deliberately displayed the terno in their campaigns to present a nonthreatening Filipina modernity. This terno-wearing suffragist sartorially demonstrated a deep investment in normative gender values that would not be threatened or erased by their enfranchisement. Through what Mina Roces calls "pañuelo activism," these terno-wearing suffragists reframed Filipina modernity. The terno, as a fashionable and therefore modern garment, allowed elite Filipinas to create an appearance of modernity associated with respectability.[117]

The anxieties centered on the flapper of the 1920s and the coed of the 1930s were not just about protecting women or, rather, protecting societal norms from unruly women. They were also anxieties about class formations. Because more men occupied more roles in civil governance, they had the potential to elevate the statuses of their families. Women, particularly the matriarchs of these families, supplemented family incomes, and at times earned more than their husbands, which allowed families to send multiple children to universities in Manila.[118] Estefanía Aldaba-Lim and her ten siblings all attended university in Manila. Her father was a provincial treasurer and received a monthly salary of 290 pesos—"a lot of money then," she contends, but not enough to live comfortably and pay for college tuition.[119] But her mother created a diamond business that was so lucrative that she "was able to fund the family needs."[120] Beyond fulfilling needs, Aldaba-Lim recounts, her mother's business allowed them to "afford a certain amount of luxury," such as having enough money to purchase a wardrobe so that the eldest sister was "considered one of the best-dressed colegialas of her time" at Philippine Women's University.[121]

The rising numbers of Filipinas attending schools and finding white-collar work in Manila sparked new forms of contact and interaction between middle-class and elite Filipinas. The creation and enforcement of dress regulations in schools and workplaces became one strategy to mitigate the tensions and debates over modern femininity and new class formations. Education officials and supporters promoted the enforcement of school uniforms as a means of working toward a modern and more democratic society. In a speech delivered at the Teachers' Convention at Santa Clara School in Manila in 1928, Paz Mendoza-Guazón, an affluent, well-respected doctor, writer, and suffragist, extolled the virtues of a uniform. Reflecting on her own experiences in school and later in the health profession, she argued that "the uniform broke down social differences, because every one of us felt that we were friends and co-workers."[122] Mendoza-Guazón repeated the democratizing spirit of the uniform in an essay about young women and "good manners," published in 1931, in which she writes, "You go to school or to the office to work and study, not to display the wealth of your wardrobe."[123] While personal style could convey one's class and social status with details like a long train, the type of fabric one's clothes were made of, and the presence or lack of embellishments, uniforms would erase sartorial difference. The elimination of clothing's semiotic details, according to Mendoza-Guazón, would allow Filipina students and professionals from different social classes to forge relationships with one another and, perhaps more importantly, to focus on work and studying. The kinds of petty politics of wearing one's status and asserting hierarchies of difference, she asserted, distracted students from doing good work.

The need for Mendoza-Guazón and others to vocalize a defense of the uniform emerged from resistance to the regulation of dress practices. To erase class and social differences was perceived as threatening the hierarchies of power that structured much of Philippine society. Catherine Ceniza Choy notes that much like the initial families recruited for the School of Household Industries, American-established nursing schools originally targeted elite Filipino families. But these Filipinas and their families "opposed the use of [the] American-style nursing uniform, as its absence of a long train signified lower-class status."[124] Despite Mendoza-Guazón's message about uniforms' potential for democratization, fears over the blurring of class distinctions persisted. Elites' investment in maintaining their status prompted other methods of policing dress practices to sustain class boundaries. Although the US colonial regime did not enforce sumptuary laws, Filipino elites regarded dressing as someone of a higher class or "passing" as an elite to be taboo.[125] Unlike uniforms, dress practices in social settings could not be officially regulated through policy. However, circulating messages about dress expectations could use the normalization of sartorial practices as a policing tactic. Mendoza-Guazón—despite advocating for school uniforms to make Filipina students appear equal—warned Filipinas, "Wear as fine clothes as you can afford; be as fashionable as you like; but consider *Place, Time, Occasion, Age* and the *Size of your Income.*"[126] She underscored her point by commanding her readers to "dress according to your means."[127] She went on to say, "A Poor boy or girl who exhibits dresses that only the well-to-do can afford arouses suspicion."[128] Mendoza-Guazón presumes that those who would feel suspicion are those of the elite classes, who possessed the authority to judge and police dress practices. The members of the privileged class, whom Mendoza-Guazón simply refers to as "people," "sometimes know how much money you have in your pocket, how much your parents are worth without telling anyone. So, if by adopting the airs of a millionaire or heiress you think you could deceive people, you are simply deceiving yourself."[129] Even within the context of a growing movement toward democratization and women's suffrage, Filipino elites were deeply invested in maintaining distinct class lines.[130] Equality through education and access to labor and capital could only go so far. In urban Manila, where people of different classes constantly came in contact with one another, performing one's proper class through dress was crucial. This class exclusion reinforced the exceptionality of Filipina high fashion. For women, the predominant dress of the well-to-do was the terno. Mendoza-Guazón reinforced the idea that only women of the upper echelons of society could wear these glamorous and luxurious garments. The creation of high fashion occurred tangentially to the crystallization of a Filipino high society based in Manila. Both high fashion and high society depended on a notion of exclusivity. Defining precisely who could legitimately wear Filipiniana formal dresses contributed to the exclusivity of a high-fashion system.

Efforts to distinguish class hierarchies also intersected with ethnic differences. Filipina elites defined the boundaries of Filipina high fashion along ethnic lines. The selection of the terno as the style of Filipina high fashion not only demarcated elite dress, but it also constructed hierarchies that categorized other kinds of ethnic garb as *probinsyana* (provincial), unmodern, and unfashionable. The *balintawak*, for example, was very similar to the traje de mestiza and the terno, with its stiff, oversized butterfly sleeves and separate skirt. This skirt, however, was much shorter than the formal gown and did not have a train. Historian Alfredo Roces's encyclopedia of Filipino heritage echoes early twentieth-century attitudes: "The *terno* should be distinguished from such other Filipina dresses as the informal *balintawak* and the *patadyong*. Lacking the *terno*'s svelte sophistication, these rural costumes are worn mainly by barefoot dancers of the *tinikling* and by carabao-riding maidens in the landscapes of Amorsolo."[131] Similarly, fashion spreads and society pages excluded other forms of dress practiced throughout the archipelago. Textiles, clothing, and accessories worn in the hundreds of non-Christian communities like the Bagobo, T'boli, Mandaya, or B'laan in Southern Mindanao were presented not as fashion or dress but as ethnic "costumes." On the rare occasion that fashion platforms such as the media and public-facing events like the Manila Carnival mentioned dress practices outside the urban landscape, they adopted racist anthropological language, portraying these particular ethnic groups as strange and exotic.[132] As a result, the fashion system contributed to the minoritization of ethnic and religious groups who were not part of the larger Christian Filipino hegemonic majority that determined what constituted Filipino identity. Conscious of their shifting roles—a direct result of white American racism and changes in class dynamics—elite Filipinas felt similar to their ilustrado predecessors. Like the educated and often elite Filipinos of the late nineteenth century, elite Filipinas of the 1920s and 1930s resented race and class misrepresentations of their privileged status.[133] Revamping Filipina formal gowns into a distinctly Filipina high fashion allowed Filipinas to negotiate racial, class, and gender ideologies. Creating a system of high fashion helped elite Filipinas redefine Philippine—and more specifically, Manila—high society.

## Dressing for a Nation-to-Be: The Commonwealth Period

The linked economies of the Philippines and the United States that precipitated urbanization and the emergence of new, glamorous lifestyles during World War I were met, at the beginning of 1921, with the challenges of the economic recession. Although the Philippines began to crawl out of the recession toward the end of the 1920s, the global economic depression caused a plummet in exports in 1929 and 1930. In both urban and rural areas of the Philippines, movements against the uneven distribution of wealth spread. Laborers and unions organized strikes. At the same time, the push for Philippine independence from US colonialism persisted with varying and often competing visions of a future nation. The 1934 Tydings-McDuffie Act set into motion a ten-year phased schedule that would "prepare" the Philippines for eventual independence. Consequently, the Philippines became a commonwealth in 1935. Economic depression, the impending loss of a US export market, machinations by the US to retain its economic benefits, and questions over what the next ten years and the promise of independence would hold created an uncertain future for Filipinos.[134]

The 1930s terno played a key role in navigating the shifting social, economic, and political systems. Both the terno and its production became fertile grounds on which to construct a narrative of nationalist progress and maturation that simultaneously evoked a sense of readiness for independence and obfuscated the destruction of US colonialism. Nationalist narratives expressed through the terno combated the political and economic uncertainty of the 1930s. The terno was a sartorial declaration of national identity and tradition as well as a method for measuring Filipina modernity. Feminist scholars like Lauren Berlant, Norma Alarcón, Caren Caplan, and Minoo Moallem have shown the key role that gender played in the formation of a national identity, such as the ways in which the "maternal-beloved feminine imagery" came to represent the national body.[135] Reynaldo Ileto and others have shown how *Inang Bayan*, the image of the nation as mother, was used to create a new collective Filipino identity during the Revolution.[136] In these imaginings of the nation, the symbolic woman is one-dimensional and unchanging, representing an essential past that is held up as the heart of an imagined community. But in the 1930s, the fashion system—embodied in the terno—provided a narrative of movement and momentum toward a "coming of age." The terno and stories about Filipina fashion underscored a rising awareness of the colonial government's efforts to move into a commonwealth period and to close off US markets; competing political parties were vying for control over a nation in the making. Unlike a national costume—a garment revered as a snapshot frozen in time—the terno celebrated change and new styles.[137] In this way, the terno and its ever-evolving form came to designate the Philippines as a modern nation.

Filipina elites' sartorial performances via the terno communicated a specific type of Filipina modernity. Colonial projects presented the modernization of Filipinas as a universal process. Filipina elites, however, worked to distinguish their own brand of modernity that rested on urbanity, glamour, and cosmopolitanism to convey respectability as well as Filipina nationalism. In addition to signifying luxury, the terno also represented modesty, an important part of the Filipina feminine ideal. Ligaya Victorio-Reyes, a celebrated fiction writer who also wrote about fashion and society for various Manila publications, addressed the terno's power in a 1938 article, "Feminina." The caption accompanying a staged studio photograph of a young woman reads, "With her hair up and in the J. M. Roa version of the famous costume, Rosario is the Maria Clara of a modern Ibarra's dreams (Photo by Juan de la Cruz Studio)."[138] Maria Clara, the famous character from Jose Rizal's canonical novel, *Noli me tangere*, a late nineteenth-century critique of the corruption of Spanish friars in the Philippines, signified ideal Filipina femininity.[139] She was revered for her beauty, her demure nature, her modesty, and her piety. Because of the association between Maria Clara and ideal Filipina beauty and femininity, the traje de mestiza was also referred to as the Maria Claria gown. The Maria Clara gown signified beauty and modesty in its careful covering of its wearer's body while also emphasizing the prestige of mestiza Filipinas. Victorio-Reyes's reference to Maria Clara and Juan Crisostomo Ibarra evokes these revered qualities. At the same time, Victorio-Reyes modified the trope—as the gown itself was modified—highlighting its modern qualities as a fashionable and stylish dress. Victorio-Reyes argued that while elite women became modernized, they still upheld the revered qualities embodied by Maria Clara. Through the terno, Filipinas maintained gender norms while also presenting the image of a respectable modern Filipina—a new national image that mediated the "traditional" and the "modern." As a national dress, the terno simultaneously represented ideal Filipina femininity in an emerging Philippine nation and Filipina high fashion.

Later in 1938, Victorio-Reyes published a long-form piece titled "Evolution of the Mestiza Dress." In this piece, Victorio-Reyes contends that the "mestiza dress," a catchall phrase that encompassed the traje de mestiza and the terno, was "one of the most beautiful creations that fashion ever played with."[140] She supports her point by detailing the constantly shifting styles of the terno.[141] Victorio-Reyes traces the fashion history of the terno over the years, starting in the mid-1800s. She reviews the style of dress in each decade, highlighting the changes and similarities between the gowns, noting "the demure simplicity of the eighties, the coquettish fussiness of the nineties, the graceful daring frankness of the twentieth century."[142] Victorio-Reyes points to specific moments that, in her view, reflect significant changes in Filipina character. She notes one such critical moment for Filipina fashion in the 1920s, explaining that Filipina fashion began to bloom in that decade, like a young girl in the first moments of womanhood. Victorio-Reyes argues that this maturation marks a new awareness of high fashion. But Reyes believes that Filipina fashion came into its own in the 1930s when it "declared alliance with universal style which generations of dreamers all over the world had perfected."[143] It was at this moment, she maintains, that the "mestiza dress in all its possibilities of charm, reach[ed] a glorified height which only the changes in the Filipino woman herself can hope to surpass."[144] Reyes portrays this maturation as Filipina fashion finally connecting to global systems of high fashion and finally living up to its full potential as a modern gown.

The metaphor of fashion as a little girl growing into the full blossom of womanhood is a progress narrative. The idea of maturation mirrored the language and attitudes of Filipino readiness for self-governance. During the 1930s, in particular, preserving distinctly Filipina characteristics while also exhibiting cosmopolitan qualities helped to construct the modern woman-hood envisioned by Filipina elites. During this decade, nationalist discourses intensified the idea that the terno symbolized Filipino national identity. In 1934, the newly formed National Economic Protectionism Association (NEPA) organized a fashion show that exhibited ternos as well as European-style gowns made of local fabrics. Impressed with the gowns at the fashion show—and in particular, the "Commonwealth Terno"—Walter Robb, editor of the *American Chamber of Commerce Journal*, wrote to Carmen Melencio, "[Your terno] breathed style.... I may add that to me it was the first suc-cess with the Philippine costume I have ever seen. ... You are the first, in my opinion, to make the costume what it should be; namely a stylish dress—I mean one that would be stylish anywhere—yet at the same time highly na-tional. Please accept our warm congratulations."[145] This note attempted to legitimize Filipina fashion from an American perspective. However, Filipina fashion had long claimed its style authority as distinct from American influ-ence and did not therefore need American approval. The approach of inde-pendence and the heightened pressure to construct a cohesive Philippine national identity resulted in the creation of a "Commonwealth Terno," which was deliberately designed to represent a Filipino national identity in both style and fabric used for the gown.[146] The Commonwealth terno was made of local textiles only—like piña and jusi—and had a new "modern" silhouette that did away with the traditional train to allow for greater freedom of move-ment. The design responded to earlier criticisms made by US officials that long trains prevented women and girls from being efficient and productive in their work.[147] NEPA positioned the gown as emblematic of the promise of a modern Philippine nation. It promoted the use of local materials, and its unique cut was up to date rather than "traditional" and stagnant.[148] For the members of the American Chamber of Commerce, using Philippine textiles while also making changes to the terno's style signified the maturation of the Filipina fashion system.

The promotion of local materials also demonstrated the influence of eco-nomic developments on the Filipina fashion system. At the same time, using local textiles reflected a greater sense of urgency around funneling capital into Philippine industries. The Commonwealth terno and the NEPA fashion show played key parts in attempts to mitigate the damage of the global eco-nomic depression that was further exacerbated by the way that the US gov-ernment structured "independence." The Great Depression not only made US markets vulnerable, it also devastated the Philippines.[149] By 1935, the Com-monwealth government was attempting to strengthen a Philippine economy that was structured to be completely dependent on the United States. The Tydings-McDuffie Act dictated that US exports to the Philippines were to be free from tariffs and duties, and it placed stringent quotas on Philippine exports to the United States. For the Commonwealth, imminent independence also meant losing access to US markets and economic support.[150] As a result, the new Commonwealth government felt pressured to encourage economic growth.[151] In addition to its efforts toward diversifying exports, modernizing the manufacturing and energy industries, and modernizing the agricultural sector, the Commonwealth government also hoped expand domestic business.[152] Thus, made-to-order and ready-to wear ternos were enfolded into proto-nationalist economic strategies, bolstering the use of the Filipina dress to increase the demand for locally produced textiles and local labor. NEPA strongly encouraged the use of Philippine-made textiles for Filipiniana gowns through print campaigns and spectacles like the Commonwealth fashion show during the Philippine Exposition. These "special programs" were organized to "inculcate a spirit of economic nationalism."[153]

Popular media also bolstered these economic initiatives. Fashion pages promoted piña and jusi, declaring that these textiles were as luxurious as imported materials, if not more so.[154] The March 1933 issue of *Graphic* ran an article titled "'Pinocpoc' and Piña: Smart Substitutes for Linen, Organdy, and Taffeta," which endorsed local fabrics by comparing them to fancy imported textiles. It contended that "*jusi* or *piña* can vie with such rich fabrics as satin, charmeuse, velvet, lace, crepe, and tissue cloth in attractiveness and elegance for a skirt for evening wear as shown by the '*terno*' worn by Pacita de los Reyes in the Fashion Show held at the auditorium of the last Manila Carnival."[155] The article gave a detailed comparison of Philippine and foreign textiles, encouraging both dressmakers and consumers to opt for local products, calling them the fabrics of choice when trying to look fashionable. These fabrics garnered much "admiration" and "attracted the most attention" at functions held at the University Club, the place where "Manila's most popular debutantes went."[156] Elite organizations also bolstered "made in the Philippines" protectionist efforts. While many club events had already implemented dress codes, they now required that ternos be made from "piña and other native weaves."[157]

The terno and the high-fashion system in the Philippines thus animated nationalist frameworks and provided a steady narrative of progress and maturation. At the same time, the terno and fashion writing about Filipina fashion asserted Filipinas' place in the formation of a Philippine nation. During the Commonwealth period, Filipina feminists and suffragists organized to enfranchise women and earn the right to vote, a right which they would not gain until 1937. The suffrage question was a fraught and critical political issue in the 1930s. Historian Mina Roces argues that because suffragists deliberately and regularly wore the terno and pañuelo to official occasions and to work, the terno also became identified with suffragists who were referred to as *"pañuelo* actvists."[158] For fashion writers like Ligaya Victorio-Reyes, the terno and the changes in Filipina fashion were not just about the evolution of the Philippine nation; the story was specifically about recognizing modern Filipinas as equal citizens. Victorio-Reyes posited that fashion was "like a little girl grown tall," likening fashion to a girl maturing into womanhood as a metaphor for the making of a nation. But she went on to state that the "mestiza dress is not only a faithful record of the changing fashions in the Philippines"; the dress also "mirrors the struggles of a womanhood emerging from inhibitions and impositions of olden times to attain its state of present-day freedom."[159] For Victorio-Reyes, the story of the "Evolution of the Mestiza Dress" was about "the dream of beauty," and the "possibilities" offered by fashion, the nation, and Filipinas themselves.[160]

### The Global Reaches and Limits of Filipina High Fashion

The global dimensions of Filipina high fashion went beyond importing foreign materials and styles to the Philippines. The circulation of Filipina gowns was not prohibited by the boundaries of the islands. Instead, the terno and its material and aesthetic elements took on different meanings when they circulated in transnational currents. Different systems of race, gender, and class influenced how Filipina fashions were received. As such, while the terno lived up to Filipina cosmopolitan aspirations by moving beyond Philippine borders, it still faced the limitations of colonialism and white supremacy that created structural and systemic regimes of power and impeded Filipina fashion systems from being recognized as *global* high fashion.

Minh-hà Phạm describes hegemonic structures of fashion as instituting a "very specific authorial labor relationship where the West is the authorial source of global fashion."[161] Authorship in Western hegemonic fashion systems, argues Phạm, perpetuates notions of "entitlement" that manifest in "citational colonialism."[162] That is, Western fashion systematically erases non-Western authorship and perpetuates the idea that fashion cannot originate or come from nonwhite creators. In this system, Western designers claim "inspiration" from non-Western styles of dress, incorporate elements into their own designs, and profess this as a form of elevation. European haute couture designers, in other words, enacted orientalist fantasies. One of the more noted examples of this kind of fashion colonialism was Paul Poiret's harem pants, which he claimed were inspired by *Arabian Nights*.[163] Perhaps less well-known is the influence of Filipina formal dress styles on evening gowns created for American women. The March 1, 1936, issue of *Vogue* ran an article, "Fashion: Extremes Meet at Paris Spring Collections," on sheer evening gowns for the spring season. The extremes in the article referred to both the proportions of the evening gown sleeves and its mimicry of the terno's butterfly sleeves. A caption for one dress sketch describes a "big-sleeved, slim-lined dinner-dress . . . made of rosy red organza with a lovely white flower design penciled over it. The flare in the skirt balances the width in the sleeves and gives a very chic look—a bit like the frocks worn by Filipino women."[164] According to the magazine, this gown could be purchased at high-end boutiques like I. Magnin (San Francisco), Hattie Carnegie (New York City), and Martha Weathered (Chicago). This 1936 *Vogue* article built on and perpetuated American images and descriptions of Filipina appearance and dress that circulated widely in the early years of the US colonialization through travel literature, stereographs, and newspapers. But here, the beauty regime of empire had shifted so that dress was not just a marker of difference but became an extractable form for imitation. *Vogue*'s promotion of 1936 Paris spring collections demonstrated that American women could readily wear styles that were imitations of the Filipina fashion they had once considered beneath them in race, culture, style, and taste.[165]

The process of making foreign "costumes" into haute couture required the authority of the European designer. Just as Lanvin had made *chinoiserie* popular among American and European consumers, French designer Madeleine Vionnet drew from Filipina styles for her 1936 spring collection. *Vogue* called the Filipina styles featured in the collection "extreme."[166] However, the article declared that the haute couture designer had the power to transform what were deemed radically different styles into fashion, stating, "Credit this season goes to the designer and not to history or art. If a designer varies his ideas, it is not because he is confused but because he is inspired."[167] The article went on to describe how garments from Vionnet's collection showed her "weakness for high shouldered Filipino sleeves with square folded fullness."[168] In the following issue, *Vogue* again referenced Filipina butterfly sleeves, claiming that mannequins "with shoulders built out like Filipino girls" could be found in Paris salons.[169] The magazine lauded Vionnet's ingenuity, stating, "always queen of dramatic, subtle cut, Vionnet gives the world this year a new shoulder—a crisp folded one not unlike a Filipino woman's."[170]

Because of the deeply racist treatment of nonwhite dress as ethnic costumes that were frozen in time and therefore unfashionable in Western fashion systems, these styles became fashionable only when interpreted and used by Western designers. Vionnet, as a French designer, could claim credit for creating "new" types of cuts and silhouettes. As such, Western—and in particular, Parisian—high-fashion systems profited from taking styles from "exotic costumes" and transforming them into haute couture.

Vogue's illustration looks a lot like the Filipina gowns pictured in Manila-based magazines, such as Belen's dresses in Woman's World. The bell-like sleeves and mermaid silhouettes that flared at the knees were popular styles worn by fashionable women in both the Philippines and the United States. It is difficult to trace the provenance of formal gowns. For example, Women's World claimed the combination of bell sleeves and mermaid silhouette was a Filipina design inspired by Spanish styles, while Vogue described it as a Western frock with traces of Filipina influence. Either way, there are similarities between these gowns that articulate transnational exchange, appropriation, and translation on both ends. In the dominant global fashion systems, though, these similarities were often attributed to colonial imitation and aping. The absence of Filipina/o designers from global fashion systems demonstrates the limitations placed on Filipina fashion, with the exception of Ramon Valera.[171]

Despite the limits set by hegemonic Western-based systems of high fashion, Filipinas continued to wear the terno. As in the Philippines, elite Filipinas circulating in the United States wore ternos only for special occasions.[172] Historian Sarah Steinbock-Pratt examines how Filipina pensionadas (sponsored students) who attended American colleges and universities wore ternos strategically to make claims to a Filipino national identity.[173] In an interview, Alicia Syquia de Quirino recalls, "Estando en América, . . . asistíamos a los bailes . . . [y] siempre trajeadas a la mestiza, aun con aquel frio de invierno, a dieciocho grados bajo cero" (While in America, . . . we attended dances [and] always dressed in the mestiza style, even in the cold of winter, at eighteen degrees below zero).[174] There are a number of reasons why de Quirino and other Filipino women would choose to wear a terno while attending events in the United States. Some wore the terno to perform their Filipino identity. The selection of the terno was also a sartorial statement of beauty. De Quirino professed, "Usted no puede imaginarse la admiración que causábamos cuando entrábamos en el salón con aquel traje vaporoso. Les oíamos a los concurrentes cuchichear" (You cannot imagine the admiration that we drew when we entered the room with that floaty dress. I heard those in attendance whispering).[175] De Quirino took pleasure in the reactions her gown elicited.

Even if American women did not consider the gown high fashion, de Quirino was recognized and reveled in their admiring gaze. In a published interview between Caroline Crawford, who represented the Young Women's Christian Association, and Solita Garduño, a Filipina pensionada whom the organization hoped to sponsor, Crawford expressed her admiration for Garduño's terno. She remarked, "If all the native costumes are as fascinating and as charming as Miss Garduño's, I should think they would cling to them. No evening gown of ours could be more captivating."[176] Similarly, an article celebrating "Filipino Night," an event showcasing "bits of Philippine life" and held on October 22, 1926, claimed, "Filipino girls in native costume were the main attraction."[177] The US social terrain was different from Manila's. These Filipino women were navigating the specific racist and gendered hierarchies of the metropole. Nevertheless, much like their counterparts in the Philippines, they used the terno as a form of empowerment. They had confidence in the glamour of the terno and the artistry of its design. They used beauty and fashion aggressively to gain admiration and to take pleasure from it.

The 1920s and 1930s witnessed dramatic changes to systems of Filipina dress, style, and regimes of beauty. Fashion allowed elite Filipinas to maneuver through significant ruptures in the colonial Philippine cultural, social, political, and economic landscapes. For Filipinas of the elite class, the formal Filipiniana gown signified an ideal Filipina woman, one associated with wealth, mestiza identity, and cosmopolitanism. Through the terno, elite Filipinas also responded to the racist and segregationist logics of US racial paradigms that were pervasive throughout the empire. At the same time, they carved out an elite identity that was distinct from that of the growing middle class. In contrast to the country dresses of the provinces, the terno— with its luxurious fabric, elaborate details, and distinct cut—embodied an elite mestiza style.

EPILOGUE

*Protectionism and Preparedness*

*under Overlapping Empires*

This book began with stories of sartorial confrontations and tensions that highlight the messy links between the suspension of Philippine independence, the transition from a Spanish to a US imperial regime, and the Philippine-American War. Such tensions were shaped by the uncertainty of Philippine nationhood, a new colonial regime, and warfare. I end this book at another moment that mirrored the uncertainty of the turn of the century. The 1930s was also a time of heightened precarity for Filipinos, characterized by economic instability, a murky future as a possible independent nation, and another war on the horizon: World War II. The Philippines once again found itself caught in the overlap between two empires, this time between the United States and Japan.

The beauty regime framework draws attention to how Filipinos and the Philippines as a commonwealth preparing for independence witnessed and experienced the operations of the US and Japanese empires. Although the fashion and beauty economies of the 1920s and 1930s in many ways affirmed these decades as the "golden age" of Philippine history, in the years leading up to World War II and Japanese colonial occupation, the fashion and beauty world also took on an atmosphere of protection and preparedness. The dual threads of protectionism and preparedness emerged as anxieties rose in the 1930s. During the Commonwealth period, postcolonial anticipation about what nationhood and independence would look like generated anxiety. This uncertainty resulted from the decades-long US colonialism that had built a "system of production that aggravated conditions of underdevelopment" in the Philippines for the economic benefit of the United States—a disparity that would endure long after "independence."[1] With political sovereignty looming on the horizon, the future of the nation of the Philippines remained precarious.

The imperial competition between the United States and Japan manifested in many ways even prior to the start of World War II. For example, market competition in textiles turned into contentious battles over consumers in the Philippines. The newly formed Commonwealth government struggled to find ways to protect the Philippine economy when it was still very much dependent on the United States. When the tensions and competition between two empires expanded beyond market competition and trade agreements, and when it became clear that war was on its way, news reporting explicitly told Filipinas that new modes of self-styling would prepare them to navigate a war when it emerged.[2] New wartime fashion, it seemed, would offer protection to Filipinas. In their everyday lives, Filipinas would have been aware of tensions between the two empires, and they would have increasingly felt anticipation and anxiety over their uncertain future.

## Fashioning Protectionism

After the signing of the Independence Act or the Tydings-McDuffie Act in 1934 and the subsequent formation of the Philippine Commonwealth in 1935, the anticipation of Philippine independence, no matter how delayed, brought into question what trade relations would look like between the Philippines, the United States, and other competitors—namely, Japan. Up to that point, the United States had enjoyed a duty-free import-export system, which allowed cheap manufactured goods, including fashion commodities, to be imported into the United States from the Philippines. This system had also enabled US textiles, namely cotton, to take advantage of a huge market expansion in the Philippines.

The economic depression of the 1930s hit all facets of the US economy and made maintaining an export economy in the Philippines all the more imperative for US textile manufacturers and exporters. At that time, cotton was the second largest manufacturing industry in the United States; it had been built on the centuries-old white supremacist oppressive system of enslaved Black labor and relied on the continuance of exploitative labor systems well into the twentieth century.[3] Like so many other industries, US-based cotton manufacturers relied on exports into markets outside of the continental United States. Cotton was a principal import between the Philippines and the United States. While cotton was used in a number of products, it was primarily used for the garments constructed in the Philippines and sold to American consumers.[4] Cotton was also marketed as a lightweight and durable textile for everyday use and as a staple fabric for ready-to-wear clothing in the Philippines. While Filipiniana gowns signified high fashion, cotton dresses were worn at schools, in workplaces, for informal daytime social occasions such as luncheons, and for play at leisurely sports. Children's clothing was also made from an array of cotton-derived textiles. The changing social world of the colonial Philippines demanded changing clothes, and the United States promised to outfit modern subjects properly. The Philippines was a vital market precisely because, as a colony, tariffs did not cut into US manufacturers' profits. Even as the Philippines transitioned into a commonwealth and moved toward independence, the Tydings-McDuffie Act protected US economic interests by keeping US imports free of tariffs and duties while imposing quotas and taxes on Philippine exports to the US.[5]

At the same time, this colony in transition was impacted by the growing power of another empire. The Philippines felt and saw the emergence of the Japanese empire well before it was invaded by the Japanese military in December 1941. During the Commonwealth period, Japanese power was present in the material culture of beauty regimes. According to American cotton manufacturers, competition from Japanese textile exporters and impending Philippine independence were the causes of sharp declines in American profits in the Philippines. For the most part, the Tydings-McDuffie Act produced a substantial increase in the United States' share of all imported products to the Philippines, except cotton textiles.[6] On July 9, 1935, Governor-General Frank Murphy reported the declining numbers to the chief of the Bureau of Insular Affairs. Murphy stated that in regard to cotton imports into the Philippines, the decline on a quantity basis went from 72 percent of the total imports in 1932, to 67 percent in 1933, to 40 percent in 1934. Up to that point in 1935, the US share was only 30 percent of the total number of cotton imports.[7]

Individual companies and textile associations, such as the Textiles Exporters Association wrote to state representatives and directly to the Bureau of Insular Affairs that American cotton could neither compete with the dramatically lower prices of cotton imported from Japan nor with Japan's increasing production of a cheaper and sturdier textile, rayon.[8] As part of their imperial expansion and colonialism in Asia and the Pacific, Japan had taken over textile mills in China and India and became a direct competitor to other imperial powers like the United States and Britain.[9] In 1933, prior to the passing of the Tydings-McDuffie Act, Edgar Hesslein, president of the textile company Neuss, Hesslein & Co., Inc., forwarded a cablegram from another textile firm to the Bureau of Insular Affairs. The text warned that "Japanese and Chinese grey and white goods will inevitably crowd out our merchandise. Japanese boycott weakening. Bringing all pressure possible to increase Philippine tariff."[10] American manufacturers had greatly benefited from Chinese merchants' boycott of Japanese goods, a show of protest and resistance against Japanese imperialism and the colonization of China. But the waning boycott and the low cost of Japanese products worried American manufacturers who feared Japan's hold on other industries, like rubber shoes.[11] As Japan's economic threat seemed only to strengthen over time, American textile importers continued to express their frustration to the Bureau of Insular Affairs. A year later, another letter from Hesslein that was copied and shared with several US agencies declared, "The United States cotton textile trade has fallen off not only in the Philippine islands but in practically all other areas of the world during the past year due to Japanese competition. During this period the Japanese have made substantial gains in this trade on the mainland of the United States. Several factors contribute to this, one of which is undoubtedly dependent upon the efficiency of the cotton textile industry in the United States."[12] United States cotton manufacturers proposed a number of different methods for preserving their profits and markets in the Philippines. They called for protectionist strategies typically associated with national and domestic tactics, such as a quantitative allocation that guaranteed the Philippines would import the majority of their textiles from the United States. From 1933 to 1935, US cotton manufacturers aggressively lobbied for the United States to press legislators in the Philippines to either increase tariffs on Japanese imports or institute a quota system. United States manufacturers expressed deep frustration with what they considered nonaction and a lack of sympathy from government officials in the Bureau of Insular Affairs and the State Department. The State Department replied to the governor-general that it was "inconsistent with the economic policy of the US to initiate measures for radically increasing or blocking trade."[13]

In 1935, US government agents across departments formed an interdepartmental committee to address the complexities of the ties between Japan, the Philippines, and the United States.[14] By July of that year, Murphy, who had previously stated that he did not believe Japan posed a serious threat to American textile manufacturers, reversed his stance. Murphy wrote to the Secretary of War, "It is believed that a satisfactory adjustment of our trade relations with the United States would be materially aided and facilitated by an affective adjustment of import duties on textiles and other products that would afford prompt relief to American and Philippine interests, without subjecting other countries to unfair treatment or imposing unreasonable and excessive burdens on the consuming public."[15] Murphy framed raising tariffs and duties on Japanese imports as being equally favorable to the Philippines, Filipino consumers, and the United States. He also carefully worded his letter to portray such changes as fair to US competitors and Filipino consumers. The circumspect wording reflects Murphy's desire to assuage American textile lobbyists and maintain favorable diplomatic relations with Japan.[16] United States officials reasoned that "the question of cotton textile trade in the Philippines islands is being very carefully studied by the Interdepartmental Committee," and that careful and slow proceedings were necessary to find "mutually acceptable" "adjustments" between both Japan and the United States.[17] United States government officials felt the need to tread carefully in negotiations with Japan because, as Creed Cox wrote in a memorandum to the Secretary of War, the "relationship to Japanese–United States trade should not be lost of sight. The trade between Japan and the United States in 1934 was over $325,000,000, about two-thirds of which were purchases by Japan from the United States, one third being purchases by the United States from Japan."[18] The mutually acceptable adjustments, however, did not include the perspective of Filipino officials. An editorial, "Colonial Pilates," published in the *Philippines Herald* on August 3, 1935, described trade negotiations over the Philippine market as deliberately excluding Filipinos. The editorial stated, "Japan wants a portion of [the Philippine market] and America also wants a portion of it. And where does the Philippines get in? Well the Philippines gets in nowhere. There is no business of the Filipinos, but of America's and Japan's exclusively."[19] The rhetoric and actions of US officials provide a different picture from that of the United States as determined rescuer of the Philippines from Japan's grip.

The confidence American textile industry leaders had in gaining favorable legislation in the Philippines both before and after the establishment of the Commonwealth government speaks to the kind of power and authority the US continued to have over the Philippines. Textile associations' appeals to the Bureau of Insular Affairs and the United States Congress warned that the US government's inattention would lead to the decimation of the textile industry and the loss of American jobs at mills and processing centers.

In their pleas for the implementation of protectionist policies, American cotton exporters and their supporters created a sense of urgency that was amplified, in part, through their use of racist discourse in portraying the Japanese threat to the US economy. Lobbyists used broad generalities that mirrored the language of Yellow Peril to make their case.[20] A private report from Neuss, Hesslein & Co., Inc., to Governor-General Frank Murphy urgently demanded that "Japan must be stopped and our Government awaked to this critical and alarming condition of affairs."[21] Most literature on American racism against people of Japanese heritage focuses on the "Japanese threat" in the form of military aggression, as "fifth columns" planted in the United States, or in terms of Japanese farmers who threatened white American jobs. Here, however, the threats posed were in the realm of fashion and imitation.[22]

American textile companies attempted to smear Japanese manufacturers' reputations by labeling them "notoriously incompetent" yet cunning in their deceit. A letter from New York–based textile exporter Neuss, Hesslein & Co., Inc., to the chief of the Bureau of Insular Affairs enumerated the problems with Japanese textiles. The letter variously charged that the "cloths [the Japanese] produce are imitations of American productions"; "[the Japanese] are notoriously incompetent in the way of invention but are all the best imitators"; "[the fabrics] are most inferior quality and wear on the average, only half as long as similar American fabrics"; and "[the Japanese] are ruthless and hit below the belt continuously."[23] As Minh-hà Phạm has pointed out in her work on imitation and fashion authorship, "Not all copying is valued equally," as "fashion's spectrum of originality is coded in different ways."[24] It is difficult to trace the actual "origins" of cotton textiles, weaves, and patterns. However, US-based companies' accusations built on the myth of origins, which presumes white Western authority and superiority. This discourse contributed to the notion that Asians' capacity for valuable production was limited to the level of copying and imitation they performed. Moreover, rather than presenting imitation in terms of the common Western practices of "homage" or "inspiration," it was seen instead as an underhanded form of theft. The threat of Japanese deceit, warned American textile companies, would eventually lead to the "total subjugation and eventual extermination of Western civilization."[25]

American textile companies also claimed to be advocating for the protection of unsuspecting Filipino consumers. A detailed letter accompanied by a dozen swatches of Japanese textiles from the Manila-based general manager of Neuss, Hesslein & Co., Inc., relied on another racist trope to fuel their call for protectionist policies, claiming, "While the quality is not here [Japanese textile companies] do everything possible to give their goods the appearance of American goods so that the average native is distracted by ridiculously low prices and is too easily deceived."[26] Playing on the stereotype of the naive and childlike Filipino supported the portrayal of the United States as benevolent savior.[27] Even as the proposed trade policies would heavily favor the United States, the Americans purported to be acting in the best interests—for the safekeeping and well-being—of Filipinos. Thus, according to American textile lobbyists and manufacturers, it was the US government's duty to protect its citizens by pressuring the Philippine Commonwealth to pass policies that would limit Japanese imports and favor the United States.

However, consumers and merchants in the Philippines were *not* naive. Rather, they held complex attitudes and positions in relation to the competing empires. As previously mentioned, trade reports show that there was, in fact, a dramatic dip in the consumption of Japanese cotton in 1932—the result of Chinese merchants based in the Philippines boycotting all Japanese imports to protest Japanese imperial aggression and colonialism in Manchuria in 1931. But as the boycott waned and as Japanese imports became more widely available, Filipino consumers increasingly purchased Japanese textiles. On July 30, 1935, the *Philippines Herald* reported that Filipino textile dealers disclosed that "cheap but satisfactory Japanese goods are a blessing to generally poor natives."[28] Here, Filipino merchants and consumers appear to be anything but gullible dupes; rather, they understood their economic vulnerability and made their purchases based on an assessment of both quality and cost. The author of a separate article in the *Manila Tribune* stated that while he was "personally in favor of giving American textiles adequate protection in our markets," such policies should remain "within the limit of our people's capacity to absorb and pay for that added protection."[29] Filipino consumers and political leaders understood their delicate position between two empires, and they also understood the likely cost that Filipino consumers would pay to fulfill US textile manufacturers' demands for protectionist policies against Japanese textiles. Manuel Quezon, who was at the time the president of the Philippine Senate, dodged the pressure from both the United States and Japan by stating that the Philippine legislature "is in no position to take action now" and about to take a recess.[30]

Taking seriously the detrimental impact of long-term colonialism and forms of neocolonial oppression, it is important to carefully approach

Americanization as a systematic and persistent effort to leave Filipinos few options. As mentioned previously, local textile production was suppressed and replaced almost entirely by imported goods. Further, textile trade reports show that cost and affordability played a huge determining factor in Filipinos' consumption practices and that the lower price of Japanese textiles undermined the presumed Filipino desire for all things American. Japanese textiles were cheaper because they practiced similar labor practices to those employed by the United States: they used colonial labor to drive down production costs and flooded their colonial markets with imports. Moreover, decades of US colonialism created an economic structure that made the Philippines dependent on the US purchase of exports such as sugar, coconut oil, and cordage. An article in the *Manila Tribune* asserted that the Philippines could not "alienate American sympathy by favoring Japanese imports."[31]

The Commonwealth period was very much about constructing a Philippine nation; but extricating itself from the United States was not so easy.[32] Protectionist policies and projects enacted by the Commonwealth government, such as the National Economic Protectionism Association (NEPA), were intertwined with US agendas to secure economic structures that would continue to protect US economic interests well beyond the end of formal colonialism.[33]

At the same time that legislation on trade tilted toward continued US domination of Philippine markets, other forms of more recognizable protectionist strategies emerged. Rather than major land reform, the Commonwealth government sought to alleviate the economic depression of the 1930s by instituting protectionist policies such as buying locally produced products. Throughout the 1930s, discourse on the Philippine economy in relation to independence centered on fears of declining exports to the United States, including the exports of sartorial staples such as embroideries and buttons made from locally sourced shells. Such fears reflected questions over what kind of ruptures would result from national independence and its attendant (neo)imperial configurations. There was an awareness that little would be done by US legislators to protect the Philippine export business.

The drama over textiles brings to light the power of beauty regimes and the complexity of overlapping empires and nation formation. It also highlights a different perspective on the imperial competition between Japan and the United States over economic expansion and the shared colonial tactics that crystallized in the 1930s. The confrontation of empires did not just begin on December 8, 1941, with the bombing of Pearl Harbor and air raids on US military bases in the Philippines; it had been growing and festering, increasing tensions and fanning anxieties in the Philippines since the 1930s. Textiles, commerce, and material culture, not military confrontation, were the first grounds upon which the US and Japanese empires battled in the Philippines.

## Preparedness and Independence with War on the Horizon

In the fall of 1935, Japan and the United States settled on another "gentleman's agreement," dividing the textile market in the Philippines—without any input from Filipinos themselves.[34] A *Manila Bulletin* article, "Theoretically Practical," asserted that the agreement was successful in "avoiding a trade war and hostile negotiation."[35] However, competition and tensions remained as both Japan and the United States strove to maneuver around quotas and tariffs and increase their respective market shares. Within a few years, tensions evolved into hostility as Japanese imperialism in Asia spread through market and military expansion. In May 1939, the Philippine National Assembly created a Department of National Defense in response to the expansion of the Japanese military.[36] It was clear that war was on the horizon.

The possibility of Japanese military occupation and war stoked feelings of anxiety and anticipation in the Philippines. Beyond the establishment of the Department of National Defense, Filipinos were urged to prepare for the impact of war on their everyday lives. In July 1941, the popular Manila-based magazine *Graphic* published an issue with a Filipina model on its cover, gazing somberly into the distance and dressed in a cotton-khaki jacket nipped at the waist, with slim shoulders and large pockets, and sporting matching loose-fitting pants. A full khaki satchel rests on her right shoulder. Accompanying the image is the text "Dressed for Evacuation." The text puts the image into perspective. "Dressed for Evacuation" and the model's fixed look into the distance evoke a sense of anticipation of an impending threat. The cover expresses that if war were to come to the Philippines, Filipinos would need to evacuate, flee, and seek safety from potential bombings and air raids. And one way to prepare for the danger and turmoil of war is to dress for the occasion.

The July 1941 issue of *Graphic* offered readers sartorial advice and a "Design for Leaving." In a multipage spread, it addressed Filipina readers: "To the Woman: How will you be dressed come evacuation time? How will you bundle yourself off with neatness and dispatch to safety? Call us pessimists, if you will, but it is not too early to start growing gray hairs over these and a multitude of other questions."[37] The article presented war and evacuation as

FIGURE E.1. "Dressed for Evacuation," cover image of *Graphic*, July 10, 1941.

foregone conclusions. It also gave Filipina readers suggestions on how to manage their anticipation of war. The article offered suggestions on how to dress, such as in a suit made of "thick West Point khaki, a material that can do without soap and water for life if need be."[38] West Point or the US Military Academy did not produce the khaki textiles so closely associated with military uniforms. Here, however, the article invoked West Point to underscore future wartime conditions' demands for utility and durability. By promoting the purchase of outfits made from American khaki, the article suggested transforming women's wear as a means of preparing for impending war. The article promises, "In the hurry and chaos of evacuation you'll find a pair of pants as dear as life itself."

But khaki pants were not just life-saving attire, they were also the dress of colonial brutality. During the Second Afghan War of 1878, the British military stationed in South Asia co-opted the term *khaki*, a Persian and Hindi term meaning "dust-colored," dying their white uniforms with local materials. These new khaki-colored uniforms, designed to camouflage—as opposed to the flamboyant military uniforms more commonly used by the British Army—came to be the style of the British military and, thus, the style of colonial violence.[39] By the turn of the twentieth century, khakis also became the norm for American military uniforms in the Philippine-American War.

As World War II threatened to come to the Philippines in 1941, khaki came to signify preparedness and protection. Through the militarization of everyday feminine clothing styles, Filipinas prepared for invasion by the Japanese empire. Fearing the prospect of evacuation, they sought protection in the fabric of a familiar US empire. The *Graphic* article insisted a woman civilian might need a coat to be as "tough as the elements," as evacuation would entail leaving the shelter of a home.[40] She would also benefit from wearing pants with utility pockets and a cap that could serve as a bag to hold rations such as canned foods, presumably imported from the United States. As a young teenager preparing to evacuate her home, Helen Mendoza meticulously curated what was necessary for evacuation and calculated the amount she could carry herself. She listed packing three sets of clothes, two pairs of socks, a pair of slippers, and an extra pair of rubber shoes.[41] Fashion and consumption offered ways to deal with the anxiety and uncertainty that came with the prospect of another empire. While under US colonial rule and during the uncertainty of the Commonwealth period, Filipinos had also dealt with the fear of war. Japan already had a presence in the Philippines, with small numbers of Japanese migrant communities residing in the Manila area and Japanese markets expanding through the increased importation of commodities and goods.[42] Japanese imperial military aggression heightened dramatically in 1941. For the Japanese empire, these efforts were part of a larger project of Japanese settler colonialism.[43]

In 1941, the Philippines' involvement in the Pacific War appeared inescapable. Philippine news outlets addressed the possibility of war and what this would mean for Filipino civilians.[44] News reports on Filipino economic interests and building a nation appeared side-by-side with news of fascism in Europe, Japanese imperialism and military aggression throughout Asia, and the expansion of US militarization to "defend" their imperial interests in Asia and the Pacific against Japan. The spectacular events, fairs, and celebrations that had come to mark Filipino nationalism, its capacity for self-government, and its modernity assumed a somber atmosphere. The sixth annual Commonwealth festivities held in November 1941 were "calculated to impress Mr. Average Citizen with the idea of preparedness for emergency" to "keep in step with the times."[45] Even the pageantry of the winners of Miss Commonwealth and the feting of "four beautiful girls, all prominent members of Manila," took on a more staid feeling. Their style of dress undergirded the message of civilian preparedness. Photo captions describing the beauty queens' gowns mirrored the militarization of women's fashion: "At the right is a dress that can be military if it wants . . . a pleated flounce and a prim file of buttons down front would be contributing factors."[46] Just a little over a week after *Graphic* published its coverage on the Commonwealth pageant, on December 8, 1941, Japan invaded the Philippines. The Philippines once again became a battlefield, caught between two empires.

Buying khaki clothing might have given Filipinos a sense of preparedness, a method by which to assuage feelings of anticipation and anxiety about impending war and further deferment of independence. But khakis and militarized dress would provide little protection. Filipinos could not have known the extent of the violence and devastation of World War II. The golden age of *alta sociedad* was over. The "impasse" of Commonwealth transition had ended. And the age of World War II and Japanese occupation had begun.

Sartorial preparedness and the systems of fashion and beauty exposed the contours of overlapping imperial regimes and the tricky landscape of Philippine national formation in the years leading up to World War II. As at the turn of the century, the clash of empires and anticolonial nation-building efforts produced feelings of anxiety and uncertainty as well as a sense of anticipation for an unforeseeable future. And just as in the moment of imperial transition between Spain and the United States, fashion, dress, and beauty served as important tools with which to navigate the shifting terrains of power. Indeed, beauty regimes—from the wearing of the traje de mestiza to the donning of the militarized khaki ensemble—embodied the entangled formations of fashion and beauty systems, power, multiple empires, and nation-building projects. Beauty regimes create a space for documenting and understanding the beauty and fashion practices and forms of labor that operate on individual, national, and global scales.

INTRODUCTION

1 "A Queen Is Crowned: Guia Balmori, Daughter of a Manila Labor Leader, Crowned Guia I, Miss Philippines of 1938 and Queen of the Philippine Exposition," *Graphic*, February 24, 1938, 8, 18–19.

2 "Queen Is Crowned," 18.

3 Burns, "Your Terno's Draggin'," 201.

4 For more on definitions of the *terno*, see Burns, "'Your Terno's Draggin','" 199–217; Coo, "Clothing and the Colonial Culture of Appearances"; Cruz, *The Terno*; Steinbock-Pratt, "'It Gave Us Our Nationality'"; M. Roces, "Gender, Nation and the Politics of Dress."

5 "Queen Is Crowned."

6 Ambeth R. Ocampo, "The Philippines' First Beauty Queen," *Philippine Daily Inquirer*, February 3, 2017, https://opinion.inquirer.net/101348/philippines -first-beauty-queen#ixzz5vYlDijGI; Cannell, *Power and Intimacy*; Clutario, "Pageant Politics"; David and Cruz, "Big, *Bakla*, and Beautiful"; Johnson, *Beauty and Power*.

7 Tourism Secretary Vicente Ramos (1994), quoted in Banet-Weiser, *Most Beautiful Girl in the World*, 200.

8 David, "Transgender Archipelagos," 337. According to Robert Diaz, *bakla* "often denotes gay male identity, male-to-female transgender identity, effeminized or hyperbolic gay identity, and gay identity that belongs to the lower class." R. Diaz, "The Limits of *Bakla* and Gay," 721.

9 I use the designation *Filipinx* when referring to present-day circumstances. When addressing developments of the late nineteenth and early twentieth centuries, I use "Filipino" and "Filipina" to underscore the historical processes of identity constructions. A growing number of communities, scholars, and activists use the term *Filipinx*. More than a term of gender neutrality, the "x" in Filipinx, as Sony Corañez Bolton argues, "opens up a colonial relationality between histories of Spanish colonialism and US imperialism" and recognizes that "the simple act of altering one letter of the historically colonial language of Spanish and its ordering of binary gender, encourages an ethics of solidarity that brings Filipinx and Latinx peoples together." Bolton, "Tale of Two X's," 187.

10 R. Diaz, "Biyuti from Below," 417.

11 Manalansan, *Global Divas*, 90.

12  Banet-Weiser, "'I'm Beautiful the Way I Am'"; Lee, "Beauty between Empires."

13  Nash, "Writing Black Beauty," 105. See also Blain Roberts on the pleasures of connection, community, and care between Black women in beauty parlors. Roberts, *Pageants, Parlors, and Pretty Women*, 97.

14  Weinbaum et al., *The Modern Girl around the World*, 31.

15  My work builds on the growing scholarship on race, gender, and the politics of beauty and fashion. Craig, *Ain't I a Beauty Queen?*; Ford, *Liberated Threads*; Greer, *Represented*; Lee, Moon, and Nguyen Tu, *Fashion and Beauty in the Time of Asia*; Nguyen, "Biopower of Beauty," 362; Ochoa, *Queen for a Day*; Roberts, *Pageants, Parlors, and Pretty Women*; Saraswati, *Seeing Beauty, Sensing Race*; Nguyen Tu, *The Beautiful Generation*.

16  Nguyen, *Promise of Beauty*.

17  Kant, *Observations on the Feeling of the Beautiful and Sublime*. For a critique on Kant's approaches to beauty, see Armstrong, "The Effects of Blackness."

18  Finnane, *Changing Clothes in China*; Kang, *Managed Hand*; Phạm, *Asians Wear Clothes on the Internet*, 81; Tarlo, *Clothing Matters*; Weinbaum et al., *Modern Girl around the World*.

19  Tadiar, *Fantasy Production*, 30.

20  Nguyen, "Right to Be Beautiful."

21  Nguyen, "Biopower of Beauty," 361.

22  Vanita Reddy's work on the power of beauty and fashion in formations of Indian diaspora underscores how "practices associated with beauty are socializing in the way that they make possible new racialized subject formations, affiliations, and forms of diasporic belonging." Reddy, *Fashioning Diaspora*, 19.

23  M. Roces, "Women in Philippine Politics and Society," 172.

24  Manalansan, *Global Divas*, 15.

25  I thank Heather Lee, Naoko Shibusawa, and Lili Kim for their input on the naming and shaping of this framework.

26  Raymundo, "Beauty Regimens, Beauty Regimes," 103.

27  Grewal, *Transnational America*, 3, 126.

28  Many thanks to Anonymous Reader 1 for this language.

29  Keeley, "Toward a Foucauldian Analysis of International Regimes."

30  Strange, "Cave! Hic Dragones."

31  Novadona Bayo, Santoso, Purna Samadhi, *In Search of Local Regime in Indonesia*, 16–17.

32  Hall, *Policing the Crisis*, xi.

33  Hall and Morley, *Essential Essays*, 365.

34  Barthes, *Fashion System*, 8–9.

35  For more on histories of nationalism under both Spanish and US colonial regimes, see Agoncillo, *Filipino Nationalism, 1872–1970*; Constantino, *Neocolonial Identity and Counter-Consciousness*; Cullinane, *Ilustrado Politics*; Doran, "Women, Nationalism and the Philippine Revolution"; Ileto, *Pasyon*

*and Revolution*; Mojares, *Brains of the Nation*; Quibuyen, *Nation Aborted*; Schumacher, *Making of a Nation*.

36 Lowe, *Intimacies*, 5, 8.

37 I am indebted to the labors of transnational, women of color, and third world feminist scholars and their groundbreaking work in studies of colonialism, globalization, and empire. In addition to the works cited above and elsewhere in this book, such works include Alexander and Talpade Mohanty, *Feminist Genealogies, Colonial Legacies*; Hill Collins, *Black Feminist Thought*; Briggs, *Reproducing Empire*; Davis, *Women, Race, and Class*; García-Peña, *Borders of Dominicanidad*; Grewal and Kaplan, *Scattered Hegemonies*; Kang, *Managed Hand*; Mahmood, *Politics of Piety*; Najmabadi, *Women with Mustaches*; Salazar Parreñas, *Force of Domesticity*; Wu, *Radicals on the Road*.

38 Here, I draw from Stephen Krasner's definition of political regimes. Krasner, *International Regimes*, 3.

39 Cruz, "Global Mess and Glamour"; Manalansan, "The 'Stuff' of Archives."

40 Here, the Philippine Exposition refers to the commerce and business exposition that was part of the festivities of the Manila Carnival, an annual fair modeled after the world's fairs and in which the Manila Carnival Queen contest served as the crowning point of the one- to two-week-long event.

41 M. Kerkvliet, *Manila Workers' Unions*.

42 Anderson, *Imagined Communities*.

43 For more on the United States' imperial projects of benevolent assimilation, see Agoncillo, *Filipino Nationalism*; Cullinane, *Ilustrado Politics*; Greenberg, *Manifest Manhood*; Hoganson, *Fighting for American Manhood*; Ileto, *Pasyon and Revolution*; Karnow, *In Our Image*; Kramer, *Blood of Government*; Miller, *Benevolent Assimilation*.

44 Rafael, *Promise of the Foreign*, 19.

45 Capazzola, *Bound by War*; Caronan, *Legitimizing Empire*; McCoy and Scarano, *Colonial Crucible*; Poblete, *Islanders in the Empire*.

46 Scholars of Filipino immigration have examined the ambivalent position of Filipinos who migrated to the United States and other US territories such as Hawai'i. Isaac, *American Tropics*. For more on immigration and Filipinos' legal status as "nationals," see Baldoz, *Third Asiatic Invasion*; Lowe, *Immigrant Acts*; Ngai, *Impossible Subjects*.

47 Karnow, *In Our Image*; Miller, *Benevolent Assimilation*.

48 Mojares, "Formation of Filipino Nationality," 12.

49 Michelle Mitchell and Naoko Shibusawa provide an insightful synthesis of gender, labor, capitalism, and imperialism. Mitchell and Shibusawa, "Introduction." Cedric Robinson's groundbreaking work put forth the idea of "racial capitalism," which argues that the very formations of capital and capitalism are intrinsically linked to and motivated by racism and race. Robinson, *Black Marxism*.

50 Ancheta and Beltran-Gonzalez, *Filipino Women in Nation Building*. For a detailed analysis of biographies and writings promoting the Filipina women's

movement, see D. Cruz, *Transpacific Filipinas*, 21–27; Aquino, "Filipino Women and Political Engagement," 36–37; Winkelmann, *Dangerous Intercourse*.

51 My framing of performance draws from the work of Diana Taylor. Taylor, *Disappearing Acts*.

52 Francisco, "From Subjects to Citizens," 113. For descriptions of women's status in precolonial Philippines, see Alzona, *Filipino Woman*; Camagay, "Women through Philippine History," 31–32; and Subido, *Feminist Movement in Philippines*.

53 Roces and other citations on suffrage, on civic groups, on Filipina education. M. Roces and Edwards, "Is the Suffragist an American Colonial Construct"; M. Roces, "Gender, Nation and the Politics of Dress"; M. Roces, "Filipino Elite Women and Public Health."

54 Hartman, "Venus in Two Acts," 3.

55 See for example the work of Arondekar, *For the Record*.

56 Lowe, *Intimacies*, 5.

57 For more on the structure of archives, mislabeling, and the disappearing of women from the archive, see Vicuña Gonzalez, *Empire's Mistress*, 8–12. See also Mendoza, *Metroimperial Intimacies*, 29.

58 While there are many languages and dialects in the Philippines, most of the sources made available to me were written in Tagalog.

59 Mitra, *Indian Sex Life*, 4.

60 Arondekar, *For the Record*, 3. Marisa Fuentes's work on gender, women, and slavery in the Caribbean interrogates the implications of archival obsessions with particular forms of violence inflicted upon Black women that obscure other kinds of brutality. The hypervisibility of some narratives consequently renders other histories invisible. Fuentes, *Dispossessed Lives*, 128–29.

61 Brewer and Medcalf, *Researching the Fragments*.

62 Clutario, "World War II and the Promise of Normalcy."

## 1. TENSIONS AT THE SEAMS

1 The original iteration of the second Philippine Commission, often referred to as the Taft Commission, was composed of William Taft, Henry Clay Ide, Luke Wright, Dean Worcester, and Bernard Moses. Between 1900 and 1916, more Americans and Filipinos would join the Commission. These members included Benito Legarda, Trinidad Pardo de Tavera, Jose de Luzuriaga, James Francis Smith, William Cameron Forbes, William Morgan Shuster, Newton W. Gilbert, Rafael Palma, Gregoria Araneta, Juan Sumulong, Fran Branagan, Charles Elliot, Francis Burton Harrison, Victorino Mapa, Jaime C. de Veyra, Vicente Ilustre, Vicente Singson Encarnacion, Henderson Martin, Clinton L. Riggs, Eugene Elliott Reed, and Wilford Denison. Most Filipinos who took part in the Commission were Partido Federal (Federal Party) members. In addition to staff and a few Filipino and American journalists, a few wives, sisters, and children accompanied the Commission. While the Com-

mission toured the entire archipelago, this chapter focuses on their time in Manila, Luzon, and the Western Visayas. R. Paredes, "The Partido Federal."

2  Shaw and Francia, *Vestiges of War*.

3  Go, *American Empire*, 25–54; Kramer, *Blood of Government*, 171, 305–8; R. Paredes, *Philippine Colonial Democracy*.

4  The designation "elite" rapidly took on new meanings during the latter half of the nineteenth century with the consolidation of Chinese and Spanish mestizo identity formations that deliberately sought to create clear demarcations of class, racial, and cultural difference from various people and communities that were often referred to as the *tao* (the masses), *indios* (the Spanish term for native peoples), and non-Christians. For more on Chinese mestizos see Chu, *Chinese and Chinese Mestizos of Manila*; Doran, "Spanish and Mestizo Women of Manila"; Cullinane, *Ilustrado Politics*; R. Reyes, *Love, Passion and Patriotism*.

5  Moses, *Unofficial Letters*, 19. This chapter relies heavily on the published letters of Edith Moses, Helen Taft's memoir, and the unpublished and up to this point overlooked letters of Mabel LeRoy. These sources exclude the names of the individual Filipinas that they encountered in the Philippines. However, a close examination of white women's descriptions of Filipinas' gestures, utterances, and acts provide insight into their subjectivity, feelings, attitudes, and viewpoints.

6  Coo, *Clothing the Colony*, 260.

7  Ngai, *Ugly Feelings*, 5–6.

8  Balce, *Body Parts of Empire*, 129.

9  Anthony, *Nellie Taft*, 194.

10  Anthony, *Nellie Taft*, 22–82.

11  Aguilar, *Clash of Spirits*; Aguilar, "Fulcrum of Structure-Agency."

12  Yamaguchi, "The New 'American' Houses."

13  Historian Augusto Espiritu describes how elites at the end of the nineteenth century and throughout the early twentieth century displayed wealth and power and expressions of Hispanism through conspicuous consumption. Espiritu, "American Empire, Hispanism," 168.

14  Kalaw, *Aide-de-Camp to Freedom*, 1–2; quoted in Espiritu, "American Empire, Hispanism," 168.

15  Mabel Leroy to her parents, John Pound and Elizabeth Maria Pound, March 21, 1900, Travelogue Account of Trip to the Philippines (hereafter TATP), 1900–1901 Folder, Box 1, James Alfred LeRoy Papers, Bentley Historical Collections, University of Michigan, Ann Arbor (hereafter JAL). I have chosen to use the dates that appear on transcribed letters. The documents date the letters from the year 1900 although some of the events described in Mabel LeRoy's letters appear to overlap and coincide with incidents noted in James LeRoy's letters and manuscript notes, which sometimes list the year 1900 and in other points mark the year as 1901, as well as Edith Moses's letters, which date such events in 1901.

16  Phạm, *Asians Wear Clothes on the Internet*, 59.

17 Vanita Reddy challenges the dismissal of beauty as a serious subject of inquiry. Reddy, *Fashioning Diaspora*, 17.

18 Tulloch, *Birth of Cool*, 4.

19 Burns, *Puro Arte*, 22.

20 Rafael, "Colonial Domesticity"; Samonte, "Obtaining 'Sympathetic Understanding,'" 14; Winkelmann, *Dangerous Intercourse*.

21 Clutario, "World War II and the Promise of Normalcy," 241–43.

22 By *intimacies* I refer to the range of colonial relations forged out of proximity that can refer to interiority or domesticity, but also the connections and encounters formed in public view and spaces. For more on expansive definitions of intimacies in relation to capitalism and empire, see Lowe, *Intimacies*, 17.

23 Taft, *Recollections*, 158.

24 M. Pratt, *Imperial Eyes*, 7.

25 M. Pratt, *Imperial Eyes*, 6–8.

26 Ngai, *Ugly Feelings*, 130.

27 Tarlo, *Clothing Matters*, 8.

28 Tanisha Ford's methodological approach to the history of dress and fashion shaped my thinking and analysis of dress practices. Ford's work on the global Black Freedom struggle urges readers to "think critically about dress as a political strategy." Ford, *Liberated Threads*, 3. For more on the relationship between politics and dress, see also Cohn, *Colonialism and Its Forms of Knowledge*, 114; Lee, Moon, and Tu, *Fashion and Beauty*, 5.

29 Hall, "Encoding/Decoding," 163.

30 Entwistle, "Fashion and the Fleshy Body," 325.

31 Kristin Hoganson provides important perspectives on gender and cosmopolitanism in her examination of American women's conspicuous consumption and to convey worldly knowledge. Hoganson, *Consumers' Imperium*, 13–15.

32 Lowe, *Intimacies*, 48.

33 On December 21, 1898, with the signing of the Treaty of Paris, Spain formally ceded the Philippines, along with its other territories and colonies, like Guam and Puerto Rico, to the United States. Exactly one month later on January 21, 1899, when Filipino nationalists declared independence and the establishment of a Philippine state, the United States dismissed these declarations and argued that Filipino naivety and backwardness made them unfit for self-governance. Less than one month later, on February 4, 1899, a new war began—the Philippine-American War. For more on the Philippine-American War, see Churchill, "Life in a War of Independence"; Capozzola, *Bound by War*; Ileto, "Philippine Wars and the Politics of Memory"; Shaw and Francia, *Vestiges of War*; Silbey, *War of Frontier and Empire*.

34 Mojares, "Formation of Filipino Nationality."

35 Campomanes, "1898 and the Nature of the New Empire"; DeLisle, "Navy Wives/Native Lives"; V. Diaz, *Repositioning the Missionary*; Ferrer, *Insurgent Cuba*; García-Peña, *Borders of Dominicanidad*; Oberiano, "Territorial Discontent"; Thompson, *Imperial Archipelago*.

36  Byrd, *Transit of Empire*; Karuka, *Empire's Tracks*.

37  Arvin, *Possessing Polynesians*; Saranillio, *Unsustainable Empire*; Camacho, "Homomilitarism."

38  Chang, "Circulating Race and Empire"; Day, "Being or Nothingness"; Hartman, *Scenes of Subjection*; Smallwood, "Reflections on Settler Colonialism."

39  Karuka, *Empire's Tracks*, 15.

40  DeGuzmán, *Spain's Long Shadow*, 139.

41  Doran, "Women in the Philippine Revolution."

42  Gates, "Hang the Dogs," 850–51.

43  Abinales, *Making Mindanao*, 105.

44  The Philippine Revolution and the Philippine-American War were not just waged or led by elite nationalists. Anticolonial and revolutionary movements were also organized by peasant leaders in rural areas, Muslim leaders, and labor activists in the south, and urban labor activists. Aguilar, "Fulcrum of Structure-Agency"; Ileto, *Pasyon and Revolution*.

45  LeRoy, *Philippine Life in Town and Country*, 57. The Philippine Commission would be replaced by a Senate and House of Representatives in 1916 as part of Governor Harrison's Filipinization efforts.

46  Go, *American Empire*, 49.

47  Gonzalez, "Illicit Labor," 94.

48  At the same time, the Philippine Commission's project maintained its tutelary charge. Through interactions with local elites, colonial authorities provided a political education in American colonial principles. Go, *American Empire*, 49.

49  Abinales, "Progressive-Machine Conflict," 155.

50  Scholarship on gender and empire has explored the history of white women as imperial agents and attended to their investments in white womanhood. See Burton, *Burdens of History*; Jacobs, *White Mother to a Dark Race*; Sinha, *Specters of Mother India*; Sneider, *Suffragists in an Imperial Age*.

51  In her article on gender and the US Foreign Service during the first half of the twentieth century, Molly Wood argues that the wives of diplomats wielded authority and significant influence in their roles as wife, mother, homemaker, hostess, and model of white respectability. Her analysis of diplomatic wives shows how gender helped project a positive image of American diplomacy and foreign relations. Wood, "Diplomatic Wives," 143–44.

52  Taft, *Recollections*, 58.

53  "Wardrobe for Philippines/Note Paper, Seal Rings, Dinner Coat," *Vogue*, September 27, 1900, 16.

54  Taft, *Recollections*, 58.

55  Purtschert, Falk, and Lüthi, "Switzerland and 'Colonialism without Colonies'"; Rafael, "Colonial Domesticity," 56.

56  Stoler, *Carnal Knowledge*, 14–15. Stoler points out that the motif of white women dressed in white clothing also appears in Marguerite Duras's later novel, *The Lover*, where Duras also uses detailed imagery of wearing and removing white linen dresses and undergarments from a white woman to set

the scene of miscegenation, illicit intimacy, and colonialism. Duras, *Sea Wall*, 135; Duras, *Lover*, 19, 38.

57  McClintock, *Imperial Leather*, 211.

58  Tadiar, *Fantasy Production*, 9.

59  Newman, *White Women's Rights*; Rafael, "Colonial Domesticity," 52–75.

60  Allan Isaac puts forward the term "American Tropics" to describe the regulatory tropes and narratives of US imperialism and the dislocated American island spaces. Isaac addresses 1898 colonial acquisitions, protectorates, and current territorial landscapes, including the Philippines, Guam, Hawai'i, Puerto Rico, Cuba, Haiti, the Dominican Republic, American Samoa, the Federated States of Micronesia, the Northern Mariana Islands, the Marshall Islands, Palau, and the US Virgin Islands. Isaac, *American Tropics*, 2.

61  "Wardrobe for Philippines," 16.

62  In her letters, Edith Moses notes that it took forty-six days to journey from San Francisco to Manila. This included stops in Honolulu and Hong Kong. Moses, *Unofficial Letters*, 1.

63  Antonia Finnane's work on fashion in nineteenth-century China and Thuy Linh Nguyen Tu's transnational research on Asian Americans and fashion complicate the dominant historical trajectory made by Western fashion and costume scholars that presumed fashion developed in the West, closed off from any global or intercultural, East-West relationships. Finnane, *Changing Clothes in China*, 10; Tu, *Beautiful Generation*, 114–24.

64  Isaac, *American Tropics*, 3.

65  Kaplan and Pease, *Cultures of United States Imperialism*, 473; Mitchell, "'Black Man's Burden.'"

66  V. Mendoza, *Metroimperial Intimacies*, 4–5.

67  For more on turn of the century travel literature about the Philippines, see Balce, "Bile of War."

68  Anthony, *Nellie Taft*, 125.

69  For more on colonial travel writing, see C. Kaplan, *Questions of Travel*; M. Pratt, *Imperial Eyes*.

70  Blair, *The Philippine Islands*; Sawyer, *Inhabitants of the Philippines*; Worcester, *Philippine Islands and Their People*; Olivares, *Our Islands and Their People*.

71  Isaac, *American Tropics*, 87.

72  Balce, *Body Parts of Empire*, 36. Also see, for example, the many images of indigenous women in the Philippines found in various photograph collections from the late nineteenth and early twentieth centuries. These photographers and scientists regarded photography as a way to document and categorize Filipino "types" and ethnic groups, providing insight into everyday life in the Philippines. Dean C. Worcester, *Photographs of the Philippine Islands*, E. Murray Bruner Philippine Image Collection, Wisconsin Philippines Image Collection, University of Wisconsin, Madison.

73  Balce, *Body Parts of Empire*, 131.

74 Rice, *Dean Worcester's Fantasy Islands*, 168.

75 Mark Rice quoting Alfred McCoy, on colonial photography. Rice, *Dean Worcester's Fantasy*, 161. McCoy, "Orientalism of the Philippine Photograph."

76 Said, *Orientalism*. The following scholars build on Edward Said's formative work on orientalism and the process of constructing the "orient" as the "other" to the "occident" in the colonial Philippine context. McKenna, *American Imperial Pastoral*; Halili, *Iconography of the New Empire*.

77 Taft, *Recollections*, 33.

78 Taft, *Recollections*, 33.

79 Samonte, "Obtaining 'Sympathetic Understanding,'" 4.

80 Wood, "Diplomatic Wives," 143–44.

81 "Wardrobe for Philippines," 16.

82 Moses, *Unofficial Letters*, 1.

83 "Ladies" designated the adult women who were wives, daughters, and sisters of the higher-ranking officials. James Alfred LeRoy, "Notes for March 1–2, 1901," Manuscript of Travelogue Account of Trip to the Philippine Islands (hereafter MTPI), 142, February 12–March 9, 1901 Folder, Box 1, JAL.

84 Lowe, *Intimacies*, 38.

85 Burton, *Burdens of History*, 2, 41; Prieto, "'Stepmother America.'"

86 DeGuzmán, *Spain's Long Shadow*, xii, 34.

87 Mabel LeRoy to her parents, John Pound and Elizabeth Maria Pound, August 12, 1900, TATP, 1900–1901 Folder, Box 1, JAL.

88 Du Bois, "Worlds of Color"; Kaplan and Pease, *Cultures of United States Imperialism*, 473; Mitchell, "'Black Man's Burden'"; Silkey, *Black Woman Reformer*.

89 Moses, *Unofficial Letters*, 73.

90 Moses, *Unofficial Letters*, 74.

91 Moses, *Unofficial Letters*, 74.

92 Moses, *Unofficial Letters*, 43.

93 Moses, *Unofficial Letters*, 89–90.

94 Moses, *Unofficial Letters*, 90.

95 Moses, *Unofficial Letters*, 90.

96 R. Reyes, *Love, Passion and Patriotism*, 10–11.

97 Moses, *Unofficial Letters*, 90.

98 Schirmer and Shalom, *Philippines Reader*, 40.

99 US Philippine Commission, "The Organization of Provincial Governments," in *Report of the United States Philippine Commission to the Secretary of War, December 1 1900 to October 15, 1901, Part 1: Annual Reports for the War Department for the Fiscal Year ended June 30, 1901* (Washington, DC: US Government Printing Office, 1901), 11–12.

100 Sharpe, *Allegories of Empire*, 6, 86; Cacho, "Presumption of White Innocence."

101 For more on the concept of colonial maternalism, see Jacobs, *White Mother to a Dark Race*.

102 Taft, *Recollections*, 154.

103 James LeRoy, March 13, 1900, TATP, 1900–1901 Folder, Box 1, JAL.

104 Tayabas is a city located in Quezon Province, Luzon, Philippines.

105 James LeRoy, March 13, 1900, TATP, 1900–1901 Folder, Box 1, JAL.

106 Mabel LeRoy to her parents, John Pound and Elizabeth Maria Pound, April 1, 1900, TATP, 1900–1901 Folder, Box 1, JAL.

107 Balce, *Body Parts of Empire*, 129.

108 Mojares, *War against the Americans*, 7.

109 Mojares, *War against the Americans*, 23.

110 Mabel LeRoy to her parents, John Pound and Elizabeth Maria Pound, April (n.d.), 1900, TATP, 1900–1901 Folder, Box 1, JAL.

111 Mabel LeRoy to her parents, April (n.d.), 1900.

112 Mabel LeRoy to her parents, April (n.d.), 1900.

113 Mabel LeRoy to her parents, April (n.d.), 1900.

114 Go, *American Empire*, 47.

115 Mojares, *War against the Americans*, 7.

116 Mojares, *War against the Americans*, 8.

117 Go, *American Empire*, 62. Tanisha Ford addresses gendered performances of socioeconomic position in her study of elite urban women in South Africa. Ford, *Liberated Threads*, 169.

118 Fernandez, "Pompas y Solemnidades," 118.

119 Wendt, "Philippine Fiesta"; Fernandez, "Pompas y Solemnidades," 139.

120 Eva Johnson to Bertha Schaffer, July 21, 1902, Mixed Material, 1898, Bertha Schaffer Letters, Bentley Historical Collection, University of Michigan, Ann Arbor.

121 Mabel LeRoy to her parents, John Pound and Elizabeth Maria Pound, March 13, 1900, TATP, 1900–1901 Folder, Box 1, JAL.

122 James Alfred LeRoy, March 13, 1901, "Notes for March 10–April 3, 1901," MTPI, 142.

123 Eric Cruz explains that at the turn of the century, when women wore materials in blue and red, it was called "Escuadra Americana," and when they wore "red and yellow," it was "Escuadra Española." Cruz, *Terno*, 6. Mabel LeRoy to her parents, March 13, 1900.

124 Cruz, *Terno*, 4–7.

125 Mabel LeRoy to her parents, March 21, 1900. James Alfred LeRoy's notes also consist of many descriptions of towns flying American flags and local bands playing "The Star-Spangled Banner." James Alfred LeRoy, "Notes for March 1–2, 1901," MTPI, 139–45.

126 Mabel LeRoy to her parents, March 13, 1900; James Alfred LeRoy, "Notes for March 1–2, 1901," MTPI, 143.

127 Paredes, *Philippine Colonial Democracy*, 43.

128 Constantino and Constantino, *History of the Philippines*, 236–39.

129 Constantino and Constantino, *History of the Philippines*, 236–37.

130 Bascara, "Collaboration, Co-prosperity," 91.

131 Bascara, "Collaboration, Co-prosperity," 91.

132  Ileto, "Friendship and Forgetting," 7.

133  Go, *American Empire*, 95.

134  Go, *American Empire*, 96–97.

135  Kramer, *Blood of Empire*, 185.

136  Wendt, "Philippine Fiesta," 7.

137  Wendt, "Philippine Fiesta," 6.

138  R. Diaz, *Confetti of Ordinary Dreams*.

139  Fernandez, "Pompas y Solemnidades," 130. Ferdinand Lopez refers to the common and frequent local practices of fiestas of the nineteenth, twentieth, and twenty-first centuries as a "fiesta complex." Lopez argues that displays and celebrations organized and orchestrated usually by matriarchs and women were indicative of local power. Women showcased family heirlooms, expensive silverware, porcelain dishes, religious statues ornamented with fine fabrics and jewels, and luxurious gowns, musicians with the intention of making good impressions and impressions of family wealth and power. Ferdinand Lopez, conversation with the author, July 14, 2021.

140  R. Reyes, *Love, Passion and Patriotism*, 29.

141  Go, *American Empire*, 95.

142  In her letters, Mabel LeRoy remarks that she is one of the few women accompanying the commission who could speak Spanish. Mabel LeRoy to her parents, John Pound and Elizabeth Maria Pound, April 11, 1900, TATP, 1900–1901 Folder, Box 1, JAL.

143  Mabel LeRoy to her parents, April 11, 1900.

144  Mabel LeRoy to her parents, John Pound and Elizabeth Maria Pound, September 14, 1901, TATP, 1900–1901 Folder, Box 1, JAL.

145  Coo, "Clothing and the Colonial Culture," 51.

146  Moses, *Unofficial Letters*, 77.

147  Moses, *Unofficial Letters*, 77. In the eighteenth century, Sèvres emerged as the leading European maker of porcelain pieces purchased mostly by the European aristocracy. In the nineteenth century, Sèvres ware stamped with family monograms continued to symbolize luxury, refinement, and taste in the Philippines. Importers personally visited haciendas in the provinces to sell the delicate wares. Fernandez, *Tikim*, 213.

148  Mabel LeRoy to her parents, John Pound and Elizabeth Maria Pound, April 12, 1900, TATP, 1900–1901 Folder, Box 1, JAL.

149  Nineteenth-century Spanish colonial policies and economic arrangements transformed the Philippines from a cash crop to an agricultural export economy. The nineteenth century's impact could be felt all over the islands and across class, ethnic, racial, and gender lines. R. Reyes, *Love, Passion and Patriotism*, 4–5; Cullinane, *Ilustrado Politics*, 11; Dery, *History of the Inarticulate*; Camagay, *Working Women of Manila*.

150  Wickberg, "Chinese Mestizo," 165–68.

151  Nagano, *State and Finance in the Philippines*, 23–24.

152  Larkin, "International Face of the Philippine Sugar Industry," 46.

153 Aguilar, *Clash of the Spirits*, 105–6.

154 Aguilar, *Clash of the Spirits*, 103–4, 106.

155 I am drawing from a specific genealogy of mestiza and mestizo identity in the Philippines. The nineteenth century witnessed economic, social, and political developments that led to the rise of a colonial elite class composed of indios, Chinese and Spanish mestizos, and a few creoles. *Mestizo* refers to Filipinos of mixed heritage including Spanish Filipinos, Chinese Filipinos, and American Filipinos. Mestizo identity in the Philippine context also refers to the performance of a particular elite identity associated with wealth, a Hispanic heritage, and "cosmopolitanism." Rafael, *The Promise of the Foreign*, 6–8; R. Reyes, *Love, Passion and Patriotism.*

156 Such displays of social status were grounded in wealth as well as whiteness. Even as elites straddled multiple racial categories, such as Chinese (Sangley) and Spanish mestizos, they generally sought to distinguish themselves from the "*massa*," *tao*, and *indio* and claim power and privilege through proximity to Hispanicism and whiteness. Katigbak, *Legacy*, 20–25; Chu, *Chinese Mestizos of Manila*, 20, 249.

157 Arrizón, *Queering Mestizaje*; Rafael, *Promise of the Foreign*, 96–97.

158 R. Reyes, *Love, Passion and Patriotism*, 12–13.

159 R. Reyes, *Love, Passion and Patriotism*, 39–67.

160 R. Reyes, *Love, Passion and Patriotism*, 53.

161 Rizal, *Reminiscences and Travels of Jose Rizal*, 239–56, quoted in R. Reyes, *Love, Passion and Patriotism*, 53.

162 Coo, *Clothing and the Colonial Culture*, 251–52; R. Reyes, *Love, Passion and Patriotism*, 9.

163 Katigbak, *Legacy*, 31.

164 Mabel LeRoy to her parents, April 12, 1900.

165 Moses, *Unofficial Letters*, 84.

166 Mabel LeRoy to her parents, April 12, 1900. Felicia Santa María details the kind of jewelry and accessories that were popular in the late nineteenth century. These include hair combs and pins made of gold and silver, and decorated with jewels and seed pearls, and gold crucifixes on corresponding chains. Santa María, *Household Antiques and Heirlooms*, 202–3.

167 Moses, *Unofficial Letters*, 119.

168 Villegas, *Hiyas*, 129–30.

169 Reyes, *Love, Passion and Patriotism*, 26.

170 Mojares, *Brains of the Nation*, 469.

171 Taft, *Recollections*, 87; Moses, *Unofficial Letters*, 206.

172 Moses, *Unofficial Letters*, 206; Coo, *Clothing and the Colonial Culture*, 199.

173 Coo, *Clothing and the Colonial Culture*, 87–88.

174 Coo, *Clothing and the Colonial Culture*, 88. Alicia Arrizón describes the *terno* as the material link that connected mestizos to "privilege, affirming the identity constructed by adopting the Hispanic legacy." Arrizón, *Queering Mestizaje*, 146.

175 According to Eric Cruz, the María Clara gown entailed a skirt of heavy satin cut in multiple panels of contrasting colors and a long *cola*, or train, a waist-length camisa, and a pañuelo with wide sleeves stiffened with starch to "achieve the effect of airiness." Caroline Hau examines long-enduring twinned intellectual and popular discourse and debates about María Clara as both a model of Filipina femininity and a victim of colonialism. Cruz, *Terno*, 5; Hau, "Afterlives of María Clara."

176 *El bello sexo*, January 14, 1891, referenced in Bernal and Escaler, *Patterns for the Filipino Dress*, 16; Coo, *Clothing and the Colonial Culture*, 88. According to Coo, prior to 1880, women wore Victorian-styled ball gowns for formal events. This changed as notions of *patria*, Filipino identity, and nationalist movements took shape.

177 Coo, *Clothing and the Colonial Culture*, 111.

178 R. Reyes, *Love, Passion and Patriotism*, 11; Camacho, "Public Transcendence of Intimacy."

179 Hau, "'Patria é Intereses.'"

180 Hau, "'Patria é Intereses,'" 27.

181 R. Reyes, *Love, Passion and Patriotism*, 21.

182 Espiritu, "American Empire and Hispanism," 158.

183 Karnow, *In Our Image*.

184 Camagay, *Working Women of Manila*, 121.

185 R. Reyes, *Love, Passion and Patriotism*, 65.

186 Lopez, *Lopez Family*, 2, xliii.

187 Lopez, *Lopez Family*, xliii.

188 James Alfred Leroy, "Notes March 14, 1901," MTPI, 13, February 12–March 9, 1901 Folder, Box 1, JAL.

189 Rafael, *Promise of the Foreign*, 2.

190 Mabel LeRoy to her parents, March 21, 1900.

191 Moses, *Unofficial Letters*, 66.

192 James Alfred LeRoy, "Notes March 1, 1901," MTPI, 13, February 12–March 9, 1901 Folder, Box 1, JAL.

193 Mendoza-Guazón, *Development and Progress of the Filipino Women*, 28; Santa María, *Household Antiques and Heirlooms*, 13.

194 Mabel LeRoy to her parents, March 21, 1900.

195 Cohn, "Cloth, Clothes, and Colonialism," 405; Edwards, "Restyling Colonial Cambodia," 391.

196 Finnane, "Yangzhou's 'Mondernity,'" 402; Tarlo, *Clothing Matters*, 1, 6.

197 Tu, *Beautiful Generation*, 7.

198 Rafael, "Colonial Domesticity," 60–61.

199 Mabel LeRoy to her parents, March 21, 1900.

200 From a wealthy mestizo family, Benito Legarda was originally Emilio Aguinaldo's cabinet member; however, with the change to American colonial control, he allied himself with the new American colonial government.

201 Moses, *Unofficial Letters*, 167.

202 Hoganson, *Consumers' Imperium*, 58, 97.

203 Mabel LeRoy to her parents, March 21, 1900.

204 Mabel LeRoy to her parents, March 21, 1900.

205 Mabel LeRoy to her parents, March 21, 1900.

206 Choy, "A Filipino Woman in America," 135.

207 Samonte, "Obtaining 'Sympathetic Understanding,'" 4; Wexler, *Tender Violence*, 53.

208 Mabel LeRoy to her parents, April 12, 1900.

209 Mabel LeRoy to her parents, April (n.d.) 1900.

210 Mabel LeRoy to her parents, April 12, 1900; Prieto, "Delicate Subject."

211 Mabel LeRoy to her parents, February 3, 1900.

212 Mabel LeRoy to her parents, April 12, 1900.

213 Ngai, *Ugly Feelings*, 130.

214 Samonte, "Obtaining 'Sympathetic Understanding,'" 10.

215 Taft, *Recollections*, 166.

216 Taft, *Recollections*, 128.

217 Taft, *Recollections*, 147.

218 Moses, *Unofficial Letters*, 184.

219 Moses, *Unofficial Letters*, 344–45.

220 Tadiar, *Fantasy Production*, 2–3.

221 Moses, *Unofficial Letters*, 174.

222 Moses, *Unofficial Letters*, 119.

223 The sense of failed mimicry of Spanish or European styles can be found in other white American writings concerning the Philippines. For example, Mary H. Fee, a Thomasite in the Philippines, expressed similar sentiments in her diary. Describing the way that elite Filipinas dressed their children for state occasions, Fee claimed that Filipino children were "inducted into raiment which their deluded mothers fancy is European and stylish; but there is always something wrong." Fee, *Woman's Impressions of the Philippines*, 79.

224 Moses, *Unofficial Letters*, 88.

225 Taft, *Recollections*, 123.

226 Taft, *Recollections*, 146–47.

227 Elias, "Palate of Power," 49.

228 Abinales and Amoroso, *State and Society in the Philippines*, 115; McCoy, *Policing America's Empire*.

229 Elsie Clews Parsons, "American Snobbishness in the Philippines," *The Independent* 60 (February 8, 1906): 332–33, in 1875–1909 Newspaper Clippings folder, 1905, concerning the travels of Secretary of War William H. Taft in the Philippine Islands (1), Box 1, JAL.

230 Parsons, "American Snobbishness in the Philippines," 332.

231 Parsons, "American Snobbishness in the Philippines," 332. Kiyoko Yamaguchi discusses how racial tensions and racial segregation impacted architecture, home buying, the creation of neighborhoods, and the lack of social interaction

between elite Filipinos and Americans in Manila. Yamaguchi, "New 'American' Houses," 431.

232 Love, *Race over Empire*, 160–65, 199; Ngozi-Brown, "African-American Soldiers and Filipinos," 42–53.

233 Parsons, "American Snobbishness in the Philippines," 332.

234 Kramer, *Blood of Government*, 294–95.

235 Parsons, "American Snobbishness in the Philippines," 333.

236 *San Francisco Argonaut*, October 9, 1905, in 1875–1909 Newspaper Clippings folder, 1905, concerning the travels of Secretary of War William H. Taft in the Philippine Islands (1), Box 1, JAL.

237 *San Francisco Argonaut*, October 9, 1905.

238 Teodoro Kalaw originally addressed the emergence of what he called "La Girl Filipina," a new type of young Filipina who was a product of a "strange personality that American culture was creating for [Filipinos]," in an essay published in the Spanish-language Filipino nationalist newspaper *El Renacimiento*, in 1904. The essay was translated to English and published in a collection of Kalaw's essays. Kalaw, *Aide-de-Camp to Freedom*, 41–43.

239 Parsons mentioned and paraphrased Bishop Charles Brent in her article. Parsons, "American Snobbishness in the Philippines," 333.

## 2. QUEEN MAKERS

1 At the time of her interview, Pura Villanueva Kalaw was married. As was custom, she changed her surname, Villanueva, to her middle name and took on the name of Kalaw as her surname. Although she was unmarried at the time of her coronation, I refer to her as Villanueva Kalaw throughout the chapter.

2 Marina, "Pura Villanueva Kalaw," *La vanguardia*, September 19, 1934. This interview was republished in Marina, *Lo que ellas dicen*, 34. This text was a compilation of interviews of prominent women in the Philippines that a journalist, Marina (a pseudonym), conducted and published originally in the Spanish-language Manila-based newspaper *La vanguardia*, between 1934 and 1937.

3 Marina, "Pura Villanueva Kalaw."

4 Marina, "Pura Villanueva Kalaw," 34.

5 M. Roces, "Gender, Nation and the Politics of Dress"; Cannell, *Power and Intimacy*.

6 Farrales, "Repurposing Beauty Pageants," 47.

7 Mabalon, *Little Manila Is in the Heart*, 176.

8 Similarly, Judy Tzu-Chun Wu argues that ethnic beauty pageants and the idealization of womanhood reflect the intersections between culture and power in Wu, "Loveliest Daughter." For more on ethnic beauty pageants in the United States see Roberts, *Pageants, Parlors, and Pretty Women*; Craig, *Ain't I a Beauty Queen?*; King-O'Riain, *Pure Beauty*.

9  Arleen de Vera and Dawn Mabalon have written on the importance of beauty contests in forming Filipino communities in California, articulating the performance of nationalism within the diasporic context. See Vera, "Rizal Day Queen Contests"; Mabalon, "Beauty Queens, Bomber Pilots."

10  Abinales and Amoroso, *State and Society in the Philippines*, 135.

11  For more on the Philippine Commission and its role in the formation of the Insular Government, see chapter 1.

12  Kramer, *Blood of Government*, 195.

13  Gleeck, *Manila Americans*, 197; Kramer, *Blood of Government*, 289. McCoy, *Policing America's Empire*, 140; Torres, *Americanization of Manila*, 28–74.

14  Contemporary international news outlets have deemed the Philippines as a pageant "powerhouse" and a "queen maker"—a play on the phrase "king maker" used in political writings and histories of monarchies. In the 2010s, the Philippines ranked just behind Venezuela and Colombia in numbers of international beauty pageant titles held. In 2016, Pia Wurtzbach won the title of Miss Universe in a memorable contest that ended with pageant host Steve Harvey's public gaffe in which he accidentally announced Ariadna Gutiérrez, Miss Colombia, as winner. The Philippines currently holds the longest winning streak in the Big Four (Miss World, Miss International, Miss Earth, and Miss Universe) from 2013 to 2017. News pieces and blog posts exposed a multitude of boot camps to train beauty queens scattered across the country. In 2018, Catriona Gray won Miss Universe again for the Philippines. Katrina Angco, "How PH Became the Top Beauty Pageant Country in the World," ABS-CBN News, December 14, 2017, http://news.abs-cbn.com/life/12/14/17/how-ph-became-the-top-beauty-pageant-country-in-the-world; Amee Enriquez, "Philippines: How to Make a Beauty Queen," BBC News, February 2, 2014, https://www.bbc.co.uk/news/world-asia-25550425; Alexa Villano, "Beauty Queens on PH as Pageant Powerhouse," *Rappler*, January 26, 2016, https://www.rappler.com/life-and-style/specials/miss-universe/119894-pia-wurtzbach-miss-universe-international-pageants-powerhouse.

15  A. E. Litiatco, "Meet the 'Misses': Presenting the National Beauties of 1930," *Graphic*, February 26, 1930, 20.

16  M. Johnson, *Beauty and Power*; David, "Transgender Archipelagos," 332–35.

17  Sarah Banet-Weiser describes contemporary beauty pageants as a "vast and varied infrastructure that supports, sustains, and simultaneously reinvent[ed]" beauty. Banet-Weiser, *Most Beautiful Girl in the World*, 6.

18  Burns, *Puro Arte*, 7–9; Fernandez, *Palabas*, 2–26.

19  David and Cruz, "Big, *Bakla*, and Beautiful," 29–33; Farrales, "Repurposing Beauty Pageants," 46–48.

20  *Graphic*, July 9, 1936; *Philippines Free Press*, August 8, 1931.

21  Over the years, the Manila Carnival Queen contests would employ different rules and guidelines for beauty contests. Some contests employed a ballot system, while other years used a board of judges to select winners.

22  Alex R. Castro has an entire blog dedicated to the history of the Manila Carnival Queen contests and the Miss Philippines pageants. The blog also serves as an incredibly rich digital archive filled with photographs, pamphlets, news clippings, and other primary sources. Alex R. Castro, *Manila Carnivals: 1908–1939: A Pictorial History of the "Greatest Annual Event in the Orient"* (blog), http://manilacarnivals.blogspot.com/. Castro, *Aro Katimyas Da!*, 11.

23  Mabalon, *Little Manila Is in the Heart*, 174–79.

24  Villarama, *Sunday Beauty Queen*; Piocos, "Queer Promise of Pageantry."

25  R. Diaz, "Queer Unsettlements."

26  Billig, *Banal Nationalism*.

27  Here, I borrow from Marcia Ochoa's work on transwomen in Venezuela and the lure and the resistant power of beauty and glamour in beauty pageants. Ochoa examines the production of the "mass-mediated beauty pageant in the same analytic frame as the everyday accomplishment of femininity." Ochoa, *Queen for a Day*, 5.

28  Cohen, Wilk, and Stoeltje, *Beauty Queens on the Global Stage*.

29  Burns, *Puro Arte*, 12.

30  Burns, *Puro Arte*, 12; Tolentino, "Transvestites and Transgressions," 334.

31  Chapter 1 goes into greater detail on the relationship between pageantry and religious practices. Mina Roces also addresses how town fiestas and annual religious celebrations produced platforms for Filipino pageantry that celebrated beauty, social status, and feminine norms. M. Roces, "Women in Philippine Politics and Society," 161. Fenella Cannell explains that the history of beauty pageants can be traced back to the Spanish colonial period wherein wealthy families enrolled their daughters in pageants in the hope that, by winning a title, the family could secure advantageous marriage arrangements. Cannell, *Power and Intimacy*, 204.

32  Most of the members of the first Manila Carnival Association were white American men. As the planning of the event became more complex, the Association created subcommittees, which began to include Filipino businessmen and political leaders. For example, Arsenio Luz took the position of director general of the Manila Carnival in 1921, and one popular magazine referred to Luz as the Manila Carnival's "lord and master." "The Carnival Is Coming," *Graphic*, November 10, 1928, 16.

33  For more on the Philippine village, largest of the "living exhibits" at the 1904 St. Louis World's Fair, see Rydell, *All the World's a Fair*; Burns, *Puro Arte*, 21–48; Sarmiento, "To Return to St. Louis"; Kramer, "Making Concessions"; Talusan, "Music, Race, and Imperialism."

34  "True Carnival Spirit Now Prevails," *Manila Times*, February 1, 1907.

35  At a promotional banquet for the first Manila Carnival held in September 1907, attended by 150 Filipino, American, and European investors and entrepreneurs and officials, Governor-General James Francis Smith stated that "though the Carnival would look like it was for pleasure, it was really for business."

36 *El renacimiento*, September 10, 1907, reprinted and translated in Katigbak, *Legacy*, 87.

37 Katigbak, *Legacy*, 132.

38 1909 Manila Carnival Promotional Pamphlet, Records of the Bureau of Insular Affairs, RG 350, series 5453–13, container 415, NARA.

39 1909 Manila Carnival Promotional Pamphlet.

40 Harry Debnam, "The Philippine Carnival: Being an Official Report of Its Organization, Purpose and Success," May 19, 1908, RG 350, series 5453–9, container 415, NARA.

41 Miller, *Benevolent Assimilation*.

42 1909 Manila Carnival Promotional Pamphlet.

43 1909 Manila Carnival Promotional Pamphlet.

44 1909 Manila Carnival Promotional Pamphlet.

45 Philippine Carnival, Manila, February 5 to 14, Promotional Pamphlet, 1910, RG 350, series 5453–12, container 415, NARA.

46 Debnam, "The Philippine Carnival."

47 McCoy and Roces, *Philippine Cartoons*, 24.

48 Among these newspapers were *Cablenews-American, The Manila Times, Philippine Free Press, Daily Bulletin, Manila Opinion, Philippines Gossip, El comercio, El mercantil, El renacimiento, Libertas, La democracia, Mercurio, Asemblea Filipina, Lipag calabaw*, or *Vida Filipina*. A list was found in *Muling pagsilang*, December 9, 1907, reprinted and translated in Katigbak, *Legacy*, 88; "For Queen of the Carnival," *Manila Times*, December 5, 1907, 5.

49 "Queen of the Carnival," 3.

50 McCoy and Roces, *Philippine Cartoons*, 25.

51 M. Roces, "Women in Philippine Politics and Society," 171.

52 Drery, "Prostitution in Colonial Manila."

53 Carnival was also a European Christian adaptation of Dionysian revelry. Anna Kasafi Perkins gives a detailed and insightful genealogy of Carnivale or Canvale in "Carne Vale (Goodbye to Flesh?)." Perkins, "Carne Vale."

54 Cruz-Lucero, "Judas and His Phallus."

55 Said, "The Imperial Spectacle."

56 1909 Manila Carnival Promotional Pamphlet.

57 1909 Manila Carnival Promotional Pamphlet.

58 Carnivals, as interruptions of everyday life manifested in seasonal celebrations (typically before the Lenten season), have a long and rich history; their elements can be traced back even to pre-Christian Rome. Carnivals of medieval Europe, in general, describe festivities that included forms of shocking entertainment that pushed at the boundaries of what would be considered socially acceptable. The shocking components of carnivalistic festivities were often called "misrule," an aberration of normal life or social order. Bakhtin, "Carnival and the Carnivalesque," 250–52; Humphrey, *Politics of Carnival*, 40.

59 1909 Manila Carnival Promotional Pamphlet; Philippine Carnival, Manila, February 5 to 14, Promotional Pamphlet, 1910.

60 The documents pertaining to the first Manila Carnival Queen competition use only the married names of Jones and Beck. The way the articles address the contestants deliberately highlights their social status and influence, as their married or family names clearly indicate their backgrounds. For example, Baldasano was the daughter of the Spanish consul, and Mrs. Israel Beck's husband was a wealthy American businessman. Moreover, the participation of these women reflected the Carnival Association's need for the support and capital of wealthy and influential families to ensure the success of the first Manila Carnival.

61 *Muling pagsilang*, December 9, 1907, published in Katigbak, *Legacy*, 88.

62 Documentation on the Manila Carnivals does not reveal whether or not this Union continued to function after the first Manila Carnival Queen contest.

63 "For the Filipina Queen," *Manila Times*, December 12, 1907, 3.

64 "Cosas del Carnaval: La Prensa Diaria Retira los Cupones—Se Suspende le Eleción de la Reina—Noble Actitud de las Candidates—¿Que Pasa?," *El renacimiento*, January 4, 1908, n.p.

65 "Cosas del Carnaval."

66 "Mrs. Beck Withdraws—Is No Longer a Candidate for the Queen of the Carnival," *Manila Times*, January 2, 1908, 1.

67 *El renacimiento*, December 14, 1907, n.p., published in Katigbak, *Legacy*, 89.

68 McCoy and Roces, *Philippine Cartoons*, 24.

69 McCoy and Roces, *Philippine Cartoons*, 23.

70 Debnam, "The Philippine Carnival."

71 "Life in Manila," *Muling pagsilang*, February 29, 1908, reprinted and translated in Katigbak, *Legacy*, 125.

72 "Pequeños Lunares," *El renacimiento*, February 29, 1908, n.p. For more on the Nacionalista party and the significance of Spanish-language publications in anticolonial nationalist movements in the Philippines, see Cano, "Filipino Press between Two Empires."

73 "Pequeños Lunares."

74 "Pequeños Lunares."

75 Choy, *Empire of Care*, 19.

76 McFerson, "Filipino Identity and Self-Image," 13.

77 *El renacimiento*, February 28, 1908.

78 Fernandez, *Palabas*; Mojares, "Formation of Filipino Nationality"; Rodell, "Philippine 'Seditious Plays'"; Rafael, "White Love."

79 Governor-General James Francis Smith to Unknown, extract from cablegram, Manila, Philippine Islands, March 5, 1908, RG 350, series 5453–5, container 415, NARA.

80 "Method of Choosing Queens," *Manila Times*, January 15, 1909, n.p.

81 Frank Holland, "The Philippines Exposition," *Philippine Monthly*, August 1911, n.p.

82 "The Carnival: Filipino Day and Night," *Philippine Monthly* 2 (January 19, 1912): 22.

83 Fernandez, "Pompas y Solemnidades," 115.

84 "The Carnival: Filipino Day and Night," 22.

85 "Carnival: Filipino Day and Night," 22.

86 "Carnival: Filipino Day and Night," 22.

87 The 1912 Carnival crowned Paz Marquez as Manila Carnival Queen. The 1909 Manila Carnival crowned two queens: an American Queen of the Occident and a Filipina Queen of the Orient. In 1920, Manila Carnival officials crowned then Governor-General Francis Burton Harrison's daughter, Virginia Harrison, Manila Carnival Queen. *Colonial and the Philippines Monthly Review* 3, no. 3 (January 1912): 24.

88 The procedures for selecting Manila Carnival Queens changed several times. The methods ranged from public balloting across the Philippines to the closed selection of young women from prominent families by the Manila Carnival Association. In 1929, the regulations changed again, and Carnival Queen candidates were chosen to represent their college or university.

89 Alex Castro provides detailed descriptions of various celebrations in Manila and Pampanga, including Rizal Day and fêtes for "School Muses" and "Club Muses" from the growing number of colleges and universities. Castro, *Aro Katimyas Da!*, 30–33.

90 "What Price Bathing Suits? About a New Phase of Local Beauty Contests," *Graphic*, February 26, 1930, 2.

91 M. Roces, "Women in Philippine Politics and Society," 172.

92 M. Roces, "Women in Philippine Politics and Society," 172.

93 "Rules Governing 1931 Free Press Beauty Contest," *Philippine Free Press*, August 8, 1931, 43.

94 Litiatco, "Meet the 'Misses,'" 20.

95 Chu, *Chinese and Chinese Mestizos of Manila*.

96 Enriqueta David, "Carnival Beauty Chaperons [sic] Tell Their Story," *Graphic*, January 28, 1931, 7; "A Queen Is Crowned," *Graphic*, February 24, 1938, 8.

97 Licuanan, *Paz Marquez Benitez*, 6.

98 David, "Carnival Beauty Chaperons," 7; "Queen Is Crowned," 8.

99 David, "Carnival Beauty Chaperons," 7; "Queen Is Crowned," 8.

100 David, "Carnival Beauty Chaperons," 7; "Queen Is Crowned," 8.

101 Litiatco, "Meet the 'Misses,'" 20.

102 Litiatco, "Meet the 'Misses,'" 20.

103 Kellner and Durham, "Adventures in Media and Cultural Studies," 8–9.

104 Kramer, *Blood of Government*, 5–6.

105 According to Reynaldo Ileto, *ilustrado* elites of the late nineteenth century constructed a nationalist identity based on a "nostalgia" for Filipino origins. In their writings, including those of José Rizal, they depicted a precolonial Philippines as a lost civilization. Ileto, *Filipinos and Their Revolution*, 31. See also Agoncillo, *Revolt of the Masses*; Quibuyen, *Nation Aborted*.

106 Aguilar, "Tracing Origins."

107 I use the terms *native* and *indio* as they were both used to refer to people, ethnic groups outside of Manila and the lowland provinces, as well as to con-

cepts of "tradition" and "indigeneity" during the U.S. colonial period. Prior to the U.S. regime, Spanish colonizers referred to people in the islands that they would call the Philippines as indio, a term they used for indigenous peoples in their colonies. Indio, native, and "Indigenous" have complex meanings in the Philippines and change over time. As Oona Paredes writes, in the contemporary moment, the "concept of indigeneity carries distinct political connotations in the Republic of the Philippines. Indigeneity is not only defined legally by the national Indigenous Peoples' Rights Act [1997], it is also used to refer to ethnic minorities who are widely regarded by the general public as not merely culturally differentiated but also racially distinct from the mainstream Filipino population." O. Paredes, "Preserving 'Tradition,'" 86.

108 For photographs of each Manila Carnival Queen, see Nuyda and Reyes, *Beauty Book*.

109 Flores, "Prohibiting the Presentation of Pride."

110 Aguilar, "Tracing Origins," 614.

111 Burns, "Your Terno's Draggin'," 205; M. Roces, "Dress, Status, and Identity in the Philippines," 358–59.

112 Arrizón, *Queering Mestizaje*, 146.

113 A. E. Litiatco, "Memories of the First Carnival as Told by Mrs. Pura Villaneuva-Kalaw (First Filipino Carnival Queen)," *Graphic*, February 12, 1930, 4.

114 "Queen Manolita I," *Evangelina E. Lewis Collection of Postcards*, Newberry Library, Chicago.

115 Nuyda and Reyes, *Beauty Book*, 28.

116 Nuyda and Reyes, *Beauty Book*, 28.

117 See chapter 4 in Clutario, "The Appearance of Filipina Nationalism."

118 Sobritchea, "American Colonial Education," 70.

119 Calata, "Role of Education in Americanizing Filipinos," 89; Coloma, "Disidentifying Nationalism."

120 "The Majesty the Empress," *Colonial and the Philippines Monthly Review* 3, no. 3 (January 1912): 24.

121 "The Majesty the Empress," 24.

122 Enriqueta David, "Carnival Beauties Talk: Intimate Glimpses of Seven of the Carnival Beauty Contestants Are Revealed in Interviews Had with a Charming Yong [sic] Newspaper Woman Enriqueta David," *Graphic*, January 14, 1931, 6. In this chapter, I continue to use the name Maria Kalaw, although she might also be recognized by her later married name, Maria Kalaw Katigbak.

123 Doeppers, *Feeding Manila in Peace and War*, 3.

124 D. Cruz, *Transpacific Femininities*, 22, 72.

125 Laguio, *Our Modern Woman*, 5.

126 D. Reyes, "History of Divorce Legislation in the Philippines since 1900"; D. Cruz, *Transpacific Femininities*, 100.

127 Burns, "Your Terno's Draggin'," 323; D. Cruz, *Transpacific Femininities*, 104.

128 M. Roces, "Rethinking 'the Filipino Woman,'" 41.

129 D. Cruz, *Transpacific Femininities*, 68.

130  D. Cruz, *Transpacific Femininities*, 87–98.
131  M. Roces, "Rethinking 'the Filipino Woman,'" 34–38.
132  "The Eternal Queen," *Philippine Free Press*, February 7, 1931, 1.
133  "The Majesty the Empress," 24.
134  Litiatco, "Memories of the First Carnival," 5.
135  Litiatco, "Memories of the First Carnival," 5.
136  Litiatco, "Memories of the First Carnival," 5.
137  For more on the history of feminism in the Philippines and Pura Villanueva's role, see Aquino, "Filipino Women and Political Engagement"; Blackburn, "A Century of Women's Activism in the Philippines," 21–33; Roces, "Rethinking 'The Filipino Woman,'" 34–62; and Subido, *The Feminist Movement in the Philippines.*
138  "Memories of the First Carnival," 5.
139  M. Roces, "Women in Philippine Politics and Society," 161.
140  "Queen Is Crowned," 8.
141  David, "Carnival Beauties Talk," 6; David, "Carnival Beauty Chaperons," 7.
142  Rodrigo C. Lim, "Carnival Queens of By-Gone Days," *Graphic*, December 8, 1928, 33.
143  "Miss Philippines 1926 Is December Bride," *Graphic*, November 26, 1927, 25; Lim, "Carnival Queens of By-Gone Days," 33.
144  Cannell, *Power and Intimacy*, 204.
145  M. Roces, "Women in Philippine Politics and Society," 159.
146  Lim, "Carnival Queens of By-Gone Days, 33.
147  Lim, "Carnival Queens of By-Gone Days, 33.
148  For more on internationalism and the formation of the PPWA, see Paisley, *Glamour in the Pacific.*
149  The Pan-Pacific Research Institution, *Mid-Pacific Magazine*, Volume 46–47 (1933), 3.
150  "Maria Kalaw Katigbak," Barbour Scholars, University of Michigan, accessed August 14, 2019, https://rackham.umich.edu/project/maria-kalaw-katigbak/; Reymann L. Guevarra, "Maria Kalaw Katigbak: Senator and Beauty Queen," National Historical Commission of the Philippines, September 4, 2012, http://nhcp.gov.ph/maria-kalaw-katigbak-beauty-queen-and-senator/.
151  M. Roces, "Women in Philippine Politics and Society," 161.
152  Hinojosa and Carle, "From Miss World to World Leader: Beauty Queens, Paths to Power, and Political Representations"; M. Roces, *Women, Power, and Kinship Politics*, 172.
153  M. Roces, *Women, Power, and Kinship Politics*, 172.
154  At the time of her coronation, Paz Marquez was a single young woman. By the time she wrote her short story "Dead Stars" in 1925, she had married and had changed her name. Marquez Benitez, "Dead Stars."
155  Grout, "Between Venus and Mercury"; Latham, "Packaging Woman."
156  "What Price Bathing Suits?," 2.
157  "What Price Bathing Suits?," 2.

158 "What Price Bathing Suits?," 2.
159 "There Are Queens and 'Queens,'" photo caption published in Lim, "Carnival Queens of By-Gone Days," 37.
160 Ochoa, *Queen for a Day*, 5.
161 Victor Mendoza's work on sexuality and intimacy during the US colonization of the Philippines offers an important methodology on queer archives. Mendoza argues that "intimacies emerged in various forms of largely neglected state and cultural productions: a strange archive, that is seemingly disparate archival material." Piecing together archival material also "necessitates a queer-of-color reading practice that gets at how such governance emerged in a negative (or even roundabout) yet nonetheless effective form." V. Mendoza, *Metroimperial Intimacies*, 29, 43.
162 Mina Roces argues that the Filipina beauty queen, starting from the early twentieth century up until the present, offers an image of female power. M. Roces, "Women in Philippine Politics and Society," 172.
163 "Manila's Great Carnival Opens the Eyes of the Entire Orient," *New York Herald*, April 12, 1908.
164 Several different converging forces during the early twentieth century caused the development of various and shifting icons of beauty. Industrialization and new technologies, what historian Doreen Fernandez calls "the intensification of communication technologies," in the Philippines led to the growth of print media and visual culture. Fernandez, "Mass Culture and Cultural Policy," 297. Ramon Roces, editor of *Liwayway* and *Graphic* magazine, insisted that during the 1920s, "there [was] a big field in these Islands for an up to date illustrated weekly, one devoted almost entirely to pictured news." For R. Roces, "news pictures reflected reality." Within five years of the first pictorial weekly, he pointed out that numbers of readers for *Liwayway*, which included pictorials, increased steadily; it was the first publication to ever exceed a readership of 30,000, and by 1927, it averaged a circulation of 60,000 every week. R. Roces's editorial expressed a shift toward the visual in public media and reception. Ramon Roces, "To the Reading Public," *Graphic*, July 2, 1927, 1; Encanto, *Constructing the Filipina*.
165 During the early twentieth century, *Manila Times* readership consisted mostly of white Americans living in Manila. *El renacimiento*, which later became *La vanguardia*, targeted a Filipino audience, in particular, those of the Spanish-speaking, educated class. Later, English language publications like *Graphic* provided pictorials and articles to an American, educated Filipino readership.
166 "Miss Philippines 1926 Is December Bride," *Graphic*, November 26, 1927, 25; Lim, "Carnival Queens of By-Gone Days," 33; "Beauties: 1938 Models," *Graphic*, February 24, 1938.
167 M. Roces, "Women in Philippine Politics and Society," 191, 204.
168 "Beauties: 1938 Models."
169 "Beauties: 1938 Models."

170 Castro, *Aro Katimyas Da!*, 11.
171 Lim, "Carnival Queens of By-Gone Days," 33; *Graphic*, August 20, 1927, 11–15; Quimpo and Cordero, "Cruel (Dedicado a la Srta. Guia Balmori)."
172 "Tribute to Beauty," *Graphic*, July 9, 1936.
173 Evangelina E. Lewis Collection of Postcards, Newberry Library, Chicago.
174 David, "Carnival Beauty Chaperons," 6.
175 David, "Carnival Beauty Chaperons," 7.
176 "Miss Batangas Leads," *Philippine Free Press*, September 19, 1931, 37.
177 Taylor, *Disappearing Acts*, ix.
178 The concept of nationalism as a process of community and identity formation is borrowed from Benedict Anderson's influential work, *Imagined Communities*.
179 *El Tiempo*, March 3, 1908, n.p., reprinted and translated in Katigbak, *Legacy*, 129.
180 *El renacimiento*, December 19, 1907, n.p., reprinted and translated in Katigbak, *Legacy*, 129.
181 *Muling pagsilang*, December 18, 1907, reprinted and translated in Katigbak, *Legacy*, 128; *El renacimiento*, December 19, 1907, 129.
182 Letter published in *El Abalid, Iloilo*, December 19, 1907, reprinted and translated in Katigbak, *Legacy*, 91.
183 *Muling pagsilang*, December 18, 1907, 128; *El renacimiento*, December 19, 1907, 129.
184 "Your Final Chance to Vote: Last Ballots in Free Press Beauty Contests This Week," *Philippine Free Press*, October 29, 1932, 28.
185 "Your Final Chance to Vote," 28.
186 "Miss Batangas Leads: Voting Continuous Merrily in the Free Press Beauty Contest," *Philippine Free Press*, September 19, 1931, n.p.
187 "Miss Batangas Leads."
188 Myles A. Garcia, "And You Thought You Knew Everything about Beauty Pageants," *Positively Filipino*, January 27, 2016, http://www.positivelyfilipino.com/magazine/and-you-thought-you-knew-everything-about-beauty-pageants.
189 Nuyda and Reyes, *The Beauty Book*, 18.
190 Here I draw from Millian Kang's work on race, transnational feminism, and labor in beauty service work. Kang argues that the labor of beautification also takes place in the public and highly racialized spaces of service work. Kang, *Managed Hand*, 15–16.
191 Philippine Carnival, Manila, February 5 to 14, Promotional Pamphlet, 1910.
192 David, "Carnival Beauty Chaperons," 6.
193 David, "Carnival Beauty Chaperons," 6.
194 David, "Carnival Beauty Chaperons," 6.
195 Litiatco, "Meet the 'Misses,'" 20.
196 Litiatco, "Meet the 'Misses,'" 20.
197 David, "Carnival Beauties Talk," 6.
198 "Queen Is Crowned," 18; Nuyda and Reyes, *Beauty Book*, 45.

199 "Queen Is Crowned," 18.
200 "Queen Is Crowned," 18–19.
201 See chapter 4 in Clutario, "The Appearance of Filipina Nationalism."

3. PHILIPPINE LINGERIE

1  The film *Luzon Lingerie* (1920) was produced by Burton Holmes and shot and directed by cinematographer Herford T. Cowling. It is unclear when the film was filmed in the Philippines. In his published travelogues, Holmes indicates that he first traveled to Manila in the early 1900s, before the publication of the book in 1908. However, some of the scenes from the film suggest that Holmes returned to the Philippines as the subjects on screen reflect fashion and details that could be attributed to the late 1910s. See Holmes, *Burton Holmes Travelogues*. For more on the culture of travel and entertainment in the United States, see Barber, "The Roots of Travel Cinema."

2  Holmes, *Luzon Lingerie*.

3  This title flashed on the screen immediately after a shot of young Filipino men and boys cutting patterns to be used by embroiderers. As in the United States, pattern makers and cutters were usually men who earned higher wages than the embroiderers and seamstresses. However, women and girls made up the majority of workers in the embroidery and garment industries. Holmes, *Luzon Lingerie*.

4  For more on travel literature, gender, racism, whiteness, and cultures of imperialism, see Grewal, *Home and Harem*, 26; Kaplan, *Anarchy of Empire*, 23–50.

5  Holmes, *Luzon Lingerie*. Roland Sintos Coloma addresses the white American colonial gaze and the desire for viewing Filipinas as part of a tropical and exotic landscape. Coloma, "White Gazes, Brown Breasts," 252.

6  Phạm, *Asians Wear Clothes*, 71.

7  Elson and Pearson, "Nimble Fingers Make Cheap Workers"; Safa, "Runaway Shops and Female Employment," 419.

8  Enloe, "Women Textile Workers," 409.

9  Corpuz, *Economic History of the Philippines*, 222.

10  Milgram, "Piña Cloth"; Que, Review of *Textiles in the Philippine Colonial Landscape*; Ramos, "Filipina Bordadoras"; M. Roces, "Dress, Status, and Identity," 341–72.

11  Commons et al., *History of Labour in the United States*, 106–7; Laurie, *Artisans into Workers*, 15–46.

12  Lowe, *Intimacies*, 5, 8.

13  Tadiar, "Empire," 114.

14  Phạm, *Asians Wear Clothes*, 76.

15  Doeppers, *Manila 1900–1941*, 23.

16  Corpuz, *Economic History of the Philippines*, 219–21; Ventura, "From Small Farms to Progressive Plantations."

17  Root, *A Report of the Secretary of War*, 6.
18  Root, *A Report of the Secretary of War*, 6.
19  Coo, *Clothing the Colony*, 173.
20  Bernal and Encanto, *Patterns for the Filipino Dress*, 10.
21  Bernal and Encanto, *Patterns for the Filipino Dress*, 10–11.
22  European style fine needlework proliferated in the Philippines. At the same time, Filipino embroiderers adapted and localized needlework methods to ornament locally made textiles such as jusi and piña. Filipinas, particularly those of the upper and middle classes, took up this needlework as part of their domestic duties. Embroidery also evolved into a profession for Filipinas. Although embroidery work was difficult, embroiderers were paid very little. Coo, *Clothing the Colony*, 172.
23  Milgram, "Piña Cloth"; L. Reyes, *Textiles of Southern Philippines*.
24  Canta, "Of Cambayas, Custas and Calicos," 127–28; Capistrano-Baker, Keurs, and Castro, *Embroidered Multiples*, 20.
25  Ramos, "Filipina Bordadoras," 26, 27; Montinola, *Piña*, 94.
26  Montinola, *Piña*, 94–95; Ramos, "Filipina Bordadoras," 26.
27  Hernandez, *Homebound*, 39.
28  Coo, *Clothing the Colony*, 132.
29  Coo, *Clothing the Colony*, 132.
30  Doeppers, *Manila 1900–1941*, 23; Camagay, *Working Women of Manila*, 39–42.
31  Camagay, *Working Women of Manila*, 40.
32  Funtecha, "Iloilo's Weaving Industry," 177–78.
33  A feeling of indebtedness that stems from a long-standing genealogy of patronage. Rafael, *Contracting Colonialism*, 121–35.
34  Coo, "Clothing and the Colonial Culture," 415.
35  Fr. Joaquin Martinez de Zuñiga, *Estadismo de las filipinas o mis viajes por esto pais*, vol. 1 (Madrid: n.p., 1893), 294–95, quoted in Camagay, *Working Women of Manila*, 39.
36  Capistrano-Baker et al., *Embroidered Multiples*, 18; Lynne, "Piña Cloth."
37  Coo, "Clothing and the Colonial Culture," 415.
38  Coo, "Clothing and the Colonial Culture," 405, 420.
39  Tessa P. Liu describes French lingerie production as "a mass industry which employed women to produce for women." Liu, "Commercialization of Trousseau Work," 180; Wilkes, *Narrative of the United States Exploring Expedition*, 475.
40  Wilkes, *Narrative of the United States Exploring Expedition*, 296.
41  Liu, "Commercialization of Trousseau Work," 180.
42  LaFeber, *New Empire*; Schirmer and Shalom, *Philippines Reader*.
43  Fujita Rony, *American Workers, Colonial Power*; Baldoz, *Third Asiatic Invasion*; España-Maram, *Creating Masculinity*.
44  Choy, *Empire of Care*.
45  Parreñas, *Servants of Globalization*; Francisco-Menchavez, *The Labor of Care*; G. Pratt, "From Registered Nurse to Registered Nanny."

46 Many thanks to Mae Ngai for encouraging me to connect Philippine embroidery to the history of immigrant women in New York and the US garment industry. Textile and garment industries have garnered much attention from historians. Labor historians and scholars of material culture alike have shown how industrialization and immigration shaped the contours of garment work in cities like New York. Enstad, *Ladies of Labor*; Waldinger, "Another Look at the International Ladies' Garment Workers' Union"; Bender, *Sweated Work*.

47 Waldinger, "Another Look at the International Ladies' Garment Workers' Union," 165; Bender, *Sweated Work*, 2.

48 Walton, "Working Women."

49 Doeppers, *Manila 1900–1941*, 23.

50 Museums and museum publications on textiles document the global trade of textiles produced in different regions in the Philippines even prior to the US colonial period. Seafaring and trade routes like that of the Manila Galleon facilitated the purchase of textiles, such as piña, as luxurious souvenirs and gifts, as well as the practice of displaying textiles in homes and museums and later, in the nineteenth century, at world's fairs. Montinola, *Piña*.

51 Pante, "Quezon's City."

52 Consul General George E. Anderson, Hong Kong, "Development of Philippine Embroidery Trade," *Daily Consular and Trade Reports*, no. 190 (Bureau of Foreign and Domestic Commerce and Department of Commerce, August 15, 1913), 913–16, Folder: Embroidery & Textiles, Box 869, Entry 5, RG 350, NARA.

53 Coo, "Clothing and the Colonial Culture," 135.

54 Nerissa Balce addresses the ways in which US racial discourse portrayed Filipino bodies as "grotesque," "hideous," and "malnourished," to underscore the "primitiveness" of the tropics. Balce, *Body Parts of Empire*, 142.

55 Balce, *Body Parts of Empire*, 142–45. Conger, *Ohio Woman*, 60.

56 Conger, *Ohio Woman*, 60.

57 Balce, *Body Parts of Empire*, 142.

58 This discourse reflected nineteenth- and early twentieth-century ideologies of biological racism. Eugenicist logics promoted notions of a "natural" hierarchy of races. (Philippines) Bureau of Education, *Lace Making and Embroidery*, 9.

59 (Philippines) Bureau of Education, *Lace Making and Embroidery*, 9.

60 Walter W. Marquardt, "America's Contribution to Philippine Education," October 1944, Folder: Papers re Philippine Education, Box 7, Walter W. Marquardt Papers, Bentley Historical Collections, University of Michigan, Ann Arbor (hereinafter WM).

61 Holmes, *Luzon Lingerie*.

62 Boomer, "Philippine Embroidery," 153–54; Gleeck, *American Business*, 69.

63 Stoler, *Along the Archival Grain*.

64 Parreñas, "Migrant Filipina Domestic Workers"; Ong, "Gender and Labor Politics of Postmodernity."

65 Gleeck, *American Business*, 72. White, "Introduction," 7.

66  Pérez, *War of 1898*, xii.

67  Corpuz, *Economic History of the Philippines*, 220.

68  A brief trade report in *Women's Wear Daily* stated, "Imports into the United States from the Philippine Islands in 1908, the last year prior to the enactment of the law in question, were $9,243,244 in value. In 1911, 20,212,917: while domestic exports to those islands were in 1908, 9,904,097, and in 1911 20,896,029, both imports and exports having thus more than doubled in value in the period between 1908 and 1911. The law in question was enacted in August, 1909, the calendar year 1908 being the last full year prior to its enactment." "General News: Washington D.C.—Trade of the United States with the Philippine Islands," *Women's Wear Daily* 4, no. 46 (February 26, 1912): 4.

69  "The Tariff," *Women's Wear Daily* 5, no. 126 (November 29, 1912): 10–11.

70  Onofre Corpuz focuses on products and raw materials, but here I emphasize that the insular government's economic plan also largely targeted the extraction of cheap labor. Corpuz, *Economic History of the Philippines*, 220.

71  M. D. C. Crawford, "Design Department: Adapting Philippine Embroidery to Needs of American People Expanded Consumption of Hand-Made Underwear in This Country," *Women's Wear Daily* 19, no. 62 (September 12, 1919): 2.

72  "Fashion: Soft and Lacy Underwear at Unusual Prices," *Vogue* 51, no. 9 (May 1, 1918): 77, 78.

73  Gleeck, *American Business and Philippine Economic Development*, 72.

74  United States Tariff Commission, "The Insular Case," in *Colonial Tariff Policies*, 580–600.

75  Ngai, *Impossible Subjects*, 96–126; Baldoz, *The Third Asiatic Invasion*, 32–39, 150–57.

76  "Filipino Lingerie Brought to US by Big Syndicate," *Women's Wear Daily* 12, no. 23 (January 28, 1916): 16.

77  Department of Commerce and Communications and Bureau of Commerce and Industry, "The Philippine Embroidery Industry," reprint from the *Commerce and Industry Journal* 2, no. 7 (1926), revised December 31, 1929, 21519/19, Box 869, RG 350, NARA.

78  P. N. Sturtevant, "Some Effects of the European War on Industrial Work in the Philippines," *Philippine Craftsman* 4, no. 4 (October 1915): 262–63.

79  Blackhawk, *Violence over the Land*, 39–41; Cook-Lynn, *Separate Country*, 34–50, 147–59; Deloria, *Behind the Trail of Broken Treaties*; Jacobson, *Barbarian Virtues*, 7; Estes, "Wounded Knee."

80  Beck and Tolnay, "The Killing Fields of the Deep South"; Johnson, *River of Dark Dreams*; Hunter, *To 'Joy My Freedom*, 81–97.

81  "Anniversary Number," *Manila Times*, February 1910, quoted in Gleeck, *American Business*, 70.

82  "Anniversary Number," quoted in Gleeck, *American Business*, 69.

83  Gleeck, *American Business*, 70.

84  Gleeck, *American Business*, 69.

85  "Embroideries," *Women's Wear Daily* 5, no. 34 (August 9, 1912): 11.

86   Doeppers, *Manila 1900–1941*, 3.

87   Doeppers, *Manila 1900–1941*, 23.

88   Doeppers, *Manila 1900–1941*, 22.

89   Hugo H. Miller, "Review of the Industrial Conferences, Baguio, May 3–7, 1915," *Philippine Craftsman* 4, no. 1 (July 1915): 38.

90   "Embroideries," 11.

91   Crawford, "Design Department," 2.

92   Ong, *Spirits of Resistance*, xvii.

93   Doeppers, *Manila 1900–1941*, 22; Camagay, *Working Women of Manila*, 39.

94   Industry growth depended on quickly creating a labor force during a period that US officials regarded as a crisis of the lack of workers. Bankoff, "Wants, Wages, and Workers."

95   Kang, "Manicures," 184.

96   Powis-Brown was one of the prominent early firms to emerge in the 1910s. Other firms were Ollendorf's, Elaine Elser, Elico Embroidery, Art Embroidery (later Daisy), and George Borgfeldt and Co. Gleeck, *American Business*, 71.

97   Elsie Cleveland Mead, "She Made a Million Dollars," *The Delineator* 100 (June 1922): 13.

98   Mead, "She Made a Million Dollars," 13

99   Mead, "She Made a Million Dollars," 13.

100  Mead, "She Made a Million Dollars," 13.

101  Mead, "She Made a Million Dollars," 13.

102  Anderson, "Development of Philippine Embroidery Trade," 913.

103  For more on the contradictions of copyright and plagiarism in the fashion industry see Phạm, "Feeling Appropriately."

104  Assistant Secretary of War Henry Breckinridge to the US Secretary of State, July 15, 1913, Box 869, Entry 5, RG 350, NARA.

105  "U. S. Imports of Hand-Embroidery Made in Islands of World Reported Falling," *Women's Wear Daily* 31, no. 140 (December 14, 1925): 39, 44; Gleeck, *American Business*, 72.

106  "Undergarments," *Women's Wear Daily* 15, no. 7 (July 10, 1917): 5.

107  Gleeck, *American Business*, 72.

108  Crawford, "Design Department," 2.

109  Gleeck, *American Business*, 72. I elaborate on the establishment of the School of Household Industries in chapter 4.

110  "Undergarments," 5.

111  In the early years of a transnational Philippine embroidery industry, manufacturers focused on "waists," or blouses designed to be tucked into the waist of floor-length skirts. However, by the mid-1910s, this style of blouse fell to the wayside. Embroidery became more focused on undergarments.

112  "U.S. Imports of Hand-Embroidery," 39, 44.

113  The report only accounted for the total value of exports. "U.S. Imports of Hand-Embroidery," 39, 44.

114  "Undergarments," 5.

115  "Filipino Lingerie Brought to U.S. by Big Syndicate," *Women's Wear Daily* 12, no. 23 (January 28, 1916): 16.

116  Crawford, "Design Department," 2.

117  Crawford, "Design Department," 2.

118  "Undergarments," 5.

119  "Undergarments," 5.

120  "Undergarments," 5.

121  Crawford, "Design Department," 2.

122  See chapter 1 for more on the impact of Spanish colonialism and fashion in the Philippines.

123  Thuy Linh Nguyen Tu argues that even in the late twentieth and into the twenty-first centuries, fashion marketing strategies of what she calls "Asian Chic" need to be "familiar enough to be consumable, but distinctive enough to still be desirable." Tu, *Beautiful Generation*, 121.

124  "Fashion: Soft and Lacy Underwear at Unusual Prices," *Vogue* 51, no. 9 (May 1, 1918): 77, 78.

125  "Advertisement for Macy's Annual January Sales," *New York Times*, January 3, 1926, 11.

126  "Fashion," *Vogue* 47, no. 1 (January 1, 1916): 57.

127  I want to thank Anne Cheng for pointing out the power of consumer desire for the handmade garment.

128  "Blouses: Rapid Advance under American Supervision Breaks Down Distinctions between Types of Island Handwork," *Women's Wear Daily* 19, no. 109 (November 8, 1919): 14, 18.

129  "Undergarments," 5.

130  "Undergarments," 5.

131  "Fashion: Soft and Lacy Underwear at Unusual Prices," 77, 78.

132  Thompson, "Aesthetics and Empire," 3, 23.

133  Balce, *Body Parts of Empire*, 80; Holt, *Colonizing Filipinas*, 10–11.

134  Boris, *Home to Work*.

135  Doeppers, *Manila 1900–1941*, 22.

136  Advertisement (Powis-Brown Co., Inc.), *Women's Wear Daily* 23, no. 126 (November 30, 1921), 11.

137  Holmes, *Luzon Lingerie*; Hoganson, *Consumers' Imperium*, 137–38.

138  Hoganson, *Consumers' Imperium*, 137.

139  "Realistic Exhibit Shows Natives at Work on Dainty Embroideries," *Women's Wear Daily* 22, no. 106 (May 7, 1921): 25.

140  R. Reyes, "Modernizing the Manileña"; Nava, "Modernity's Disavowal."

141  "Realistic Exhibit Shows Natives at Work on Dainty Embroideries," 25; "Undergarments: Philippine Embroidery Exhibit at Coast Shop Publication," *Women's Wear Daily* 25, no. 58 (September 8, 1922), 14.

142  "Undergarments: Philippine Embroidery Exhibit," 14.

143  "Undergarments: Philippine Embroidery Exhibit," 14.

144 "Undergarments: Philippine Embroidery Exhibit," 14.

145 For more American perceptions of Filipinos' racial strangeness and queerness as colonial and liminal subjects, see Mendoza, *Metroimperial Fantasies*, 28.

146 Lim, *Brown Boys and Rice Queens*, 160.

147 Anne Cheng addresses the construction of glamour and the commodification of women of color. Cheng, "Shine," 1037, 1038; Cheng, *Ornamentalism*, 22.

148 "Laces and Embroideries," *Women's Wear Daily* 21, no. 31 (August 6, 1920): 21, 36.

149 "Laces and Embroideries," 36.

150 "Laces and Embroideries," 36.

151 "Laces and Embroideries," 36.

152 "Laces and Embroideries," 36.

153 "Laces and Embroideries," 36.

154 "Laces and Embroideries," 21.

155 "Laces and Embroideries," 21.

156 "Laces and Embroideries," 21.

157 "Laces and Embroideries," 21.

158 For more on labor unions in the Philippines, see M. Kerkvliet, *Manila Workers' Unions*; Scrase, "Precarious Production," 452.

159 For more on women's histories on informal labor, resistance, and labor organizing, see Cobble, "More Intimate Unions."

160 Chiba, "Cigar-Makers"; M. Kerkvliet, *Unbending Cane*; Sibal, "Century of the Philippine Labor Movement."

161 American Chamber of Commerce of the Philippines, *American Chamber of Commerce Journal* 2, no. 1 (January 1922): 33

162 "Exchange Rate Hurts U.S. Trade in Philippines," *Women's Wear Daily* 22, no. 34 (February 10, 1921): 13.

163 *American Chamber of Commerce Journal* 2, no. 1 (January 1922): 33.

164 "Says Embroidery Industry in the Philippines Is Hit Hard," *Women's Wear Daily* 23, no. 42 (August 19, 1921): 41, 48.

165 Doeppers, *Manila 1900–1941*, 23.

166 "Philippine Embroidery Industry," *New York Times*, December 13, 1925, 21; "U.S. Imports of Hand-Embroidery Made in Islands of World Reported Falling," *Women's Wear Daily* 31, no. 140 (December 14, 1925): 39, 44; "Philippine Embroidery Reported Hard to Sell," *Women's Wear Daily* 31, no. 93 (October 19, 1925): 45.

167 Frank White to Frank McIntyre, November 17, 1924, and July 15, 1925, 21510/81, Folder: Embroidery Inquiries, Box 869, Entry 5, RG 350, NARA.

168 "Lingerie: Philippine Lingerie Importer Decries Cheapened Merchandise Standards," *Women's Wear Daily* 28, no. 122 (May 23, 1924): 9.

169 "Lingerie: Majority Opinion Favors Proposed Philippine Lingerie Legislation," *Women's Wear Daily* 29, no. 89 (October 14, 1924): 10, 47.

170 Frank White to Frank McIntyre, November 17, 1924, and July 15, 1925.

171 Tadiar, "Life-Times of Disposability within Global Neoliberalism."

172 *American Chamber of Commerce Journal* 2, no. 1 (January 1922): 33.

173 *American Chamber of Commerce Journal* 2, no. 1 (January 1922): 33.

174 *American Chamber of Commerce Journal* 2, no. 1 (January 1922): 33.

175 Gleeck, *American Business and Philippine Economic Development*, 70.

176 US Department of Commerce, *Women's Muslin-Underwear Industry*, 27, 115–17.

177 "Undergarments: Philippine Work Better Than Ever but Cannot Compete with Best of French Work," *Women's Wear Daily* 19, no. 71 (September 23, 1919): 9.

178 "Undergarments: Philippine Work Better Than Ever," 9.

179 "Undergarments: Philippine Work Better Than Ever," 9.

180 Scott, *Weapons of the Weak*, xv–xvi.

181 I use the term *multisited* as *multinational* glosses over the historical specificity of colonialism.

182 Ofreneo, "Philippine Garment Industry."

183 Ofreneo, "Philippine Garment Industry," 162–63.

184 Rodriguez, *Migrants for Export*, xii.

185 Gleeck, *American Business and Philippine Economic Development*, 70.


4. BEAUTY REGIMENS

1 Alzate, *Convict Labor*, 21.

2 Holmes, *Luzon Lingerie*.

3 "Prison System in the Philippines Proving Merit: Director Tells Salt Lake City Congress of Industrial Activities," *Christian Science Monitor*, August 18, 1924, 4.

4 Victorio, *Prison Reform in the Philippines*, 78.

5 Here I draw from Michel Foucault's work that connects the distribution of disciplinary space to the "individualizing fragmentation of labour power" and industrialization. Foucault, *Discipline and Punish*, 145.

6 Raymundo, "Beauty Regimens, Beauty Regimes," 103–5.

7 D. Rodriguez, *Forced Passages*, 44.

8 Neferti Tadiar calls this "life-times of disposability" or "life-producing practices of social experience of surplus populations." Tadiar, "Life-Times of Disposability."

9 Philippines, Department of Public Instruction, *Report of the Secretary of Public Instruction*, 10.

10 Colonial education officials referred to industrial school students as "pupil workers," a term that reflected both their industrial trade training and that their wares were sold in local markets and urban trade fairs and expositions. May, *Social Engineering in the Philippines*, 153. The term "convict labor" was regularly used by government officials, prison officials, and Filipino and American social scientists to describe the system work performed by prisoners. See, for example, Alzate, *Convict Labor*.

11  Elihu Root, Secretary of War, response to "A Dispatch from Judge Taft Dated January 9, 1901," in *Reports of the Philippine Commission . . . 1900–1903*, 27.

12  "Results from Domestic Science," *Philippine Craftsman* 2, no. 7 (January 1914): 451.

13  Conception Torres, "Domestic Science in Bago, Occidental Negros," *Philippine Craftsman* 4, no. 3 (September 1915): 158; "Resolutions of Industrial Conferences," *Philippine Craftsman* 2, no. 9 (March 1914): 729–30.

14  Moral, *Negotiating Empire*, 28; Francisco, "From Subjects to Citizens"; Martin, "Pedagogy," 90–100; Schueller, "Colonial Management, Collaborative Dissent."

15  Cruz, *Transpacific Femininities*, 6–7.

16  Coloma, "Destiny Has Thrown."

17  David Barrows, quoted in LeRoy, *Philippine Life*, 231.

18  Coloma, "Destiny Has Thrown," 513.

19  Steinbock-Pratt, *Educating the Empire*, 192.

20  May, *Social Engineering*, 153.

21  Bankoff, "Wants, Wages, and Workers," 59–86.

22  May, "Business of Education," 151.

23  May, "Business of Education," 151.

24  May, "Business of Education," 154.

25  Glenn, *Unequal Freedom*.

26  Teachers approached household labor as a kind of science, borrowing from the movement for domestic sciences in the United States. Goldstein, *Creating Consumers*; Leon, "Home Economics Curricular Reforms." See also May, "Social Engineering in the Philippines," 137; McKenna, *American Imperial Pastoral*, 49–74.

27  See chapter 3 for the development and expansion of the Philippine embroidery industry. US manufacturers imported materials to be cut, embroidered, and finished in the Philippines and then shipped back to the United States for American consumers.

28  Frank McIntyre to James Hay, Representative in Congress, January 9, 1912, RG 94, NARA.

29  (Philippines) Bureau of Education, *Lace Making and Embroidery*, 9.

30  (Philippines) Bureau of Education, *Lace Making and Embroidery*, 9.

31  See chapter 3 for more on the genealogy of needlework in the Philippines.

32  Frank Carpenter to Frank McIntyre, March 11, 1912, Box 869, RG 350, NARA.

33  Carpenter to McIntyre, March 11, 1912.

34  Carpenter to McIntyre, March 11, 1912.

35  Herbert D. Fisher, "Evolution of Industrial Supervision," *Philippine Craftsman* 5, no. 2 (August 1916): 86.

36  Fisher, "Evolution of Industrial Supervision," 86.

37  See chapter 3 for the gendered racialization of Filipina embroiderers. Fisher, "Evolution of Industrial Supervision," 86.

38  Fisher, "Evolution of Industrial Supervision," 86.

39  Fisher, "Evolution of Industrial Supervision," 87.

40  See *Acts of the Second Philippine Legislature*, 42.

41  Frank Carpenter to Frank McIntyre, June 26, 1912, Box 869, RG 350, NARA. By "cacique type," Carpenter refers to the women who were part of politically and socially influential families.

42  After attending trade schools, these worker-pupils would then return to their hometowns to work in trade centers, continuing to create handcrafts for sale on the global market. Walter W. Marquardt, "America's Contribution to Philippine Education," October 1944, Folder: Papers re Philippine Education, Box 7, Walter W. Marquardt Papers, Bentley Historical Collections, University of Michigan, Ann Arbor (hereinafter WM).

43  Marquardt, "America's Contribution to Philippine Education."

44  Carpenter to McIntyre, March 11, 1912.

45  Carpenter to McIntyre, March 11, 1912.

46  Camilo Osias, "The School Is the Nucleus of Cooperative Work," *Philippine Craftsman* 5, no. 1 (July 1916): 35.

47  Sinamayeras were usually Filipina women who owned shops that sold sinamay, a woven material made from abaca fibers and other textiles.

48  (Philippines) Bureau of Education, *School of Household Industries*, 15.

49  (Philippines) Bureau of Education, *School of Household Industries*, 15.

50  (Philippines) Bureau of Education, *School of Household Industries*, 16.

51  (Philippines) Bureau of Education, *School of Household Industries*, 18.

52  (Philippines) Bureau of Education, *School of Household Industries*, 18.

53  Carpenter to McIntyre, June 26, 1912.

54  Carpenter to McIntyre, June 26, 1912.

55  Norah M. Wise, "School of Household Industries," *Philippine Craftsman* 5, no. 3 (September 1916): 188.

56  Wise, "School of Household Industries," 188.

57  Wise, "School of Household Industries," 192.

58  Mimi Nguyen astutely addresses the way that liberal empire uses debt as a form of colonial control as it mobilizes the colonizer as the giver of so-called gifts and the colonized as left in a cycle of being indebted even if colonialism deliberately falls short of empire's promises. Nguyen, *Gift of Freedom*, 5, 181.

59  Hugo H. Miller, "The Commercialization of Industrial Work," *Philippine Craftsman* 5, no. 8 (February 1917): 547. Glenn May notes that this portion of the American colonial period saw a significant shift in the Philippine Bureau of Education: "having adopted commercialization and standardization as its mantra, [the bureau] . . . took on many of the characteristics of a mammoth business operation." May, *Social Engineering in the Philippines*, 153; Miller, "Commercialization of Industrial Work," 547.

60  Miller, "Commercialization of Industrial Work," 547.

61  Philippines Governor General, "Bureau of Education," in *Report of the Governor General of the Philippine Islands, 1916* (Washington, DC: US Government Printing Office, 1917), 19.

62  Philippines Governor General, "Bureau of Education," 30.

63  Julian Meliton, "Cooperation of Local Dealers in the Sale of School Made Industrial Articles," *Philippine Craftsman* 5, no. 1 (July 1916): 26–27.

64  Hugo Miller explained that Act 2629 forbade competition and ruled that once household centers were "well organized" they would be turned over to merchants. Exceptions were made when small sample orders were taken for "experimental purposes only, with the understanding that the Bureau [of Education] considered itself under no obligations to accept large orders from such parties." The Act also allowed the General Sales Department of the Bureau of Education to purchase and carry in stock goods not exceeding 30,000 pesos in value. Miller, "Commercialization of Industrial Work," 553–54.

65  Miller, "Commercialization of Industrial Work," 553–54.

66  Miller, "Commercialization of Industrial Work," 551–52.

67  Hugo Miller, "Teacher Pensionados Assigned to the General Office for the School Year 1914–15," *Philippine Craftsman* 4, no. 1 (July 1915): 2.

68  *Pensionada/o* typically referred to government-sponsored students and is usually associated with students from the Philippines matriculating in US colleges and universities. Here, *teacher pensionada* refers to Filipinas educated in the US colonial education system, most likely the Philippine Normal School, who were then assigned to teach in small towns in provinces outside of Manila throughout the Philippines.

69  Gracia Urquiza, "The Supervision of Needlework," *Philippine Craftsman* 5, no. 2 (August 1916): 105.

70  Urquiza, "Supervision of Needlework," 105.

71  Urquiza, "Supervision of Needlework," 105.

72  Urquiza, "Supervision of Needlework," 105.

73  Urquiza, "Supervision of Needlework," 106.

74  W. H. H. Liesch, "Résumé of the Vacation Assembly, 1916," 5, no. 2 (August 1916): 105.

75  Urquiza, "Supervision of Needlework," 107–8.

76  "Editorial, Cooperation," *Philippine Craftsman* 5, no. 2 (August 1916): 65.

77  Victoria Ciudadano, "Bobbin Lace," *Philippine Craftsman* 5, no. 7 (January 1917): 485.

78  Fisher, "Evolution of Industrial Supervision," 93.

79  G. Glenn Lyman, "Points to Be Noted When Inspecting Industrial Classes," 5, no. 2 (August 1916): 98; G. Glenn Lyman, "Embroidery," *Philippine Craftsman* 5, no. 7 (January 1917): 490.

80  Camilo Osias, "Industrial Supervision," *Philippine Craftsman* 5, no. 2 (August 1916): 93.

81  Lyman, "Embroidery," 490.

82  George T. Shoens, Victoria Ciudano, and Ward B. Gregg, "In Bobbin Lace Classes," *Philippine Craftsman* 4, no. 7 (January 1916): 486.

83  Leroy Martin, "Some Results from Having Specialized in Embroidery," *Philippine Craftsman* 5, no. 3 (September 1916): 205.

84  Bureau of Education, *School of Household Industries*, 11.

85 Bureau of Education, *School of Household Industries*, 6, 12.

86 Gleeck, *American Business*, 70.

87 Bureau of Education, *School of Household Industries*, 8.

88 Bureau of Education, *School of Household Industries*, 8.

89 Urquiza, "Supervision of Needlework," 107.

90 Child, *Boarding School Seasons*; Coleman, *American Indian Children at School*.

91 Woolford, *This Benevolent Experiment*.

92 Eittreim, *Teaching Empire*, 25.

93 Steinbock-Pratt, *Educating the Empire*, 176.

94 "Industrial Notes," *Philippine Craftsman* 5, no. 5 (November 1916): 373–74.

95 (Philippines) Bureau of Education, *Good Manners and Right Conduct*.

96 Marquardt, "America's Contribution to Philippine Education."

97 (Philippines) Bureau of Education, *Good Manners and Right Conduct*.

98 Paulet, "To Change the World."

99 Campomanes, "Images of Filipino Racialization"; Blanco, "Race as Praxis"; Vergara, *Displaying Filipinos*; Rice, *Dean Worcester's Fantasy Islands*.

100 Paulet, "To Change the World," 20.

101 Marquardt, "America's Contribution to Philippine Education."

102 Choy, *Empire of Care*, 25.

103 Kalaw, *Aide-de-Camp to Freedom*, 41–43.

104 Carpenter to McIntyre, June 26, 1912.

105 *Philippine Education, Vol. 20* (Philippines: F. R. Lutz, 1923), 179, Folder: Philippines—Women, RG 350, NARA.

106 Cruz, *Transpacific Femininities*, 97.

107 Mendoza-Guazon, *My Ideal Filipino Girl*, 31.

108 Mendoza-Guazon, *My Ideal Filipino Girl*, 31.

109 O. Garfield Jones, "Bilibid Industrial School," *Philippine Craftsman* 3, no. 2 (August 1914): 69.

110 Jones, "Bilibid Industrial School," 70.

111 Jones, "Bilibid Industrial School," 70.

112 Salman, "'The Prison That Makes Men Free,'" 117.

113 The number of incarcerated Filipinas would only increase slightly over the years. By 1928, it was reported that roughly one hundred Filipinas produced embroidery, crocheting, and lace in Bilibid. Lamont and Hopkins, "Prison Industries," 68.

114 Haley, *No Mercy Here*, 39.

115 Sarah Haley points out that prison reform resulted in the replacement of the convict leasing system with chain gang labor and new systems of exploitation through the public-private partnerships. Haley, *No Mercy Here*, 3, 119–55.

116 Davis, "Race, Gender, and Prison History," 35–45; Gilmore, *Golden Gulag*, 14.

117 Mallari, "Bilibid Prison," 174.

118 D. Rodriguez, *Forced Passages*, 40.

119 Jones, "Bilibid Industrial School," 72.

120 While vaguely phrased as a seemingly banal hygienic practice, forced bathing has a long history as a method of dehumanization. Typically, forced disinfecting baths in prisons involved stripping the prisoners naked before hosing them off with frigid water and sometimes harmful chemicals as a form of ritualized and corporeal humiliation. Jones, "Bilibid Industrial School," 72; Molina, *Fit to Be Citizens?*, 49.

121 Campomanes, "Images of Filipino Racialization."

122 Many thanks to Ben Weber for generously sharing with me his photographs of intake records from Bilibid Prison from his archival research in the Philippines. These records have yet to be cataloged and are stored at the Bureau of Corrections Museum, New Bilibid Prison, in Matinlupa, Metro Manila. Bureau of Prisons, Philippine Islands, Bilibid Prison, Bertillon Signaletic Prison Intake Record, no date, Bureau of Corrections Museum, New Bilibid Prison, Metro Manila.

123 Jones, "Bilibid Industrial School," 70.

124 Jones, "Bilibid Industrial School," 73; Gillin, *Taming the Criminal*, 44.

125 Jones, "Bilibid Industrial School," 70.

126 Jones, "Bilibid Industrial School," 70.

127 Department of Public Instruction, Bureau of Prisons, *Catalogue of Products of the Industrial Division of Bilibid*, 4.

128 Frederic J. Haskin, "Bilibid Prison," *Los Angeles Herald*, March 28, 1910.

129 Haskin, "Bilibid Prison."

130 Haskin, "Bilibid Prison."

131 Alzate, *Convict Labor*, 25–26.

132 During the mid-nineteenth century, Bilibid Prison was linked to a network of Spanish penitentiaries in Spain and throughout its empire. Pike, "Penal Servitude in the Spanish Empire."

133 Kramer, *Blood of Government*, 316.

134 Alzate, *Convict Labor*, 25–26.

135 Kramer, *Blood of Government*, 316.

136 Kramer, *Blood of Government*, 316.

137 Despite narratives of difference between the United States and Spain, the United States extended some of the prison features put into place by the Spanish regime, namely the practice of convict labor. Unlike provincial prisons, which placed mainly short-term convicts in hard labor, such as building roads and other infrastructural projects, Bilibid expanded the Spanish convict labor system of production that had prisoners produce "trinkets" and cheap furniture. Jones, "Bilibid Industrial School," 74.

138 McLennan, *Crisis of Imprisonment*, 88.

139 Jones, "Bilibid Industrial School," 78.

140 *Acts of the Philippine Commission, No. 1–1800*, 102.

141 US Philippine Commission, *Report of the United States Philippine Commission to the Secretary of War, 1912* (Washington, DC: Government Printing Office, 1912), 43.

142 Coloma, "White Gaze, Brown Breasts," 256.

143 Industrial education played a central role in fashioning incarcerated Filipinos into a Filipino workforce. For men incarcerated for the long term, industrial schooling entailed a rigid schedule that included formal training in manufacturing and handicraft as well as classes in physical education, English language, and arithmetic. Salman, *Embarrassment of Slavery*; Gutierrez, "Studying Criminality."

144 Alzate, *Convict Labor*, 88–90.

145 Department of Public Instruction, Bureau of Prisons, *Catalogue of Products of the Industrial Division of Bilibid*, 23, 45.

146 Jones, "Bilibid Industrial School," 89.

147 Mallari, "Bilibid Prison," 165–92.

148 Jones, "Bilibid Industrial School," 69.

149 Guttierez, "The Influence of Cesare Lombroso on Philippine Criminology," 324–41.

150 Theresa Ventura investigates the devastating land-reform legislation that the US colonial state passed in 1906. Ventura, "From Small Farms to Progressive Plantations."

151 M. Roces, "Woman in Philippine Society and Politics," 172.

152 Gillin, *Taming the Criminal*, 48, 62.

153 Although adultery was by law a crime for both men and women, gendered norms resulting from the *querida* system in the Philippines, a concubinage system that developed during the Spanish colonial period, normalized the practice of men having multiple sexual and intimate relationships outside of marriage. Thus, men generally faced few legal consequences for adultery. By contrast, societal norms aimed to contain women's sexuality within the bounds of marriage in order to uphold the feminine ideal of pious and devout Filipina-ness. Winkelmann, *Dangerous Intercourse*; Sabanpan-Yu, "*Querida Mia*," 236–37.

154 J. D. Long, M. D., Director of Health, The Government of the Philippine Islands Department of Public Instruction, Philippine Health Service, *Report of the Philippine Health Service for the Fiscal Year From (January 1 to December 31, 1917)* (Manila: Bureau of Printing, 1918), 29.

155 Alzate, *Convict Labor*, 67, 73; Gillin, *Taming the Criminal*; Gutierrez, "Petty Crimes," 1; Dery, "Prostitution in Colonial Manila."

156 Santiago, *Sexuality and the Filipina*, 29.

157 Carpenter to McIntyre, March 11, 1912.

158 Worcester, *Philippines Past and Present*, 535.

159 Worcester, *Philippines Past and Present*, 340.

160 McCoy, *Policing Empire*, 156; Worcester, *Philippines Past and Present*, 135; Malcolm, *The Commonwealth of the Philippines*, 31; Bajá, *Philippine Police System*, 349–54.

161 Aguilar, *Clash of Spirits*, 328.

162 The larger industrial and sales system of Bilibid and the Department of Public Instruction generated income and profit yearly, contributing to the capital needed to sustain the operations of these institutions.

163 Salman, "Nothing without Labor," 116.

164 Victorio, *Prison Reform in the Philippines*, 15.

165 Alzate, *Convict Labor*, 35–36.

166 Mallari, "Bilibid Prison," 182; Davis and Shaylor, "Race, Gender, and the Prison Industrial Complex"; Davis, *Are Prisons Obsolete?*

167 Department of Public Instruction, Bureau of Prisons, *Catalogue of Products of the Industrial Division of Bilibid*, 45.

168 Mallari, "Bilibid Prison," 188.

169 Mallari, "Bilibid Prison," 184; Dauncey, *Englishwoman in the Philippines*, 135.

170 Dauncey, *Englishwoman in the Philippines*, 135; Gillin, *Taming the Criminal*, 36–37; Department of Public Instruction, Bureau of Prisons, *Catalogue of Products of the Industrial Division of Bilibid*, 7.

171 Frank McIntyre to Joseph P. McHugh & Co., August 14, 1909, Box 640, RG 350, NARA. The provisions referred to Section 49 of the McKinley Act, which stated "That all goods, wares, articles, and merchandise manufactured wholly or in part in any foreign country by convict labor, shall not be entitled to entry at any of the ports of the United States."

172 Holmes, *Luzon Lingerie*.

173 Frank Carpenter, *Report of the Executive Secretary the Government of the Philippine Islands Executive Bureau Manila*, September 16, 1912, in *Report of the United States Philippine Commission to the Secretary of War* (Washington, DC: US Government Printing Office, 1912), 43.

174 Carpenter, *Report of the Executive Secretary*, 43.

175 Bureau of Prisons, Philippine Islands, Bilibid Prison, Bertillon Signaletic Prison Intake Record, no date, Bureau of Corrections Museum, New Bilibid Prison, Metro Manila.

176 Haley, *No Mercy Here*, 15, 122.

177 Gillin, *Taming the Criminal*, 47.

178 Philippines Department of Health, *Report. Philippines: Philippines Department of Health, 1916*, 53–58.

179 Bureau of Prisons, "Report from the Bureau of Prisons," in *Report of the United States Philippine Commission to the Secretary of War 1910* (Washington, DC: Government Printing Office, 1910), 195.

180 Luisa Camagay's work shows that this was particularly true of peasant and working classes. But even in the upper echelons of society, women and girls participated in wage-earning occupation and entrepreneurship. Camagay, *Working Women of Manila*, 124–25.

181 Hila, Reyes, and Feleo, *Garment of Honor*, 158.

182 Hila, Reyes, and Feleo, *Garment of Honor*, 158; *Journal of Prison Discipline and Philanthropy* 57 (March 1918): 6.

183  Garrison-Mencken correspondence, May 3, 1922, box 5, F. H. Garrison pa-
     pers, Ms c 166, History of Medicine Division, National Library of Medicine,
     Bethesda, Maryland, quoted in W. Anderson, *Colonial Pathologies*, 135.

184  Gillin, *Taming the Criminal*, 47.

185  Long, *Report of the Philippine Health Service for the Fiscal Year from Janu-
     ary 1 to December 31, 1917*.

186  Long, *Report of the Philippine Health Service for the Fiscal Year from January 1 to
     December 31, 1917*.

187  Long, *Report of the Philippine Health Service for the Fiscal Year from January 1
     to December 31, 1917*.

188  Gillin, *Taming the Criminal*, 47, 53.

189  Heiser, *Annual Report of the Bureau of Health for the Philippine Islands*, 101;
     "Bureau of Health, Report of the Secretary of the Interior," in *Report of the
     United States Philippine Commission to the Secretary of War 1914* (Washing-
     ton, DC: Government Printing Office, 1914), 124.

190  Pan-Pacific Research Institution, *Mid-Pacific Magazine* 27 (1924): 272.

191  Murray, "Century of Tuberculosis"; Moralina, "State, Society, and Sickness."

192  Murray, "Century of Tuberculosis."

193  Ventura, "Medicalizing *Gutom*," 44.

194  Naomi Paik argues that one of central features of US imperial practices of
     biopower is the systematic and persistent devaluing of colonial subjects' lives.
     Paik, *Rightlessness*, 101–2.

195  Moralina, "State, Society, and Sickness," 201–2.

196  Moralina, "State, Society, and Sickness," 201–2.

197  "Prisons Sanitation Division," in Bureau of Health for the Philippine Islands,
     *Annual Report of the Bureau of Health, 1911*, 156.

198  Moralina, "State, Society, and Sickness," 201–2.

199  Frank McIntyre to Frank Carpenter, May 16, 1912, Box 869, RG 350, NARA.

200  May, *Social Engineering in the Philippines*, 153.

201  American colonial officials in the Philippines borrowed disciplinary tech-
     nologies of cultural genocide from Indian boarding schools of the nineteenth
     century. Child, *Boarding School Seasons*; Coleman, *American Indian Children
     at School*; May, *Social Engineering*.

202  "Editorial," *Philippine Craftsman* 4, no. 1 (July 1915): 46–47.

203  Torres, "Domestic Science in Bago," 161.

204  Carpenter, *Report of the Executive Secretary the Government of the Philippine
     Islands Executive Bureau, Manila*, September 16, 1912, in *Report of the United
     States Philippine Commission, 1912*, 42.

205  Carby, "Policing the Black Woman's Body," 746.

206  Carpenter to McIntyre, March 11, 1912.

207  Act 3579 authorized the establishment of the Correctional Institute for
     Women in Mandaluyong, Rizal, in 1931. In 1931, 270 women were transferred
     from Bilibid Prison to the Correctional Institute for Women. Women serv-
     ing more than three years of imprisonment were housed at the Correctional

Institute for Women. See Celso Bravo, in United Nations Asia and Far East Institute for the Prevention of Crime and the Treatment of Offenders, *Annual Report for 2012*, 155–56.

208 Tu, *Beautiful Generation*; Bonacich, *Global Production*.

209 Guevarra, *Marketing Dreams, Manufacturing Heroes*.

## 5. "THE DREAM OF BEAUTY"

1 Quirino, NEPA *Handbook*, 154.

2 E. Cruz, *Terno*, 8. Lucy San Pablo Burns and Ana Labrador address the genealogy of the term *Filipiniana*. They point out that it is a "contradictory term for all things Filipino as it influences more the foreign influences" in "iconic" Filipino/a fashions and dress. Burns, "Your Terno's Draggin'," 202. Labrador, "Project of Nationalism," 59.

3 Abinales and Amoroso, *State and Society in the Philippines*, 139–52.

4 Corpuz, *Economic History of the Philippines*.

5 Quirino, NEPA *Handbook*, 155.

6 Lucy Burns looks at Filipiniana formal gowns in the context of Filipino elites' efforts to consolidate power under the US colonial regimes. It should be noted that the use of the terno to convey elite power is still very much evident in contemporary SONA (Philippines State of the Nation Address) red-carpet entrance and fashion terno displays. Burns, "Your Terno's Draggin'," 205.

7 Barthes, *Fashion System*, 6–12.

8 Tarlo, *Clothing Matters*, 8.

9 In the introduction and in the previous chapter, I discuss how constructing textiles and clothing were part of Filipinas' roles in the domestic setting. The American colonial regime reaffirmed such feminine roles by instituting home economics classes for young Filipina girls. American educators viewed home economics courses as a way to train Filipinas to run a proper household.

10 R. Reyes, "Modernizing Manileños," 194. Doeppers, *Manila 1900–1910*, 10.

11 Doeppers, *Manila 1900–1910*, 137.

12 Anderson, "Cacique Democracy," 11.

13 Anderson, *Imagined Communities*, 11. Leon Maria Guerrero also argues that many foreign commentators in the late nineteenth century witnessed a Manila-based, cosmopolitan, and elite society. Guerrero, *First Filipino*.

14 Bernal, Encanto, and Escaler, *Patterns for the Filipino Dress*, 20.

15 Kalaw-Ledesma, *And Life Goes On*, 281.

16 Kalaw-Ledesma, *And Life Goes On*, 281.

17 Burns, "Your Terno's Draggin'," 202.

18 Bernal, Encanto, and Escaler, *Patterns for the Filipino Dress*, 25.

19 Bernal, Encanto, and Escaler, *Patterns for the Filipino Dress*, 25.

20 Sewing machines had been available in the Philippines prior to the 1920s. However, it was in the 1920s that electricity became more widely available in

Manila and machinery became more widely used. R. Reyes, "Modernizing the Manileña," 197.

21  "New Orientation in Our Educational Policy," *Woman's World*, March 1936, 28.

22  "New Orientation in Our Educational Policy," 28.

23  The term *matapobré* literally translates to *mata*, or eyes, in Tagalog, and *pobré*, or poor, in Spanish. The term combines the two words to mean "to look down at those less fortunate," presumably the wealthier looking down at the poorer. Kerkvliet, "Everyday Resistance to Injustice."

24  M. Roces, "Dress, Status, and Identity," 341–72.

25  Quirino, NEPA *Handbook*, 149.

26  Katigbak, *Legacy*, 27.

27  Bernal, Encanto, and Escaler, *Patterns for the Filipino Dress*, 19; Santa María, *Fountain of Gold*, 195.

28  Bernal, Encanto, and Escaler, *Patterns for the Filipino Dress*, 19.

29  Doeppers, *Manila 1900–1941*, 3.

30  E. Cruz, *The Terno*, 8.

31  Juanita Mina-Roa, J. Jayme-Fernandez, and Bert Hernandez, "Evolution of the Elegant Philippine Costume," 30, in Encarnacion Alzona Papers, Ateneo Library of Women's Writings, Rizal Library, Ateneo University, Philippines.

32  A. Roces, *Filipino Heritage vol. 10*, 2540.

33  Santa María, *Fountain of Gold*, 195.

34  "La 'reina de la aguja'" (The 'Queen of the Needle'), *Woman's Home Journal*, January 1932.

35  "La 'reina de la aguja'" (The 'Queen of the Needle').

36  Juanita Mina-Roa, quoted in Quirino, NEPA *Handbook*, 155.

37  Phạm, "China," 61.

38  Phạm, "China." See also Tu, *Beautiful Generation*.

39  The primary and secondary sources switch between the terms "designer" and "couturiere/couturier."

40  As quoted in A. Roces, "Ins-and-Outs of the Terno," 2540.

41  Ligaya Victorio-Reyes, "Evolution of the Mestiza Dress," 1938, Folder: Women & Women's Work in the Philippines Press Clippings, 17087–8, Box 871, RG 350, NARA.

42  Victorio-Reyes, "Evolution of the Mestiza Dress."

43  Victorio-Reyes, "Evolution of the Mestiza Dress."

44  "Queen Is Crowned," *Graphic*, February 24, 1938.

45  "Queen Is Crowned."

46  Gale, "Ramon Valera," 16.

47  Quirino, NEPA *Handbook*, 156.

48  "La 'reina de la aguja'" (The 'Queen of the Needle'), 29–32.

49  "Fashion Gleanings," *Woman's World*, July 1938, 33.

50  "Fashion Gleanings," 33.

51  "Fashion Gleanings," 33.

52  Quirino, NEPA *Handbook*, 156.

53 Jeanne Paquin was a leading Parisian couturiere during the early twentieth century. "La 'reina de la aguja'" (The 'Queen of the Needle'), 29.

54 Antonia Finnane carefully traces the role and power of clothing and fashion in the articulation of nationalism and nation-building. Finnane, *Changing Clothes in China*.

55 "Woman's Fashion," *Woman's Journal*, April 1920.

56 As quoted in Santa María, *Fountain of Gold*, 199.

57 "La 'reina de la aguja'" (The 'Queen of the Needle'), 29.

58 In her interview, Longos said, "De Paris tambien me vienen directamente revistas de modas" (I also get fashion magazines directly from Paris). "La 'reina de la aguja'" (The 'Queen of the Needle'), 29.

59 Encarnacion Alzona, "Philippine Collegian, October 31, 1927," in Camagay, *Encarnacion Alzona*, 6.

60 "'Pinocpoc' and Piña: Smart Substitutes for Linen, Organdy, and Taffeta," *Graphic*, March 29, 1933.

61 Vera West, "The Latest in the Fashion World—Universal Studios," *Woman's World*, December 1935, 37; "Glamorous Ginger Rogers' Styles," *Woman's World*, January 1936, 40–41.

62 "A Woman's Fancy: Knock-Knocks," *Commonwealth Advocate* 11, no. 17 (November 1936): 18–19.

63 "The Vogue in Fashionable Manila," *Graphic*, April 1, 1931, 18.

64 Lolita Sollee, "Well-Dressed Manilan Could Feel at Home in Paris or New York: Miss Gloria Luzan and Paz Longos, Foremost Manila Modestes, Creating Styles Embodying Cleverness, Originality and Beauty," *Graphic*, March 31, 1928, 10–11.

65 Victorio-Reyes, "Evolution of the Mestiza Dress."

66 Laguio, *Our Modern Woman*, 5.

67 Tu, *Beautiful Generation*, 15.

68 Mina-Roa, Jayme-Fernandez, and Hernandez, "Evolution of the Elegant Philippine Costume," 23.

69 Belen Gana, "Creations by Belen: Grecian Lines Influence Filipino Dress," *Woman's World*, January 1936, 54–55.

70 A. B. Legislator, "Weekly Mirror of Thoughts and Events, March 4–10, 1928," *Graphic*, March 17, 1928, 3.

71 Legislator, "Weekly Mirror of Thoughts and Events," 3.

72 During the first half of the twentieth century, in advertisements, literature, and other forms of print culture, the "modern girl" was associated with "frivolous pursuits of consumption, romance, and fashion." Weinbaum et al., *Modern Girl around the World*, 9.

73 Kramer, *Blood of Government*, 71.

74 Gleeck, *Manila Americans*, 147.

75 Romulo, *Manila Hotel*.

76 See the previous chapter on the racialized discourse of dress for a better understanding of how white supremacy operated in the Philippines.

77 Bernal, Encanto, and Escaler, *Patterns for the Filipino Dress*, 10.

78 Photo editorial, *Woman's World*, December 1935, 30.

79 Photo editorial, *Woman's World*, December 1935, 30.

80 Photo editorial, *Woman's World*, January 1936, 30.

81 "Revue 1936 Carnival," *Graphic*, March 1936, 47.

82 "Revue 1936 Carnival," 47.

83 Thayer Sidel, *Capital, Coercion, and Crime*; McCoy, *Anarchy of Families*.

84 "Revue 1936 Carnival," 47.

85 "Revue 1936 Carnival," 47.

86 "Fashion of Manila," *Graphic*, March 1936, 34.

87 "Enchanting Ensembles for Late Afternoons and Evenings," *Graphic*, August 5, 1931, n.p.

88 Santa María, *Fountain of Gold*, 194.

89 Mina-Roa, Jayme-Fernandez, and Hernandez, "Evolution of the Elegant Philippine Costume," 30.

90 Roland Barthes argues that fashion description is "by definition the very information which photography or drawing cannot transmit," and these descriptions emphasize certain elements to "stress their value." See Barthes, *Fashion System*, 13–15.

91 Ligaya Victorio-Reyes, "Feminina," *Woman's World*, July 1938, n.p.

92 Victorio-Reyes, "Feminina."

93 Sobritchea, "American Colonial Education." See also Buhain, *History of Publishing in the Philippines*; D. Fernandez, "Philippine Press System."

94 Doeppers, *Manila 1900–1941*, 23; A. Roces, *Filipino Heritage vol. 10*, 2540.

95 Mina-Roa, Jayme-Fernandez, and Hernandez, "Evolution of the Elegant Philippine Costume," 30.

96 A. Roces, *Filipino Heritage vol. 10*, 2540.

97 A. Roces, *Filipino Heritage vol. 10*, 2540.

98 Doeppers, *Manila 1900–1941*, 59.

99 Doeppers, *Manila 1900–1941*, 62.

100 Choy, *Empire of Care*, 19.

101 Choy, *Empire of Care*, 23–24.

102 Weinbaum et al., *Modern Girl around the World*, 9.

103 Weinbaum et al., *Modern Girl around the World*, 9. For descriptions of the Filipina modern girl of the 1920s and 1930s, who was "trim, polished, and glamorous," see R. Reyes, "Modernizing Manileños," 209.

104 R. Reyes, "Modernizing Manileños," 213.

105 "'Kiri' nga kaya ang kahulugan ng salitang 'flapper'?" ("Flirt" Is It the Meaning of the Word "Flapper"?), *Graphic*, October 27, 1927, 23.

106 "'Kiri' nga kaya ang kahulugan ng salitang 'flapper'?" ("Flirt" Is It the Meaning of the Word "Flapper"?), 23.

107 "'Kiri' nga kaya ang kahulugan ng salitang 'flapper'?" ("Flirt" Is It the Meaning of the Word "Flapper"?), 23.

108 D. Cruz, *Transpacific Femininities*, 89.

109 Joaquin, *One Woman's Liberating*, 26.

110  D. Cruz, *Transpacific Feminities*, 89.

111  Laguio, *Our Modern Woman*, 5. Denise Cruz's examination of Laguo's text traces how the literary figure of Maria Clara came to stand in as the embodiment of ideal Filipina femininity in the 1920s and the 1930s. Historian Nick Joaquin and cultural critic and journalist Carmen Guerrero Nakpil argue that the "cult of Maria Clara" developed in the decades after *Noli me tangere's* publication in 1887. Joaquin points specifically to the 1920s as the period in which the trope of Maria Clara consolidated in popular discourse. D. Cruz, *Transpacific Femininities*, 67–110; Joaquin, *Naval de Manila*, 65–76; Nakpil, "Maria Clara," 34.

112  D. Cruz, *Transpacific Femininities*, 92.

113  Laguio, *Our Modern Women*, 5.

114  D. Cruz, *Transpacific Femininities*, 90–95.

115  See for example, Encarnacion Alzona, "Feminine Valor," Address for Philippine Women's University, January 25, 1939, Encarnacion Alzona Papers, Folder Speeches and Messages, Ateneo Library of Women's Writings, Rizal Library, Ateneo University, Philippines. For more on Encarnacion Alzona, see Catherine Ceniza Choy, "A Filipino Woman in America: The Life and Work of Encarnacion Alzona," *Genre: Forms of Discourse and Culture* 39, no. 3 (2006): 127–40.

116  D. Cruz, *Transpacific Feminism*, 95.

117  M. Roces, "Gender, Nation and the Politics of Dress," 365.

118  See chapter 1 for common practices of entrepreneurship among Filipino women and the organization of gendered labor in families.

119  Joaquin, *One Woman's Liberating*, 10.

120  Joaquin, *One Woman's Liberating*, 10.

121  Joaquin, *One Woman's Liberating*, 10.

122  Mendoza-Guazón, *My Ideal Filipino Girl*, 96.

123  Mendoza-Guazón, *My Ideal Filipino Girl*, 31.

124  Choy, *Empire of Care*, 25.

125  R. Reyes, *Love, Passion and Patriotism*, 11–14.

126  Mendoza-Guazón, "On Good Manners: To the Young Women of the Philippines," in *My Ideal Filipino Girl*, 31.

127  Mendoza-Guazón, "On Good Manners," 31.

128  Mendoza-Guazón, "On Good Manners," 31.

129  Mendoza-Guazón, "On Good Manners," 31.

130  Raquel Reyes discusses how, even in the nineteenth century, Filipinos of the *ilustrado* class felt anxious about mixing of classes in Manila. "Ilustrado criticism of popular lower-class culture was borne out from the messy reality of Manila culturally hybrid urban environment where people of all classes lived together, maintained a range of sexual arrangement and followed fluid, sometimes conflicting forms of desire." R. Reyes, *Love, Passion and Patriotism*, 20.

131  A. Roces, *Filipino Heritage*, vol. 10, 2537.

132  Mendoza-Guazón, *Development and Progress of the Filipino Women*, 3.

133 Kramer, *Blood of Government*, 71.

134 For more on political history of the US colonial period in the Philippines see McCoy, "Quezon's Commonwealth"; Salamanca, *Filipino Reaction to American Rule*.

135 Lauren Berlant, quoted in Kaplan, Alarcón, and Moallem, *Between Woman and Nation*, 13.

136 Ileto, *Pasyon and Revolution*, 129–36.

137 Steinbock-Pratt, "'It Gave Us Our Nationality,'" 565–88.

138 Ligaya Victorio-Reyes, "Feminina," *Woman's World* (January 1939), 38. Maria Clara and Ibarra refer to the main protagonists of José Rizal's novel, *Noli me tangere*, María Clara de los Santos and Juan Crisóstomo Ibarra y Magsalin.

139 Rizal, *Noli me tangere* (*Touch Me Not*).

140 Victorio-Reyes, "Evolution of the Mestiza Dress."

141 Fashion experts and scholars argued fashion was defined by constant change, an obsession with the new, and a desire to stay current. See Barthes, *Fashion System*; Wilson, *Adorned in Dreams*.

142 Victorio-Reyes, "Evolution of the Mestiza Dress."

143 Victorio-Reyes, "Evolution of the Mestiza Dress."

144 Victorio-Reyes, "Evolution of the Mestiza Dress."

145 Walter Robb to Carmen Melencio, in Mina-Roa, Jayme-Fernandez, and Hernandez, "Evolution of the Elegant Philippine Costume," 32.

146 E. Cruz, *Terno*, 9.

147 See chapter 4 for the discourse of critique.

148 E. Cruz, *Terno*, 9.

149 Colonial policies including the Tydings-McDuffie Act made the Philippine economy dependent on US prices and demands for export commodities. The Tydings-McDuffie Act, which was lobbied for American farm blocs and pro-independence advocates, declared that US exports would continue to be free of tariffs and duties but placed a stringent quota on Philippine exports to the United States. Doeppers, *Manila 1900–1946*, 16.

150 B. Anderson, *Imagined Communities*, 12.

151 Hoganson, *Consumers' Imperium*, 96.

152 Corpuz, *Economic History of the Philippines*, 256.

153 Doeppers, *Manila 1900–1946*, 29.

154 Mina-Roa, Jayme-Fernandez, and Hernandez, "Evolution of the Elegant Philippine Costume," 32.

155 "'Pinocpoc' and *Piña*," n.p.

156 "'Pinocpoc' and *Piña*," n.p.

157 Doeppers, *Manila 1900–1941*, 29. "Made in the Philippines Week," *Tribune*, 12 August 1924; "Made in the Philippines Week," *Manila Tribune*, August 17, 1934, and *Philippine Herald*, August 17, 1934; "Balmaceda Talks at Eastern U," *Manila Tribune*, August 22, 1934.

158 M. Roces, "Gender, Nation and Politics of Dress," 362.

159 Victorio-Reyes, "Evolution of the Mestiza Dress."
160 Victorio-Reyes, "Evolution of the Mestiza Dress."
161 Phạm, "China," 45.
162 Phạm, "China," 45.
163 Phạm, "Paul Poiret's Magical Techno-Oriental Fashions."
164 "Fashion: Extremes Meet at Paris Spring Collections," *Vogue* 87, no. 5 (March 1, 1936): 52.
165 See chapter 1 for the sartorial friction and tensions between white American women and Filipina elites.
166 "Fashion: Extremes Meet at Paris Spring Collections," 52.
167 "Fashion: Extremes Meet at Paris Spring Collections," 53.
168 "Fashion: Extremes Meet at Paris Spring Collections," 53.
169 "Fashion: 'I Dress as I Please,'" *Vogue* 87, no. 6 (March 15, 1936), 59.
170 "Fashion: 'I Dress as I Please,'" 59, 144.
171 An article celebrating Valera's life and work noted that Cristobal Balenciaga, a famous haute couture designer from Madrid, invited Valera to serve as chief designer of a proposed Asian fashion house. However, Valera turned down the offer, and the fashion house never came to fruition. Gale, "Ramon Valera," 15.
172 Marina, "Alicia Syquia de Quirino: El traje vaporoso de mestiza" (Alicia Syquia de Quirino: The Vaporous Mestiza Dress), *La vanguardia*, December 22, 1934, as reprinted in Marina, *Lo que ellas dicen*, 48.
173 Steinbock-Pratt, "'It Gave Us Our Nationality,'" 571.
174 Marina, "Alicia Syquia de Quirino," 48.
175 Marina, "Alicia Syquia de Quirino," 48.
176 Caroline Crawford, "The Present Filipino Women," *Filipino Student Bulletin* 4, no. 5 (January 1926): 48.
177 "Filipino Girls, the Main Attraction of a Night," *Filipino Student Bulletin* 6, no. 2 (December 1926): 8.

6. EPILOGUE

1 Nadal, "Literary Remittance," 608–9.
2 Clutario, "World War II and the Promise of Normalcy," 241–58.
3 Fields, "Slavery, Race and Ideology"; Foley, *White Scourge*; Henry and Danns, "W. E. B. DuBois"; Jenkins, "Ghosts of the Past"; Sell, *Trouble of the World*, 72–84.
4 Embroidery cloth coming from the United States for processing in the Philippines and reshipment back to the United States technically falls under the heading of import. See chapter 3. "Theoretically Practical," *Manila Bulletin*, October 15, 1935, Folder C-1094–119: P. I. Textile Duties on Inquiries, Box 123, RG 350 NARA.
5 MacIsaac, "The Struggle for Economic Development in the Philippine Commonwealth," vol. 147.

6 Creed Cox, Memorandum to Oliver Grimes, June 5, 1935, Folder C-1094–119: P. I. Textile Duties on Inquiries, Box 123, RG 350, NARA.

7 Radiogram from Frank Murphy to Creed Cox, July 9, 1935, C-1094–116, Folder C-1094–131: Cotton Textiles Part I, Box 123, RG 350, NARA.

8 "Theoretically Practical."

9 Copy of letter by A. G. Kempt, January 9, 1934, sent and enclosed in letter to Frank Murphy, February 16, 1934, Folder C-1094–119: P. I. Textile Duties on Inquiries, Box 123, RG 350, NARA; "Theoretically Practical"; Duus, "Zaikabo."

10 Brune Pottberg & Co. to Textile Exporters Association, July 7, 1933, Folder C-1094–119: P. I. Textile Duties on Inquiries, Box 123, RG 350, NARA; Letter from Edgar Hesslein to Colonel W. C. Short, July 18, 1933, Folder C-1094–119: P. I. Textile Duties on Inquiries, Box 123, RG 350, NARA.

11 A. G. Kempt, Neuss, Hesslein & Co., Inc., to Frank Murphy, "Private and Confidential Report," February 23, 1934, Folder C-1094–119: P. I. Textile Duties on Inquiries, Box 123, RG 350, NARA.

12 Edgar J. Hesslein to Frank Murphy, May 27, 1935, Folder C-1094–119: P. I. Textile Duties on Inquiries, Box 123, RG 350, NARA.

13 Cable No. 201, April 27, 1934, "Textiles," Folder C-1094–119: P. I. Textile Duties on Inquiries, Box 123, RG 350, NARA.

14 Quiason, "Japanese Community in Manila," 184.

15 Frank Murphy to the Secretary of War, July 9, 1935, Folder C-1094–116: P. I. Textile Duties, Box 123, RG 350, NARA.

16 In July 1935, the US State Department and the Bureau of Insular Affairs reprimanded Frank Murphy for supporting Senate Resolution 163 and House Resolution 280. After much pressure from the US textile industry, the Senate and the House passed identical resolutions to pressure the Philippine Senate president and the Philippine Assembly to pass new policies and sanctions that would dramatically reduce Japanese textiles imported into the Philippines and protect the United States' hold on the textile market there. Japanese representatives expressed their displeasure to the State Department, inciting concern about difficulties in maintaining diplomatic trade negotiations between the United States and Japan. Radiogram from Creed Cox to Frank Murphy, July 2, 1935, Folder 1094–116: P. I. Textiles Duty, Box 123, RG 350, NARA; Creed Cox, Memorandum to the Secretary of War, July 8, 1935, Folder 1094–116: P.I. Textile Duty, Box 123, RG 350, NARA.

17 Memorandum to the Executive Assistant to the Secretary of War, June 5, 1935, Folder C-1094–116: P.I. Textiles Duty, Box 123, RG 350, NARA.

18 Memorandum to the Executive Assistant to the Secretary of War, June 5, 1935.

19 "Colonial Pilates," Philippines Herald, August 3, 1935, Folder C-1094–116: P.I. Textile Duty, Box 123, RG 350, NARA.

20 Azuma, "Japanese Immigrant Settler Colonialism"; Lee, "The 'Yellow Peril.'"

21 A. G. Kempt, Neuss, Hesslein & Co., Inc., "Private and Confidential Report to His Excellency, Governor General Frank Murphy."

22 Azuma, Between Two Empires.

23  A. G. Kempt, Neuss, Hesslein & Co., Inc., "Private and Confidential Report to His Excellency, Governor General Frank Murphy."

24  Phạm, "China," 61.

25  A. G. Kempt, Neuss, Hesslein & Co., Inc., "Private and Confidential Report to His Excellency, Governor General Frank Murphy."

26  A. G. Kempt, Neuss, Hesslein & Co., Inc., "Private and Confidential Report to His Excellency, Governor General Frank Murphy."

27  Ignacio et al., *Forbidden Book,* 23–33.

28  "Washington, Tokyo Ignore Philippines: Negotiations on Textile Exports to P.I. in Progress," *Philippines Herald,* July 30, 1935, n.p.

29  *Manila Tribune,* July 19, 1935, n.p., clipping under "Cotton Textiles (Legislation)," Folder C-1094–131: Cotton Textiles, Box 123, RG 350, NARA.

30  *Manila Tribune,* July 19, 1935, n.p.

31  *Manila Tribune,* July 19, 1935, n.p.

32  In the 1930s, the Philippines experienced political turmoil, economic tension and anger, labor movements, and peasant revolts. For more on the Commonwealth period of the Philippines, see Abinales and Amoroso, *State and Society in the Philippines,* 147–58; McCoy, "Philippine Commonwealth and Cult of Masculinity."

33  Lumba, *Monetary Authorities;* Nagano, *State and Finance in the Philippines.*

34  After rising tensions and anti-Japanese attitudes and violence on the US West Coast, Japan and the United States consented to The Gentleman's Agreement of 1907. This was an informal diplomatic agreement between Japan and the United States that recognized the United States' right to restrict further immigration from Japan. At the same time, the San Francisco School Board withdrew its order to segregate schools between Asian and white children. "Theoretically Practical."

35  "Theoretically Practical."

36  Abinales and Amoroso, *State and Society in the Philippines,* 36; *Philippine Magazine* 26 (1939): 253.

37  "Dressing for Evacuation," *Graphic,* July 10, 1941, cover.

38  "Design for Leaving," *Graphic,* July 10, 1941, 30–31.

39  Galster and Nosch, "Textile History and the Military," 2–3.

40  "Design for Leaving," 30–31.

41  H. Mendoza, *Memories of the War Years,* 29.

42  Hayase, "American Colonial Policy."

43  Azuma, *In Search of Our Frontier,* 127, 207; Lu, *Making of Japanese Settler Colonialism,* 14, 174.

44  "Headlines," *Woman's Home Journal,* February 1939, 2.

45  "NEPA Spirit," *Graphic,* November 27, 1941, n.p.

46  "NEPA Spirit," n.p.

ARCHIVES AND ABBREVIATIONS

Ateneo de Manila University, Philippines
  Alzona, Encarnacion, Papers, Ateneo Library of Women's Writings (ALIWW),
    Rizal Library
  American Historical Collection, Rizal Library
Bureau of Corrections Museum, New Bilibid Prison, Metro Manila, Philippines
Evangelina E. Lewis Collection of Postcards, Newberry Library, Chicago
Filipinas Heritage Library, Ayala Museum, Manila, Philippines
Lopez Memorial Museum, Metro Manila, Philippines
Mario Feir Filipiniana Library, Metro Manila, Philippines
National Archives and Records Administration, College Park, MD (NARA)
  Records of the Adjutant General's Office (RG 94)
  Records of the Bureau of Insular Affairs, General Classified Files 1898–1945 (RG
    350)
University of Michigan, Ann Arbor
  Bentley Historical Collections
    LeRoy, James Alfred, Papers (JAL)
      Manuscript of Travelogue Account of Trip to the Philippine Islands (MTPI)
      Travelogue Account of Trip to the Philippines (TATP)
    Marquardt, Walter W., Papers (WM)
    Schaffer, Bertha, Letters
University Library, University of the Philippines, Diliman
  Special Collections
  Filipiniana Books
  Serials
Worcester, Dean C. *Photographs of the Philippine Islands*, E. Murray Bruner Phil-
  ippine Image Collection, Wisconsin Philippines Image Collection, University of
  Wisconsin, Madison


PERIODICALS

*American Chamber of Commerce Journal*
*BBC News*
*Bulletin of the Pan American Union*
*Christian Science Monitor*

*Colonial and the Philippines Monthly Review*
*Commerce and Industry Journal*
*Commonwealth Advocate*
*Delineator*
*El bello sexo*
*El renacimiento*
*Filipino Student Bulletin*
*Independent*
*La vanguardia*
*Liwayway*
*Los Angeles Herald*
*Manila Bulletin*
*Manila Times*
*Manila Tribune*
*Mid-Pacific Magazine*
*Muling pagsilang* (Tagalog portion of the newspaper *El renacimiento*)
*New York Herald*
*New York Times*
*Philippine Daily Inquirer*
*Philippine Free Press*
*Philippine Magazine*
*Philippine Monthly*
*Philippines Herald*
*Positively Filipino*
*Rappler*
*San Francisco Argonaut*
*The Terno*
*Vogue*
*Woman's Home Journal*
*Women's Wear Daily*
*Woman's World*


FILMS

Holmes, Burton. *Luzon Lingerie*. Directed by Herford T. Cowling. Manila, 1920.
Villarama, Baby Ruth, dir. *Sunday Beauty Queen*. Manila: Voyage Studios and
    Solar Pictures, 2016.


SONGS

Quimpo, T., and V. V. Cordero. "Cruel (Dedicado a la Srta. Guia Balmori)." Crystal
    Arcade, Manila: Lira de Oro, 1938.

*Acts of the Philippine Commission, No. 1–1800.* Washington, DC: Government Printing Office, 1907.

*Acts of the Second Philippine Legislature: Second and Special Sessions, and of the Philippine Commission* (nos. 2076 to 2187, inclusive). Washington, DC: Government Printing Office, 1912. https://hdl.handle.net/2027/hvd .32044085007292.

Bureau of Foreign and Domestic Commerce and Department of Commerce. *Daily Consular and Trade Reports.* Washington, DC: Government Printing Office, 1903–1913.

Bureau of Health for the Philippine Islands. *Annual Report of the Bureau of Health for the Philippine Islands, 1911.* Manila: Bureau of Printing, 1911.

Department of Public Instruction, Bureau of Prisons. *Catalogue of Products of the Industrial Division of Bilibid.* Manila: Bureau of Printing, 1915.

Heiser, Victor. *Annual Report of the Bureau of Health for the Philippine Islands, July 1, 1912 to June 30, 1913.* Manila: Bureau of Printing, 1913.

Lamont, R. P., and O. P. Hopkins. "Prison Industries." In *Domestic Commerce Series*, No. 27. Washington, DC: Government Printing Office, 1929.

Long, J. D., Director of Health, Government of the Philippine Islands Department of Public Instruction, Philippine Health Service. "Report of the Philippine Health Service for the Fiscal Year From (January 1 to December 31, 1917)." Manila: Bureau of Printing, 1918, 29.

(Philippines) Bureau of Education. *Good Manners and Right Conduct for Use in Primary Grades.* Manila: Bureau of Printing, 1913.

(Philippines) Bureau of Education. *Lace Making and Embroidery.* Bulletin No. 34. Manila: Bureau of Printing, 1911. https://hdl.handle.net/2027/njp .32101049926692.

(Philippines) Bureau of Education. *The Philippine Craftsman.* Manila: Bureau of Education, 1912–1917.

(Philippines) Bureau of Education. *School of Household Industries*, Bulletin No. 45. Manila: Bureau of Printing, 1912.

Philippines, Department of Health. *Report.* Manila: Bureau of Printing, 1916.

(Philippines) Department of Health, *Report. Philippines: Philippines Department of Health.* Manila: Bureau of Printing, 1920.

Philippines, Department of Public Instruction. *Annual Report of the Secretary of Public Instruction to the Philippine Commission.* Manila: Bureau of Printing, 1907. https://hdl.handle.net/2027/hvd.hn47rl.

Philippines Governor General. *Report of the Governor General of the Philippine Islands, 1916.* Washington, DC: US Government Printing Office, 1917.

Quirino, Eliseo. *NEPA Handbook.* Manila: National Economic Protectionism Association, 1938.

Root, Elihu. *A Report of the Secretary of War, Containing the Reports of the Taft Commission, Its Several Acts of Legislation, and Other Important Information*

*Relating to the Conditions and Immediate Wants of the Philippine Islands.*
Washington, DC: US Government Printing Office, 1901.

United Nations Asia and Far East Institute for the Prevention of Crime and the
Treatment of Offenders. *Annual Report for 2012 and Resource Material Series,
No. 90.* Tokyo: United Nations Asia and Far East Institute, 2013.

United States Department of Commerce. *The Women's Muslin-Underwear Industry: Report on the Cost of Production of Women's Muslin Underwear in the
United States.* Washington, DC: Government Printing Office, 1915. https://hdl
.handle.net/2027/hvd.li5cjf.

United States Philippine Commission. *Report of the Philippine Commission to the
Secretary of War.* Washington, DC: Government Printing Office, 1901–16.

United States Philippine Commission. *Reports of the Philippine Commission, the
Civil Governor, and the Heads of the Executive Departments of the Civil Government of the Philippine Islands, 1900–1903.* Washington, DC: Government Printing Office, 1904. https://hdl.handle.net/2027/hvd.tz1ppx.

United States Tariff Commission. *Colonial Tariff Policies.* Washington, DC: Government Printing Office, 1922. https://hdl.handle.net/2027/nyp.33433024582730.

White, Frank R. "Introduction." In *Lace Making and Embroidery,* by (Philippines)
Bureau of Education, 7–8. Manila: Bureau of Printing, 1911. https://hdl.handle
.net/2027/njp.32101049926692.


PUBLISHED BOOKS, ESSAYS, AND ARTICLES

Abinales, Patricio. *Making Mindanao: Cotabato and Davao in the Formation of
the Philippine Nation-State.* Quezon City: Ateneo de Manila University Press,
2020.

Abinales, Patricio. "Progressive-Machine Conflict in Early-Twentieth-Century U.S.
Politics and Colonial-State Building in the Philippines." In *The American Colonial
State in the Philippines,* edited by Julian Go and Anne L. Foster, 148–81. Dur-
ham, NC: Duke University Press, 2003.

Abinales, Patricio, and Donna Amoroso. *State and Society in the Philippines.* 2nd ed.
State and Society in East Asia. Lanham, MD: Rowman and Littlefield, 2017.

Agoncillo, Teodoro A. *Filipino Nationalism, 1872–1970.* Quezon City: R. P. Garcia,
1974.

Agoncillo, Teodoro A. *The Revolt of the Masses: The Story of Bonifacio and the
Katipunan.* Quezon City: University of the Philippines Press, 1956.

Aguilar, Filomeno V. *Clash of Spirits: The History of Power and Sugar Planter Hegemony on a Visayan Island.* Honolulu: University of Hawai'i Press, 1998.

Aguilar, Filomeno V. "The Fulcrum of Structure-Agency: History and Sociology
of Sugar Haciendas in Colonial Negros." *Philippine Sociological Review* 61, no. 1
(2013): 87–122.

Aguilar, Filomeno V. "Tracing Origins: Ilustrado Nationalism and the Racial Science of Migration Waves." *Journal of Asian Studies* 64, no. 3 (2005): 605–37.
https://doi.org/10.1017/S002191180500152X.

Alexander, M. Jacqui, and Chandra Talpade Mohanty. *Feminist Genealogies, Colonial Legacies, Democratic Futures*. New York: Routledge, 1997.

Alzate, M. A. *Convict Labor in the Philippine Islands Presented at the Ninth International Prison Congress held in London, August, 1925*. Manila: Bureau of Printing, 1926.

Alzona, Encarnación. *The Filipino Woman: Her Social, Economic, and Political Status, 1565–1933*. Manila: University of the Philippines Press, 1934.

Ancheta, Herminia M., and Michaela Beltran-Gonzalez. *Filipino Women in Nation Building: A Compilation of Brief Biographies*. Quezon City: Phoenix Publishing House, 1984.

Anderson, Benedict. "Cacique Democracy and the Philippines: Origins and Dreams." *New Left Review*, no. 169 (1988): 3–32.

Anderson, Benedict R. *Imagined Communities: Reflections on the Origin and Spread of Nationalism*. Rev. ed. ACLS Humanities E-Book. London: Verso, 2006.

Anderson, Warwick. *Colonial Pathologies: American Tropical Medicine, Race, and Hygiene in the Philippines*. Durham, NC: Duke University Press, 2006.

Anthony, Carl Sferrazza. *Nellie Taft: The Unconventional First Lady of the Ragtime Era*. New York: William Morrow, 2005.

Aquino, Belinda A. "Filipino Women and Political Engagement." *Review of Women's Studies* 4, no. 1 (1994): 32–53.

Armstrong, Meg. "'The Effects of Blackness': Gender, Race, and the Sublime in Aesthetic Theories of Burke and Kant." *Journal of Aesthetics and Art Criticism* 54, no. 3 (1996): 213–36. https://doi.org/10.2307/431624.

Arondekar, Anjali R. *For the Record: On Sexuality and the Colonial Archive in India*. Durham, NC: Duke University Press, 2009.

Arrizón, Alicia. *Queering Mestizaje: Transculturation and Performance*. Ann Arbor: University of Michigan Press, 2006.

Arvin, Maile. *Possessing Polynesians: The Science of Settler Colonial Whiteness in Hawai'i and Oceania*. Durham, NC: Duke University Press, 2019.

Azuma, Eiichiro. *Between Two Empires: Race, History, and Transnationalism in Japanese America*. New York: Oxford University Press, 2005.

Azuma, Eiichiro. *In Search of Our Frontier: Japanese America and Settler Colonialism in the Construction of Japan's Borderless Empire*. Berkeley: University of California Press, 2019.

Azuma, Eiichiro. "Japanese Immigrant Settler Colonialism in the U.S.-Mexican Borderlands and the U.S. Racial-Imperialist Politics of the Hemispheric 'Yellow Peril.'" *Pacific Historical Review* 83, no. 2 (2014): 255–76. https://doi.org/10.1525/phr.2014.83.2.255.

Bajá, Emanuel Agrava. *Philippine Police System and Its Problems*. Manila: Pobre's Press, 1933.

Bakhtin, Mikhail. "Carnival and the Carnivalesque." In *Cultural Theory and Popular Culture: A Reader*, edited by John Storey, 250–60. Athens: University of Georgia Press, 1998.

Balce, Nerissa. *Body Parts of Empire: Visual Abjection, Filipino Images, and the American Archive*. Ann Arbor: University of Michigan Press, 2016.

Baldoz, Rick. *The Third Asiatic Invasion: Empire and Migration in Filipino America, 1898–1946*. New York: New York University Press, 2011.

Banet-Weiser, Sarah. "'I'm Beautiful the Way I Am': Empowerment, Beauty, and Aesthetic Labour." In *Aesthetic Labour*, edited by Ana Sofia Elias, Rosalind Gill, and Christina Scharff, 265–82. London: Palgrave Macmillan, 2017.

Banet-Weiser, Sarah. *The Most Beautiful Girl in the World: Beauty Pageants and National Identity*. Berkeley: University of California Press, 1999.

Bankoff, Greg. "Wants, Wages, and Workers." *Pacific Historical Review* 74, no. 1 (2005): 59–86. https://doi.org/10.1525/phr.2005.74.1.59.

Barber, X. Theodore. "The Roots of Travel Cinema: John L. Stoddard, E. Burton Holmes and the Nineteenth-Century Illustrated Travel Lecture." *Film History* 5, no. 1 (1993): 68–84.

Barthes, Roland. *The Fashion System*. Translated by Matthew Ward and Richard Howard. Berkeley: University of California Press, 1990.

Bascara, Victor. "Collaboration, Co-prosperity, and 'Complete Independence': Across the Pacific (1942), across Philippine Palimpsests." In *Filipino Studies: Palimpsests of Nation and Diaspora*, edited by Martin F. Manalansan and Augusto Espiritu, 87–105. New York: New York University Press, 2020.

Beck, E. M., and Stewart E. Tolnay. "The Killing Fields of the Deep South: The Market for Cotton and the Lynching of Blacks, 1882–1930." *American Sociological Review* 55, no. 4 (1990): 526–39. https://doi.org/10.2307/2095805.

Bender, Daniel E. *Sweated Work, Weak Bodies: Anti-sweatshop Campaigns and Languages of Labor*. New Brunswick, NJ: Rutgers University Press, 2004.

Bernal, Salvador, Georgina R. Encanto, and Francis L. Escaler. *Patterns for the Filipino Dress: From the Traje de Mestiza to the Terno, 1890s–1960s*. Manila: Cultural Center of the Philippines, 1992.

Billig, Michael. *Banal Nationalism*. London: Sage, 1995.

Blackhawk, Ned. *Violence over the Land: Indians and Empires in the Early American West*. Cambridge, MA: Harvard University Press, 2006.

Blair, Emma Helen. *The Philippine Islands, 1493–1803: Explorations by Early Navigators, Descriptions of the Islands and Their Peoples, Their History and Records of the Catholic Missions, as Related in Contemporaneous Books and Manuscripts*. Cleveland: A. H. Clark, 1903. http://nrs.harvard.edu/urn-3:HUL.FIG:004199173.

Blanco, John D. "Race as Praxis in the Philippines at the Turn of the Twentieth Century." *Tōnan Ajia Kenkyu* 49, no. 3 (2011): 356–94. https://doi.org/10.20495/tak.49.3_356.

Bolton, Sony Coráñez. "A Tale of Two X's: Queer Filipinx and Latinx Linguistic Intimacies." In *Filipinx American Studies: Reckoning, Reclamation, Transformation*, edited by Rick Bonus and Antonio T. Tiongson Jr., 284–290. New York: Fordham University Press, 2022.

Bonacich, Edna. *Global Production: The Apparel Industry in the Pacific Rim*. Philadelphia: Temple University Press, 1994.

Boomer, J. F. "Philippine Embroidery: A New Industry for Women in the Islands." *Bulletin of the Pan American Union*, vol. LIII (1921): 153–63.

Boris, Eileen. *Home to Work: Motherhood and the Politics of Industrial Homework in the United States*. Cambridge: Cambridge University Press, 1994.

Brewer, Carolyn, and Anne-Marie Medcalf. *Researching the Fragments: Histories of Women in the Asian Context*. Quezon City: New Day, 2000.

Briggs, Laura. *Reproducing Empire: Race, Sex, Science, and U.S. Imperialism in Puerto Rico*. Berkeley: University of California Press, 2002.

Buhain, Dominador. *A History of Publishing in the Philippines*. Quezon City: Rex Bookstore, 1998.

Burns, Lucy Mae San Pablo. *Puro Arte: Filipinos on the Stages of Empire*. New York: New York University Press, 2013.

Burns, Lucy Mae San Pablo. "Your Terno's Draggin': Fashioning Filipino American Performance." *Women and Performance* 21, no. 2 (2011): 199–217. https://doi.org /10.1080/0740770X.2011.607597.

Burton, Antoinette. *Burdens of History: British Feminists, Indian Women, and Imperial Culture, 1865–1915*. Chapel Hill: University of North Carolina Press, 1994.

Byrd, Jodi A. *The Transit of Empire: Indigenous Critiques of Colonialism*. Minneapolis: University of Minnesota Press, 2011.

Cacho, Lisa Marie. "The Presumption of White Innocence." *American Quarterly* 66, no. 4 (2014): 1085–90. https://doi.org/10.1353/aq.2014.0078.

Calata, Alexander A. "The Role of Education in Americanizing Filipinos." In *Mixed Blessing: The Impact of the American Colonial Experience on Politics and Society in the Philippines*, edited by Hazel M. McFerson, 89–98. Westport, CT: Greenwood Press, 2002.

Camacho, Keith L. "Homomilitarism: The Same-Sex Erotics of the US Empire in Guam and Hawai'i." *Radical History Review* 123 (2015): 144–75. https://doi.org /10.1215/01636545-3088192.

Camacho, Maria Svetlana R. "The Public Transcendence of Intimacy: The Social Value of Recogimiento in Urbana at Feliza." In *More Pinoy Than We Admit: The Social Construction of the Filipina*, edited by Maria Luisa T. Camagay, 295–300. Quezon City: Vibal Foundation, 2010.

Camagay, Maria Luisa T. *Encarnacion Alzona: An Anthology*. Quezon City: Office of Research Coordination, University of the Philippines, 1996.

Camagay, Maria Luisa T. "Women through Philippine History." In *An Anthology of Studies on the Filipino Woman*, edited by Amaryllis T. Torres, 31–32. Metro Manila, Philippines: Unesco, 1986.

Camagay, Maria Luisa T. *Working Women of Manila in the Nineteenth Century*. Quezon City: University of the Philippines Press and the University Center for Women Studies, 1995.

Campomanes, Oscar V. "1898 and the Nature of the New Empire." *Radical History Review* 73 (1999): 130–46. https://doi.org/10.1215/01636545-1999-73-130.

Campomanes, Oscar V. "Images of Filipino Racialization in the Anthropological Laboratories of the American Empire: The Case of Daniel Folkmar." *PMLA:*

*Publications of the Modern Language Association of America* 123, no. 5 (2008): 1692–99. https://doi.org/10.1632/pmla.2008.123.5.1692.

Cannell, Fenella. *Power and Intimacy in the Christian Philippines*. New York: Cambridge University Press, 1999.

Cano, Glòria. "Filipino Press between Two Empires: El Renacimiento, a Newspaper with Too Much Alma Filipina." *Tōnan Ajia Kenkyu* 49, no. 3 (2011): 395–430. https://doi.org/10.20495/tak.49.3_395.

Canta, Marilyn. "Of Cambayas, Custas and Calicos: The Indo-Philippine Textile Connection." In *Manila: Selected Papers of the 17th Annual Manila Studies Conference, August 13–14, 2008*, edited by Bernardita Reyes Churchill, 127–28. Quezon City: Manila Studies Association, 2009.

Capistrano-Baker, Florina H., Pieter ter Keurs, and Sandra B. Castro. *Embroidered Multiples: 18th–19th Century Philippine Costumes from the National Museum of Ethnology, Leiden, the Netherlands*. Manila: Royal Netherlands Embassy, 2007.

Capozzola, Christopher. *Bound by War: How the United States and the Philippines Built America's First Pacific Century*. New York: Basic Books, 2020.

Carby, Hazel. "Policing the Black Woman's Body in an Urban Context." *Critical Inquiry* 18, no. 4 (1992): 738–55. https://doi.org/10.1086/448654.

Caronan, Faye. *Legitimizing Empire: Filipino American and U.S. Puerto Rican Cultural Critique*. Urbana: University of Illinois Press, 2015.

Castro, Alex R. *Aro Katimyas Da! A Memory Album of Titled Kapampangan Beauties (1908–2012)*. Angeles City, Philippines: Center for Kapampangan Studies, Holy Angel University, 2012.

Castro-Baker, Sandra. *Textiles in the Philippine Landscape: A Lexicon and Historical Survey*. Quezon City: Ateneo de Manila University Press, 2018.

Chang, Kornel. "Circulating Race and Empire: Transnational Labor Activism and the Politics of Anti-Asian Agitation in the Anglo-American Pacific World, 1880–1910." *Journal of American History* 96, no. 3 (2009): 678–701. https://doi.org/10.1093/jahist/96.3.678.

Cheng, Anne Anlin. *Ornamentalism*. New York: Oxford University Press, 2019.

Cheng, Anne Anlin. "Shine: On Race, Glamour, and the Modern." *PMLA: Publications of the Modern Language Association of America* 126, no. 4 (October 2011): 1022–41. https://doi.org/10.1632/pmla.2011.126.4.1022.

Chiba, Yoshihiro. "Cigar-Makers in American Colonial Manila: Survival during Structural Depression in the 1920s." *Journal of Southeast Asian Studies* 36, no. 3 (2005): 373–97. https://doi.org/10.1017/S0022463405000214.

Child, Brenda J. *Boarding School Seasons: American Indian Families, 1900–1940*. Lincoln: University of Nebraska Press, 2000.

Choy, Catherine Ceniza. "A Filipino Woman in America: The Life and Work of Encarnacion Alzona." *Genre* 39, no. 3 (2006): 127–40. https://doi.org/10.1215/00166928-39-3-127.

Choy, Catherine Ceniza. *Empire of Care: Nursing and Migration in Filipino American History*. Durham, NC: Duke University Press, 2003.

Chu, Richard T. *Chinese and Chinese Mestizos of Manila: Family, Identity, and Culture, 1860s–1930s*. Boston: Brill, 2010.

Churchill, Bernadita Reyes. "Life in a War of Independence: The Philippine Revolution, 1896–1902." In *Daily Lives of Civilians in Wartime Asia: From the Taiping Rebellion to the Vietnam War*, edited by Stewart Lone. Westport, CT: Greenwood Press, 2007.

Clutario, Genevieve. "Pageant Politics: Tensions of Power, Empire, and Nationalism in Manila Carnival Queen Contests." In *Gendering the Trans-Pacific World*, edited by Catherine Ceniza Choy and Judy Tzu-Chun Wu, 257–83. Leiden: Brill, 2017. https://doi.org/10.1163/9789004336100_014.

Clutario, Genevieve Alva. "The Appearance of Filipina Nationalism: Body, Nation, Empire." PhD diss., University of Illinois at Urbana-Champaign, 2014.

Clutario, Genevieve Alva. "World War II and the Promise of Normalcy: Overlapping Empires and Everyday Lives in the Philippines." In *Crossing Empires: Taking U.S. History into Transimperial Terrain*, edited by Kristin L. Hoganson and Jay Sexton, 241–58. Durham, NC: Duke University Press, 2020. https://doi.org/10.1515/9781478007432-013.

Cobble, Dorothy Sue. "More Intimate Unions." In *Intimate Labors: Cultures, Technologies, and the Politics of Care*, edited by Rhacel Salazar Parreñas and Eileen Boris, 280–96. Palo Alto, CA: Stanford University Press, 2020. https://doi.org/10.1515/9780804777278-020.

Cohen, Colleen Ballerion, Richard Wilk, and Beverly Stoeltje. *Beauty Queens on the Global Stage: Gender, Contests, and Power*. New York: Routledge, 2013.

Cohn, Bernard S. "Cloths, Clothes, and Colonialism: India in the Nineteenth Century." In *European Intruders and Changes in Behaviour and Customs in Africa, America and Asia before 1800*, edited by Murdo J. MacLeod and Evelyn Sakakida Rawski, 189–239. London: Routledge, 1998. https://doi.org/10.4324/9781315255934-11.

Cohn, Bernard S. *Colonialism and Its Forms of Knowledge: The British in India*. Princeton, NJ: Princeton University Press, 1996.

Coleman, Michael C. *American Indian Children at School, 1850–1930*. Jackson: University Press of Mississippi, 1993.

Coloma, Roland Sintos. "'Destiny Has Thrown the Negro and the Filipino under the Tutelage of America': Race and Curriculum in the Age of Empire." *Curriculum Inquiry* 39, no. 4 (2009): 495–519. https://doi.org/10.1111/j.1467-873X.2009.00454.x.

Coloma, Roland Sintos. "Disidentifying Nationalism." In *Revolution and Pedagogy: Interdisciplinary and Transnational Perspectives on Educational Foundations*, edited by E. Thomas Ewing, 19–37. New York: Palgrave Macmillan, 2005. https://doi.org/10.1057/9781403980137_2.

Coloma, Roland Sintos. "White Gazes, Brown Breasts: Imperial Feminism and Disciplining Desires and Bodies in Colonial Encounters." *Paedagogica Historica* 48, no. 2 (2012): 243–61. https://doi.org/10.1080/00309230.2010.547511.

Commons, John R., David J. Saposs, Helen L. Sumner, E. B. Mittelman, H. E. Hoagland, John B. Andrews, and Selig Perlman. *History of Labour in the*

*United States*. New York: Macmillan, 1935. https://hdl.handle.net/2027/mdp .35128001423449.

Constantino, Renato. *Neocolonial Identity and Counter-Consciousness: Essays on Cultural Decolonization*. New York: Routledge, 1978. https://doi.org/10.4324 /9781315177946.

Constantino, Renato, and Letizia R. Constantino. *A History of the Philippines: From the Spanish Colonization to the Second World War*. New York: Monthly Review Press, 1975.

Coo, Stephanie. *Clothing the Colony: Nineteenth-Century Philippine Sartorial Culture, 1820–1896*. Quezon City: Ateneo de Manila University Press, 2019.

Coo, Stéphanie Marie R. "Clothing and the Colonial Culture of Appearances in Nineteenth Century Spanish Philippines (1820–1896)." PhD diss., Université Nice Sophia Antipolis, 2014.

Cook-Lynn, Elizabeth. *A Separate Country: Postcoloniality and American Indian Nations*. Lubbock: Texas Tech University Press, 2012.

Corpuz, Onofre D. *An Economic History of the Philippines*. Quezon City: University of the Philippines Press, 1997.

Craig, Maxine Leeds. *Ain't I a Beauty Queen? Black Women, Beauty, and the Politics of Race*. New York: Oxford University Press, 2002.

Cruz, Denise. "Global Mess and Glamour: Behind the Spectacle of Transnational Fashion." *Journal of Asian American Studies* 19, no. 2 (2016): 143–67.

Cruz, Denise. *Transpacific Femininities: The Making of the Modern Filipina*. Durham, NC: Duke University Press, 2012.

Cruz, Eric V. *The Terno: Its Development and Identity as the Filipino Women's National Costume*. Quezon City: U. P. College of Home Economics, 1982.

Cruz-Lucero, Rosario. "Judas and His Phallus: The Carnivalesque Narratives of Holy Week in Catholic Philippines." *History and Anthropology* 17, no. 1 (2006): 39–56. https://doi.org/10.1080/02757200500395568.

Cullinane, Michael. *Ilustrado Politics: Filipino Elite Responses to American Rule, 1898–1908*. Quezon City: Ateneo de Manila University Press, 2003.

Dauncey, Mrs Campbell. *An Englishwoman in the Philippines*. London: J Murray, 1906.

David, Emmanuel. "Transgender Archipelagos." *Transgender Studies Quarterly* 5, no. 3 (2018): 332–54. https://doi.org/10.1215/23289252-6900724.

David, Emmanuel, and Christian Joy P. Cruz. "Big, *Bakla*, and Beautiful: Transformations on a Manila Pageant Stage." *Women's Studies Quarterly* 46, nos. 1–2 (2018): 29–45. https://doi.org/10.1353/wsq.2018.0006.

Davis, Angela Y. *Are Prisons Obsolete?* New York: Seven Stories Press, 2011.

Davis, Angela Y. "Race, Gender, and Prison History: From the Convict Lease System to the Supermax Prison." In *Prison Masculinities*, edited by Don Sabo, Terry A. Kupers, and Willie London, 35–45. Philadelphia: Temple University Press, 2001.

Davis, Angela Y. *Women, Race, and Class*. New York: Knopf Doubleday, 2011.

Davis, Angela Y., and Cassandra Shaylor. "Race, Gender, and the Prison Industrial Complex: California and Beyond." *Meridians* 2, no. 1 (September 1, 2001): 1–25. https://doi.org/10.1215/15366936-2.1.1.

Day, Iyko. "Being or Nothingness: Indigeneity, Antiblackness, and Settler Colonial Critique." *Critical Ethnic Studies* 1, no. 2 (2015): 102–21. https://doi.org/10.5749 /jcritethnstud.1.2.0102.

DeGuzmán, María. *Spain's Long Shadow: The Black Legend, Off-Whiteness, and Anglo-American Empire.* Minneapolis: University of Minnesota Press, 2005.

DeLisle, Christine Taitano. "Navy Wives/Native Lives: The Cultural and Historical Relations between American Naval Wives and Chamorro Women in Guam, 1898–1945." PhD diss., University of Michigan, 2008.

Deloria, Vine. *Behind the Trail of Broken Treaties: An Indian Declaration of Independence.* New York: Delacorte Press, 1974.

Dery, Luis C. *A History of the Inarticulate: Local History, Prostitution, and Other Views from the Bottom.* Quezon City: New Day Publishers, 2001.

Dery, Luis C. "Prostitution in Colonial Manila." *Philippine Studies* 39, no. 4 (1991): 475–89.

Diaz, Robert. "Biyuti from Below." *Transgender Studies Quarterly* 5, no. 3 (2018): 404–24. https://doi.org/10.1215/23289252-6900781.

Diaz, Robert. *Confetti of Ordinary Dreams: Queer Filipinos and Reparative Acts.* Durham, NC: Duke University Press, forthcoming.

Diaz, Robert. "Queer Unsettlements: Diasporic Filipinos in Canada's World Pride." *Journal of Asian American Studies* 19, no. 3 (2016): 327–50. https://doi.org/10 .1353/jaas.2016.0030.

Diaz, Robert. "The Limits of *Bakla* and Gay: Feminist Readings of My Husband's Lover, Vice Ganda, and Charice Pempengco." *Signs: Journal of Women in Culture and Society* 40, no. 3 (2015): 721–45. https://doi.org/10.1086/679526.

Diaz, Vicente M. *Repositioning the Missionary: Rewriting the Histories of Colonialism, Native Catholicism, and Indigeneity in Guam.* Honolulu: University of Hawai'i Press, 2010.

Doeppers, Daniel F. *Feeding Manila in Peace and War, 1850–1945.* Madison: University of Wisconsin Press, 2016.

Doeppers, Daniel F. *Manila 1900–1941: Social Change in a Late Colonial Metropolis.* Quezon City: Ateneo de Manila University Press; New Haven, CT: Yale University Press, 1984.

Doran, Christine. "Spanish and Mestizo Women of Manila." *Philippine Studies* 41, no. 3 (1993): 269–86.

Doran, Christine. "Women in the Philippine Revolution." *Philippine Studies* 46, no. 3 (1998): 361–75.

Doran, Christine. "Women, Nationalism and the Philippine Revolution." *Nations and Nationalism* 5, no. 2 (1999): 237–58.

Drery, Luis. "Prostitution in Colonial Manila." *Philippine Studies* 39, no. 4 (1991): 475–89.

Du Bois, W. E. B. "Worlds of Color." *Foreign Affairs* 3, no. 3 (1925): 423–44. https://doi.org/10.2307/20028386.

Duras, Marguerite. *The Lover*. Translated by Barbara Bray. New York: Pantheon Books, 1985.

Duras, Marguerite. *The Sea Wall*. Translated by Herma Briffault. New York: Farrar, Straus and Giroux, 1967.

Duus, Peter. "Zaikabo: Japanese Cotton Mills in China, 1895–1937." In *The Japanese Informal Empire in China, 1895–1937*, edited by Peter Duus, Ramon H. Myers, and Mark R. Peattie, 65–100. Princeton, NJ: Princeton University Press, 1991. https://doi.org/10.1515/9781400847938.65.

Edwards, Louise, and Mina Roces. "Rethinking 'the Filipino Woman': A Century of Women's Activism in the Philippines, 1905–2006." In *Women's Movements in Asia: Feminisms and Transnational Activism*, edited by Mina Roces and Louise Edwards, 44–62. London: Routledge, 2010. https://doi.org/10.4324/9780203851234-8.

Edwards, Penny. "Restyling Colonial Cambodia (1860–1954): French Dressing, Indigenous Custom and National Costume." *Fashion Theory* 5, no. 4 (2001): 389–416. https://doi.org/10.2752/136270401778998909.

Eittreim, Elisabeth M. *Teaching Empire: Native Americans, Filipinos, and US Imperial Education, 1879–1918*. Lawrence: University Press of Kansas, 2019.

Elias, Megan. "The Palate of Power: Americans, Food and the Philippines after the Spanish-American War." *Material Culture* 46, no. 1 (2014): 44–57.

Elson, Diane, and Ruth Pearson. "'Nimble Fingers Make Cheap Workers': An Analysis of Women's Employment in Third World Export Manufacturing." *Feminist Review* 7, no. 1 (1981): 87–107. https://doi.org/10.1057/fr.1981.6.

Encanto, Georgina R. *Constructing the Filipina: A History of Women's Magazines (1891–2002)*. Quezon City: University of the Philippines Press, 2004.

Enloe, Cynthia. "Women Textile Workers in the Militarization of Southeast Asia." In *Women, Men, and the International Division of Labour*, edited by June Nash and María Patricia Fernández Kelly, 407–25. Albany: SUNY Press, 1983.

Enstad, Nan. *Ladies of Labor, Girls of Adventure: Working Women, Popular Culture, and Labor Politics at the Turn of the Twentieth Century*. New York: Columbia University Press, 1999.

Entwistle, Joanne. "Fashion and the Fleshy Body: Dress as Embodied Practice." *Fashion Theory* 4, no. 3 (2000): 323–47. https://doi.org/10.2752/136270400778995471.

España-Maram, Linda. *Creating Masculinity in Los Angeles's Little Manila: Working-Class Filipinos and Popular Culture, 1920s–1950s*. New York: Columbia University Press, 2006.

Espiritu, Augusto. "American Empire, Hispanism, and the Nationalist Visions of Albizu, Recto, and Grau." In *Formations of United States Colonialism*, edited by Alyosha Goldstein, 157–79. Durham, NC: Duke University Press, 2014.

Estes, Nick. "Wounded Knee: Settler Colonial Property Regimes and Indigenous Liberation." *Capitalism, Nature, Socialism* 24, no. 3 (2013): 190–202. https://doi.org/10.1080/10455752.2013.814697.

Farrales, May. "Repurposing Beauty Pageants: The Colonial Geographies of Filipina Pageants in Canada." *Environment and Planning D: Society and Space* 37, no. 1 (2019): 46–64. https://doi.org/10.1177/0263775818796502.

Fee, Mary H. *A Woman's Impressions of the Philippines*. Chicago: A. C. McClurg, 1910.

Fernandez, Doreen G. "Mass Culture and Cultural Policy: The Philippine Experience." *Philippine Studies* 37, no. 4 (1989): 488–502.

Fernandez, Doreen G. *Palabas: Essays on Philippine Theater History*. Quezon City: Ateneo de Manila University Press, 1996.

Fernandez, Doreen G. "The Philippine Press System: 1811–1989." *Philippine Studies* 37, no. 3 (1989): 317–44.

Fernandez, Doreen G. "Pompas y Solemnidades: Notes on Church Celebrations in Spanish Manila." In *More Hispanic Than We Admit 2: Insights into Philippine Cultural History*, edited by Glòria Cano. Quezon City: Vibal Foundation, 2015.

Fernandez, Doreen G. *Tikim: Essays on Philippine Food and Culture*. Pasig City, Philippines: Anvil Pub, 1994.

Ferrer, Ada. *Insurgent Cuba: Race, Nation, and Revolution, 1868–1898*. Chapel Hill: University of North Carolina Press, 1999.

Fields, Barbara Jeanne. "Slavery, Race and Ideology in the United States of America." *New Left Review* 181, no. 1 (1990): 95–118.

Finnane, Antonia. *Changing Clothes in China: Fashion, History, Nation*. New York: Columbia University Press, 2008.

Finnane, Antonia. "Yangzhou's 'Mondernity': Fashion and Consumption in the Early-Nineteenth-Century World." *positions: east asia cultures critique* 11, no. 2 (2003): 395–425.

Flores, Patrick. "Prohibiting the Presentation of Pride and Patriotism: A Thesis on the Validity of Provisions within the Flag and Heraldic Code of the Philippines." PhD diss., De La Salle University–Manila, 2019.

Foley, Neil. *The White Scourge: Mexicans, Blacks, and Poor Whites in Texas Cotton Culture*. Berkeley: University of California Press, 1997.

Ford, Tanisha C. *Liberated Threads: Black Women, Style, and the Global Politics of Soul*. Chapel Hill: University of North Carolina Press, 2015.

Foucault, Michel. *Discipline and Punish: The Birth of the Prison*. Translated by Alan Sheridan. New York: Knopf Doubleday, 2012.

Francisco, Adrianne Marie. "From Subjects to Citizens: American Colonial Education and Philippine Nation-Making, 1900–1934." PhD diss., University of California, Berkeley, 2015.

Francisco-Menchavez, Valerie. *The Labor of Care: Filipina Migrants and Transnational Families in the Digital Age*. Urbana: University of Illinois Press, 2018.

Fuentes, Marisa J. *Dispossessed Lives: Enslaved Women, Violence, and the Archive*. Philadelphia: University of Pennsylvania Press, 2016.

Fujita Rony, Dorothy B. *American Workers, Colonial Power: Philippine Seattle and the Transpacific West, 1919–1941*. Berkeley: University of California Press, 2003.

Funtecha, Henry F. "Iloilo's Weaving Industry during the Nineteenth Century." *Philippine Quarterly of Culture and Society* 9, no. 4 (December 1981): 301–8.

Gale, Glenn. "Ramon Valera: A True Artist." In *Valera: Cada traje es una obra maestra*, edited by Tantoco-Rustia Foundation and National Museum. Quezon City: Tantoco-Rustia Foundation, 2005.

Galster, Kjeld, and Marie-Louise Nosch. "Textile History and the Military: An Introduction." *Textile History* 41, no. sup1 (2010): 1–5. https://doi.org/10.1179 /174329510X12646114289347.

García-Peña, Lorgia. *The Borders of Dominicanidad: Race, Nation, and Archives of Contradiction*. Durham, NC: Duke University Press, 2016.

Gates, John Morgan. "Hang the Dogs: The True History of the Balangiga Massacre." *Journal of Military History* 69, no. 3 (2005): 850–51. https://doi.org/10.1353 /jmh.2005.0161.

Gillin, John Lewis. *Taming the Criminal: Adventures in Penology*. New York: Macmillan, 1931.

Gilmore, Ruth Wilson. *Golden Gulag: Prisons, Surplus, Crisis, and Opposition in Globalizing California*. Berkeley: University of California Press, 2007. https:// doi.org/10.1525/j.ctt5hjht8.

Gleeck, Lewis E. *American Business and Philippine Economic Development*. Manila: Carmelo and Bauermann, 1975.

Gleeck, Lewis E. *The Manila Americans (1901–1964)*. Manila: Carmelo and Bauermann, 1977.

Glenn, Evelyn Nakano. *Unequal Freedom: How Race and Gender Shaped American Citizenship and Labor*. Cambridge, MA: Harvard University Press, 2002.

Go, Julian. *American Empire and the Politics of Meaning: Elite Political Cultures in the Philippines and Puerto Rico during U.S. Colonialism*. Durham, NC: Duke University Press, 2008.

Goldstein, Carolyn M. *Creating Consumers: Home Economists in Twentieth-Century America*. Chapel Hill: University of North Carolina Press, 2012.

Gonzalez, Vernadette Vicuña. "Illicit Labor: MacArthur's Mistress and Imperial Intimacies." *Radical History Review* 2015, no. 123 (2015): 87–114. https://doi.org /10.1215/01636545-3088168.

Greenberg, Amy S. *Manifest Manhood and the Antebellum American Empire*. Cambridge: Cambridge University Press, 2005.

Greer, Brenna Wynn. *Represented: The Black Imagemakers Who Reimagined African American Citizenship*. Philadelphia: University of Pennsylvania Press, 2019.

Grewal, Inderpal. *Home and Harem: Nation, Gender, Empire, and the Cultures of Travel*. Durham, NC: Duke University Press, 1996.

Grewal, Inderpal. *Transnational America: Feminisms, Diasporas, Neoliberalisms*. Durham, NC: Duke University Press, 2005.

Grewal, Inderpal, and Caren Kaplan. *Scattered Hegemonies: Postmodernity and Transnational Feminist Practices*. Minneapolis: University of Minnesota Press, 1994.

Grout, Holly. "Between Venus and Mercury: The 1920s Beauty Contest in France and America." *French Politics, Culture and Society* 31, no. 1 (2013): 47–68. https://doi.org/10.3167/fpcs.2013.310103.

Guerrero, Leon Ma. *The First Filipino: A Biography of José Rizal*. Manila: Publications of the National Heroes Commission, 1977.

Guevarra, Anna Romina. *Marketing Dreams, Manufacturing Heroes: The Transnational Labor Brokering of Filipino Workers*. New Brunswick, NJ: Rutgers University Press, 2009.

Gutierrez, Filomeno. "Petty Crimes in the late 19th Century Manila." *Manila* 4, no. 1 (2008). http://www.ejournals.ph/form/cite.php?id=3019. Accessed December 2, 2015.

Gutierrez, Filomeno. "Studying Criminality and Criminal Offenders in the Early Twentieth-Century Philippines." In *International Handbook of Criminology*, edited by Shlomo Giora Shoham, Paul Knepper, and Martin Kett, 369–400. Boca Raton, FL: CRC Press, 2010. https://doi.org/10.1201/9781420085525-21.

Haley, Sarah. *No Mercy Here: Gender, Punishment, and the Making of Jim Crow Modernity*. Chapel Hill: University of North Carolina Press, 2016.

Halili, Servando D. *Iconography of the New Empire: Race and Gender Images and the American Colonization of the Philippines*. Manila: University of the Philippines Press, 2006.

Hall, Stuart. "Encoding/Decoding." In *Media and Cultural Studies: Keyworks*, edited by Meenakshi Gigi Durham and Douglas M. Kellner, 2nd ed., 163–73. Malden: Blackwell, 2006.

Hall, Stuart. *Policing the Crisis: Mugging, the State, and Law and Order*. 2nd ed. Basingstoke: Palgrave Macmillan, 2013.

Hall, Stuart, and David Morley. *Essential Essays, Volume 1: Foundations of Cultural Studies. Stuart Hall: Selected Writings*. Durham, NC: Duke University Press, 2019.

Hoganson, Kristin L. *Fighting for American Manhood: How Gender Politics Provoked the Spanish-American and Philippine-American Wars*. New Haven, CT: Yale University Press, 1998.

Hartman, Saidiya V. *Scenes of Subjection: Terror, Slavery, and Self-Making in Nineteenth-Century America*. New York: Oxford University Press, 1997.

Hartman, Saidiya V. "Venus in Two Acts." *Small Axe: A Caribbean Journal of Criticism* 26, no. 26 (2008): 1–14. https://doi.org/10.2979/SAX.2008.-.26.1.

Hau, Caroline S. "The Afterlives of María Clara." *Humanities Diliman* 18, no. 1 (2021): 118–61.

Hau, Caroline Sy. "'Patria é Intereses': Reflections on the Origins and Changing Meanings of Ilustrado." *Philippine Studies* 59, no. 1 (2011): 3–54.

Hayase, Shinzo. "American Colonial Policy and the Japanese Abaca Industry in Davao, 1898–1941." *Philippine Studies* 33, no. 4 (1985): 505–17.

Henry, Paget, and George Danns. "W. E. B. DuBois, Racial Capitalism and Black Economic Development in the United States." *CLR James Journal* 26, no. 1 (2020): 267–91. https://doi.org/10.5840/clrjames2020261/26.

Hernandez, Eloisa May P. *Homebound: Women Visual Artists in Nineteenth Century Philippines*. Quezon City: University of the Philippines Press, in cooperation with the National Commission for Culture and the Arts, 2004. https://hdl .handle.net/2027/heb.04462.

Hila, Ma Corazon Alejo, Mitzi Marie Aguilar Reyes, and Anita B. Feleo. *Garment of Honor, Garment of Identity*. Manila: EN Barong Filipino, 2008.

Hill Collins, Patricia. *Black Feminist Thought: Knowledge, Consciousness, and the Politics of Empowerment*. 2nd ed. New York: Routledge, 2000.

Hinojosa, Magda, and Jill Carle. "From Miss World to World Leader: Beauty Queens, Paths to Power, and Political Representations." *Journal of Women, Politics and Policy* 37, no. 1 (2016): 24–46. https://doi.org/10.1080/1554477X.2016.1116298.

Hoganson, Kristin L. *Consumers' Imperium: The Global Production of American Domesticity, 1865–1920*. Chapel Hill: University of North Carolina Press, 2007.

Holmes, Burton. *Burton Holmes Travelogues*. New York: McClure, 1908.

Holt, E. M. *Colonizing Filipinas: Nineteenth-Century Representations of the Philippines in Western Historiography*. Quezon City: Ateneo de Manila University Press, 2002.

Humphrey, Chris. *The Politics of Carnival: Festive Misrule in Medieval England*. Manchester, UK: Manchester University Press, 2001.

Hunter, Tera W. *To 'Joy My Freedom: Southern Black Women's Lives and Labors after the Civil War*. Cambridge, MA: Harvard University Press, 1997.

Ignacio, Abe, Enrique B. de la Cruz, Jorge A. Emmanuel, and Helen Toribio. *The Forbidden Book: The Philippine-American War in Political Cartoons*. San Francisco: T'Boli, 2004.

Ileto, Reynaldo C. *Filipinos and Their Revolution: Event, Discourse, and Historiography*. Quezon City: Ateneo de Manila University Press, 1998.

Ileto, Reynaldo C. "Friendship and Forgetting." In *Vestiges of War: The Philippine-American War and the Aftermath of an Imperial Dream 1899–1999*, edited by Luis Francia and Angel Velasco Shaw, 3–21. New York: New York University Press, 2002.

Ileto, Reynaldo C. *Pasyon and Revolution: Popular Movements in the Philippines, 1840–1910*. Quezon City: Ateneo de Manila University Press, 1979.

Ileto, Reynaldo C. "Philippine Wars and the Politics of Memory." *positions: east asia cultures critique* 13, no. 1 (2005): 215–34. https://doi.org/10.1215/10679847-13-1-215.

Isaac, Allan Punzalan. *American Tropics: Articulating Filipino America*. Minneapolis: University of Minnesota Press, 2006.

Jacobs, Margaret D. *White Mother to a Dark Race: Settler Colonialism, Maternalism, and the Removal of Indigenous Children in the American West and Australia, 1880–1940*. Lincoln: University of Nebraska Press, 2009. https://hdl.handle .net/2027/heb.08861.

Jacobson, Matthew Frye. *Barbarian Virtues: The United States Encounters Foreign Peoples at Home and Abroad, 1876–1917*. New York: Hill and Wang, 2000.

Jenkins, Destin. "Ghosts of the Past: Debt, the New South, and the Propaganda of History." In *Ghosts of the Past: Debt, the New South, and the Propaganda of History*, edited by Destin Jenkins and Justin Leroy, 185–214. New York: Columbia University Press, 2021. https://doi.org/10.7312/jenk19074-009.

Joaquin, Nick. *Naval de Manila and Other Essays*. Manila: Alberto S. Florentino, 1964.

Joaquin, Nick. *One Woman's Liberating: The Life and Career of Estefania Aldaba-Lim*. Pasig City, Philippines: Anvil Pub, 1996.

Johnson, Mark. *Beauty and Power: Transgendering and Cultural Transformation in the Southern Philippines*. London: Taylor and Francis Group, 1997.

Johnson, Walter. *River of Dark Dreams: Slavery and Empire in the Cotton Kingdom*. Cambridge, MA: Harvard University Press, 2013.

Kalaw, Teodoro M. *Aide-de-Camp to Freedom*. Translated by Maria Kalaw Katigbak. Manila: Teodoro M. Kalaw Society, 1965.

Kalaw-Ledesma, Purita. *And Life Goes On: Memoirs of Purita Kalaw-Ledesma*. Manila: Self-published, 1994.

Kang, Miliann. "Manicures as Transnational Body Labor." In *Fashion and Beauty in the Time of Asia*, edited by S. Heijin Lee, Christina H. Moon, and Thuy Linh Nguyen Tu, 184–208. New York: New York University Press, 2020.

Kang, Miliann. *The Managed Hand: Race, Gender, and the Body in Beauty Service Work*. Berkeley: University of California Press, 2010. https://doi.org/10.1525/j.ctt1ppzfz.

Kant, Immanuel, Patrick R. Frierson, and Paul Guyer. *Immanuel Kant: Observations on the Feeling of the Beautiful and Sublime and Other Writings*. Cambridge: Cambridge University Press, 2011.

Kaplan, Amy. *The Anarchy of Empire in the Making of U.S. Culture*. Cambridge, MA: Harvard University Press, 2002.

Kaplan, Amy, and Donald E. Pease. *Cultures of United States Imperialism*. Durham, NC: Duke University Press, 1993.

Kaplan, Caren. *Questions of Travel: Postmodern Discourses of Displacement*. Durham, NC: Duke University Press, 1996.

Kaplan, Caren, Norma Alarcón, and Minoo Moallem. *Between Woman and Nation: Nationalisms, Transnational Feminisms, and the State*. Durham, NC: Duke University Press, 1999.

Karnow, Stanley. *In Our Image: America's Empire in the Philippines*. New York: Random House, 1989.

Karuka, Manu. *Empire's Tracks: Indigenous Nations, Chinese Workers, and the Transcontinental Railroad*. Berkeley: University of California Press, 2019.

Katigbak, Maria Kalaw. *Legacy, Pura Villanueva Kalaw: Her Times, Life, and Works, 1886–1954*. Manila: Filipinas Foundation, 1983.

Keeley, James F. "Toward a Foucauldian Analysis of International Regimes." *International Organization* 44, no. 1 (1990): 83–105. https://doi.org/10.1017/S0020818300004653.

Kellner, Douglas M., and Meenakshi Gigi Durham. "Adventures in Media and Cultural Studies: Introducing the Keyworks." In *Media and Cultural Studies:*

*Keyworks*, edited by Meenakshi Gigi Durham and Douglas M. Kellner, 1–29. Malden: Blackwell, 2003.

Kerkvliet, Benedict J. Tria. "Everyday Resistance to Injustice in a Philippine Village." *Journal of Peasant Studies* 13, no. 2 (1986): 107–23.

Kerkvliet, Melinda Tria. *Manila Workers' Unions, 1900–1950*. Quezon City: New Day Publishers, 1992.

Kerkvliet, Melinda Tria. *Unbending Cane: Pablo Manlapit, a Filipino Labor Leader in Hawaii*. Honolulu: University of Hawai'i Press, 2002.

King-O'Riain, Rebecca Chiyoko. *Pure Beauty: Judging Race in Japanese American Beauty Pageants*. Minneapolis: University of Minnesota Press, 2006.

Knepper, Paul, and Per Jørgen Ystehede. *The Influence of Cesare Lombroso on Philippine Criminology*. New York: Routledge, 2012.

Kohlstedt, Sally Gregory. "All the World's a Fair: Visions of Empire at American International Expositions, 1876–1916. Robert W. Rydell." *Isis* 77, no. 2 (1986): 386–87. https://doi.org/10.1086/354198.

Kramer, Paul. "Making Concessions: Race and Empire Revisited at the Philippine Exposition, St. Louis, 1901–1905." *Radical History Review* 1999, no. 73 (1999): 75–114. https://doi.org/10.1215/01636545-1999-73-75.

Kramer, Paul A. *The Blood of Government: Race, Empire, the United States, and the Philippines*. Chapel Hill: University of North Carolina Press, 2006.

Krasner, Stephen D. *International Regimes*. Ithaca, NY: Cornell University Press, 1983.

Labrador, Ana. "The Project of Nationalism: Celebrating the Centenary in Philippines Contemporary Art." *Humanities Research*, no. 2 (January 1999): 53–70. https://search.informit.org/doi/abs/10.3316/informit.178938127809081.

LaFeber, Walter. *The New Empire: An Interpretation of American Expansion, 1860–1898*. Ithaca, NY: Cornell University Press, 1967.

Laguio, Perfecto E. *Our Modern Woman: A National Problem*. Manila: Pilaw Book Supply, 1931.

Larkin, John A. "The International Face of the Philippine Sugar Industry: 1836–1920." *Philippine Review of Economics* 21, nos. 1–2 (1984): 39–58.

Latham, Angela J. "Packaging Woman: The Concurrent Rise of Beauty Pageants, Public Bathing, and Other Performances of Female 'Nudity.'" *Journal of Popular Culture* 29, no. 3 (1995): 149–67.

Laurie, Bruce. *Artisans into Workers: Labor in Nineteenth-Century America*. New York: Hill and Wang, 1989.

Lee, Erika. "The 'Yellow Peril' and Asian Exclusion in the Americas." *Pacific Historical Review* 76, no. 4 (2007): 537–62. https://doi.org/10.1525/phr.2007.76 .4.537.

Lee, S. Heijin. "Beauty between Empires: Global Feminism, Plastic Surgery, and the Trouble with Self-Esteem." *Frontiers* 37, no. 1 (2016): 1–31. https://doi.org/10 .5250/fronjwomestud.37.1.0001.

Lee, S. Heijin, Christina H. Moon, and Thuy Linh Nguyen Tu, eds. *Fashion and Beauty in the Time of Asia*. New York: New York University Press, 2020.

Leon, Isidra Edralin Lopez de. "Home Economics Curricular Reforms in the Public Elementary Schools in the Philippines, 1900–1980." PhD diss., University of North Carolina at Greensboro, 1981.

LeRoy, James Alfred. *Philippine Life in Town and Country*. New York: G. P. Putnam's Sons, 1905. http://nrs.harvard.edu/urn-3:HUL.FIG:005762199.

Licuanan, Virginia Benitez. *Paz Marquez Benitez: One Woman's Life, Letters, and Writings*. Quezon City: Ateneo de Manila University Press, 1995.

Lim, Eng-Beng. *Brown Boys and Rice Queens: Spellbinding Performance in the Asias*. New York: New York University Press, 2014.

Liu, Tessie P. "Commercialization of Trousseau Work: Women Workers in the French Lingerie Trade." In *A Woman's Hands in Industrializing Craft*, edited by Daryl M. Hafter, 179–97. Bloomington: Indiana University Press, 1995.

López, Oscar M. *The Lopez Family*. Manila: Eugenio López Foundation, 1982.

Love, Eric T. L., and L. Love. *Race over Empire: Racism and U.S. Imperialism, 1865–1900*. Chapel Hill: University of North Carolina Press, 2004.

Lowe, Lisa. *Immigrant Acts: On Asian American Cultural Politics*. Durham, NC: Duke University Press, 2012.

Lowe, Lisa. *The Intimacies of Four Continents*. Durham, NC: Duke University Press, 2015.

Lu, Sidney Xu. *The Making of Japanese Settler Colonialism: Malthusianism and Trans-Pacific Migration, 1868–1961*. New York: Cambridge University Press, 2019.

Lumba, Allan. *Monetary Authorities: Capitalism and Decolonization in the American Colonial Philippines*. Durham, NC: Duke University Press, 2022.

Mabalon, Dawn Bohulano. "Beauty Queens, Bomber Pilots, and Basketball Players: Second-Generation Filipina Americans in Stockton, California, 1930s to 1950s." In *Pinay Power: Peminist Critical Theory; Theorizing the Filipina-American Experience*, edited by Melinda L. De Jesus, 102–16. New York: Routledge, 2005.

Mabalon, Dawn Bohulano. *Little Manila Is in the Heart: The Making of the Filipina/o American Community in Stockton, California*. Durham, NC: Duke University Press, 2013.

MacIsaac, Steve. "The Struggle for Economic Development in the Philippine Commonwealth, 1935–1940." *Philippine Studies* 50, no. 2 (2002): 141–67.

Mahmood, Saba. *Politics of Piety: The Islamic Revival and the Feminist Subject*. Princeton, NJ: Princeton University Press, 2011.

Malcolm, George A. *The Commonwealth of the Philippines*. New York: D. Appleton-Century, 1936.

Mallari, Aaron Abel T. "The Bilibid Prison as an American Colonial Project in the Philippines." *Philippine Sociological Review* 60 (2012): 165–92.

Manalansan, Martin F. *Global Divas: Filipino Gay Men in the Diaspora*. Durham, NC: Duke University Press, 2003.

Manalansan, Martin F. "The 'Stuff' of Archives: Mess, Migration, and Queer Lives." *Radical History Review* 2014, no. 120 (2014): 94–107. https://doi.org/10.1215/01636545-2703742.

Marina. *Lo que ellas dicen: Recopilacion de entrevistas publicadas en la vanguardia durante los anos 1934–1935–1936–1937.* Manila: Islas Filipinas, 1938.

Marquez Benitez, Paz. "Dead Stars." In *Brown River, White Ocean: An Anthology of Twentieth-Century Philippine Literature in English,* edited by Luis H. Francia, 3–12. New Brunswick, NJ: Rutgers University Press, 1993.

Martin, Isabel Pefianco. "Pedagogy: Teaching Practices of American Colonial Educators in the Philippines." *Kritika Kultura* 1 (2002): 90–100.

May, Glenn Anthony. "The Business of Education in the Colonial Philippines, 1909–1930." In *Colonial Crucible: Empire in the Making of the Modern American State,* edited by Alfred W. McCoy and Francisco A. Scarano, 151–62. Madison: University of Wisconsin Press, 2009.

May, Glenn Anthony. "Social Engineering in the Philippines: The Aims and Execution of American Educational Policy, 1900–1913." *Philippine Studies* 24, no. 2 (1976): 135–83.

May, Glenn Anthony. *Social Engineering in the Philippines: The Aims, Execution, and Impact of American Colonial Policy, 1900–1913.* Westport, CT: Greenwood Press, 1980.

McClintock, Anne. *Imperial Leather: Race, Gender, and Sexuality in the Colonial Contest.* London: Taylor and Francis Group, 1995.

McCoy, Alfred W. *An Anarchy of Families: State and Family in the Philippines.* Madison: University of Wisconsin Press, 1993.

McCoy, Alfred W. "Orientalism of the Philippine Photograph: America Discovers the Philippine Islands." 2004. https://dcstatic.library.wisc.edu/Collections/docs/OrientalismOfThePhilippinePhotograph.pdf.

McCoy, Alfred W. *Philippine Cartoons: Political Caricature of the American Era, 1900–1941.* Quezon City: Vera-Reyes, 1985.

McCoy, Alfred W. "Philippine Commonwealth and Cult of Masculinity." *Philippine Studies* 48, no. 3 (2000): 315–46.

McCoy, Alfred W. *Policing America's Empire: The United States, the Philippines, and the Rise of the Surveillance State.* Madison: University of Wisconsin Press, 2009.

McCoy, Alfred W. "Quezon's Commonwealth: The Emergence of Philippine Authoritarianism." *Philippine Colonial Democracy* 1, no. 1 (1989): 4–1.

McCoy, Alfred W., and Francisco A. Scarano. *Colonial Crucible: Empire in the Making of the Modern American State.* Madison: University of Wisconsin Press, 2009.

McFerson, Hazel M. "Filipino Identity and Self-Image in Historical Perspective." In *Mixed Blessing: The Impact of the American Colonial Experience on Politics and Society in the Philippines,* edited by Hazel M. McFerson, 13–42. Westport, CT: Greenwood Publishing Group, 2002.

McKenna, Rebecca Tinio. *American Imperial Pastoral: The Architecture of US Colonialism in the Philippines.* Chicago: University of Chicago Press, 2017.

McLennan, Rebecca M. *The Crisis of Imprisonment: Protest, Politics, and the Making of the American Penal State, 1776–1941.* Cambridge: Cambridge University Press, 2008.

Mendoza, Helen N. *Memories of the War Years: A Teenage Girl's Life in the Philippines under Japanese Rule*. Quezon City: Pantas, 2016.

Mendoza, Victor Román. *Metroimperial Intimacies: Fantasy, Racial-Sexual Governance, and the Philippines in U.S. Imperialism, 1899–1913*. Durham, NC: Duke University Press, 2015.

Mendoza-Guazón, María Paz. *The Development and Progress of the Filipino Women*. Manila: Bureau of Printing, 1928.

Mendoza-Guazón, María Paz. *My Ideal Filipino Girl*. Manila: University of the Philippines College of Medicine, 1931.

Milgram, B. Lynne. "Piña Cloth, Identity and the Project of Philippine Nationalism." *Asian Studies Review* 29, no. 3 (2005): 233–46. https://doi.org/10.1080/10357820500270144.

Miller, Stuart Creighton. *"Benevolent Assimilation": The American Conquest of the Philippines, 1899–1903*. New Haven, CT: Yale University Press, 1982.

Mitchell, Michele. "'The Black Man's Burden': African Americans, Imperialism, and Notions of Racial Manhood 1890–1910." *International Review of Social History* 44, no. S7 (1999): 77–99. https://doi.org/10.1017/S0020859000115202.

Mitchell, Michele, and Naoko Shibusawa, with Stephan F. Miescher. "Introduction: Gender, Imperialism and Global Exchanges." *Gender and History* 26, no. 3 (2014): 393–413. https://doi.org/10.1111/1468-0424.12081.

Mitra, Durba. *Indian Sex Life: Sexuality and the Colonial Origins of Modern Social Thought*. Princeton, NJ: Princeton University Press, 2020.

Mojares, Resil B. "Artist, Craftsman, Factory Worker: Concerns in the Study of Traditional Art." *Philippine Quarterly of Culture and Society* 14, no. 3 (1986): 177–88.

Mojares, Resil B. *Brains of the Nation: Pedro Paterno, T. H. Pardo de Tavera, Isabelo de Los Reyes, and the Production of Modern Knowledge*. Quezon City: Ateneo de Manila University Press, 2006.

Mojares, Resil B. "The Formation of Filipino Nationality under US Colonial Rule." *Philippine Quarterly of Culture and Society* 34, no. 1 (2006): 11–32.

Mojares, Resil B. *The War against the Americans: Resistance and Collaboration in Cebu, 1899–1906*. Quezon City: Ateneo de Manila University Press, 1999.

Molina, Natalia. *Fit to Be Citizens? Public Health and Race in Los Angeles, 1879–1939*. Berkeley: University of California Press, 2006.

Montinola, Lourdes R. *Piña*. Manila: Amon Foundation, 1991.

Moral, Solsiree del. *Negotiating Empire: The Cultural Politics of Schools in Puerto Rico, 1898–1952*. Madison: University of Wisconsin Press, 2013.

Moralina, Aaron Rom O. "State, Society, and Sickness: Tuberculosis Control in the American Philippines, 1910–1918." *Philippine Studies* 57, no. 2 (2009): 179–218. https://www.jstor.org/stable/42634008.

Moser, Patrick. "Charles Wilkes, *Narrative of the United States Exploring Expedition*." In *Pacific Passages: An Anthology of Surf Writing*, edited by Patrick Moser, 96–97. Honolulu: University of Hawaiʻi Press, 2017.

Moses, Edith. *Unofficial Letters of an Official's Wife*. New York: D. Appleton, 1908.

Murray, John F. "A Century of Tuberculosis." *American Journal of Respiratory and Critical Care Medicine* 169, no. 11 (2004): 1181–86. https://doi.org/10.1164/rccm .200402-1400E.

Nadal, Paul. "A Literary Remittance: Juan C. Laya's His Native Soil and the Rise of Realism in the Filipino Novel in English." *American Literature* 89, no. 3 (2017): 591–626. https://doi.org/10.1215/00029831-4160906.

Nagano, Yoshiko. *State and Finance in the Philippines, 1898–1941: The Mismanagement of an American Colony.* Singapore: NUS Press, 2015.

Najmabadi, Afsaneh. *Women with Mustaches and Men without Beards: Gender and Sexual Anxieties of Iranian Modernity.* Berkeley: University of California Press, 2005.

Nakpil, Carmen Guerrero. *Woman Enough and Other Essays.* Quezon City: Ateneo de Manila University Press, 1999.

Nash, Jennifer C. "Writing Black Beauty." *Signs: Journal of Women in Culture and Society* 45, no. 1 (2019): 101–22. https://doi.org/10.1086/703497.

Nash, June C., and María Patricia Fernández-Kelly. *Women, Men, and the International Division of Labor.* Albany: SUNY Press, 1983.

Nava, Mica. "Modernity's Disavowal: Women, the City and the Department Store." In *Modern Times: Reflections on a Century of Modernity*, edited by Mica Nava and Alan O'Shea, 38–76. London: Routledge, 1996.

Newman, Louise Michele. *White Women's Rights: The Racial Origins of Feminism in the United States.* New York: Oxford University Press, 1999.

Ngai, Mae M. *Impossible Subjects: Illegal Aliens and the Making of Modern America.* Princeton, NJ: Princeton University Press, 2014.

Ngai, Sianne. *Ugly Feelings.* Cambridge, MA: Harvard University Press, 2005.

Ngozi-Brown, Scot. "African-American Soldiers and Filipinos: Racial Imperialism, Jim Crow and Social Relations." *Journal of Negro History* 82, no. 1 (1997): 42–53. https://doi.org/10.2307/2717495.

Nguyen, Mimi. *The Promise of Beauty.* Durham, NC: Duke University Press, forthcoming.

Nguyen, Mimi. "The Right to Be Beautiful." *Account Magazine*, no. 6 (2016). https://theaccountmagazine.com/article/the-right-to-be-beautiful/.

Nguyen, Mimi Thi. "The Biopower of Beauty: Humanitarian Imperialisms and Global Feminisms in an Age of Terror." *Signs: Journal of Women in Culture and Society* 36, no. 2 (2011): 359–83. https://doi.org/10.1086/655914.

Nguyen, Mimi Thi. *The Gift of Freedom: War, Debt, and Other Refugee Passages.* Durham, NC: Duke University Press, 2012.

Novadona Bayo, Longgina, Purwo Santoso, Willy Purna Samadhi, Yayasan Obor Indonesia, Universitas Gadjah Mada Research Centre for Politics and Government, and Universitetet i Oslo. *In Search of Local Regime in Indonesia: Enhancing Democratisation in Indonesia.* Jakarta: Yayasan Pustaka Obor Indonesia in cooperation with PolGov Fisipol UGM and University of Oslo, 2018.

Nuyda, Doris G., and Pablo Reyes. *The Beauty Book.* Manila: Mr. and Ms. Pub. Co., 1980.

Oberiano, Kristin. "Territorial Discontent: Chamorros, Filipinos, and the Making of the United States Empire on Guam." PhD diss., Harvard University, 2021.

Ochoa, Marcia. *Queen for a Day: Transformistas, Beauty Queens, and the Performance of Femininity in Venezuela.* Durham, NC: Duke University Press, 2014.

Ofreneo, Rosalinda Pineda. "The Philippine Garment Industry." In *Global Production: The Apparel Industry in the Pacific Rim*, edited by Edna Bonacich, Lucie Cheng, Norma Chinchilla, Nora Hamilton, and Paul Ong, 162–79. Philadelphia: Temple University Press, 2009.

Olivares, José de. *Our Islands and Their People as Seen with Camera and Pencil.* Vol. 2. New York: Thompson Publishing, 1899.

Ong, Aihwa. *Spirits of Resistance and Capitalist Discipline: Factory Women in Malaysia.* Albany: SUNY Press, 2010.

Ong, Aihwa. "The Gender and Labor Politics of Postmodernity." *Annual Review of Anthropology* 20, no. 1 (1991): 279–309. https://doi.org/10.1146/annurev.an.20 .100191.001431.

Paik, A. Naomi. *Rightlessness: Testimony and Redress in U.S. Prison Camps since World War II.* Chapel Hill: University of North Carolina Press, 2016.

Paisley, Fiona. *Glamour in the Pacific: Cultural Internationalism and Race Politics in the Women's Pan-Pacific.* Honolulu: University of Hawai'i Press, 2009.

Pante, Michael D. "Quezon's City: Corruption and Contradiction in Manila's Prewar Suburbia, 1935–1941." *Journal of Southeast Asian Studies* 48, no. 1 (2017): 91–112. https://doi.org/10.1017/S0022463416000497.

Paredes, Oona. "Preserving 'Tradition': The Business of Indigeneity in the Modern Philippine Context." *Journal of Southeast Asian Studies* 50, no. 1 (2019): 86–106. https://doi.org/10.1017/S0022463419000055.

Paredes, Ruby R. *Philippine Colonial Democracy.* Quezon City: Ateneo de Manila University Press, 1989.

Paredes, Ruby Rivera. "The Partido Federal, 1900–1907: Political Collaboration in Colonial Manila (Volumes I and II)." PhD diss., University of Michigan, 1989.

Parreñas, Rhacel Salazar. "Migrant Filipina Domestic Workers and the International Division of Reproductive Labor." *Gender and Society* 14, no. 4 (2000): 560–80. https://doi.org/10.1177/089124300014004005.

Parreñas, Rhacel Salazar. *Servants of Globalization: Migration and Domestic Work.* 2nd ed. Stanford, CA: Stanford University Press, 2015.

Parreñas, Rhacel Salazar. *The Force of Domesticity: Filipina Migrants and Globalization.* New York: New York University Press, 2008.

Paulet, Anne. "To Change the World: The Use of American Indian Education in the Philippines." *History of Education Quarterly* 47, no. 2 (2007): 173–202. https://doi.org/10.1111/j.1748-5959.2007.00088.x.

Pérez, Louis A., Jr. *War of 1898: The United States and Cuba in History and Historiography.* Chapel Hill: University of North Carolina Press, 1998.

Perkins, Anna Kasafi. "Carne Vale (Goodbye to Flesh?): Caribbean Carnival, Notions of the Flesh and Christian Ambivalence about the Body." *Sexual-*

*ity and Culture* 15, no. 4 (December 1, 2011): 361–74. https://doi.org/10.1007
/s12119-011-9106-1.

Phạm, Minh-hà T. *Asians Wear Clothes on the Internet: Race, Gender, and the
Work of Personal Style Blogging*. Durham, NC: Duke University Press, 2015.

Phạm, Minh-hà T. "China: Through the Looking Glass: Race, Property, and the
Possessive Investment in White Feelings." In *Fashion and Beauty in the Time
of Asia*, edited by S. Heijin Lee, Christina H. Moon, and Thuy Linh Nguyen Tu,
41–68. New York: New York University Press, 2019.

Phạm, Minh-hà T. "Feeling Appropriately: On Fashion Copyright Talk and
Copynorms." *Social Text* 34, no. 3 (2016): 51–74. https://doi.org/10.1215
/01642472-3607576.

Phạm, Minh-hà T. "Paul Poiret's Magical Techno-oriental Fashions (1911): Race,
Clothing, and Virtuality in the Machine Age." *Configurations* 21, no. 1 (2013):
1–26. https://doi.org/10.1353/con.2013.0003.

Pike, Ruth. "Penal Servitude in the Spanish Empire: Presidio Labor in the Eighteenth Century." *Hispanic American Historical Review* 58, no. 1 (1978): 21–40.
https://doi.org/10.1215/00182168-58.1.21.

Piocos, Carlos M. "The Queer Promise of Pageantry: Queering Feminized Migration and the Labor of Care in Sunday Beauty Queen (2016)." *Feminist Media
Studies*, 1–16. https://doi.org/10.1080/14680777.2021.1906297.

Poblete, JoAnna. *Islanders in the Empire: Filipino and Puerto Rican Laborers in
Hawai'i*. Urbana: University of Illinois Press, 2014.

Pratt, Geraldine. "From Registered Nurse to Registered Nanny: Discursive Geographies of Filipina Domestic Workers in Vancouver, B.C." *Economic Geography*
75, no. 3 (1999): 215–36. https://doi.org/10.1111/j.1944-8287.1999.tb00077.x.

Pratt, Mary Louise. *Imperial Eyes: Travel Writing and Transculturation*. London:
Routledge, 1992.

Prieto, Laura R. "A Delicate Subject: Clemencia López, Civilized Womanhood, and
the Politics of Anti-imperialism." *Journal of the Gilded Age and Progressive Era*
12, no. 2 (2013): 199–233. https://doi.org/10.1017/S1537781413000066.

Prieto, Laura R. "'Stepmother America': The Woman's Board of Missions in the
Philippines, 1902–1930." In *Competing Kingdoms*, edited by Gilbert M. Joseph,
Emily S. Rosenberg, Kathryn Kish Sklar, Connie A. Shemo, and Barbara Reeves-
Ellington, 342–66. Durham, NC: Duke University Press, 2020.

Purtschert, Patricia, Francesca Falk, and Barbara Lüthi. "Switzerland and 'Colonialism without Colonies': Reflections on the Status of Colonial Outsiders." *Interven-
tions* 18, no. 2 (2016): 286–302. https://doi.org/10.1080/1369801X.2015.1042395.

Que, Gilbert Jacob S. Review of *Textiles in the Philippine Colonial Landscape: A
Lexicon and Historical Survey*, by Sandra Castro. *Philippine Studies: Historical
and Ethnographic Viewpoints* 67, no. 2 (2019): 261–64.

Quiason, Serafin D. "The Japanese Community in Manila, 1898–1941." *Philippine
Historical Review* 3 (1970): 184–222.

Quibuyen, Floro C. *A Nation Aborted: Rizal, American Hegemony, and Philippine
Nationalism*. Quezon City: Ateneo de Manila University Press, 1999.

Rafael, Vicente L. "Colonial Domesticity." In *White Love and Other Events in Filipino History*. Durham, NC: Duke University Press, 2014.

Rafael, Vicente L. *The Promise of the Foreign: Nationalism and the Technics of Translation in the Spanish Philippines*. Durham, NC: Duke University Press, 2005.

Rafael, Vicente L. "White Love: Census and Melodrama in the United States Colonization of the Philippines." *History and Anthropology* 12, no. 1 (1999): 265–98.

Ramos, Marlene Flores. "The Filipina Bordadoras and the Emergence of Fine European-Style Embroidery Tradition in Colonial Philippines, 19th to Early-20th Centuries." PhD diss., Mount Saint Vincent University, 2016.

Raymundo, Emily. "Beauty Regimens, Beauty Regimes: Korean Beauty on YouTube." In *Fashion and Beauty in the Time of Asia*, edited by S. Heijin Lee, Christina H. Moon, and Thuy Linh Nguyen Tu, 103–26. New York: New York University Press, 2019.

Reddy, Vanita. *Fashioning Diaspora Beauty, Femininity, and South Asian American Culture*. Philadelphia: Temple University Press, 2016.

Reyes, Deogracias T. "History of Divorce Legislation in the Philippines since 1900." *Philippine Studies* 1, no. 1 (1953): 42–58.

Reyes, Lynda Angelica N. *The Textiles of Southern Philippines: The Textile Traditions of the Bagobo, Mandaya and Bilaan from Their Beginnings to the 1900s*. Quezon City: University of the Philippines Press, 1992.

Reyes, Raquel A. G. *Love, Passion and Patriotism: Sexuality and the Philippine Propaganda Movement, 1882–1892*. Singapore: NUS Press; Seattle: University of Washington Press, 2008.

Reyes, Raquel A. G. "Modernizing the Manileña: Technologies of Conspicuous Consumption for the Well-to-Do Woman, circa 1880s–1930s." *Modern Asian Studies* 46, no. 1 (2012): 193–220. https://doi.org/10.1017/S0026749X1100062X.

Rice, Mark. *Dean Worcester's Fantasy Islands: Photography, Film, and the Colonial Philippines*. Ann Arbor: University of Michigan Press, 2014.

Rizal, José. *Noli me tangere (Touch Me Not)*. Translated by Harold Augenbraum. New York: Penguin, 2006.

Roberts, Blain. *Pageants, Parlors, and Pretty Women: Race and Beauty in the Twentieth-Century South*. Chapel Hill: University of North Carolina Press, 2014.

Robinson, Cedric J. *Black Marxism: The Making of the Black Radical Tradition*, 3rd rev. ed. Chapel Hill: University of North Carolina Press, 2021.

Roces, Alfredo R. *Filipino Heritage: Birth of a Nation (1941–1946)*. Vol. 10. Manila: Lahing Pilipino Publishing, 1978.

Roces, Mina. "Dress, Status, and Identity in the Philippines: Pineapple Fiber Cloth and Ilustrado Fashion." *Fashion Theory* 17, no. 3 (2013): 341–72. https://doi.org/10.2752/175174113X13597248661828.

Roces, Mina. "Filipino Elite Women and Public Health in the American Colonial Era, 1906–1940." *Women's History Review* 26, no. 3 (2017): 477–502. https://doi.org/10.1080/09612025.2016.1194076.

Roces, Mina. "Gender, Nation and the Politics of Dress in Twentieth-Century Philippines." *Gender and History* 17, no. 2 (2005): 354–77. https://doi.org/10.1111/j.0953-5233.2006.00385.x.

Roces, Mina. "Rethinking 'the Filipino Woman': A Century of Women's Activism in the Philippines, 1905–2006." In *Women's Movements in Asia: Feminisms and Transnational Activism*, edited by Mina Roces and Louise P. Edwards, 34–52. New York: Routledge, 2010.

Roces, Mina. "Women in Philippine Politics and Society." In *Mixed Blessing: The Impact of the American Colonial Experience on Politics and Society in the Philippines*, edited by Hazel M. McFerson, 159–84. Westport, CT: Greenwood Press, 2002.

Roces, Mina. *Women, Power, and Kinship Politics: Female Power in Post-war Philippines*. Westport, CT: Praeger, 1998.

Roces, Mina, and Louise Edwards. "Is the Suffragist an American Colonial Construct? Defining 'the Filipino Women' in Colonial Philippines." In *Women's Suffrage in Asia: Gender, Nationalism and Democracy*, 24–58. New York: Routledge, 2004.

Rodell, Paul A. "Philippine 'Seditious Plays.'" *Asian Studies* 12, no. 1 (1974): 88–118.

Rodriguez, Dylan. *Forced Passages: Imprisoned Radical Intellectuals and the U.S. Prison Regime*. Minneapolis: University of Minnesota Press, 2006.

Rodriguez, Robyn Magalit. *Migrants for Export: How the Philippine State Brokers Labor to the World*. Minneapolis: University of Minnesota Press, 2010.

Romulo, Beth Day. *The Manila Hotel: The Heart and Memory of a City*. Manila: B. D. Romulo, 1977.

Rydell, Robert W. *All the World's a Fair: Visions of Empire at American International Expositions, 1876–1916*. Chicago: University of Chicago Press, 1984.

Sabanpan-Yu, Hope. "Querida Mia: The Mistress in Cebuano Women's Short Fiction." In *More Pinay Than We Admit: The Social Construction of the Filipina*, edited by Luisa Camagay. Manila: Vibal Foundation, 2010.

Sabo, Donald F., Terry Allen Kupers, and Willie James London. *Prison Masculinities*. Philadelphia: Temple University Press, 2001.

Safa, Helen I. "Runaway Shops and Female Employment: The Search for Cheap Labor." *Signs: Journal of Women in Culture and Society* 7, no. 2 (1981): 418–33. https://doi.org/10.1086/493889.

Said, Edward W. *Orientalism*. 25th anniversary ed. New York: Vintage Books, 2003.

Said, Edward W. "The Imperial Spectacle." *Grand Street* 6, no. 2 (1987): 82–104. https://doi.org/10.2307/25006961.

Salamanca, Bonifacio S. *The Filipino Reaction to American Rule, 1901–1913*. Quezon City: New Day Publishers, 1984.

Salman, Michael. "'Nothing without Labor': Penology, Discipline, and Independence in the Philippines under United States Rule." In *Discrepant Histories: Translocal Essays on Filipino Cultures*, edited by Vicente Rafael, 113–29. Philadelphia: Temple University Press, 1995.

Salman, Michael. *The Embarrassment of Slavery: Controversies over Bondage and Nationalism in the American Colonial Philippines.* Berkeley: University of California Press, 2001.

Salman, Michael. "'The Prison That Makes Men Free': The Iwahig Penal Colony and the Simulacra of the American State in the Philippines." In *Colonial Crucible: Empire in the Making of the Modern American State,* edited by Alfred McCoy and Francisco A. Scarano, 116–28. Madison: University of Wisconsin Press, 2009.

Samonte, Cecilia. "Obtaining 'Sympathetic Understanding': Gender, Empire, and Representation in the Travel Writings of American Officials' Wives, 1901–1914." *Journal of Transnational American Studies* 3, no. 2 (2011): 1–14.

Santa María, Felice. *Fountain of Gold: The Club Filipino Story.* San Juan, Metro Manila: The Club, 1983. http://catalog.hathitrust.org/api/volumes/oclc /15653465.html.

Santa María, Felice. *Household Antiques and Heirlooms.* Quezon City: G. C. F. Books, 1983.

Santiago, Lilia Quindoza. *Sexuality and the Filipina.* Quezon City: University of the Philippines Press, 2007.

Saranillio, Dean Itsuji. *Unsustainable Empire: Alternative Histories of Hawai'i Statehood.* Durham, NC: Duke University Press, 2018.

Saraswati, L. Ayu. *Seeing Beauty, Sensing Race in Transnational Indonesia.* Honolulu: University of Hawai'i Press, 2013.

Sarmiento, Thomas Xavier. "To Return to St. Louis: Reading the Intimacies of the Heartland of U.S. Empire through 'The Dogeater.'" *Amerasia Journal* 46, no. 2 (2020): 218–35. https://doi.org/10.1080/00447471.2020.1852701.

Sawyer, Frederic Henry Read. *The Inhabitants of the Philippines, by Frederic H. Sawyer.* London: Samson Low, Marston and Co., 1900. https://hdl.handle.net /2027/hvd.32044083336867.

Schirmer, Daniel B., and Stephen Rosskamm Shalom, eds. *The Philippines Reader: A History of Colonialism, Neocolonialism, Dictatorship, and Resistance.* Boston: South End Press, 1999.

Schueller, Malini Johar. "Colonial Management, Collaborative Dissent: English Readers in the Philippines and Camilo Osias, 1905–1932." *Journal of Asian American Studies* 17, no. 2 (2014): 161–98. https://doi.org/10.1353/jaas.2014.0018.

Schumacher, John N. *The Making of a Nation: Essays on Nineteenth-Century Filipino Nationalism.* Manila: Ateneo de Manila University Press, 1991.

Scott, James C. *Weapons of the Weak: Everyday Forms of Peasant Resistance.* New Haven, CT: Yale University Press, 1985. https://hdl.handle.net/2027/heb.02471.

Scrase, Timothy J. "Precarious Production: Globalisation and Artisan Labour in the Third World." *Third World Quarterly* 24, no. 3 (2003): 449–61. https://doi .org/10.1080/0143659032000084401.

Sell, Zach. *Trouble of the World: Slavery and Empire in the Age of Capital.* Chapel Hill: University of North Carolina Press, 2021. https://doi.org/10.5149 /9781469660479_sell.

Sharpe, Jenny. *Allegories of Empire: The Figure of Woman in the Colonial Text.* Minneapolis: University of Minnesota Press, 1993.

Shaw, Angel Velasco, and Luis Francia. *Vestiges of War: The Philippine-American War and the Aftermath of an Imperial Dream, 1899–1999.* New York: New York University Press, 2000.

Sibal, Jorge V. "A Century of the Philippine Labor Movement." *Illawarra Unity-Journal of the Illawarra Branch of the Australian Society for the Study of Labour History* 4, no. 1 (2004): 29–41.

Sidel, John T. *Capital, Coercion, and Crime: Bossism in the Philippines.* Palo Alto: Stanford University Press, 1999.

Silbey, David. *A War of Frontier and Empire: The Philippine-American War, 1899–1902.* New York: Hill and Wang, 2007.

Silkey, Sarah L. *Black Woman Reformer: Ida B. Wells, Lynching, and Transatlantic Activism.* Athens: University of Georgia Press, 2015.

Sinha, Mrinalini. *Specters of Mother India: The Global Restructuring of an Empire.* Radical Perspectives. Durham, NC: Duke University Press, 2006.

Smallwood, Stephanie E. "Reflections on Settler Colonialism, the Hemispheric Americas, and Chattel Slavery." *William and Mary Quarterly* 76, no. 3 (2019): 407–16. https://doi.org/10.5309/willmaryquar.76.3.0407.

Sneider, Allison L. *Suffragists in an Imperial Age: U.S. Expansion and the Woman Question, 1870–1929.* Oxford: Oxford University Press, 2008.

Sobritchea, Carolyn Israel. "American Colonial Education and Its Impact on the Status of Filipino Women." *Asian Studies* 27 (1989): 70–91.

Steinbock-Pratt, Sarah. *Educating the Empire: American Teachers and Contested Colonization in the Philippines.* Cambridge: Cambridge University Press, 2019.

Steinbock-Pratt, Sarah. "'It Gave Us Our Nationality': US Education, the Politics of Dress and Transnational Filipino Student Networks, 1901–45." *Gender and History* 26, no. 3 (2014): 565–88. https://doi.org/10.1111/1468-0424.12089.

Stoler, Ann Laura. *Along the Archival Grain: Epistemic Anxieties and Colonial Common Sense.* Princeton, NJ: Princeton University Press, 2009.

Stoler, Ann Laura. *Carnal Knowledge and Imperial Power: Race and the Intimate in Colonial Rule.* Berkeley: University of California Press, 2002.

Strange, Susan. "Cave! Hic Dragones: A Critique of Regime Analysis." *International Organization* 36, no. 2 (1982): 479–96. https://doi.org/10.1017/S0020818300019020.

Subido, Tarrosa. *The Feminist Movement in the Philippines, 1905–1955: A Golden Book to Commemorate the Golden Jubilee of the Feminist Movement in the Philippines.* Philippines: National Federation of Women's Clubs, 1955.

Tadiar, Neferti Xina M. "Empire." *Social Text* 27, no. 3 (2009): 112–17.

Tadiar, Neferti Xina M. *Fantasy Production: Sexual Economies and Other Philippine Consequences for the New World Order.* London: Eurospan, 2004.

Tadiar, Neferti Xina M. "Life-Times of Disposability within Global Neoliberalism." *Social Text* 31, no. 2 (2013): 19–48. https://doi.org/10.1215/01642472-2081112.

Taft, Helen Herron. *Recollections of Full Years*. New York: Dodd, Mead & Company, 1914.

Talusan, Mary. "Music, Race, and Imperialism: The Philippine Constabulary Band at the 1904 St. Louis World's Fair." *Philippine Studies* 52, no. 4 (2004): 499–526.

Tantoco-Rustia Foundation and National Museum (Philippines). *Valera: Cada traje es una obra maestra*. Quezon City: Tantoco-Rustia Foundation, 2005. http://books.google.com/books?id=8teBAAAAMAAJ.

Tarlo, Emma. *Clothing Matters: Dress and Identity in India*. Chicago: University of Chicago Press, 1996.

Taylor, Diana. *Disappearing Acts: Spectacles of Gender and Nationalism in Argentina's "Dirty War."* Durham, NC: Duke University Press, 1997.

Thayer Sidel, John. *Capital, Coercion, and Crime: Bossim in the Philippines*. Stanford, CA: Stanford University Press, 1999.

Thompson, Lanny. "Aesthetics and Empire: The Sense of Feminine Beauty in the Making of the US Imperial Archipelago." *Culture and History Digital Journal* 2, no. 2 (2013): e027. https://doi.org/10.3989/chdj.2013.027.

Thompson, Lanny. *Imperial Archipelago: Representation and Rule in the Insular Territories under U.S. Dominion after 1898*. Honolulu: University of Hawai'i Press, 2010.

Tolentino, Rolando B. "Transvestites and Transgressions: Panggagaya in Philippine Gay Cinema." *Journal of Homosexuality* 39, no. 3–4 (2000): 325–37. https://doi .org/10.1300/J082v39n03_17.

Torres, Cristina Evangelista. *The Americanization of Manila, 1898–1921*. Quezon City: University of the Philippines Press, 2010.

Tu, Thuy Linh Nguyen. *The Beautiful Generation: Asian Americans and the Cultural Economy of Fashion*. Durham, NC: Duke University Press, 2010.

Tulloch, Carol. *The Birth of Cool: Style Narratives of the African Diaspora*. London: Bloomsbury, 2016.

Ventura, Theresa. "From Small Farms to Progressive Plantations: The Trajectory of Land Reform in the American Colonial Philippines, 1900–1916." *Agricultural History* 90, no. 4 (2016): 459–83. https://doi.org/10.3098/ah.2016.090.4.459.

Ventura, Theresa. "Medicalizing *Gutom*: Hunger, Diet, and Beriberi during the American Period." *Philippine Studies, Historical and Ethnographic Viewpoints* 63, no. 1 (2015): 39–69. https://doi.org/10.1353/phs.2015.0000.

Vera, Arleen de. "Rizal Day Queen Contests, Filipino Nationalism, and Femininity." In *Asian American Youth: Culture, Identity and Ethnicity*, edited by Jennifer Lee and Min Zhou, 81–96. New York: Routledge, 2004.

Vergara, Benito Manalo. *Displaying Filipinos: Photography and Colonialism in Early 20th Century Philippines*. Quezon City: University of the Philippines Press, 1995.

Victorio, Ramon. *Prison Reform in the Phillipines; a Compilation of Lectures, Speeches, Memoranda, Articles, and Press Interviews*. Manila: n.p., 1927.

Vicuña Gonzalez, Vernadette. *Empire's Mistress, Starring Isabel Rosario Cooper*. Durham, NC: Duke University Press, 2021.

Villegas, Ramon N. *Hiyas: Philippine Jewellery Heritage*. Pasay City, Metro Manila, Philippines: Guild of Philippine Jewellers, 1997. http://books.google.com/books ?id=-B3WAAAAMAAJ.

Waldinger, Roger. "Another Look at the International Ladies' Garment Workers' Union: Women, Industry Structure and Collective Action." In *Women, Work and Protest: A Century of US Women's Labor History*, edited by Ruth Milkman, 86–109. Boston: Routledge, 1985.

Walton, Whitney. "Working Women, Gender, and Industrialization in Nineteenth-Century France: The Case of Lorraine Embroidery Manufacturing." *Journal of Women's History* 2, no. 2 (1990): 42–65. https://doi.org/10.1353 /jowh.2010.0117.

Weinbaum, Alys Eve, Lynn M. Thomas, Priti Ramamurthy, Uta G. Poiger, Madeleine Yue Dong, Tani E. Barlow, and The Modern Girl around the World Research Group. *The Modern Girl around the World: Consumption, Modernity, and Globalization*. Durham, NC: Duke University Press, 2008.

Wendt, Reinhard. "Philippine Fiesta and Colonial Culture." *Philippine Studies* 46, no. 1 (1998): 3–23.

Wexler, Laura. *Tender Violence: Domestic Visions in an Age of U.S. Imperialism*. Chapel Hill: University of North Carolina Press, 2000.

Wickberg, E. "The Chinese Mestizo in Philippine History." In *The Chinese Diaspora in the Pacific*, edited by Anthony Reid, 137–75. New York: Routledge, 2008. https://doi.org/10.4324/9781315240756-6.

Wilkes, Charles. *Narrative of the United States Exploring Expedition during the Years 1838, 1839, 1840, 1841, 1842*. New York: G. P. Putnam, 1856.

Wilson, Elizabeth. *Adorned in Dreams: Fashion and Modernity*. Berkeley: University of California Press, 1987.

Winkelmann, Tessa. *Dangerous Intercourse: Gender and Interracial Relations in the American Colonial Philippines, 1898–1946*. Ithaca, NY: Cornell University Press, forthcoming.

Wood, Molly M. "Diplomatic Wives: The Politics of Domesticity and the 'Social Game' in the US Foreign Service, 1905–1941." *Journal of Women's History* 17, no. 2 (2005): 142–65. https://doi.org/10.1353/jowh.2005.0025.

Woolford, Andrew John. *This Benevolent Experiment: Indigenous Boarding Schools, Genocide, and Redress in Canada and the United States*. Lincoln: University of Nebraska Press, 2015.

Worcester, Dean C. *The Philippine Islands and Their People; a Record of Personal Observation and Experience, with a Short Summary of the More Important Facts in the History of the Archipelago, by Dean C. Worcester*. New York: Macmillan, 1899. https://hdl.handle.net/2027/uc2.ark:/13960/tojs9rw1b.

Worcester, Dean C. *The Philippines Past and Present*. New York: MacMillan Company, 1930.

Wu, Judy Tzu-Chun. "'Loveliest Daughter of Our Ancient Cathay!' Representations of Ethnic and Gender Identity in the Miss Chinatown U.S.A. Beauty Pageant." *Journal of Social History* 31, no. 1 (1997): 5–31.

Wu, Judy Tzu-Chun. *Radicals on the Road: Internationalism, Orientalism, and Feminism during the Vietnam Era*. Ithaca, NY: Cornell University Press, 2013.

Yamaguchi, Kiyoko. "The New 'American' Houses in the Colonial Philippines and the Rise of the Urban Filipino Elite." *Philippine Studies* 54, no. 3 (2006): 412–51.

Zapanta-Manlapaz, Edna. "A Feminist Reading of Paz Marquez-Benitez's 'Dead Stars.'" *Philippine Studies: Historical and Ethnographic Viewpoints* 41, no. 4 (1993): 523–28.

"Dressed for Evacuation" (*Graphic* magazine feature), 231–33
Dress Reform Clubs, 165
Du Bois, W. E. B., 31
Duggan, Helen, 133
Duras, Marguerite, 30, 243n.56

earnings, convict labor and gender inequality with, 176–77
economic conditions in Philippines: agricultural exports and, 45–46, 247n.149; elite Filipinos and, 50–52; Filipina fashion industry and, 216–18; global economic depression and, 213–18, 223–25, 230; import-export economy and, 16–17, 207, 264n.88; protectionist policies and, 224–31; Tydings-McDuffie Act and, 10, 100
educational achievements, of beauty pageant contestants, 88–95
educational system in Philippines: Department of Public Instruction and, 141–47; embroidery industry and, 17, 111, 117–21, 124, 137; emerging middle class and, 206–13; gendered hierarchies in, 88; home economics courses in, 277n.9; US colonial organization of, 33; workforce creation using, 147–55. *See also* industrial education
elite Filipinos: American colonial encounters with, 40–59; American women's encounters with, 15–16, 20–25, 27–34, 39–40, 41–59; classification of, 241n.4; colonialism and, 19–25, 65; embroidery industry linked to, 111; encouragement of embroidery industry by, 129–32; European ties of, 45–48, 50; fashion design in Philippines and, 191–205; fiestas and pageants as expressions of power, 42–44; Filipinization strategy and, 59–62; gender dynamics among, 51–52; influx in Manila by, 186–88; luxury textile consumption by, 112; Manila Carnival Queen contest and, 72–80, 93–95; middle class as threat to, 205–13; Philippine-American War and, 26–27; in Philippine Revolution, 44; power consolidation by, 184–86; racial

boundaries between US occupiers and, 59–62; School of Household Industries and, 148–55; as Second Commission members, 42–43; Second Philippine Commission misrecognition of, 36–37; terno as symbol of, 17, 86–87, 220–21; terno industry and, 186–99; US military social exclusion of, 36; World War II and decline of, 234–35
*El renacimiento* newspaper, 74–75, 77–80, 93, 99, 259n.165
embroidery industry in Philippines: communication, surveillance and regimented discipline in, 156–65; convict labor for, 169–71, 174–77; Department of Public Instruction and scale-up of, 141–47; development of, 16–17, 105, 107–21, 269n.27; in Filipina clothing, 42, 47–54; legacy and unfulfilled promise of, 180–82; prison labor in, 165–71; quality control and, 158–65; School of Household Industries as labor source, 148–55; Spanish colonization and development of, 110; terno production and, 189–90. *See also* transnational embroidery industry
Embroidery Section circular, 137
Embroidery Trading Company, 120
empire: beauty regimes and, 14–18, 22–25; Filipino beauty and fashion and role of, 3–8; in historical context, 9–12; nationalism and, 9; pageants as tool of, 14; transnational embroidery industry and geographies of, 136–37; US expansion of, 25–26
Encanto, Georgina R., 187, 189
"Enchanting Ensembles for Late Afternoons and Evenings" (*Graphic* magazine), 204
entertainment, beauty queens as, 103–5
Escarole, Francis L., 187, 189
*escuadra Americana* gown, 41–42, 246n.123
Escurdia, Pura, 191, 193–95
España Maram, Linda, 114
Espiritu, Augusto, 241n.13
ethnic hierarchies: beauty aesthetics and, 84–95; beauty contests and, 100–102; clothing in beauty contests and, 86; elite Filipina establishment of, 44–45; fashion and, 212–13

educational opportunities for, 206–13; embroidery industry myths about labor of, 117–23; European ties of, 46–47; as fashion designers, 183–86; financial power of, 50–52, 210–11; flapper era and, 207–8; formation of, 11–12; gender norms for, 72–80, 91–95; hosting of American women by, 41–54; ideal image of, 90–95; modernity embraced by, 207–13; morality rates for Bilibid prisoners, 178–80; as nurses, exploitation of, 114; obsession with appearance among, 14, 24–25; Philippine-American War and, 26; preparation for postcolonial life and, 25–34; prisoners as workforce, 139–41, 272n.113; prominence in Manila Carnival of, 83; racist American stereotypes of, 31–34; refusals of exploitation by, 134–35; romanticization of labor by, 128–32; sartorial competition with American women and, 21–25, 39–40, 47–59; School of Household Industries recruitment of, 148–55; standards of beauty for, 84–95; terminology, 237n.9; transnational embroidery industry and, 16–17, 105, 107–10, 121–32

Filipiniana style, 17, 163, 183, 190, 196, 203–4, 212, 217, 221, 225, 277n.2, 277n.6

Filipinisque, evolution of, 121–32

Filipinization strategy, 59–62, 184–86, 206–7

Filipino Americans, beauty contest and, 67–68, 252n.9

Filipino Day and Night (Manila Carnival), 82–83

Filipino diaspora, beauty pageants and, 67–69, 99–102, 252n.9

Filipinx, defined, 237n.9

Fisher, Herbert D., 147

Flag Law (Philippines), 80

flapper era, emerging Filipino middle class and, 207

Flores de Mayo performances, 72

Forbes, William Cameron, 71–72, 81, 88–89

forced bathing, for Filipina women prisoners, 167, 273n.120

Ford, Tanisha, 242n.28, 246n.117

Foucault, Michel, 268n.5

Fuentes, Marisa, 240n.60

Fujita Rony, Dorothy, 114

Fuller, Alice, 169–70

Gala des Diademes, 201

gambling, Filipina women accused of, 171–73

Gana, Belen, 199, 220

Garduño, Solita, 221

garment industry: decline of Philippine embroidery industry and, 132–35; history of, 263n.46, 265n.111; labor unrest in, 115; technology's impact in, 205–13

gay and transgender beauty pageants, 2, 237n.8

gender: beauty aesthetics and, 84–95; empire-building and national identity and, 11–12, 243nn.50–51; Filipina fashion design and, 199–205, 218–21; Filipino vs. US concepts of, 55; industrial education and, 17; Manila Carnival and disruption of Filipino norms of, 72–80, 91–95; national identity and, 214; of performance, 15–16; textile production labor and, 16–17; transnational embroidery industry and, 108–14, 127–32

Gentleman's Agreement of 1907, 228, 285n.34

geographies of empire, 9–12

Gillin, John Lewis, 171, 177

global capitalism: limits of Filipina high fashion in, 218–21; transnational embroidery industry and, 109–10

Go, Julian, 40

*Good Manners and Right Conduct for Use in Primary Grades* (Bureau of Education), 162–65

*Graphic* magazine: beauty contest coverage in, 1–2, 9–10, 85, 89–90, 92, 97–103, 234, 259n.164; evacuation preparedness features in, 231–33; fashion coverage in, 193, 197, 202–5; flapper era in, 207–8; local textiles promoted by, 217; popularity contest of, 67; readership for, 259n.165

Grau, Corazon E., 192–93

Gray, Catriona, 2, 252n.14

"Grecian Lines Influence Filipino Dress" (*Woman's World* feature), 199

Grewal, Inderpal, 5

Manila Carnival, 63, 239n.40; clothing of Filipinas exhibited at, 161, 213; economic impact of, 67, 253n.35; Filipino-American tensions at, 64–66, 76–80; history of, 65; industrial showcasing at, 116–17; institutionalization of, 80–83; as merchandising venue, 153; politics and, 69–72; racial tensions in, 65–66, 72–80; urbanization and role of, 186

Manila Carnival Association, 65, 69–81, 84; white and Filipino members of, 253n.32

Manila Carnival Queen contest: balloting for, 74–75, 81, 99–100, 252n.21, 256n.87; bathing suit category for, 94–95; blog about, 253n.22; cosmopolitanism of, 71–72; criticism of, 72–80, 96–102; ethnic clothing in, 86; Filipino, American, and Spanish winners of, 82, 256n.87; Filipino-American tensions at, 64–66, 72–80; Filipino nationalism and, 64–69, 86, 96–102; gowns of, 104–5; history of, 255n.60; institutionalization of, 80–83; media coverage of, 96–102; *mestiza* features favored in, 84–86; prominence of Filipina women in, 83; public obsession with, 96–102; rules and guidelines for contests, 252n.21, 256n.87; as social and cultural capital, 103–5; standard of beauty for, 84–95

Manila Galleon, 263n.50

*Manila Times*, 75, 259n.165

*Manila Tribune*, 209, 230

María Clara iconography, 48, 90–91, 93, 214–15, 249n.175, 281n.111

Marina, 91, 251n.2

marketing strategies for Philippine lingerie industry, 126–32, 266n.123; Bureau of Education role in, 152–55

Marquardt, Walter William, 117, 123, 163

Marquez, Paz, 82, 85, 88–89, 94, 256n.87, 258n.154

marriage, Filipina beauty queens and, 91–92

Marshall Field and Company, 116, 128, 133

martial law in Philippines, US military imposition of, 35–36

Martinez, Consuelo, 104–5

*matapobré*, 190, 278n.23

maternalism, in American women's writing about Philippines, 38

Max Factor, 2, 104

McClintock, Anne, 30

McCoy, Alfred, 76

McGee, Fannie, 169–70

McKinley, William, 27

McKinley Act, 275n.171

media industry in Philippines: beauty contest coverage in, 92–95; Filipina fashion design in, 191–96, 201–5; Filipina hypervisibility in, 14; gowns of beauty queens in, 104–5; growth of middle class and, 205–13; local textiles promoted by, 217–18; public obsession with beauty queens and, 96–104, 259n.164; ranking of beauty contests by, 252n.14; texts and images of Philippines in, 31–34; US narrative of embroidery industry in, 122; written clothing in, 7

"Meet the 'Misses,'" 84

Mendoza, Helen, 233

Mendoza, Victor, 32, 259n.161

Mendoza-Guazón, Paz, 164–65, 211–12

*mestizaje* identity: American women's perceptions of, 55–59; beauty aesthetics and, 85–95; colonialism and, 19–25; cosmopolitanism of, 48–50, 248n.156; fashion design linked to, 197, 200–205, 214–18; formation of, 241n.4, 248n.155; sartorial practices as reflection of, 47–54, 56–59; Spanish colonialism and, 46–47; terno as symbol of, 17; terno linked to, 189

*mestizo* elites. *See* elite Filipinos

middle class in Philippines: cosmopolitanism of, 48–50; fashion and threat of, 205–13

*Mid-Pacific Magazine*, 179

military occupation of Philippines, terror inflicted by American soldiers during, 56; martial law imposed by US military, 35–36; racism of US military, 35–37, 127

mimicry: beauty pageants and, 68–69; in transnational embroidery industry, 125

Mina-Roa, Juanita, 191–92, 194, 199, 204, 205

Miss Cebu contest, 97

social order, postcolonial Filipino focus on, 15–18

Sollee, Lolita, 197

Spanish-American War, 15–16, 25–26, 31, 58–59, 168

Spanish colonization of Philippines: American women's perspectives on, 58–59, 250n.223; economic impact of, 45–46, 247n.149; embroidery industry and, 110, 116–17; end of, 15–16; Filipino elite Hispanism and, 21–25, 43–44, 46, 48, 241n.13; Filipino national identity and, 10–12; *indio* groups and, 256n.107; Manila as nucleus of, 186; prison systems and, 166–68, 273n.132, 273n.137; racial system under, 46; Second Philippine Commission image-making about, 35–40; US imperial expansion and, 26

Spanish Penal Code, 139

state actors: Manila Carnival and, 65; US empire and, 7

Steinbock-Pratt, Sarah, 220

St. Louis World's Fair, 69, 128–29; clothing of Filipinas exhibited at, 161

Stoler, Ann Laura, 30, 243n.56

Strange, Susan, 5–6

style: beauty queens as arbiters of, 103–4; transnational embroidery industry discourse of, 125

sub-debs in Filipino society, 9–10

suffragist movement: Filipina-American women's collaboration and, 61–62; Philippine nationalism and, 210, 217–18

sugar industry, Philippines economic shift to, 45–46

Sultana of Mindanao, 82

supercodes of clothing, 7

surveillance: of Filipina student embroiderers and lacemakers, 156–65; in Philippine prisons, 167–68

Tadiar, Neferti, 30, 109

Taft, Charley, 20

Taft, Helen, 20–21, 28–29, 32, 34–35, 38, 55–57, 58–59, 241n.5

Taft, William, 20–21, 27, 33

Taft Commission. *See* Second Philippine Commission

Tagalog community, racist depictions of, 32–34

*tapatnaloob* (loyalty), 99

tariff laws: corporate interests and colonialism and, 118–21; US protectionism in Philippines and, 225–31

Tarlo, Emma, 23

teachers: criticism of industrial education by, 153–55; industrial education in Philippines and role of, 147–48, 153–55, 269n.26; surveillance of embroidery students by, 160–65

technology, Filipina fashion industry and, 205–13, 277n.20

*terno* (formal Filipina gown): construction of, 191–92; elite status linked to, 17, 86–87, 201–5, 212–13; evolution of, 183–86; Filipino designers innovations for, 196–99; global exposure of, 218–21; hybridization of, 199; media focus on, 104–5; nationalism linked to, 1, 213–18; political power of, 210; social status of, 199–205; technology and growing accessibility of, 205–13; as *traje de mestiza* adaptation, 188–89; urbanization and rise of, 186–99

Textile Importers Association, 225–26

textiles: beauty contest clothing and, 87; corporate interests and colonization and, 118–21; decline of Philippine embroidery industry and, 132–35; Filipino luxury textiles, 21, 47–48, 201–5; global trade in, 263n.50; history of, 263n.46; imperial competition and, 17–18; industrial education and workforce production for, 144–47; Japanese expansion into, 224–26, 284n.16; labor exploitation in Philippines and, 111–21; Manila Carnival showcasing of, 116–17; marketing strategies for, 125–26; national identity linked to, 216–18; protectionism and, 224–31; Spanish colonization and development of, 110–11; transnational embroidery industry, 107–10, 112–21, 124–32; US-Japanese competition in, 224, 284n.16

theft, Filipina women accused of, 171–73

"Theoretically Practical" (*Manila Bulletin*), 231

Printed in the USA
CPSIA information can be obtained
at www.ICGtesting.com
LVHW021522200823
755747LV00003B/162